HARMONISING EU COMPETITION LITIGATION

This volume in the Swedish Studies in European Law series, produced by the Swedish Network for European Legal Studies, heralds the new harmonised regime of private enforcement of EU competition law. In 2013, the Commission issued a Communication and Practical Guide to the quantification of harm in antitrust litigation and a Recommendation on collective redress. In 2014, the long-awaited Directive on actions for damages for infringements of EU competition law was finally adopted. In 2016, the Commission is expected to issue guidelines on the passing-on of overcharges. This book examines these recent developments and offers the perspectives of judges, officials, practitioners and academics.

With a preface by Judge Carl Wetter of the General Court, the book explores five different themes. In section one, the main policy issues and challenges are presented. In section two, the new regime is placed in the bigger picture of recent EU law developments. In section three, the nexus between private enforcement and transparency is investigated. A comparative perspective is offered in section four, by looking into private enforcement in five Member State jurisdictions. Finally, issues relating to causation, harm and indirect purchasers are explored in section five.

Harmonising EU Competition Litigation

The New Directive and Beyond

Swedish Studies in European Law
Volume 8

Edited by
Maria Bergström
Marios Iacovides
and
Magnus Strand

• HART •
PUBLISHING
OXFORD AND PORTLAND, OREGON
2018

Hart Publishing
An imprint of Bloomsbury Publishing Plc

Hart Publishing Ltd
Kemp House
Chawley Park
Cumnor Hill
Oxford OX2 9PH
UK

Bloomsbury Publishing Plc
50 Bedford Square
London
WC1B 3DP
UK

www.hartpub.co.uk
www.bloomsbury.com

Published in North America (US and Canada) by
Hart Publishing
c/o International Specialized Book Services
920 NE 58th Avenue, Suite 300
Portland, OR 97213-3786
USA

www.isbs.com

First published in hardback, 2016
Paperback edition, 2018

British Library Cataloguing-in-Publication Data
A catalogue record for this book is available from the British Library.

ISBN: PB: 978-1-50992-116-4
HB: 978-1-84946-762-9

Library of Congress Cataloging-in-Publication Data

Names: Bergström, Maria, 1969– editor. | Iacovides, Marios C., editor. | Strand, Magnus, editor. | European Parliament. Directive 2014/104/EU of the European Parliament and of the Council of 26 November 2014 on certain rules governing actions for damages under national law for infringements of the competition law provisions of the member states and of the European Union

Title: Harmonising EU competition litigation : the new directive and beyond / edited by Maria Bergström, Marios Iacovides and Magnus Strand.

Description: Oxford ; Portland, OR : Hart Publishing, 2015. | Series: Swedish studies in European law ; volume 8 | Includes text of "Directive 2014/104/EU of the European Parliament and of the Council of 26 November 2014 on certain rules governing actions for damages under national law for infringements of the competition law provisions of the member states and of the European Union,[2014] OJ L 349/1." | Includes papers presented as a conference "EU Competition Law and the Emerging Harmonization of Private Enforcement : The Upcoming Directive and Beyond" sponsored by the Swedish Network for European Legal Studies in cooperation with the Law Department at Uppsala University, in Uppsala on 17 May 2014.—ECIP preface. | Includes bibliographical references and index.

Identifiers: LCCN 2015032036 | ISBN 9781849467629 (hardback : alk. paper)

Subjects: LCSH: European Parliament. Directive 2014/104/EU of the European Parliament and of the Council of 26 November 2014 on certain rules governing actions for damages under national law for infringements of the competition law provisions of the member states and of the European Union—Congresses. | Antitrust law—European Union countries—Congresses. | Damages—European Union countries—Congresses. | International and municipal law—European Union countries—Congresses.

Classification: LCC KJE6456.A8 H37 2015 | DDC 343.2407/21—dc23 LC record available at http://lccn.loc.gov/2015032036

Typeset by Compuscript Ltd, Shannon

Foreword

CARL WETTER*

The EU Directive on competition damages actions was finally approved by the European Parliament and the Council in November 2014.[1] It is an important step in the harmonisation of the rules governing private enforcement in the European Union.

The objective of the Directive is twofold. It seeks to optimise the interaction between public and private enforcement at the same time as it seeks to ensure full compensation for victims of anticompetitive practices.

In pursuit of the first objective, the Directive tries to strike a balance between, on the one hand, the protection of the successful public enforcement leniency programmes (which essentially allow immunity or fine reductions for voluntary confessions of cartel activities) and, on the other, the need of private parties to obtain disclosure of evidence in order to prove their case.

Although the Directive stops well short of the far-reaching legal regime for private enforcement in the United States, it contains a number of new rules that will certainly enhance the possibilities of private enforcement in Europe at the same time as providing the lawyers concerned with interesting challenges. Illustrative examples are the giving of binding force of the findings by national competition authorities or review courts for the ensuing damages cases; the attempt to regulate the passing-on defence and the rights of indirect purchasers; the clarification of the relationship between joint and several liability and leniency and the right to contribution; and, finally, the introduction of a presumption of harm from cartel infringements, the latter incidentally not being clearly defined so far.

It was therefore a welcome initiative by the Swedish Network for European Legal Studies and the Faculty of Law at Uppsala University when they together organised a two-day seminar in May 2014 on the new Directive and its scope and interpretation. I do not think that it would be an exaggeration to say that these discussions between scholars and practitioners proved to be very fruitful and also led to new insights in this complex area of law.

* Carl Wetter is Judge at the General Court of the European Union.

[1] Directive 2014/104/EU of the European Parliament and of the Council of 26 November 2014 on certain rules governing actions for damages under national law for infringements of the competition law provisions of the Member States and of the European Union [2014] OJ L349/1.

The organisers are to be congratulated that they have now, together with Hart Publishing, been able to collect these interesting contributions in a book. I am convinced that it will prove interesting and valuable reading for all those who will be confronted with the often tricky challenges in the crossroads between public and private competition law enforcement in this new legal environment.

Carl Wetter
Luxembourg

Editors' Preface

On behalf of the Swedish Network for European Legal Studies, we are proud to present the eighth volume in the series *Swedish Studies in European Law*, which has been issued by the Network since 2006.

This edited volume is a collection of contributions springing from a conference on the Draft Directive held by the Network in cooperation with the Faculty of Law at Uppsala University, in Uppsala on 17 May 2014. Since then, the Draft Directive has been adopted as Directive 2014/104/EU of 26 November 2014 (the Directive).[1] It is to be transposed into the national laws of the Member States by 27 December 2016. The timing of this edited volume could therefore not be better.

The topic of the Uppsala conference was 'EU Competition Law and the Emerging Harmonization of Private Enforcement: The Upcoming Directive and Beyond'. The aim of the conference was to appeal to a wider public than the one that usually attends competition law conferences. It also aimed to engage with scholars, practitioners, and stakeholders from other disciplines both within and outside EU law that could identify with the broader, in particular constitutional, issues raised by the Directive: the limits of harmonisation and the choice of legal basis, the choice of legal instrument (Directive rather than Regulation), the impact of the Directive on national rules on transparency and procedure, the interplay between the public and private enforcement of EU law, and the manageability of complex rules dealing with quantification of damages.

Exploring a multitude of aspects of the Directive, and charting what may lie beyond its strict scope proved popular during the conference. Indeed, the discussions confirmed our intuition that the Directive was of great interest across the board. They also revealed that the Directive has the potential to be contentious in certain crucial ways and that the drafters of national legislation, and the lawyers and judges who will be called open to work with and to apply its rules, are equally unsure as to how best to transpose it into national law, how to implement it, and how to interpret it respectively. We hope that this edited volume, with its combination of broad scope and analytical detail, will be a useful instrument in the hands of these different actors and researchers alike.

[1] Directive 2014/104/EU of the European Parliament and of the Council of 26 November 2014 on certain rules governing actions for damages under national law for infringements of the competition law provisions of the Member States and of the European Union [2014] OJ L349/1.

In the first section, main policy issues and particular challenges are examined by Ulf Bernitz, who gives a useful overview of the Directive and provides an outline of this edited volume. Alison Jones compares EU competition law with US federal antitrust law and offers very interesting insights into the philosophy and practical application of private enforcement in both jurisdictions. Lars Henriksson analyses the Directive and relevant Swedish law from the perspective of law and economics to tease out the impact of initiatives relating to private enforcement on consumer welfare. Ingeborg Simonsson concludes this section by offering the perspective of a judge who will apply the rules of the Directive in the coming years. In that capacity, she investigates its added value for private enforcement and opens up for a dialogue with her colleagues at the Court of Justice.

The private enforcement of competition law in general and the new Directive in particular are viewed from specific—but broader than usual—contextual angles in the second section of this edited volume. Here, contributions include procedural law and intellectual property law. First in this section is Vladimir Bastidas, who evaluates the Directive from a macro-perspective, examining other enforcement measures in EU competition law, in particular those to do with public enforcement. Next is Pieter Van Cleynenbreugel, whose chapter illustrates the Directive's national procedural autonomy focus and forecasts the impact of that focus on the design and review of national procedural choices within its enforcement scheme. Lastly, Paul Torremans looks at the Directive from the perspective of the intellectual property lawyer and discusses areas of intersection of the two disciplines: competition law as a defence to intellectual property claims and injunctive relief in relation to standard setting and FRAND terms.

The third section of the book includes two analyses of the vexed issue of how to reconcile the interest of transparency with the safeguarding of effective leniency programmes. This topic proved to be one of the most controversial during the conference and one which participants felt could raise many interesting questions as to the limits of EU competition law enforcement in the future. The contributions in this section capture that feeling and offer structured ways of presenting the arguments for and against the approach of the Directive. The first contribution, by Xavier Groussot and Justin Pierce, investigates the relationship between private enforcement actions and the leniency programme, viewed through the rules on the protection or disclosure of information from one process to another. The second, authored by Björn Lundqvist and Helene Andersson, deals with the right to access documents for cartel members and cartel victims.

Practical private enforcement experiences in the Member States are the overall topic of the fourth section. The reports cover in total five Member States, in some ways diverse and in others similar. Together with Sweden, which is discussed by many of the authors in this edited volume, they form a mosaic of smaller jurisdictions that offer significant comparative insights into how private enforcement is applied in the national courts. They explore, inter alia, why private enforcement has hitherto failed to really take off in some jurisdictions despite *Courage*, *Manfredi*, and other seminal cases from the Court of Justice in this field and why it may have been successful in the Netherlands. Portugal is covered by Sofia Oliveira Pais, Poland by Anna Piszcz, Finland by Katri Havu, and Greece and the Netherlands by Agisilaos Karpetas.

Contributions in the fifth and final section are devoted to the complexity of the estimation of harm, affected as it is by passing-on and the problematic position of indirect purchasers. Elisabeth Eklund offers a typology of the varied group of indirect purchasers and outlines developments in the EU, the United States, and Sweden in relation to their standing. Magnus Strand deals with the very interesting issue of whether restitutionary redress may be an option as an alternative to damages. In the final chapter, Marios Iacovides explores the relationship of the Directive with the Practical Guide on the quantification of harm and questions the administrability of the former in light of complex economic assessments relating to rates of passing-on and the uncertainty of counterfactuals.

The Directive and the accompanying soft-law instruments undeniably give new directions to the ongoing harmonisation of private enforcement of EU and national competition law. With the inclusion of Article 114 TFEU as legal basis and the ensuing involvement of the European Parliament and the choice of legislating through a Directive in an area traditionally regulated by Regulations, these instruments also signal a different approach that may or may not be used in competition law and beyond in the future. Our view is that the process of harmonisation has only just begun. This edited volume identifies and addresses many issues to be resolved in the course of this new phase, by the EU legislator, the national legislatures, the judiciary, and private actors. We are very happy to deliver it to colleagues throughout Europe and beyond, in the hope that it may be of assistance in their efforts to cope with the new harmonised regime of private enforcement.

Maria Bergström, Marios C Iacovides and Magnus Strand
Uppsala

Contents

Foreword by Judge Carl Wetter v
Editors' Preface vii
Table of Cases xiii
Table of Legislation xxiii

Part I: Main Policy Issues and Particular Challenges

1. Introduction to the Directive on Competition Damages Actions 3
Ulf Bernitz

2. Private Enforcement of EU Competition Law: A Comparison with, and Lessons from, the US 15
Alison Jones

3. Welfare Effects of Right to Damages—A Practical Approach and the Swedish Perspective 43
Lars Henriksson

4. Challenges for Swedish Courts: Will the New Directive on Competition Damages Actions Help? 65
Ingeborg Simonsson

Part II: Private Enforcement and the New Directive in Context

5. The Damages Directive and Other Enforcement Measures in EU Competition Law 83
Vladimir Bastidas Venegas

6. Embedding Procedural Autonomy: The Directive and National Procedural Rules 99
Pieter Van Cleynenbreugel

7. Private Enforcement of Competition Law in Intellectual Property Cases 121
Paul LC Torremans

Part III: Transparency, Leniency Programmes, and Human Rights

8. Transparency and Liability in Leniency Programmes: A Question of Balancing? 143
Xavier Groussot and Justin Pierce

9. Access to Documents for Cartel Victims and Cartel Members—Is the System Coherent? 165
Björn Lundqvist and Helene Andersson

Part IV: Private Enforcement Through National Actions

10. Practical Private Enforcement: Perspectives from Portugal 187
Sofia Oliveira Pais

11. Practical Private Enforcement: Perspectives from Poland 203
Anna Piszcz

12. Practical Private Enforcement: Perspectives from Finland—Causal Links, the Principle of Effectiveness and Requirements for National Solutions 221
Katri Havu

13. Practical Private Enforcement: Perspectives from Greece and the Netherlands 235
Agisilaos Karpetas

Part V: Harm, Indirect Purchasers, and Alternative Redress

14. Indirect Purchasers—Is there Anything New in the Directive? An Introductory Overview of the Current and Future Status of Indirect Purchasers in the EU 261
Elisabeth Eklund

15. Beyond the Competition Damages Directive: What Room for Competition Law Restitution? 279
Magnus Strand

16. The Presumption and Quantification of Harm in the Directive and the Practical Guide 295
Marios C Iacovides

Appendix: Directive 2014/104/EU of the European Parliament and of the Council of 26 November 2014 on certain rules governing actions for damages under national law for infringements of the competition law provisions of the Member States and of the European Union [2014] OJ L349/1 315

Index 335

Table of Cases

European Court of Justice

Aalborg Portland and others v Commission (Joined cases C-204/00 P, C-205/00 P, C-211/00 P, C-213/00 P, C-217/00 P, C-219/00 P) [2004] ECR I-123 182

Akzo Nobel Chemicals Ltd and Akros Chemicals Ltd v Commission (Case C-550/07 P) [2010] ECR I-8301 242

Akzo Nobel v Commission (Case C-97/08 P) [2009] ECR I-8237 251

Alliance One International and Standard Commercial Tobacco v Commission and Commission v Alliance One International (Joined cases C-628/10 P and C-14/11 P) EU:C:2012:479 251

Allianz Hungária Biztositó v Gazdasági Versenyhivatal (Case C-32/11) EU:C:2013:160 286

Alstom v Commission (Case T-164/12 R) EU:T:2014:1089 174

Amministrazione delle Finanze dello Stato v San Giorgio (Case 199/82) [1983] ECR 3595 230

Andrea Francovich and Daniela Bonifaci and others v Italian Republic (Joined cases C-6/90 and C-9/90) [1991] ECR I-5357 103

Ansaldo Energia v Administrazione delle Finanze dello Stato (Joined cases C-279/96 to C-281/96) [1998] ECR I-5025 .... 291, 292

Antoine Boxus and others v Région wallonne (Joined cases C-128/09 to C-131/09, C-134/09 and C-135/09) [2011] ECR I-9711 117

Automec v European Commission (Case T-24/90) [1992] ECR II-2223 87

Belasco v Commission (Case 246/86) [1989] ECR 2117 303

Belgische Radio en Televisie v SV SABAM (Case 127/73) [1974] ECR 51 .... 5, 27, 86, 292

Belgium v Commission (Case C-110/03) [2005] ECR I-2801 149

Brahim Samba Diouf v Ministre du Travail, de l'Emploi et de l'Immigration (Case C-69/10) [2011] ECR I-7151 117

Brasserie du Pêcheur v Bundesrepublik Deutschland and R v Secretary of State for Transport ex parte Factortame (Joined cases C-46/93 and C-48/93) [1996] ECR I-1029 .... 4, 8, 231

British Broadcasting Corp & BBC Enterprises Ltd v Commission (Magill TV Guide Ltd intervening) (Case T-70/89) [1991] ECR II-536 126

Bundeswettbewerbsbehörde and Bundeskartellanwalt v Schenker (Case C-681/11) EU:C:2013:404 159

Bundeswettbewerbsbehörde v Donau Chemie (Case C-536/11) EU:C:2013:366 .... 11, 30, 32, 36, 92–3, 96, 97, 100, 152, 153, 157, 160, 169, 212, 222, 227, 231, 234, 240, 243
CDC Hydrogene Peroxide v Commission (Case T-437/08) [2011] ECR II-8251 .... 32, 149, 151, 170, 190
Cimenteries CBR v Commission (Case T-25/95) [2000] ECR II-491 182
Commission v Agrofert Holding (Case C-477/10) EU:C:2012:394 .... 150, 152
Commission v Bavarian Lager (Case C-28/08) [2010] ECR I-6055 157
Commission v Éditions Odile Jacob (Case C-404/10) EU:C:2012:393 .... 150, 152, 172
Commission v EnBW Energie Baden-Württemberg (Case C-365/12) EU:C:2014:112 .... 32, 150, 152, 162, 170, 172, 175, 176
Commission v Fresh Marine (Case C-472/00 P) [2003] ECR I-7541 223
Competition Authority v Beef Industry Development Society Ltd and Barry Brothers (Carrigmore) Meats Ltd (Case C-209/07) [2008] ECR I-8637 300
Courage v Crehan (Case C-453/99) [2001] ECR-I-6297 .... 5, 28, 29, 30, 48, 60, 87, 92, 94, 100, 101, 104, 105, 153, 160, 166, 188, 222, 224, 225, 226, 227, 231, 261, 264, 265, 286, 287, 290, 301
Danfoss A/S and Sauer-Danfoss v Skatteministeriet (Case C-94/10) [2011] ECR I-9963 282
Dole Food Company Inc and Dole Germany OHG v Commission (Case T-588/08) EU:T:2013:130 300
Eco Swiss Time Ltd v Benetton International NV (Case C-126/97) [1999] ECR I-3055 56
Edis v Ministero delle Finanze (Case C-231-96) [1998] ECR I-4951 .... 291, 292
Europemballage Corporation and Continental Can Company v Commission (Case 6/72) [1973] ECR 215 49
Europese Gemeenschap v Otis NV (Case C-199/711) EU:C:2012:684 .... 9, 72, 104, 222, 225, 227, 271, 295
Evonik Degussa v Commission and Council (Case C-266/06 P) EU:C:2008:295 148
Expedia v Autorité de la concurrence (Case C-226/11) EU:C:2012:795 300
Firma Molkerei -Zentrale Westfalen/Lippe GmbH v Hauptzollamt Paderborn (Case 28/67) [1968] ECR 211 102

GlaxoSmithKline Services v Commission (Joined cases C-501/06 P, C-513/06 P, C-515/06 P and C-519/06 P) [2009] ECR I-9291 .... 49, 50
Groupement des cartes bancaires (CB) v Commission (Case C-67/13 P) EU:C:2014:2204 300
GT-Link A/S v De Danske Statsbaner (DBS) (Case C-242/95) [1997] ECR I-14449 280
Hans Just v Danish Ministry for Fiscal Affairs (Case 68/79) [1980] ECR 3595 230
Huawei v ZTE (Case C-170/13) EU:C:2014:2391 .... 134, 136–7
IMS Health v Commission (Case T-184/01 R) [2001] ECR II-3193 127–8
IMS Health v NDC Health (Case C-418/01) [2004] ECR I-5039 .... 125, 129, 130, 131
Independent Television Publications Ltd v Commission (Magill TV Guide Ltd intervening) (Case T-76/89) [1991] ECR II-575 126
Intel v Commission (Case T-286/09) EU:T:2014:547 .... 263, 303
Inuit Kanatami v European Parliament and Council (Case C-583/11 P) EU:C:2013:625 290
Knauf Gips v Commission (Case C-407/08 P) [2010] ECR I-6375 182–3
Kone Oyj v Commission (Case C-510/11) EU:C:2013:696 147
Kone v ÖBB-Infrastruktur (Case C-557/12) EU:C:2014:1317 .... 9, 12, 28, 100, 108, 157, 160, 190, 222, 225, 226, 227, 231, 232, 265
Laboratoires Pharmaceutiques Bergaderm (Case C-352/98 P) [2000] ECR I-5291 223
LG Electronics v Commission (Case T-91/13) EU:T:2015:609 263
Masco v Commission (Case T-378/10) EU:T:2013:469 147
Masterfoods v HB Ice Cream (Case C-344/98) [2000] ECR I-11369 .... 72, 245, 246
Metallgesellschaft and others and Hoechst and Hoechst (UK) v Commissioners of Inland Revenue and HM Attorney General (Joined cases C-397/98 and C-410/98) [2001] ECR I-1727 283
Milch, Fett- und Eierkontor v Hauptzollamt Saarbrücken (Case 29/68) [1969] ECR 165 102
Mitsubishi, Siemens, Toshiba v Commission (Case C-239/11 P) EU:C:2013:866 183
Mulder and Otto Heinemann v Commission (Joined cases C-104/89 and C-37/90) [2000] ECR I-203 310
NDC Health v Commission and IMS Health (Case C-481/01 P(R)) [2002] ECR I-3401 127
Netherlands v Commission (Case T-380/08) EU:T:2013:480 172

Oebmühle and Schmidt Söhne (Case C-298/96) [1998] ECR I-4767.................154
Oscar Bronner v Mediaprint Zeitungs-und Zeitschriftenverlag
(Case C-7/97) [1998] ECR I-7791 ....130, 131
Peterbroeck and others v Belgian State
(Case C-312/93) [1995] ECR I-4599 ....102, 107
Pfeiderer AG v Bundeskartellamt (Case C-360/09)
[2011] ECR I-5161..11, 32, 36, 91, 93, 96, 97, 100, 106, 114, 153, 154, 155, 157, 160, 161, 162, 163, 167, 168, 169, 174, 178, 179, 212, 222, 240, 243, 263
Postbank v Commission (Case T-353/94)
[1996] ECR II-921..172
Prezes Urzedu Ochrony Konkurencji i Konsumentów v
Tel2 Polska (Case C-375/09) [2011] ECR I-3055 160
R v Secretary of State for transport ex parte Factortame
(Case C-213/89) [1990] ECR I-2433 28
Radio Telefis Eireann and Independent Television
Publications Ltd v Commission (Joined cases C-241/91
P and 242/91 P) [1995] ECR I-743...126, 130
Radio Telefis v Commission (Magill TV Guide Ltd
intervening) (Case T-69/89) [1991] ECR II-485 ....126, 130
Reagens v Commission (Case T-181/10) EU:T:2014:139..................................189
Renault v Maxicar (Case C-53/87) [1988] ECR 6039 137
Rewe-Handelsgesellschaft Nord and Rewe-Markst
Steffen v Hauptzollamt Kiel (Butter Buying Cruises)
(Case 158/80) ECR 1805...290, 291, 292
Rewe-Zentralfinanz v Landwirtschaftskammer für das
Saarland (Case C-33/76) [1976] EC 1989...28, 234
Rosalba Palmisani v Instituto nazionale della previdenza
sociale (INPS) (Case C-261/95) [1997] ECR I-4025 60
Schindler Holding Ltd v Commission (Case C-501/11)
EU:C:2013:522...148
Siemens v Commission (Case T-110/07) [2011] ECR II-477.............................183
Société de Vente de Ciments et Bétons de l' Est v
Kerpen & Kerpen (Case C-319/82) [1983] ECR 4173.............28, 280, 285, 290
Société Technique Minière v Maschinenbau Ulm
(Case C-56/65) [1966] ECR 235...28, 285
Solvay v Commission (Case C-109/10 P) [2011] ECR I-10329 182
Sot. Lelos kai Sia EE v GlaxoSmithKline (Joined cases
C-468/06 to C-478/06) [2008] ECR I-7139..49
Stergios Delimitis v Henninger Bräu (Case C-234/89)
[1991] ECR I-935...172
T-Mobile Netherlands, KPN Mobile, Orange Nederland
and Vodafone Libertel v Raad van bestuur de Nederlandse
Medegingsautoriteit (Case C-8/08) [2009] ECR I-4529 ....50, 300

Terezakis v Commission (Case T-380/04) EU:T:2008:19 ... 151
Test Claimants in the FII Group Litigation v Commissioners of Inland Revenue (Case C-446/04) [2006] ECR I-11753 ... 283–4
Trubowest Handel and Makarov (Case C-149/08 P) [2010] ECR I-2259 ... 223
Unibet (London) and Unibet (International) v Justitiekanslern (Case C-432/05) [2007] ECR I-2271 ... 290
VAG France v Établissements Magne (Case 10/86) [1986] ECR 4071 ... 280
Vebic (Case C-439/08) [2010] ECR I-12471 ... 103, 154, 158
Verein für Konsumenteninformation (Case T-2/03) [2005] ECR II-1121 ... 32
Vincenzo Manfredi and others v Lloyd Adriatico Assicurazioni and others (Joined cases C-295/04 to 298/04) [2006] ECR I-6619 ... 5, 28, 29, 30, 92, 94, 100, 105, 153, 160, 166, 222, 224, 225, 226, 227, 231, 232, 264–5, 280–1, 297, 301
Volvo v Veng (Case C-238/87) [1988] ECR 6211 ... 137
Von Colson and Kamann v Land Nordrhein-Westfalen (Case 14/83) [1984] ECR 1891 ... 28, 234
Walt Wilhelm and others v Bundeskartellamt (Case 14/68) [1969] ECR 1 ... 28, 160

European Commission Decisions

NDC Health / IMS Health (Case COMP D3/38.044) Commission Decision 2003/741/EC [2003] OJ L268/59 ... 128
Intel (Case COMP/C-3/37.990) [2009] OJ C227/13 ... 303
Rambus (Case COMP/38.636) [2010] OJ C30/17 ... 134
Google / Motorola Mobility (Case COMP/M.6381) Commission Decision 2012/02/13, not published ... 134

National Courts

Belgium

Brussels Court of First Instance, 19 September 2003 [2004] Auteurs et Media 38 ... 122

Canada

Option Consommateurs v Infineon Technologies, 2013 SCC 59 ... 268

Finland

Asphalt cartel damages claims, Helsinki District Court, 28 November 2013 .... 228, 229, 230, 233, 234
Car spare part damages claims, Helsinki District Court, L 07/33936, 31 March 2014 .... 229, 233

Germany

Huawei v ZTE, District Court of Düsseldorf, 4b O 104/12, 21 March 2013 .... 134, 136
Orange-Book-Standard, Federal Supreme Court, KZR 39/06, 6 May 2009 .... 134, 135
Pfeiderer v Bundeskartellamt, District Court of Bonn, 51 Gs 53/09, 18 January 2012 107

Greece

Athens Court of Appeal, Case 673/2009 240
Athens Court of First Instance, Case 2265/2011 252
Council of State, Case 1324/2013 240
Patras Court of Appeal, Case 18/2002 245
Supreme Court, Case 53/2002 246
Supreme Court, Case 949/2002 246
Supreme Court, Case 953/2002 241
Supreme Court, Case 21/2003 247
Supreme Court, Case 681/2007 241
Supreme Court, Case 204/2010 240
Supreme Court, Case 439/2012 252
Veria First Instance Court, Case 9/2014 241

Netherlands

ASR v Achmea, Supreme Court, 6 April 2012 NL:HR:2012:BU3784 248
CDC v Shell, The Hague District Court, 1 May 2013 NL:RBDHA:2013:CA1870 .... 242, 246
CEF v FEG, Rotterdam District Court, 7 March 2007 NL:RBROT:2007:BA0926 248
Compagnie de Manutention Ro-Ro (CdMR) v Scheldepoort, District Court of MMiddelburg, 6 July 2006 NL:RBMID:2006:AZ0501 242
Converium and others, Amsterdam Court of Appeal, 12 November 2010 NL:GHAMS:2010:BO3908; 17 January 2012 NL:GHAMS:2012:BV1026 255
Equilib v KLM, Amsterdam Court of Appeal, 24 September 2013 NL:GHAMS:2013:3013 .... 245, 246

Pilkington and Scheuten Glass v ACM, Rotterdam District Court, 3 March 2014 NL:RBROT:2014:2273 242–3
TenneT v ABB, Arnhem-Leeuwarden Court of Appeal, 2 September 2014 NL:GHARL:2014:6766 253
TenneT v ABB, East-Netherlands District Court, 16 January 2013 NL:RBONE:2013:BZ0403 .... 248, 251
TenneT v Alstom, Arnhem District Court, 16 May 2012, NL:RBARN:2012:BW7445 242
Vaal en Van't Hoft v Stichting H9 Invest e.a, Supreme Court, 15 March 2013 NL:HR:2013:BY6101 242
VVE 'Het Schip' v Otis, Centre-Netherlands District Court, 13 March 2013 NL:RBMNE:2013:CA1922 248

Poland

AB v PGE Mining and Conventional Power SA, Supreme Court, 21 December 2012 (Case V CSK 9/12) 207
Consumer Ombudsman of Warsaw v BRE Bank, Regional Court in Łódź (Case II C 1693/10) 214
Danuta K v Commune K et al, Supreme Court, 9 October 2007 (Case III CZP 46/07) 207
Housing Association in S v Power Plant, Supreme Court, 4 March 2008 (Case III CZP 135/95) 207
Knitwear Manufacturing Factory L v Alicia G-Foreign Enterprise A et al, Supreme Court, 20 November 2002 (Case II CKN 859/00) 210
Kolej Gondolowa in K v the UOKiK President, Supreme Court, 5 January 2007 (Case III SK 17/06) 207
Krakow Regional Court, 8 December 2014 (Case 1 C 932/14) 205
Miejskie Wodociągi i Kanalizacja sp z oo in K v Brewery in K, Supreme Court, 22 February 1994 (Case I CRN 238/93) 207
Municipal Heat Supply Company in O v Housing Association (Spółdzielnia Mieszkaniowa) in O, Supreme Court, 4 March 2008 (Case IV CSK 441/07) 207
PKP SA v PPH Wilan, Supreme Court, 28 April 2004 (Case III CK 521/02) 207
TPPD v State Treasury, Supreme Court, 23 July 2008 (Case III CZP 52/08) 206–7
Warsaw Apartments v Water and Sewer Utilities, Supreme Court, 14 April 2007 (CSK 454/06) 207

Portugal

ANF v IMS Health, Lisbon Court of Appeal, 3 April 2014, proc 672/11.OYRLSB 195
Carrefour v Orex Dois, Lisbon Court of Appeal, 24 November 2005, proc 6882/2005-8 192

DECO v Portugal Telecom, Supreme Court of Justice, case 03A1243, 7.10.2003 200
Sport TV case, Lisbon Judicial Court, case 7074/15.8T8LSB 192, 193–4
Toyota case, Supreme Court of Justice, 20 June 2013 proc 178/07.2TVPRT.S1 .... 192, 193

Sweden

Akzo Nobel Chemicals v CDC (Stockholm City Court case T 5285-09) 68
Akzo Nobel v CDC (Stockholm City Court case T 589-09) 68
Broform v State of Sweden/Vägverket (Svea Hovrätt Court of Appeal case T 2452-01) 57
Bromölla kommun v NCC (Stockholm City Court case T 9740-04) 70
Coinstar Inc v Scan Coin Industries AB (Hovrätten över Skåne och Blekinge Court of Appeal case T 2520-08) 56
Eka Chemicals v CDC (Stockholm City Court case T 5284-09) 68
Euroclear Sweden v Europe Investor Direct (Svea Hovrätt Court of Appeal case T 10012-08) 12, 275, 276
Fortum Värme samägt med Stockholms stad v Farsta Strand Business Center (Stockholm City Court joined cases T 1385-09 and T 8278-08) 68
Götene kommun v NCC (Stockholm City Court case T 6160-04) 70
Hydro Aluminium Sverige, Energi E2 v Staten genom affärsverket svenska kraftnät (Stockholm City Court case T 7896-02) 70
Klippans kommun v NCC (Stockholm City Court case T 6145-04) 70
Konkurrensverket v Scandorama and Ölvemarks (Stockholm City Court case T 19974-10) 76
Kristianstads kommun v NCC (Stockholm City Court case T 9744-04) 70
Linköpings kommun v NCC (Stockholm City Court case T 14898-03) 70
Linköpings kommun v NCC (Stockholm City Court case T 14900-05) 58, 69
Linköpings kommun v NCC (Stockholm City Court case T 6580-03) 70
Linköpings kommun v NCC and Skanska (Svea Hovrätt Court of Appeal case T 9597-04) 58
MD 2009:11 (Market Court, Asphalt cartel case) 53
MD 2011:28 (Market Court, Arlanda airport taxi case) 273
NJA 2008 s 120 (Supreme Court, Ystad Hamn case) 56
OÜ E-Direct and EuropeInvestor Direct v VPC (Stockholm City Court joined cases T 32799-05 and T 34227-05) 67, 69
Preem v Gävle Hamn (Stockholm City Court case T 59995-09) 68
Primeur Vin v Systembolaget (Stockholm City Court case T 11529-05) 69

SAS v Luftfartsverket (Göta Hovrätt Court of Appeal case T 33-00) 289
Skånemejerier ek för v Arla Foods (Stockholm City Court case T 21129-07) 68
Solna Biltek v Kontrollerad Bilverkstad i Sverige (Stockholm City Court case T 2679-08) 68
Tele2 Sverige v TeliaSonera (Stockholm City Court case T 10956-05) 67, 69, 71
Tranås kommun v NCC (Stockholm City Court case T 8371-03) 58, 70
Ulricehamns kommun v NCC (Stockholm City Court case T 6158-04) 70
Ulricehamns kommun v Skanska Sverige (Stockholm City Court case T 11686-05) 69
Vaggeryds kommun v NCC (Stockholm City Court case T 6155-04) 70
Vaggeryds kommun v Skanska Sverige (Stockholm City Court case T 31609-04) 70
Värnamo kommun v NCC (Stockholm City Court case T 6141-04) 70
Verisec v Pointsec Sweden (Stockholm City Court case T 10969-05) 69
Verizon Sweden AB v Tele2 Sverige (Stockholm City Court case T 20621-10) 68, 78
Yarps Network Services AB v TeliaSonera Aktiebolag (publ) (Stockholm City Court case T 15382-06) 67, 69, 71

United Kingdom

Attheraces v British Horse Racing Board Ltd [2006] FSR 20; [2007] ECC 7 132
English Welsh & Scottish Railway v EON UK [2007] EWHC 599 289
National Grid Electricity Transmission v ABB [2011] EWHC 1717 .... 173, 174, 175, 176, 183
Philips Electronics v Ingman [1998] 2 CMLR 839; [1999] FSR 112 .... 123, 125
Scandisk v Koninklijke Philips Electronics [2007] EWHC 332 (Ch); [2008] FSR 22 123
Vringo Infrastructure v ZTE (UK) [2013] EWHC 1591 135

United States

Bell Atlantic v Twombly 550 US 554 (2007) 22, 23, 25, 41
Blue Shield v McCready 457 US 465 (1982) 22
Brunswick v Pueblo Bowl-O-Mat 439 US 477 (1977) 22, 24
California v ARC 490 US 93 (1989) 21

Continental TV v GTE Sylvania 433 US 36 (1977) 23, 24
Daubert v Merell Dow Pharmaceuticals 509 US 579 (1993) 23
Eastman Kodak Co v Image Technical Services 504 US 451 (1992) 23
Financial Securities Litigation, Re 609 F2d 411 (9th Cir 1979); 446 US 929 (1980) 20
Hanover Shoe v United Shoe Machine Corp 392 US 481 (1968) 21, 22, 266, 267, 268
Hoffmann-La Roche v Empagran 542 US 155 (2004) 23
Hydrogen Peroxide Antitrust Litigation, re 552 F3d 305 (3d Cir 2008) 22
Illinois Brick v Illinois 431 US 720 (1977) 9, 21, 266–7, 268
Intel v V-ia Technologies [2003] FSR 574 (CA) 127
Japonese Electronic Products Antitrust Litigation, re 631 F2d 1069 (3rd Cir 1980) 20
Leegin Creative Leather Products v PSKS 551 US 877 (2007) 23, 25
Matsushita Electric Industrial v Zenith Radio 475 US 574 (1986) 23, 24, 41
Monsanto v Spray-Rite Service 465 US 752 (1984) 23, 24
Texas Industries v Radcliff Materials 451 US 630 (1981) 20
Verizon Communications v Law Offices of Curtis V Trinlo 540 US 398 (2004) 23
Zenith Radio v Hazeltine Research 395 US 1000 (1969) 20

Table of Legislation

European Union

Treaties

EC Treaty
Art 81 ... 3, 264
Art 81(1) ... 264–5
Art 82 ... 3
Art 85 ... 264
EU Charter of the Fundamental Rights of the European Union
Art 41(2) ... 182
Art 47 ... 234, 284, 292, 293
Treaty on the Functioning of the European Union
Art 3(3) ... 49
Art 15(3) ... 169
Art 101 ... 4, 6, 28, 31, 48, 55, 56, 87, 92, 100, 104–8, 148–50, 152–4, 158, 160, 191, 231, 264, 290, 292
Art 101(1) ... 5, 28, 86, 100, 101, 146, 300, 303, 313
Art 101(2) ... 87, 279, 284, 285, 286–7, 289
Art 101(3) ... 17, 28, 61, 146
Art 102 ... 4, 5–6, 6, 28, 31, 48, 52, 55, 86, 87, 92, 100, 105, 107, 124–6, 133, 137–8, 147, 154, 158, 191, 279, 286–7, 289–90, 292, 313
Art 103 ... 4, 33, 37
Art 114 ... ix, 33, 37
Art 234 ... 236
Art 267 ... 57, 195, 310, 312

Regulations

17/1962 [1959-1962] OJ Sp Ed 87 ... 17, 84
1049/2001 Transparency Regulation
[2001] OJ L145/43 ... 32, 152, 163, 169, 243
Recital 4 ... 151
Art 3(a) ... 170
Art 4 ... 150, 169–70, 171, 172, 177
Art 4(2) ... 151, 152, 170
Art 4(3) ... 151

1206/2001 on cooperation between courts
in civil and commercial matters 115
1/2003/EC on implementation of
rules on competition 3, 17, 27, 84, 85, 86, 150, 152, 158, 171, 204
Recital 3 87
Art 3(1) 27, 216
Art 4(3) 172
Art 5 .... 84, 85
Art 7 84
Art 7(1) 84
Art 9 .... 84, 161
Art 11 168
Art 12 168
Art 15 174
Art 15(1) 172, 173, 175, 176
Art 16 .... 31, 40, 72, 195, 217, 245
Art 16(1) 95
Art 17 84
Art 18 84
Art 20 84
Art 23 159
Art 23(1) 84
Art 27(2) 182
139/2004 on the control of concentrations between
undertakings [2004] OJ L24/1 150
Art 21(2) 17
773/2004 on the conduct of proceedings by the
Commission pursuant to Arts 81 and 82 of
the EC Treaty [2004] OJ L123/18 .... 152, 153, 171
Art 15(1) 182
622/2008 Cartel Settlement Regulation [2008] OJ L171/3 84
330/2010 Vertical Agreements Regulation [2010] OJ L102/1 287
1215/2012 on jurisdiction and recognition and enforcement of
judgments in civil and commercial matters OJ L351
Art 30 270

Directives

2004/48/EC on enforcement of intellectual
property rights [2004] OJ L157/45 .... 4, 62, 124, 166, 194
2014/104/EU Competition Damages
Directive [2014] OJ L349/1 .... v, vii, 3, 43, 65, 83, 99, 121, 153, 167, 187, 210, 221–2, 235–6, 261–78, 279 (*See appendix for full text*)
Recital 3 .... 110, 271

Recital 4 .... 66, 110
Recital 5 .... 129, 219, 264
Recitals 6–10 66
Recital 7 216
Recital 8 3
Recital 10 .... 110, 216
Recital 11 .... 118, 226, 232
Recital 12 .... 77, 216, 226
Recital 13 .... 197, 198, 201, 226
Recital 14 176
Recital 16 159
Recital 17 115
Recital 18 160–1
Recital 22 .... 155, 162
Recital 24 156
Recital 26 .... 11, 179
Recital 34 266
Recital 35 266
Recital 36 111
Recital 38 .... 8, 11
Recitals 39–41 226
Recitals 43–46 226
Recital 44 270
Recital 46 .... 73, 232
Recital 47 .... 8, 75, 299
Recital 49 263
Art 1 .... 39, 47, 110, 236, 263
Art 1(1) 8, 34, 268
Art 2 .... 226, 239
Art 2(3) 216
Art 2(4) 283
Art 2(5) 283
Art 2(6) 269
Art 2(14) 8, 298, 300
Art 2(16) 96
Art 2(20) 269
Art 2(24) 269
Arts 2–3 222
Art 3 .... 39, 48, 66, 226, 268
Art 3(1) 7, 34
Art 3(2) 35, 77, 111
Art 3(3) 7, 35, 262, 281, 304, 311
Art 4 .... 110, 232, 268–9, 301, 303
Art 5 .... 10, 35, 40, 94, 113, 176–7, 179, 238, 241
Art 5(1) 113, 177, 238, 240
Art 5(2) 113, 238
Art 5(3) 114, 177, 238

Art 5(3)(b) 244
Art 5(3)(c) 244
Art 5(4) 114, 238
Art 5(5) 114
Art 5(6) 238, 244
Art 5(7) 114, 238
Art 5(8) 113
Arts 5-8 .... 71, 216
Art 6 .... 11, 41, 94, 124, 156, 161–2, 176–7, 238
Art 6(3) 161, 179
Art 6(4) 114, 161, 238
Art 6(5) 115, 116, 162, 179, 239, 244
Art 6(6) 36, 95–6, 114, 116, 161, 178, 179, 238
Art 6(7) 96, 114, 161
Art 6(8) 180
Art 6(9) 115
Art 6(10) 114
Art 6(11) 115, 117
Art 7 .... 11, 124, 156
Art 7(1) 178, 179
Art 7(2) 115, 116, 179
Art 7(3) 116
Art 8 115
Art 9 .... 35, 40, 195, 196, 216, 295
Art 9(1) 9, 72, 95, 111, 244
Art 9(2) 72, 95, 111, 217, 245
Art 10 .... 36, 40, 60, 72, 196, 216, 246
Art 10(2) 111, 246
Art 10(3) 246, 247
Art 10(4) 111, 247
Art 11 .... 8, 36, 181, 216, 217, 248–9
Art 11(2) 112, 217–18
Art 11(3) 249
Art 11(4) 97, 218, 249, 250, 251
Art 11(5) 8, 112, 251
Art 12 .... 35, 39, 112, 270, 281, 283, 304, 311
Art 12(1) 282, 304
Art 12(2) 253, 304, 311
Art 12(5) 112, 304
Arts 12–15 94
Arts 12–16 .... 78, 226, 227, 251
Arts 12–17 222
Art 13 .... 9, 35, 251, 253, 270–1, 281, 283
Art 14 .... 9, 35, 39, 271, 282, 283
Art 14(1) 251, 311
Art 14(2) 59, 112, 304, 311
Art 15 .... 59, 94, 112, 251–2, 269–70, 282, 283, 312

Art 16 .... 10, 35, 73, 269, 304
Art 16(1) 206
Art 17 .... 40, 73, 226, 296, 298–305, 312
Art 17(1) 36, 74, 94–5, 113, 296, 301–2, 310
Art 17(2) 8, 36, 74, 95, 111, 180, 227, 233, 295, 298
Art 17(3) 113, 296, 301, 302
Art 18 254
Art 18(1) 246
Art 18(3) 111, 112, 254
Art 19 254
Art 19(1) 112, 254–5
Art 19(2) 113, 249
Art 19(3) 113, 249, 255
Art 19(4) 249
Art 20 .... 13, 117, 118
Art 21 219
Art 21(1) 3

International

Agreement on Trade-Related Aspects of Intellectual Property Rights (TRIPS) 62
European Convention on Human Rights
Art 6(1) 182

National

Finland

Competition Restrictions Act 1992 (480/1992) 228

Greece

Administrative Proceedings Code
Art 5 240
Civil Code
Art 44(1) 250
Art 71 250
Art 480 249
Art 481 250
Art 871 254
Art 904 252
Art 914 .... 237, 246, 250, 252
Art 926 250
Art 927 250
Art 937 .... 246, 247

Civil Procedure Code
Art 107 240
Art 214A 254
Art 216 241
Arts 338-440 245
Arts 450-52 240–1
Art 452(3) 241
Art 731 241
Code of Lawyers 2013 (Law 4194/2013) 254
Constitution
Art 5A 240
Art 7 250
Art 10 240
Criminal Code
Art 111 247
Art 255 247
Art 260 247
Art 261 247
Modernisation of Code of Civil Procedure 2011
(Law 3994/2011) 254
Protection of Free Competition (Law 3959/2011) 237, 239, 245, 256
Art 1 250
Art 32 245
Art 42 247
Art 42(3) 247
Art 44 247
Regulation on the Functioning and Management of
the Competition Commission 2013 (FEK B'2507/16.1.2013)
Art 15(9) 239
Art 23(4) 239

Hungary

Competition Act
s 8(8) 301

Netherlands

Civil Code
Art 3:303 237
Art 3:305 247
Art 3:305a 255
Art 3:310 247
Art 3:316 247
Art 3:317 247
Art 6:6 250

Art 6:13 ... 251
Art 6:14 ... 255
Art 6:100 ... 253
Art 6:102:1 ... 250
Art 6:162 ... 237
Art 6:229 ... 248
Art 7:900 ... 255
Art 7:907 ... 255
Civil Procedure Act
Art 21 ... 241, 242
Art 22 ... 241, 242
Art 85 ... 241
Art 126 ... 241
Art 843a ... 241, 242, 243
Art 1020 ... 255
Government Information (Public Access) Act ... 243
Art 10 ... 243
Art 10(2) ... 243
Art 11 ... 243

Norway

Competition Act
s 1 ... 50

Poland

Access to Public Information Act 2001
Art 5(2) ... 211
Cartel Act 1933 ... 203
Cartel Agreements Act 1939 ... 203
Civil Code 1964 (KC)
Art 415 ... 209
Art 441(1) ... 209
Civil Procedure Code (KPC) ... 207
Art 63 ... 210
Art 177(1)(3) ... 208
Claims in Group Proceedings Act 2009 (PCA) ... 204, 213–15
Art 1(2) ... 213
Art 2 ... 214
Competition Act 1987 ... 203–4
Competition Act 1990 ... 203, 204
Competition and Consumer Protection Act 2000 ... 204
Competition and Consumer Protection Amendment Act 2014 ... 204, 210
Competition and Consumer Protection Act 2007 (CCPA) ... 204
Art 6 ... 218

Art 70 212
Art 70(1) 212, 213
Art 70(2) 212
Art 70(3) 212
Art 70(4) 212
Art 70(5) 212–13
Art 70(6) 213
Art 73(1) 211
Art 73(2) 211
Art 73(2)(5) 211, 212, 213

Portugal

Constitution
Art 1 198
Art 52(2) 198
Civil Code
Art 498 196
Art 562 194
Civil Procedure Code
Art 11 193
Art 30 193
Art 41 193
Arts 429-42 193
Art 483 193
Art 562 193
Securities Code
Art 31 200
Law 83/95 Popular Action Act 198–9
Art 2 199
Art 3 199
Art 13 199
Art 16 199
Art 17 199
Art 18 199
Art 20 199
Art 22(2) 199
Art 22(4) 200
Art 22(5) 200
Decree Law 34/2008
Art 26.2 194
Law 19/2012 Competition Law 196, 200–1
Art 12 192
Art 22 194
Decree Law 67/2012 193

Law 72/2014
  Art 2.9 ... 194

Sweden

Arbitration Proceedings Act 1999 ... 56
Code of Judicial Procedure 1942 ... 276
  Chapter 10 ... 56
  Chapter 35 s 5 ... 57, 75
  Chapter 36 s 6 ... 62
  Chapter 38 s 2 ... 61
Collective Actions Act 2002 ... 62, 79, 276
Competition Act 1993 ... 12, 57, 60, 75, 274–5
Competition Act 2008 ... 58
  Chapter 2 s 1 ... 275
  Chapter 2 s 7 ... 275
  Chapter 3 s 25 ... 43, 55, 72, 275
  Chapter 3 s 26 ... 55, 275
  Chapter 7 s 2 ... 302
  Chapter 8 s 8 ... 302
Damages Act 1972 ... 55
Interest Act 1975
  s 4 ... 77
Patents Act 1967 ... 55
Regulation 2002:814 on competence in collective actions ... 80

United Kingdom

Competition Act 1998
  s 47A ... 31

United States

Clayton Act 1914
  s 4 ... 16, 19, 39, 40, 265–7
  s 4B ... 19, 40
  s 5(a) ... 19, 20, 40
  s 5(i) ... 19, 40
  s 16 ... 19, 39
Federal Rules of Civil Procedure
  Rule 12(b)(6) ... 24
  Rule 23 ... 199
Sherman Act 1890
  s 1 ... 25, 267
  s 2 ... 16
  s 16 ... 16

Part I

Main Policy Issues and Particular Challenges

1

Introduction to the Directive on Competition Damages Actions

ULF BERNITZ*

1. THE NEW DIRECTIVE

THE FOCAL POINT of this book is the new EU Directive on competition damages actions.[1] After years of preparations, it was finally adopted by the European Parliament and the Council in the autumn of 2014 and shall be implemented in all the Member States by 27 December 2016 at the latest.[2] The new Directive is remarkable for several important reasons.

Firstly, it is the first time the EU has issued a Directive in the field of competition law. We are all aware of the trend of the last decade towards convergence between national competition law in the Member States and the EU competition law. The convergence is partly based on the EU law requirements on national competition law and its application following from the basic EU Regulation No 1/2003 on the implementation of the competition rules laid down in the Treaty,[3] but to a very large extent the convergence is the result of decisions made independently and successively in the Member States. However, the enforcement of the right to compensation for harm resulting from infringements of Union and national competition law has been found to be uneven and dysfunctional.[4] This has triggered the application of Article 114 TFEU on the approximation of laws as the legal basis for

* Professor of European Law at Stockholm University.

[1] Directive 2014/104/EU of the European Parliament and of the Council of 26 November 2014 on certain rules governing actions for damages under national law for infringements of the competition law provisions of the Member States and of the European Union [2014] OJ L349/1.

[2] Directive 2014/104/EU, Art 21(1).

[3] Council Regulation (EC) No 1/2003 of 16 December 2002 on the implementation of the rules on competition laid down in Articles 81 and 82 of the Treaty [2003] OJ L1/1.

[4] See Directive 2014/104/EU, rec 8.

a competition damages directive in order to improve the functioning of the internal market and competition law enforcement.[5]

Secondly, the Directive contains a substantial number of rules on the right to damages. These include rules on the right to full compensation, the quantification of harm, the position of different types of claimants, joint and several liability, limitation periods, etc. It is true that the basic principles of the EU law on the right to damages had already been established by the case law of the CJEU, primarily the seminal *Brasserie du Pêcheur and Factortame* judgment of 1996.[6] However, in that judgment the Court only expressed basic principles and general directions for national courts to consider when assessing damages for infringements of Union law. The new Directive goes a great deal further. By introducing detailed rules on many aspects of the law on damages for infringements of competition law, the Union has taken a big step towards harmonising an important area of tort law.

Thirdly, the Directive contains detailed rules on a number of issues of procedural law. In general, procedural law matters are regarded as part of the competences of the Member States. This assumption is not entirely true, but it is still remarkable to find in the Directive an entire chapter with the heading Disclosure of Evidence (Chapter II). This Chapter contains detailed rules on evidence matters, primarily with the national courts as addressees. The Directive also includes Chapter VI, albeit a shorter Chapter, on Consensual Dispute Resolution. Thus, also in the area of procedural law, the Directive requires a fairly far-reaching harmonisation of national law.[7]

Naturally, the new Directive raises a large number of questions that require legal scrutiny. The aim of this book is to analyse and discuss the new legal regime established by the Directive.

2. THE BACKGROUND

The background of the Directive should be touched upon in brief. In Europe, antitrust damages actions have been, and still are, a rather underdeveloped area of law. In American antitrust law, the opposite holds true. In the US, the lion's share of all legal actions based on infringements of antitrust law are private actions in which the plaintiff(s) claim(s) damages. Normally, the

[5] In addition, the Directive cites as legal basis Art 103 TFEU, which gives certain powers to issue regulations and directives to give effect to the principles set out in Arts 101 and 102 TFEU.

[6] Joined Cases C-46/93 and C-48/93 *Brasserie du Pêcheur SA v Bundesrepublik Deutschland and The Queen v Secretary of State for Transport ex parte Factortame Ltd and others* [1996] ECR I-1029, paras 81–90.

[7] The nearest counterpart in earlier EU legislation would be Directive 2004/48/EC of the European Parliament and of the Council of 29 April 2004 on the enforcement of intellectual property rights [2004] OJ L157/45.

plaintiff is entitled to recover three-fold the damages he has sustained, ie treble damages plus litigation costs.[8] This is certainly an important factor driving private antitrust litigation and there are many cases in which large sums of damages have been awarded. Antitrust is also an area where class actions based on treble damages claims have become particularly important.

With full knowledge of the American realities, the idea to stimulate damages actions as a way of increasing the observance and impact of the competition law has long been on the agenda of the EU. The state of the law was rather uncertain for many years as no Treaty Article nor any EU Regulation on competition law contained any provisions on the right to claim damages. However, in 2001, in the seminal *Courage v Crehan* case,[9] the Court of Justice clearly stated that any individual (including undertakings) has the right to claim damages for loss caused to that person by a contract or conduct in breach of Article 101(1) TFEU. The Court recalled that Articles 101(1) and 102 TFEU produce direct effects on relationships between individuals and create rights for the individuals concerned, which the national courts must safeguard.[10] The Court based its conclusion that there is a right to damages on the necessity to secure the full effect of the competition rules.[11] It is generally agreed that the legal situation as to the right to damages is the same with regard to breaches of Article 102 TFEU, although there is still no Court of Justice judgment on that point. In the subsequent *Manfredi* case from 2006, the Court was more specific on the assessment of damages and declared that injured persons in competition law cases must be able to seek compensation not only for actual loss (*damnum emergens*) but also for loss of profit (*lucrum cessans*) plus interest.[12]

In 2005, a major law firm was commissioned to carry out a study by the Commission on the possibilities and limitations to claim damages for infringements of EU competition law in the legal systems of the Member States. The study, known as the Ashurst Study, showed that there was, in general, an astonishing diversity and underdevelopment of the laws of the Member States concerning this matter. Only a small percentage of the victims of competition law infringements appeared to obtain damages.[13] The law

[8] Clayton Act s 4. For a further comparison of competition damages actions in the EU and the US, see A Jones, ch 2 in this edited volume.

[9] Case C-453/99 *Courage Ltd v Bernard Crehan and Bernard Crehan v Courage Ltd and Others* [2001] ECR I-6297.

[10] The leading case is Case 127/73 *Belgische Radio en Televisie and société belge des auteurs, compositeurs et éditeurs v SV SABAM and NV Fonior* [1974] ECR 51; see in particular para 16.

[11] See in particular paras 23, 25 and 26.

[12] Joined Cases C-295/04 to 298/04 *Vincenzo Manfredi v Lloyd Adriatico Assicurazioni SpA et al* [2006] ECR I-6619, para 95.

[13] D Waelbroeck, D Slater and G Even-Shoshan, 'Ashurst Study on the Conditions of Claims for Damages in Case of Infringement of EC Competition Rules: Comparative Report' (Brussels, 2004), available at ec.europa.eu/competition/antitrust/actionsdamages/comparative_report_clean_en.pdf (last accessed 1 March 2015).

was found to be most developed in the United Kingdom, the Netherlands and Germany. The Ashurst Study was followed by several other studies, in particular a Green Paper and a White Paper published by the Commission. The Green Paper expressed the opinion that the low degree of compensation for antitrust damages was due to legal and procedural obstacles in the Member States and it proposed a number of options for a more efficient system of damages actions for infringements of EU competition law.[14]

The White Paper that followed in 2008 contained a number of legislative proposals to facilitate damages actions for infringements of antitrust law. It proposed, *inter alia*, the introduction of representative actions and opt-in collective actions to facilitate access to damages procedures for victims suffering small and scattered damages. Furthermore, it proposed a measure conferring binding force on decisions of national competition authorities in subsequent civil procedures. Also, it proposed a measure to make it clear to Member States, which require fault to be proven in civil procedures, that once a victim has proven a breach of Articles 101 and 102 TFEU, the infringer should be liable for the damages caused unless he demonstrates that the fault was the result of a genuine excusable error.[15]

However, it took until 2013 before the Commission presented its formal proposal for the Directive,[16] which has since been enacted by the Parliament and the Council. A major reason for the delay was probably problems related to the handling of evidence presented to the Commission as part of the leniency system. This issue will be dealt with below in Section 4.

Another reason for the delay has been differences of opinion on the introduction of a collective redress mechanism. The proposals in the White Paper concerning the introduction of Union legislation in the antitrust field on representative actions and collective opt-in collective actions in order to manage small and scattered damage claims were dropped during the legislative

[14] Commission, 'Green Paper on Damages actions for breach of the EC antitrust rules' COM(2005) 672 final. For further information about the actual status of the law and its application in different parts of the EU, see eg A Komninos, *EC Private Antitrust Enforcement* (Oxford, Hart Publishing, 2008); D Ashton, D Henry, *Competition Damages Actions in the EU: Law and Practice* (Cheltenham, Edward Elgar Publishing, 2013) and B Rodger (ed), *Competition Law Comparative Private Enforcement and Collective Redress across the EU* (Alphen aan den Rijn, Kluwer Law, 2014). See also J Basedow (ed), *Private Enforcement of EC Competition Law* (Alphen aan den Rijn, Kluwer Law, 2007); and GC Rodriguez Iglesias and L Ortiz Blanco (eds), *The Judicial Application of Competition Law: Proceedings of the FIDE XXIV Congress Madrid 2010* (vol 2, comprehensive national reports).

[15] Commission, 'White Paper on Damages actions for breach of the EC antitrust rules' COM(2008) 165 final. The White Paper was accompanied by the more comprehensive Commission, 'Staff Working Paper accompanying the White Paper on Damages actions for breach of the EC antitrust rules' SEC(2008) 404.

[16] Commission, 'Proposal for a Directive of the European Parliament and of the Council on certain rules governing actions for damages under national law for infringements of the competition law provisions of the Member States and of the European Union' COM(2013) 404 final.

process, at least partially as a result of opposition from business organisations. Instead, the deliberations have resulted in a Commission Recommendation on common principles for an injunctive and compensatory collective redress mechanism to be introduced in the Member States.[17] The Recommendation is not restricted to competition law cases but more generally framed, including consumer law cases. As a result, the Directive does not contain any provisions on collective redress.

3. AIMS AND IMPORTANT FEATURES

The basic aim of the new Directive on competition damages actions and its implementation and application in the Member States is certainly to promote the effectiveness of the prohibitions on cartels and anticompetitive behaviour and to act as a deterrent. The rules are also aimed at securing the right to compensation for natural and legal persons who have suffered harm caused by infringements of competition law but that aim seems to be regarded as somewhat secondary.

It is evident the European system established by the Directive in conjunction with existing case law of the Court of Justice will not function as a real counterpart to private litigation under American antitrust law. The European rules are aimed at full compensation, including compensation for actual loss and loss of profit, but no more;[18] there is no counterpart to the American practice of awarding treble damages. Actually, the Directive explicitly states that full compensation under the Directive shall not lead to overcompensation, whether by means of punitive, multiple or other types of damages.[19] Also, when it comes to the disclosure of evidence and litigation costs, the American system seems more favourable to the claimants. The Directive leaves the issue of litigation costs to national procedural law. In addition, there is no really workable alternative to the American class action system. Implementation of the Commission Recommendation on compensatory collective redress mechanisms is left to national law in the Member States.

However, there are important features in the Directive that should strengthen the exercise and effectiveness of antitrust damages actions in Europe, compared to the situation at present. First and foremost, all EU Member States will be obliged to have rules on damages actions and the right to compensation that fulfil the requirements set out in the Directive.

[17] Commission Recommendation 2013/396/EU of 11 June 2013 on common principles for injunctive and compensatory collective redress mechanisms in the Member States concerning violations of rights granted under Union Law [2013] OJ L201/60.

[18] Directive 2014/104/EU, Art 3(1).

[19] ibid Art 3(3).

However, the Directive is not a full harmonisation directive; Member States remain free to have/introduce more advanced rules on the possibilities to obtain damages as long as these rules do not conflict with the requirements of the Directive.

The basic aim of the Directive is to ensure that anyone who has suffered harm caused by an infringement of competition law by an undertaking can effectively exercise the right to claim full compensation for that harm from that undertaking.[20] There is no requirement concerning negligence on behalf of the infringing undertaking. Not including a criterion of fault (culpa) is in line with Union law on the right to damages.[21]

On the quantification of harm, the Directive contains an important rule on the reversed burden of proof. It is presumed that cartel infringements cause harm; however, the infringer shall have the right to rebut that presumption.[22] On this point the recitals give important additional information by pointing at price-fixing as the essential element. It is stated that cartels, in particular, have an effect on prices resulting in a rise in prices or preventing a decrease in prices which would otherwise have occurred but for the cartel. However, the presumption should not cover the actual amount of harm.[23] It is worth noting that the Directive contains a legal definition of the concept 'cartel'; a novelty in European competition law.[24] Outside the cartel area, primarily with regard to damages claims caused by the abuse of a dominant position, no presumption is applicable. It will be most interesting to see how the presumption will be applied by the national courts, in particular what will be required in order to rebut the presumption.[25]

Undertakings, which have infringed competition law through joint behaviour, are jointly and severally liable for the harm caused by the infringement.[26] In other words, the injured party has the right to require full compensation from any of them. Between the infringers, it will be possible to recover a contribution. However, there is a special derogation for small and medium-sized enterprises (SMEs). Under certain conditions they are liable only to their own purchasers. There will also be special treatment for infringers, which have been granted immunity from fines under a leniency programme. They are normally only liable for the harm caused to their own direct or indirect purchasers or providers,[27] not harm caused by other

[20] ibid, Art 1(1).
[21] *cf Brasserie* (n 6) paras 76–79.
[22] Directive 2014/104/EU, Art 17(2).
[23] ibid, rec 47.
[24] ibid, Art 2(14).
[25] For further details on the quantification of harm and the Practical Guide accompanying the Directive, see M Iacovides, ch 16 in this edited volume.
[26] Directive 2014/104/EU, Art 11.
[27] ibid, Art 11(5) second sentence and rec 38.

members of a cartel. This partial protection of whistleblowing undertakings is in line with the special limits on access to leniency documents, see below.

Another rule, aimed at enhancing the impact of the new system, is the provision on the effect of final decisions made. The Member States are obliged to ensure that an infringement of competition law found by a final decision of a national competition authority or by a review court is deemed to be irrefutably established for the purposes of an action for damages before the national courts.[28] Thus, it will not be permitted to reargue the underlying facts in a follow-on litigation about the awarding of damages.

In a recent judgment related to a major elevator cartel, the Court of Justice ruled on 'umbrella pricing', ie higher prices charged by an undertaking as a result of a prohibited cartel to which the undertaking is not a party but from which it has benefited. Stressing the importance of the full effectiveness of Article 101 TFEU, the Court stated that any individual may claim damages for loss caused to him/her, by a contract or by conduct liable to restrict or distort competition. It should be possible to claim damages also for loss resulting from umbrella pricing, as such prices are the result of a cartel managing to maintain artificially high prices.[29] In another case, also related to the elevator cartel, the Court of Justice found that the European Union, represented by the Commission, may act as plaintiff in a civil action for damages caused to the Union as a buyer concerning the activities of a cartel.[30]

Price increases caused by cartels or other infringements of competition law are often 'passed on' down the supply chain, causing harm to undertakings as indirect purchasers (eg, retailers) or consumers. The Directive is based on the principle that indirect purchasers, consumers included, are entitled to compensation by the infringer for such harm suffered.[31] On this point, the EU has opted for a solution that is different from American antitrust law. In its seminal judgment in 1977 in the *Illinois Brick* case,[32] the US Supreme Court decided to bar follow-on claimants from bringing an antitrust damages action. However, it might be difficult for follow-on claimants to prove the extent of harm caused. The fact that the Directive permits the defendant in an action for damages to invoke as a defence that the claimant passed on the whole or part of the overcharge downstream does not facilitate the assessment.[33] The rather complicated Directive rules on the

[28] ibid, Art 9(1).
[29] Case C-557/12 *Kone AG and Others v ÖBB-Infrastruktur AG* EU:C:2014:1317.
[30] Case C-199/11 *Europese Gemeenschap v Otis NV and Others* EU:C:2012:684.
[31] Directive 2014/104/EU, Art 14.
[32] *Illinois Brick Co et al v Illinois et al* 431 US 720 (1977).
[33] Directive 2014/104/EU, Art 13.

passing-on of overcharges will not be discussed here.[34] The Commission will issue guidelines in order to clarify the application.[35]

4. THE DISCLOSURE OF EVIDENCE

As mentioned above, the Directive contains specific provisions on the disclosure of evidence. This is an area where there exists in general an important difference between common law and civil law. In common law jurisdictions, rules on discovery offer claimants a broad scope regarding demands to disclose evidence. In civil law jurisdictions, requests to disclose evidence normally have to be more specific. Here, the Directive seems to have chosen a middle way. Upon the request of a claimant who has presented a reasoned justification, national courts have to be able to order not only the disclosure of specific items of evidence but also 'relevant categories of evidence'.[36] However, these have to be circumscribed as precisely and narrowly as possible on the basis of reasonably available facts. When applying these rules a proportionality test must be applied.[37] For a country like Sweden, the Directive rules on disclosure of evidence seem to be more favourable to the claimant than the present state of the law. On the other hand, the Directive rules do not seem to allow 'fishing expeditions', ie demands for large amounts of documentation in order to find out if they contain anything useful for the claimant.

An important problem that seems to have delayed the legislative process has concerned the access to leniency documents by alleged victims of antitrust infringements. Based on earlier notices, a special Commission Notice on Immunity from Fines and Reduction of Fines in Cartel Cases, the Leniency Notice, is in force.[38] The Commission's policy is to allow total immunity from fines to the first undertaking in a secret cartel to inform the Commission about the cartel activities and to impose lower fines than would otherwise be the case on undertakings that provide the Commission with further evidence that enables it to proceed more effectively with the investigation of a case. The leniency system seems to have been successful and most of the cartel cases brought by the Commission in recent years started out with information from a whistle-blower. As is clearly stated in the Leniency Notice, the immunity from or reduction of fines cannot protect

[34] See M Strand, *The Passing-On Problem in EU Law Damages and Restitution* (Uppsala University (diss) 2015). Passing-on is also discussed by many of the authors in this edited volume.

[35] Directive 2014/104/EU, Art 16.

[36] ibid, Art 5.

[37] ibid, rec 16.

[38] Commission Notice on Immunity from Fines and Reduction of Fines in Cartel Cases ('Leniency Notice') [2006] OJ C298/11, para 17.

an undertaking from the civil law consequences of its participation in an infringement of Article 101 TFEU.[39] However, the question whether, and to what extent, other undertakings are able to gain access to the evidence in relation to a private damages litigation remains an important one.

The practice of the Commission has been to refuse such access. If leniency documents were disclosed to alleged victims of antitrust infringements, it could discourage potential leniency applicants from coming forward, thus compromising cartel detection and punishment. However, the Court of Justice has rejected the idea that EU law should contain a general rule refusing such victims access to leniency documents. Instead, the Court prescribed in two cases, *Pfleiderer*[40] and *Donau Chemie*,[41] that the protected interests shall be weighed up on a case-by-case basis. In *Donau Chemie*, the Court specified that such

> weighing-up is necessary because, in competition law in particular, any rule that is rigid, either by providing for absolute refusal to grant access to the documents in question or for granting access to those documents as a matter of course, is liable to undermine the effective application of, *inter alia*, Article 101 TFEU and the rights that provision confers on individuals.[42]

These decisions by the Court were probably not too well received by the Commission and in the end seem to have contributed to speeding up the Commission's proposal for the Directive on competition damages now enacted. Articles 6 and 7 of the Directive contain detailed rules on the disclosure of evidence included in the file of a competition authority.[43] The result can be characterised as a compromise and might lead to difficulties when it comes to practical application.[44]

5. WILL THE DIRECTIVE FULFIL ITS AIMS?

In summary, there are a number of important new elements that are included in the Directive and which are aimed at enhancing the good functioning of an effective European antitrust damages action system. However, one key question remains to be answered and that is whether, and to what extent, the new Directive will prove to be a success. It is a well-known fact that it is often difficult to bring damages claims to a successful result in court. Complicated and often disputed facts have to be proven, causation and the

[39] ibid, para 39.
[40] Case C-360/09 *Pfleiderer AG v Bundeskartellamt* [2011] ECR I-5161.
[41] Case C-536/11 *Bundeswettbewerbsbehörde v Donau Chemie* EU:C:2013:366.
[42] ibid, para 31.
[43] See also Directive 2014/104/EU, recs 26 and 38.
[44] See for instance, B Lundqvist and H Andersson, ch 9 in this edited volume.

existence of harm must be established, and the size of the damage itself has to be clarified, eg the calculation of an overcharge or a profit loss. For all these points, there is often room for counterarguments of substance. As mentioned, many of the features that make the American private antitrust litigation system successful are lacking in Europe. However, national courts should bear in mind when considering competition damages claims, that it is the lodestar of the Court of Justice, as expressed in all its decisions within the field, to secure the full effectiveness and practical effect of the prohibitions laid down in Articles 101 and 102. As stated by the Court in *Kone*:

> The right of any individual to claim compensation for such a loss actually strengthens the working of the European Union competition rules, since it discourages agreements or practices, frequently covert, which are liable to restrict or distort competition, thereby making a significant contribution to the maintenance of effective competition in the European Union.[45]

Evidently, a restrictive interpretation of national law based on the Directive will not fit well with European case law as applied by the Court of Justice.

My personal view might be somewhat influenced by my knowledge of the realities in Sweden. Actually, Sweden was a pioneer in the field by introducing statutory provisions on the right to claim antitrust damages already in its Competition Act of 1993. These provisions were further clarified and expanded by certain amendments in the statutory text in 2005.[46] However, after 20 years there is only one completed case in which a Swedish court has awarded damages based on an infringement of the competition law, a Court of Appeals judgment of 2011.[47] There have also been settlements out of court in some cases, but the majority of cases brought to court have failed.[48] There are probably two major explanations behind the very limited success so far of the Swedish provisions on competition law damages. The first has to do with the many procedural and other difficulties involved in bringing competition law damages suits to court and to pursue them successfully. The second one seems to be that Sweden, like many other European countries, lacks a legal tradition and culture in this specific area.

The enactment of new national legislation implementing the Directive might mark the starting point of a rapid increase in out-of-court claims and lawsuits for antitrust damages all over the EU and the European Economic Area. There is certainly no lack of actual cases that could offer good reasons

[45] *Kone* (n 29) para 23.

[46] Prop 2004/05:117 *Skadestånd enligt konkurrenslagen, m.m.* (Swedish Government Bill on competition damages).

[47] *Svea hovrätt* (Svea Court of Appeals), judgment of 19 January 2011 in case T 10012-08, *Euroclear Sweden v Europe Invest Direct et al.*

[48] See I Simonsson, ch 4 in this edited volume. The situation in Finland, having similar legislation and legal environment, is discussed by K Havu in ch 12.

for such claims. In any case, the new Directive involves an important challenge for legal scholars to clarify and elaborate this important sector of the competition law. However, it remains to be seen whether we will experience such a development, at least in the near future. According to a final provision in the Directive, the Commission shall review it and submit a report in 2020;[49] and, if appropriate, the report shall be accompanied by a legislative proposal. I am not convinced that the present legislative text will represent the final word.

[49] Directive 2014/104/EU, Art 20.

2

Private Enforcement of EU Competition Law: A Comparison with, and Lessons from, the US

ALISON JONES*

1. INTRODUCTION

IN ORDER FOR the objectives of a competition law system to be achieved, effective enforcement of the rules must take place. Without it, the meaning of the law will not be developed and elucidated, breaches of the rules will not be halted, punished or deterred and victims of violations will not be compensated;[1] 'deterrence, compensation, and remediation'[2] will not be ensured.

A critical issue to be determined when designing or developing a competition law system is therefore how effective enforcement mechanisms can be established. Many systems rely heavily on public enforcement to protect society's interest in the efficient working of markets. The questions of how public enforcement institutions should be designed, how they can curb and deter infringements and how competition law decisions should be taken, checked and reviewed, has provoked extensive debate and a rich and wide literature.[3] This chapter, however, focuses on private enforcement

* Professor of Law, King's College London.

[1] W Wils, 'The Relationship between Public Antitrust Enforcement and Private Actions for Damages' (2009) 32 *World Competition* 3. Competition law can be conceptualised as rules to correct public wrongs, private wrongs or market failures, see N Dunne, 'The Role of Private Enforcement within EU Competition Law' (2013–14) 16 *Cambridge Yearbook for European Legal Studies* 143.

[2] See AI Gavil, 'Designing Private Rights of Action for Competition Policy Systems: The Role of Interdependence and the Advantages of a Sequential Approach' in P Lowe and M Marquis (eds), *Integrating Public and Private Enforcement of Competition Law—Implications for Courts and Agencies European Competition Law Annual 2011* (Oxford, Hart Publishing, 2014) (remediation provides means for halting offensive conduct and perhaps correcting for its adverse competitive effects, as with equitable and injunctive relief).

[3] Decision theory has prompted close scrutiny of system design and evaluation of system performance—in particular the cost of enforcement, whether it is likely to produce errors

and, in particular, on the questions of whether private enforcement of the rules by those specifically harmed by a competition law violation should be encouraged in the EU and, if so, how and how it should interact with public enforcement. These are important issues. Public enforcers have limited resources which they may concentrate principally on ensuring that serious violations which cause wide-spread harm to consumer welfare (such as cartels) are brought to an end and deterred. Accordingly they are not able to root out and prevent all violations of the rules or to ensure compensation for victims. In the EU, for example, the European Commission (the 'Commission') does not have power to award damages to those that have suffered loss in consequence of an antitrust infringement, although it has been active in trying to facilitate private actions by victims for compensation.[4] Private litigation may consequently play a fundamental part in ensuring effective enforcement of the competition law rules.

In the US, Congress made a conscious policy choice when adopting the antitrust laws to encourage private litigants to participate in their enforcement.[5] Over time, and combined with other elements of, and developments in, the US system, the net result of this choice has been that, uniquely in the world, a vast majority of antitrust enforcement in the US (approximately 90 per cent of cases)[6] emanates from private litigation rather than public enforcement. Such actions arguably play a crucial function decentralising decision-taking, democratising antitrust policy, affirming the rule of law, deterring violations and ensuring that victims obtain compensation. The system has encouraged such high volumes of litigation, however, that it has been felt necessary, through a series of steps, to adjust the system to ensure that some of its perceived excesses are moderated; in particular, to ensure that unmeritorious

(Type 1 or Type 2 errors) and the likely implications of such errors, see eg, Gavil (n 2); WE Kovacic, 'Rating the Competition Agencies: What Constitutes Good Performance?' (2000) 16 *George Mason Law Review* 903; M Trebilcock and E Iacobucci, 'Designing Competition Law Institutions' (2002) 25 *World Competition* 361.

[4] See s 3 below. But see eg OFT Press Release 88/06 'Independent Schools Agree Settlement' 19 May 2006, and the provisions on voluntary redress in the UK's Consumer Rights Act 2015, Schedule 8.

[5] See now especially Clayton Act 1914, s 4 (superseding and expanding provisions set out in the Sherman Act 1890) and s 16, as well as s 2 below.

[6] See eg, HJ Hovenkamp, 'Quantification of Harm in Private Antitrust Actions in the United States' *University of Iowa Legal Studies Research Paper*, available at http://ssrn.com/abstract=1758751; Report for the European Commission, 'Making Antitrust Damages Actions More Effective in the EU: Welfare Impact and Potential Scenarios' DG COMP/2006/A3/012D, 28 and D Crane, *The Institutional Structure of Antitrust Enforcement* (Oxford, Oxford University Press, 2011) 163. It is difficult to get completely precise statistics relating to the ratio of private to public enforcement however. Because many separate private action cases may be filed in relation to the same case before consolidation (see n 61), there may be over-counting of private actions. In contrast, as many public cases may be resolved before a case is filed, there may be under-counting of government actions.

antitrust litigation is not encouraged which may have the consequence of chilling procompetitive behaviour and so undermining the objectives of the antitrust laws.[7]

This position contrasts starkly with that which has existed in the EU. Until 2004,[8] the central role in enforcing Articles 101 and 102 (the 'antitrust' rules) was played by the Commission.[9] Although a key objective of Regulation 1/2003[10] was to allow a more decentralised enforcement system to emerge with the courts and tribunals of the individual Member States (the national courts) (as well as national competition authorities (NCAs)) participating more actively within it, a number of factors have combined to preclude private actions from developing evenly across the EU. Indeed, although litigation is growing rapidly in some Member States, particularly the UK, the Netherlands and Germany, significant barriers to private antitrust actions continue to exist in others.

For many years the Commission has taken the view that the EU situation is unsatisfactory and more needs to be done, whilst avoiding the problems that have confronted the US system, to stimulate and harmonise national rules governing private enforcement and to promote a culture of competition within the EU: 'The overall enforcement of the EU competition rules is best guaranteed through complementary public and private enforcement.'[11] In 2013, after extensive debate and discussion as to whether, and if so how, to develop a European approach to private enforcement,[12] the Commission proposed a package of measures on private antitrust actions

[7] But see eg, RH Lande, 'The Proposed Damages Directive: The Real Lessons from the United States' (2014) 2 *CPI Antitrust Chronicle* 1 and s 2 below.

[8] Prior to 2004, Regulation 17 of 1962 [1959–1962] OJ Sp Ed 87 (the first Regulation implementing Arts 101 and 102), conferred the exclusive right on the Commission to rule on the compatibility of an individual agreement with Art 101(3) and made it difficult for the national courts to take part in the enforcement process.

[9] The Directorate General for Competition ('DG Comp', currently headed by Commissioner Vestager) is responsible for competition policy and enforcement. Enforcement of the EU merger rules has, since the first EU Merger Regulation came into force, fallen exclusively to the Commission, see now Regulation 139/2004 of 20 January 2004 on the control of concentrations between undertakings [2004] OJ L24/1, Art 21(2), and cannot be enforced either by NCAs or by private persons before the national courts.

[10] Regulation 1/2003 on the implementation of the rules on competition laid down in [Articles 101 and 102 TFEU] [2003] OJ L1/1. The Commission simply does not have the resources to enforce the rules throughout the EU.

[11] Commission, 'Proposal for a Directive of the European Parliament and the Council on certain rules governing actions for damages under national law for infringements of the Competition law provisions of the Member States and the European Union' COM(2013) 404 final, Explanatory Memorandum 1.2.

[12] They deal with damages actions but not injunctions, see especially a study prepared for DG Comp by Ashurst on damages actions before national courts of the then 25 Member States ('The Ashurst Report'): D Waelbroeck, D Slater and G Even-Shoshan, 'Ashurst Study on the

including: a recommendation of non-binding principles for collective redress mechanisms for Member States;[13] a practical guide on the quantification of harm for damages to assist national courts[14] and a draft Directive[15] designed to facilitate damage claims by removing the main obstacles to full compensation for victims of antitrust violations and ensuring that private and public enforcement operate harmoniously together. The final Directive on certain rules governing actions for damages under national law for infringements of the competition law provisions of the Member States and of the European Union ('the Directive') was signed into law on 26 November 2014 and must be transposed into national law by 27 December 2016.[16]

This chapter examines the core features of this package. Its principal objective is not, however, to scrutinise these provisions in detail (this is the task of subsequent chapters). Rather, its purpose is to reflect on the questions of why, especially when compared with the position in the US, it has proved so difficult for a culture of antitrust litigation to develop in the EU, why the Commission believed that EU measures were necessary to kindle it and to consider, against that backdrop, whether the EU package is likely to achieve its stated goals. Section 2 thus commences by exploring how private enforcement has developed in the US, examining not only the factors that have facilitated and encouraged it, but the extremes widely-believed to have bedevilled and undermined it,[17] and the steps which have consequently been taken to limit and curtail it. Section 3 then examines the EU system and

Conditions of Claims for Damages in Case of Infringement of EC Competition Rules: Comparative Report' (Brussels, 2004); Commission, 'Green Paper on Damages Actions for Breach of the EC Antitrust Rules' COM(2005) 672 final; Commission, 'Staff Working Paper, Annex to the Green Paper on Damages Actions for Breach of the EC Antitrust Rules' SEC(2005) 1732; and Commission, 'White Paper on Damages Actions for Breach of the EC Antitrust Rules' COM(2008) 165 final.

[13] Commission Recommendation 2013/396/EU of 11 June 2013 on common principles for injunctive and compensatory collective redress mechanisms in the Member States concerning violations of rights granted under Union Law [2013] OJ L201/60; see also IP/13/524 and MEMO/13/530 (enabling consumers, by joining claims with others, to get access to justice and pursue infringements of competition law, where the cost of individual action may otherwise have acted as a deterrent, see rec 9). The Recommendation applies not only in the field of competition law but also horizontally to consumer protection, environmental protection, data protection, financial services and other areas where claims for injunctions or damages in respect of breaches of EU law are relevant, rec 7.

[14] Commission, 'Staff Working Document—Practical Guide on Quantifying Harm in Actions for Damages Based on Breaches of Article 101 or 102 of the Treaty on the Functioning of the European Union' SWD(2013) 205.

[15] Commission Proposal (n 11). On 17 April 2014, the Parliament adopted a text of the Directive that was agreed between it and the Council and which included some amendments to the original Commission proposal. The Directive was formally adopted in November 2014 as Directive 2014/104/EU on certain rules governing actions for damages under national law for infringements of the competition law provisions of the Member States and of the European Union [2014] OJ L349/1.

[16] ibid.

[17] '[T]he conventional wisdom in the international competition community [is] that U.S.-style private enforcement has been a disaster', Lande (n 7) 1.

seeks to unpick the different factors that have operated over time as barriers to private litigation in the EU Member States and to identify those that still exist.

Having set out the factors that have encouraged and hindered litigation in the US and the EU respectively and the pros and cons of the respective systems, it is possible to reflect more fully on the questions of whether private litigation should be further encouraged in the EU, what measures might be desirable or required to overcome the obstacles which exist to it, what measures should be avoided, whether the current package is likely to succeed, what pitfalls might be anticipated and/or what further developments and clarifications are likely to be required in the future. Section 4 concludes that the package of reforms is not likely to lead to over-enforcement or to the encouragement of unmeritorious antitrust actions in the EU. What is more of a concern, however, is whether it has done enough to boost and facilitate private damages actions and to create the level playing field across the EU sought by the Commission. Not only does the Directive not institute a completely harmonised framework, leaving a number of potential obstacles to national actions and areas of legal ambiguity outstanding, but a number of the Directive's provisions are liable to introduce considerable complexities into national proceedings. Further, scope for some significant divergences between national rules remains; such differences are likely to continue to affect where litigants choose to commence their actions and to result in forum-shopping.

2. THE PRIVATE LITIGATION SYSTEM IN THE US

The significant role played by private actions in US Antitrust law has resulted from a combination of different individual features of the US system which have developed sequentially[18] and matured over time. A first point of central importance is that the Clayton Act[19] itself encourages private enforcement of the antitrust laws by providing, for: treble damages for those injured by reason of anything forbidden in the antitrust laws;[20] injunctive relief against threatened loss or damage by a violation;[21] the use of judgments entered against the defendant as prima facie evidence against that defendant;[22] clear limitation periods;[23] and successful plaintiffs (claimants) to recover costs,

[18] See eg, Gavil (n 2).
[19] See n 5 above.
[20] Clayton Act 1914, s 4.
[21] ibid s 16.
[22] ibid s 5(a).
[23] The ordinary limitation period of four years (ibid s 4B) also gets suspended during government enforcement proceedings, s 5(i).

including reasonable attorney's fees, contrary to the ordinary rule in the US that each party bears its own attorney fees and costs.[24]

These provisions did not trigger significant volumes of private antitrust litigation on their own, however. Rather, it was not until the 1960s and 1970s that private litigation began to burgeon. Partly, this growth reflected the development of a more interventionist antitrust policy between the 1940s and 1960s, underpinned by a scepticism about the ability of firms and the markets to provide a successful economic outcome and a mistrust of big business and concentrated markets.[25] At this time the Supreme Court[26] adopted broad interpretations of the antitrust statutes (for example, making wide use of per se rules and applying lenient procedural, substantive and evidential burdens of proof)[27] which made it relatively easy for plaintiffs to win cases.[28] This, combined with the following factors, has allowed private litigation to flourish:[29]

— Wide-ranging pre-trial discovery powers exist in the US which assists the collection of relevant and essential evidence.
— Federal rules allow for consolidation of antitrust claims and for the bringing of opt-out class actions.[30]
— Lawyers regularly accept antitrust cases on a contingency fee (no win, no fee) basis;
— Many antitrust cases are tried by jury[31] (so conferring an element of 'unpredictability' to antitrust trials);
— Defendants, as joint tortfeasors, are jointly and severally liable for any damage caused with no right to contribution from co-defendants.[32]

[24] Clayton Act 1914, s 5(a).

[25] See eg E Levi, 'The Antitrust Laws and Monopoly' (1974) 14 *University of Chicago Law Review* 153; C Kaysen and D Turner, *Antitrust Policy* (Cambridge, MA, Harvard University Press, 1959).

[26] During the Warren Court Era (at this time the Chief Justice was Earl Warren (1953–1969)).

[27] For example, courts have applied lesser burdens of proof as to the amount of damages in antitrust cases eg *Zenith Radio Corp v Hazeltine Research* 395 US 100 (1969).

[28] H Hovenkamp, *The Antitrust Enterprise: Principle and Execution* (Cambridge, MA, Harvard University Press, 2005) 1.

[29] See Gavil (n 2) (explaining that 'the field of complex litigation' did not develop until mid-century).

[30] So permitting small claimants to spread costs and aggregate similar claims, making them easier and more economical to bring, see Federal Rules of Civil Procedure, r 23 (defining the standards for bringing class actions).

[31] Criminal antitrust proceedings always involve trial by jury (US Constitution, the Fifth Amendment) and both the plaintiff and the defendant can demand a jury trial in civil cases (US Constitution, the Seventh Amendment) (circuits are split on the question of whether there is a 'complexity exception' to this right, ie whether a jury trial should be denied where the complexity of the factual and legal evidence render it beyond the ability of a jury, see eg *In re Financial Securities Litigation* 609 F2d 411 (9th Cir 1979) (there can be no exception to the right), cert denied 446 US 929 (1980) and *In re Japanese Electronic Products Antitrust Litigation* 631 F2d 1069 (3rd Cir 1980) (recognising an exception)).

[32] *Texas Industries v Radcliff Materials, Inc* 451 US 630 (1981).

Further, as US public enforcement agencies have never adopted such a central role in antitrust enforcement as has their European counterpart, the European Commission, those injured by an antitrust violation have frequently had little choice but to litigate if they wish the infringement to be brought to an end.

In 1968 and 1977 respectively, the Supreme Court also handed down two important judgments, *Hanover Shoe Inc v United Shoe Machine Corp*[33] *and Illinois Brick Co v Illinois*,[34] which facilitated private litigation. These cases hold that: the possibility that a claimant might have recouped some of an anti-competitive overcharge by passing it on to its customers is *not* relevant in the assessment of antitrust damages' cases;[35] and claims brought by *indirect* purchasers should generally be refused[36] (indirect purchaser actions are however possible in a number of states under state law).[37] Although these principles might be criticised on the grounds that they may deny compensation to the real victims of the anti-competitive activity and allow direct purchasers to collect a windfall, they do concentrate antitrust claims in the hands of those most likely to sue,[38] simplify damages' litigation by allowing difficult issues of remoteness and tracing of injury to be side-stepped and reduce the process costs of litigation.[39] In establishing these principles, the Supreme Court consequently seemed to elevate the remediation and deterrent functions served by private enforcement, higher than its compensation function.

By enlisting in these ways the help of those most directly affected by anti-competitive conduct in the enforcement of the law, numerous antitrust cases have been privately litigated, providing the platform for some of the most significant principles of antitrust law to be developed and for the rapid evolution of the law. Private actions have also been able to fill enforcement gaps, offset periods of lax government enforcement, ensure compensation of victims and that disputes between private parties are resolved privately without drawing public agencies within them.

[33] *Hanover Shoe Inc v United Shoe Machine Corp* 392 US 481 (1968).

[34] *Illinois Brick Co v Illinois* 431 US 720 (1977).

[35] Otherwise such claims would become excessively complicated, private actions would be deterred and a wrongdoer in breach would be able to retain his unlawful profits and the fruits of his own illegality.

[36] If the fact that loss has been passed on by the purchaser may not be taken into account defensively in a claim between the seller and the purchaser, it should not be open to an indirect purchaser to use the passing-on principle offensively in damages proceedings. The Court set out three exceptions to this position however.

[37] Such rules are not pre-empted by federal law, *California v ARC Corp* 490 US 93 (1989).

[38] In contrast, provision for apportionment of recovery through the distribution chain, would increase the overall costs of recovery through injecting extremely complex issues into the case; at the same time such an apportionment would reduce the benefits to each plaintiff by dividing the potential recovery among a much larger group and reduce the incentive to sue.

[39] In addition, from the defendant's perspective, they preclude a multiplicity of claims and the risks of duplicate recovery from arising, but see n 37 above and text.

It is well-known, nonetheless, that the virtues of the private enforcement system are not universally extolled and that its benefits have been hotly-debated. Wide-spread concern has been articulated that, especially in the 1960s–1970s and in relation to class actions, damages actions got 'out of control' and that such litigation, motivated by private profit rather than public interest considerations, frequently did not achieve its objectives of ensuring meaningful compensation of victims, including smaller businesses and final consumers, and/or of deterring serious violations. Rather, given the combination of claimant-friendly procedural, evidential and substantive rules,[40] the system has been criticised for being prone to error and for encouraging 'anaemic' claims to be brought and settled by defendants eager to avoid protracted and expensive litigation. In addition, there has been concern that private actions might actually undermine public enforcement and deterrence, by discouraging leniency applications.

Although not all might agree with these, or all of these, criticisms, these types of anxiety have led to a dramatic recalibration of the system. Not only has the legislator stepped in in order to diminish the disincentive of submitting amnesty applications, by de-trebling antitrust damages for corporations that participate in the amnesty programme and cooperate with claimants,[41] but the Supreme Court has expressed concerns about the 'coercive'[42] elements of the antitrust system, the risk of false positives they create and handed down a series of opinions which, collectively, limit the types of antitrust claim that can successfully be brought and appreciably raise the bar for antitrust claimants.[43] In 1977, for example, in order to temper the expansive reach of the substantive rules, it introduced a requirement that plaintiffs should establish not only a violation of the law but 'antitrust injury' ('injury of the type the antitrust laws were intended to prevent ...');[44] so allowing recovery only for loss stemming from the competition-reducing aspects of the conduct. Subsequently, courts have imposed demanding standards for class certification[45] and the Supreme Court has also introduced rigorous doctrines of remoteness,[46] tough screens for introduction

[40] Especially eg, the right to treble damages, the fact that the defendant never gets its costs, even if it wins, the fact that liability is joint and several with no right to contribution from co-defendants and the expansive use by the Supreme Court of per se rules in the 1960s and 1970s. These difficulties are exacerbated by the fact that the costs of discovery may be astronomical (and are likely to be mainly borne by the defendant) and the opt-out class action system encourages huge volumes of litigation and multiple procedures being launched against alleged antitrust infringers.

[41] The Antitrust Criminal Penalty Enhancement and Reform Act 2004.

[42] See eg, *Bell Atlantic Corp v Twombly* 550 US 554 (2007) 557, n 53 below and text, and FH Easterbrook, 'Discovery as Abuse' (1989) 69 *Boston University Law Review* 635.

[43] Gavil (n 2).

[44] *Brunswick Corp v Pueblo Bowl-O-Mat, Inc* 429 US 477 (1977) 489.

[45] See eg, *In re Hydrogen Peroxide Antitrust Litigation* 552 F3d 305 (3d Cir 2008).

[46] See eg, *Blue Shield v McCready* 457 US 465 (1982) and *Hanover Shoe* (n 33).

of expert testimony[47] and been supportive of efforts to safeguard against antitrust claims having a chilling effect on competition through the use of procedural, evidential[48] and substantive rules. For example, in *Matsushita Electric Industrial Co v Zenith Radio Corp*,[49] the Supreme Court indicated that summary judgment should be granted in favour of a defendant where the plaintiff's claim makes no economic sense, is implausible, requires inferences to be drawn from ambiguous evidence, or where the evidence does not tend to exclude the possibility that the defendant acted lawfully (as opposed to illegally).[50] In *F Hoffmann-La Roche Ltd v Empagran SA*,[51] the Supreme Court reined in the circumstances in which foreign claimants are able to seek damages before the US courts. In *Verizon Communications Inc v Law Offices of Curtis V Trinko LLP*,[52] the Court, retreating from previous case law, adopted a 'skeptical stance ... toward the benefits of judicial policing of refusals to deal' and counselled generally against an undue expansion of section 2 of the Sherman Act liability. In *Bell Atlantic Corp v Twombly*,[53] the Supreme Court stepped up the standard for pleading an antitrust complaint, obtaining discovery and surviving a motion to dismiss (in that case the Court essentially dismissed a complaint on the grounds that the factual allegations made were no more likely indicative of prohibited than permitted action). Finally, in *Leegin Creative Leather Products Inc v PSKS, Inc*,[54] the Court took a further step in the retreat from per se rules commenced in *Continental TV, Inc v GTE Sylvania*[55] (where the Court held that rule of reason is the prevailing and presumptive standard under section 1 Sherman Act) and overruled the nearly century-old rule against minimum resale price maintenance, holding that such arrangements should be analysed under the rule of reason.

The developments relating to procedure have, in particular, made it easier for antitrust defendants to escape a full antitrust trial either on the basis that the complaint fails to state a claim upon which relief can be granted

[47] See eg, *Daubert v Merrell Dow Pharmaceuticals, Inc* 509 US 579 (1993) (demanding that the evidence must be relevant and reliable).

[48] ibid.

[49] *Matsushita Electric Industrial Co v Zenith Radio Corp* 475 US 574 (1986).

[50] The Court held that a plaintiff should be able to produce evidence that tends to exclude the possibility of a benign hypothesis before its case could be put to a jury. See also eg *Monsanto Co v Spray-Rite Service Corp* 465 US 752 (1984), and *Eastman Kodak Co v Image Technical Services, Inc* 504 US 451 (1992).

[51] *F Hoffmann-La Roche Ltd v Empagran SA* 542 US 155 (2004).

[52] *Verizon Communications Inc v Law Offices of Curtis V Trinko LLP* 540 US 398 (2004).

[53] *Bell Atlantic* (n 42) ('when allegations of parallel conduct are set out in order to make a § 1 claim, they must be placed in a context that raises a suggestion of a preceding agreement, not merely parallel conduct that could just as well be independent action'). The holding of this case applies more broadly than just to antitrust cases, to private actions more generally.

[54] *Leegin Creative Leather Products, Inc v PSKS, Inc* 551 US 877 (2007).

[55] *Continental TV, Inc v GTE Sylvania* 433 US 36 (1977).

(a Federal Rules of Civil Procedure (FRCP) 12(b)(6) motion)[56] or, following discovery, a FRCP 56, on the basis that 'there is no genuine issue as to any material fact' so that 'the moving party is entitled to judgment as a matter of law'.[57] Further, and crucially, there seems little doubt that the perceived 'excesses' of the treble damages system have been an important factor influencing the Supreme Court in its decision over the last 35 years to rein in the substantive reach of the antitrust laws, making it now extremely difficult for private plaintiffs not only to bring antitrust actions but to 'win' them.[58] Indeed rule of reason cases are notoriously unattractive for plaintiffs to litigate; given the complexity of the analysis required they are likely to require expert testimony on a range of issues and lengthy and costly trials.

The Supreme Court has repeatedly expressed fear that enforcement should not be permitted to 'chill the very conduct the antitrust laws are designed to protect'[59] and this concern has influenced its efforts to

> scale back the application of the US antitrust laws. The consequence of getting it wrong—or false positives—is much greater when a firm is exposed to treble, rather than single, damages for its alleged wrongdoing ... These combination of factors has led our Supreme Court to craft increasingly tough liability rules for antitrust offences and increasingly high hurdles for plaintiffs to move beyond the pleadings stage or to survive summary judgment or a directed verdict to get to a jury. The concern is not just that juries will get it wrong, but that the fear of false positives will chill business behaviour that may benefit consumers.[60]

Statistical evidence[61] reflects the impact of these recalibrating measures on antitrust litigation. They illustrate that, although private antitrust actions rose dramatically though the 1950s, 1960s and 1970s, the number peaked in 1977 (the year that *Sylvania*[62] was decided and as 'the Court began to embrace "new learning" among antitrust scholars who argued that the antitrust laws were intended to protect competition in order to promote economic efficiency and consumer welfare, not to shield small producers from larger, more efficient rivals').[63] Since then it has fallen from its apex.[64] Although the number of cases did begin to rise again for a while (mirroring

[56] A FRCP 12(b)(6) motion results in the dismissal of claims that do not allege the facts necessary to sustain a cause of action. It requires a short and plain statement of the claim showing that the pleader is entitled to relief FRCP 8(a)(2).

[57] The FRCP 56(c).

[58] W Kolasky, 'Different Roads' (2008) 11 *Global Competition Review* 17, 17.

[59] *Matsushita Electric* (n 49) 594. *Monsanto* (n 50) 762–64.

[60] Kolasky (n 58) 19.

[61] The statistics have to be treated with some caution, however, and can potentially be misleading; for example, they may lead to over-counting as numerous cases may be filed relating to the same case in different federal or state courts before getting consolidated.

[62] *Sylvania* (n 55). See also Brunswick (n 44), and accompanying text.

[63] W Kolasky, 'Antitrust Litigation: What's Changed in Twenty-Five Years?' (2012) 27 *Antitrust* 9.

[64] In contrast to federal civil claims generally which continued to increase overall, ibid 10.

perhaps increased government focus on cartel activity), after 2008 it has fallen again, most likely as a reaction to 'the long string of pro-defendant decisions in the Supreme Court, culminating in the Court's 2007 decisions in *Leegin* and *Bell Atlantic v Twombly*'.[65] In 2010, 2011, 2012 and 2013 there were 544, 475, 702 and 801 new federal private antitrust cases filed respectively,[66] figures which are considerably lower than those filed in 1977 and 2008 (in excess of 1600 and 1300 respectively).

There is now some concern that the pendulum has swung too far in the opposite direction; the rules are so rigorous and provide so little certainty that meritorious litigation may be being discouraged. As antitrust law has shifted away from clear rules, the costs of deciding antitrust cases have been increased without concern

> for the loss of certainty that had been associated with now abandoned per se rules and lenient burdens of proof and the increased party and institutional costs associated with reliance on more demanding standards of proof. Neither has it been concerned with the possibility that the incidence of false negatives could increase due to cost and lack of access to the necessary proof.[67]

Indeed, in 2013, following an important study of 60 private US antitrust cases,[68] Professors Davis and Lande[69] published a paper 'defying conventional wisdom', rejecting some or the more anecdotal and unsubstantiated concerns about private enforcement and concluding that the private actions studied demonstrated that they had played an important role both in compensating victims and deterring violations. They found not only that the cases analysed (47 of which were opt-out class actions brought through lawyers working for a contingency fee) demonstrated that significant amounts of cash (in excess of $33.8 billion) was returned to victims of anticompetitive behaviour,[70] but it was clear that they had uncovered violations which might otherwise have been undiscovered; a third of the cases examined were stand-alone actions, actions which did not follow-on from public enforcement, and a number of the follow-on cases extended significantly beyond the parameters of the original government case. This complemented and

[65] ibid. In *Leegin* (n 54) the Supreme Court overruled a nearly century-old rule that resale price maintenance was illegal per se under Sherman Act s 1.

[66] See www.uscourts.gov/uscourts/Statistics/JudicialBusiness/2013/appendices/C02ASep13.pdf.

[67] Gavil (n 2) 7–8.

[68] See RH Lande and JP Davis, 'Benefits from Private Antitrust Enforcement: An Analysis of Forty Cases' (2008) 42 *University of San Francisco Law Review* 879, and JP Davis and RH Lande 'Toward an Empirical and Theoretical Assessment of Private Antitrust Enforcement (2013) 36 *Seattle University Law Review* 1269.

[69] JP Davis and RH Lande, 'Defying Conventional Wisdom: The Case for Private Enforcement' (2013) 48 *Georgia Law Review* 1.

[70] They found that recovery levels were much higher in cases involving direct purchasers and that only 11 of the cases involved indirect purchasers.

bolstered their views, articulated in a separate paper, that private antitrust actions deter anticompetitive conduct more effectively even than criminal cartel proceedings pursued by the Department of Justice.[71]

3. BARRIERS TO PRIVATE LITIGATION IN THE EU

The US experience indicates that private actions can play an important role in the enforcement process and in ensuring that its compensatory, remediation and/or deterrence functions are achieved. Indeed, a widely held view is now that optimal enforcement requires public and private enforcement to be combined harmoniously. It also demonstrates, however, that it is a delicate and complex task to craft rules (governing procedure, evidence and substance) in a way that will achieve, and balance, the competing objectives pursued and which will minimise error costs. Further, that an important issue to be resolved may be what the primary function of private enforcement should be—deterrence of wrongs which harm society as a whole or compensation of those individuals specifically harmed by the infringement.

This section scrutinises the rights which EU law confers on individuals harmed by an infringement of Article 101 or 102 and the barriers to private litigation that have existed in the EU and which caused the Commission to conclude in 2005 that the system of damages for infringements of competition law of the Member States 'presents a picture of "total underdevelopment"'.[72] Although private enforcement has steadily been increasing, from approximately 54 decided judgments within the EU in 1999 to 146 in 2011,[73] the Commission still concluded in 2013 that '[d]espite some recent signs of improvement in a few Member States, to date most victims of infringements of the EU competition rules in practice do not obtain compensation for the harm suffered';[74] victims only commenced private actions in 25 per cent of cases where antitrust infringement decisions had been adopted by the Commission. Not all might agree that this picture indicates

[71] RH Lande and JP Davis, 'Comparative Deterrence from Private Enforcement and Criminal Enforcement of the US Antitrust Laws (2011) *Brigham Young University Law Review* 315, but see GJ Werden, SD Hammond and BA Bartlett, 'Deterrence and Detection of Cartels: Using All The Tools and Sanctions' (2011) 56 *Antitrust Bulletin* 207 and RH Lande and JP Davis, 'The Extraordinary Deterrence of Private Antitrust Enforcement: A Reply to Werden, Hammond and Barnett' (2013) 58 *Antitrust Bulletin* 173.

[72] Green Paper (n 12) 1.2. This view was based on the Ashurst Report (n 12).

[73] See B Rodgers (ed), *Competition Law: Comparative Private Enforcement and Collective Redress Across the EU* (The Hague, Wolters Kluwer, 2014) 87. Only 31% of all the cases analysed were damages claims.

[74] Proposal for a directive of the European Parliament and of the Council on certain rules governing actions for damages under national law for infringements of the competition law provision of the Member States and the European Union COM(2013) 404 final, Explanatory Memorandum, 1.2 and ibid.

that steps should be taken to stimulate private enforcement,[75] or that EU measures are required[76] and/or are a practicable means of doing so. Nevertheless, it has been seen that the Commission concluded that EU instruments to strengthen damages actions,[77] and to balance it with public enforcement, were requisite. In its view the new measures adopted will, by overcoming some barriers to effective redress, 'democratise enforcement and empower the victims of antitrust infringements to receive effective compensation…'.[78]

In order for the EU package to achieve its objectives, it must, of course, successfully tackle the obstacles that exist to national damages actions, whilst ensuring that the foundations are put in place for workable litigation systems to develop in each Member State which, without harming public enforcement, will minimise error costs. The discussion below consequently considers the combination of factors which have, over the years, conspired against the development of a coherent and uniform enforcement system across the EU and which barriers still remain.

A first important point is that, in contrast to the position in the US, the EEC Treaty, the EC Treaty and the TFEU have all been silent on the question of whether private rights of action for damages or injunctions must follow from a violation of the EU competition law rules; until the Damages Directive was adopted in 2014, no EU legislation specifically addressed private rights of action for damages (or injunctions). Rather, such rights derive, as next described, from the jurisprudence of the ECJ[79] which has developed only in a gradual and piecemeal fashion.

Second, although it has been clear since the ECJ's judgments in *Belgische Radio en Televisie v SV SABAM*[80] that Articles 101(1) and 102 have direct effect, and consequently that litigants can rely on rights derived from those provisions in private proceedings in the national courts,[81] until Regulation 1/2003 came into force in 2004, national courts could not apply

[75] See eg, W Wils, 'Should Private Antitrust Enforcement be Encouraged?' (2003) 26 *World Competition* 473 (but see now Wils (n 1) 3).

[76] Although final judgments are relatively low, these do not take account of the numerous cases that are settled. See speech by K Coates, 'Cartels and Follow On Damages Actions', Lincoln's Inn, 24 November 2014 ('Many of these cases settle. I was talking to an economist a few months ago who had advised on—he thought approximately—50 damages calculations. Not one of the cases went to final judgment') and Dunne (n 1).

[77] See s 1 above.

[78] Speech by J Almunia, 'Looking Back at Five Years of Competition Enforcement in the EU' Global Antitrust Enforcement Symposium, Washington, 10 September 2014.

[79] Which are now affirmed in Regulation 1/2003 (n 10) (providing that national courts must have the power to apply Arts 101 and 102 and for cooperation between the national courts and the Commission and consistency in interpretation of the provisions by all decision-takers).

[80] Case 127/73 *Belgische Radio en Televisie v SV SABAM* [1974] ECR 51, para 16 ('As the prohibitions of Articles [101(1) and 102] tend by their very nature to produce direct effects in relations between individuals, these articles create direct rights in respect of the individuals concerned with the national courts must safeguard').

[81] Regulation 1/2003 (n 10) Art 3(1).

Article 101(3); the Commission's exclusive right to grant exemptions under Article 101(3), coupled with its wide interpretation of Article 101(1), meant that for a number of years the Commission exercised tight control over enforcement[82] and national courts were excluded from playing a full role in antitrust cases. Third, even where Articles 101 and 102 were applied, a lack of clarity surrounded the question of what *exact* rights Articles 101 and 102 conferred upon individuals. Although the ECJ has long made it clear that national courts must protect EU rights, respect the principle of supremacy[83] and ensure the availability of adequate remedies sufficient to guarantee real and *effective* judicial protection for EU rights,[84] for some time the question of what particular remedies were required to protect rights derived under Articles 101 and 102 was a matter of acute controversy and speculation. It was only in 2001, in *Courage Ltd v Crehan*,[85] that the ECJ expressly confirmed that full compensation must, in principle, be available to those that have suffered loss in consequence of a breach of Article 101 or 102[86] and in *Manfredi v Lloyd Adriatico Assicurazioni SpA*[87] that it clarified that full compensation must include recompense not only for actual loss but also for loss of profit plus interest.[88]

Fourth, even post-*Crehan* private litigation has been, and is still being deterred by the fact that the principle of national procedural autonomy[89]

[82] See eg, speech M Monti, 'Effective Private Enforcement of EC Antitrust Law' Sixth EU Competition Law and Policy Workshop Florence, 1–2 June 2001.

[83] See Case 14/68 *Walt Wilhelm v Bundeskartellamt* [1969] ECR 1, para 9.

[84] See Case 14/83 *Von Colson and Kamann v Land Nordrhein-Westfalen* [1984] ECR 1891, especially para 23 and Case 33/76 *Rewe-Zentralfinanz eG and Rewe-Zentral AG v Landwirtschaftskammer für das Saarland* [1976] ECR 1989, para 5.

[85] Case C-453/99 *Courage Ltd v Crehan* [2001] ECR I-6297. See also joined cases C-295 & 298/04 *Manfredi v Lloyd Adriatico Assicurazioni SpA* [2006] ECR I-6619 and Case C-557/12 *Kone AG v ÖBB-Infrastruktur AG* ECLI:EU:C:2014:1317.

[86] Although the Court did not specifically deal with Art 102, it referred to the need to compensate those who have suffered loss caused to them by a contract or by conduct liable to restrict or distort competition.

[87] In *Manfredi* (n 85) paras 60, 83–100, the ECJ held that: (i) EU law did not prevent national courts from taking steps to ensure that protection of EU rights does not entail unjust enrichment of those who enjoy them but that it had to be possible to award punitive damages if such damages could be awarded pursuant to similar actions founded on domestic law; and (ii) the right to seek compensation must include compensation not only for actual loss but also for loss of profit plus interest.

[88] In Case 56/65 *Société La Technique Minière v Maschinenbau Ulm GmbH* [1966] ECR 234, 250, the ECJ clarified that individual clauses in an agreement affected by the Art 101(1)—and Art 102—prohibition are void (and that the agreement as a whole will also be void where those clauses are not severable from the remaining terms of the agreement (but that this is a matter for national law)): see Case 319/82 *Société de Vente de Ciments et Bétons de l'Est SA v Kerpen & Kerpen GmbH & Co KG* [1983] ECR 4173. In Case 213/89 *R v Secretary of State for Transport ex parte Factortame Ltd* [1990] ECR I-2433, the ECJ also made it clear that national courts must ensure that interim measures are available where necessary to protect putative EU rights.

[89] *Rewe-Zentralfinanz* (n 84) ('in the absence of Community rules on this subject, it is for the domestic legal system of each Member State to designate the courts having jurisdiction and

confers considerable latitude on the national systems and the national courts in dealing with an antitrust damages claim.[90] The protection given to EU rights is, consequently, heavily dependent on the procedural, evidential, and substantive rules governing civil litigation applicable in each particular Member State and how EU law—in particular the principles of equivalence and effectiveness[91]—is considered to constrain their operation.[92] In the absence of EU harmonising measures,[93] therefore, considerable opacity has surrounded a multiplicity of questions, including, how national claims should be framed (and in particular whether fault should or can be a constituent element of the cause of action), how causation can be established and damages calculated, whether national courts are required (or permitted) to award 'punitive' damages and whether other national rules governing the claim comply with EU law and, especially, the principle of effectiveness; for example, rules relating to standing, remoteness, illegality, a passing-on defence or setting out limitation periods. The ECJ has been requested to give rulings on some of these issues,[94] but where no specific judgment exists, the position remains subject to differing interpretations and, accordingly, uncertainty. For instance, the question of whether EU law demands that indirect purchasers should have standing to bring antitrust proceedings and/or whether defendants should be able to raise a passing-on defence, would appear to depend on how the principle of effectiveness stressed in the ECJ's *Crehan* and *Manfredi* judgments is to be construed: specifically, whether it suggests that the principal purpose of private enforcement is the attainment of corrective justice[95] –with deterrence operating merely as a socially beneficial by-product of such actions[96]—or whether it is primarily a

to determine the procedural conditions governing actions at law intended to ensure the protection of rights which citizens have from the direct effect of Community law').

[90] See obstacles identified by the Commission in its Green Paper (n 12).

[91] The rules must not be less favourable than those relating to similar claims of a domestic nature (the principle of equivalence); and must not make it virtually impossible or excessively difficult to exercise the rights that the national courts are obliged to protect (the principle of effectiveness).

[92] As many national cases settle, it is not easy to draw a picture of how national courts are resolving these issues Coates (n 76). ('That highlights one of the problems we have to deal with: although there are a number of points of law that will inevitably require clarification, there are a lot of judgment calls being made in the shadows.')

[93] The Commission recognises in its Notice on cooperation with the national courts the particular difficulties that may arise in consequence of the fact that there is no harmonisation of procedures in the Member States, see the Cooperation Notice [2004] OJ C101/54, paras 9–10.

[94] For example, in *Crehan* (n 85) para 31, the ECJ held that although the illegality of the agreement cannot operate as a general bar to claims brought between parties to a contract concluded in breach of Art 101(1), it can do so where the claimant co-contractor can be said to bear 'significant responsibility' for the breach. See also *Manfredi* (n 85).

[95] P Nebbia, 'Damages Actions for the Infringement of EC Competition Law: Compensation or Deterrence?' (2008) 33 *European Law Review* 23, 28.

[96] K Roach and MJ Trebilcock, 'Private Enforcement of Competition Laws' (1996) 34 *Osgoode Hall Law Journal* 461, 496.

tool to increase enforcement and to bring to an end and deter violations.[97] Although the Court has stressed the importance of private actions to the strengthening of the working of the competition rules and to the maintenance of effective competition,[98] in *Manfredi* the ECJ also clarified '... that any individual can claim compensation for the harm suffered where there is a causal relationship between that harm and an agreement or practice prohibited under Article [101]'.[99]

Fifth, although the principles of equivalence and effectiveness may require some rules,[100] which render nugatory the right to compensation, to be struck down or disapplied,[101] the extent to which EU law can require Member States more positively or proactively to facilitate damages claims and to put in place measures, or reform institutions in a way, which would ensure an effective enforcement framework is even less clear-cut and even more controversial.[102] In particular, the existence, or not, of specialist competition law tribunals or courts, the speed of litigation and individual national rules governing access to information and evidence, litigation costs, funding and cost rules, follow-on actions, mechanisms for collective redress and remedies for final consumers, are all factors which may dramatically affect the culture of competition and the feasibility of successfully launching private litigation. Thus, even if, for example, it were clear that EU law demands that indirect purchasers should be able to seek compensation before a national court, such a right might be worthless in a state where the national tools are inadequate to allow that right to be effectively exercised—perhaps because procedural mechanisms do not allow for actions to be grouped together collectively or for relevant evidence to be uncovered, collected or appropriately processed and assessed. In some jurisdictions individuals may simply be less litigious than in others.[103]

Indeed, it seems clear that features of the national litigation systems in the individual Member States have been deterring or constraining EU claimants. In particular:

— the cost and risk of litigation frequently operates as a deterrent, especially where claimants have not suffered much loss individually and where class or other consolidated actions and contingency fees are not

[97] See eg, F Hoseinian, 'Passing-on Damages and Community Antitrust Policy—An Economic Background' (2005) 28 *World Competition* 3, 7; Nebbia (n 95) 28; R Nazzini, 'The Objective of Private Remedies in EU Competition Law' (2011) 4 *Global Competition Litigation Review* 131, 139–40.

[98] *Crehan* (n 85) para 27; *Manfredi* (n 85) para 91.

[99] *Manfredi* (n 85) para 61.

[100] See n 94 above.

[101] Case C-536/11 *Bundeswettbewerbsbehörde v Donau Chemie* EU:C:2013:366, para 32.

[102] See Dunne (n 1).

[103] For a discussion of the position in the Member States on many of these issues, see Rodgers (n 73) especially Ch 2. For the view that individuals in Lithuania are less litigious

available[104] or where national cost rules provide disincentives to litigation (eg, where claimants are obliged to pay the defendant's legal costs if unsuccessful);[105]

— it is extremely difficult for claimants to gather the requisite evidence under many national systems; the question of when national courts can order disclosure vary considerably between Member States;[106]
— proceedings may be being deterred in some States by uncertainty over the weight to be given to decisions of NCAs; and
— many national courts have limited experience dealing with antitrust arguments and may not, consequently, be the most appropriate or understanding forum for the hearing.[107]

Sixth, a matter of specific contention in the EU has been the relationship between public and private enforcement which are closely connected. As in the US, not only do public enforcement actions by the Commission have a facilitating effect on private enforcement (a Commission decision finding a competition law infringement may be relied upon to establish the existence of a breach[108] and may provide evidence helpful in establishing causation and harm)[109] but it has been recognised that private actions can reinforce public enforcement by increasing the resources available for the prosecution of competition law infringements, the likelihood of detection and the cost of non-compliance. The interaction between the two enforcement systems

because, historically, the clutches of the Soviet Union precluded the Lithuanian legal system from development, see J Malinauskaite, 'Private Enforcement of Competition Law in Lithuania: A Story of Underdevelopment' (2013) 3 *Global Competition Law Review* 123, 133. In post-communist societies it may also take time for a fair competition culture to develop.

104 Only 0.4% of the 1268 antitrust judgments decided between 1999–2012 identified in Rodgers (n 73) 162 were aggregated/class consumer cases. Class actions may not only facilitate relief for certain victims but may produce external benefits for society as a whole: WB Rubenstein, 'Why Enable Litigation? A Positive Externalities Theory of the Small Claims Class Action' *Public Law and Legal Theory Research Paper Series, UCLA School of Law*, No 06-10, www.ssrn.com/abstract=890303.

105 See eg, J Peysner, 'Costs and Financing in Private Third Party Competition Damages Actions' (2006) 3 *Competition Law Review* 97.

106 Disclosure is recognised in the UK but does not exist in many civil law systems. National courts may ask the Commission to transmit to them information in its possession or its opinion on questions concerning the application of the EU competition law rules, see Regulation 1/2003 (n 10) Art 15(1).

107 See eg, Gavil (n 2) and Malinauskaite (n 103) 133.

108 Regulation 1/2003 (n 10) Art 16. In the UK, for example, the Competition Act 1998 s 47A also specifically allows 'follow-on' claims to be brought before the Competition Appeal Tribunal where a breach of Arts 101 or 102 (or the UK domestic equivalent) has been established in a public law decision (by the Commission or the UK's competition authority). The Directive provides that NCA infringement decisions are binding on national courts within that same Member State, see n 134 and text.

109 Wils (n 1) 15–16. The Commission is often criticised, however, for taking too long to publish its cartel and other decisions while it negotiates with the addressees of the decision about confidentiality claims.

has however become strained. In particular, tensions have arisen between the need to ensure, on the one hand, the effectiveness of the right to compensation available to victims of anticompetitive practices and, on the other, the effectiveness of the leniency programme, which constitutes a key tool for the Commission in its fight against cartels and, consequently to public enforcement.[110]

Litigants in the EU have frequently sought access to leniency evidence not only through discovery but through seeking access to a competition agency's file or by filing a claim under transparency rules.[111] Although the Commission, supported by some NCAs and Advocate General Mazák, has taken the view that access should *not* be granted to self-incriminating statements voluntarily provided by leniency applicants as this could substantially reduce the attractiveness of the leniency programme and, in turn, the effective enforcement of Article 101,[112] in *Pfleiderer AG v Bundeskartellamt*,[113] the ECJ favoured a more balanced approach to the question. It held that a national court had, in deciding whether to grant access to leniency documents, to weigh, according to national law and taking into account all the relevant factors in the case,[114] the respective interests of the leniency applicant (to have voluntarily submitted corporate statements protected) and the claimant (to have access to documents which would facilitate the claim).[115] Building on this approach, the ECJ in *Bundeswettbewerbsbehörde v Donau Chemie*,[116] held that 'in competition law ... any rule that is rigid, either by providing for absolute refusal to grant access ... or for granting access as a matter of course ... is liable to undermine the effective application of ... Article 101'.[117] Although these cases stressed that the national court should have the opportunity to consider the issues on a case-by-case basis weighing the competing interests, in *Commission v EnBW Energie Baden-Württember AG*[118] the Court recognised that access should be required only

[110] Case C–360/09 *Pfleiderer AG v Bundeskartellamt* [2011] ECR I-5161.

[111] See Regulation 1049/2001 regarding public access to European Parliament, Council and Commission documents (Transparency Regulation) [2001] OJ L145/43 and eg, Case T-2/03 *Verein für Konsumenteninformation* [2005] ECR II-1121, Case T-437/08 *CDC Hydrogen Peroxide v Commission* [2011] ECR II-8251 and Ombudsman Decision 3699/2006/ELB, 2010.

[112] *Pfleiderer* (n 110) Opinion of Mazák AG, paras 38–42. In his view an interference with the injured parties' right to an effective remedy and a fair trial was justified by the legitimate aim of ensuring the effective enforcement of Art 101 by NCAs and ultimately private litigants' possibility of obtaining an effective remedy.

[113] *Pfleiderer* (n 110).

[114] ibid para 31.

[115] ibid para 30.

[116] *Donau Chemie* (n 101).

[117] ibid para 31. It thus concluded that an Austrian law which prohibited disclosure to third parties of court files on public law competition proceedings, unless all parties to the proceedings agreed, was not compatible with the principle of effectiveness and so conflicted with EU law.

[118] Case C-365/12 P *Commission v EnBW Energie Baden-Württember AG* ECLI:EU:C:2014:112.

in cases of absolutely necessity where relevant evidence was not available from alternative mechanisms.

4. CONCLUSIONS

In Section three it has been seen that although, as cases have come before it, the ECJ has developed and clarified the rights that Articles 101 and 102 confer on private persons, uncertainty still surrounds many issues relating to how national rules should guarantee real and *effective* judicial protection for those rights and what limitations and obligations the EU imposes on national law governing the claim. Consequently, the ability of claimants to recover damages in antitrust cases diverges significantly between Member States. Further, a tension between private and public enforcement has been emerging.

Because of the close connection between private and public enforcement and their ability to impact on each other, public enforcement agencies frequently take a keen interest in the development of private enforcement. Indeed, it has been seen that, in the EU, it has been the Commission which has spearheaded the campaign to encourage greater private enforcement of the EU antitrust laws, whilst at the same time stressing that it should not adversely impact on public enforcement. It has been facilitated in this task by its unique and unusual position of having separate and central roles within the EU legal order both as a competition enforcement agency and as the EU institution which formulates most legislative proposals (including those to promote the effective application of competition law).

In considering what EU measures should be enacted to overcome the EU barriers to litigation and to stimulate, and harmonise, private damages actions, the Commission has had a tortuous path to navigate, both politically and legally. Not only has it had to convince the Parliament[119] and the Council that EU legislation was required which encroaches on traditional national litigation systems and entrenched principles developed within them,[120] but it has had to reflect on an array of factors when considering what those measures should look like and what they should cover. In addition to seeking to overcome the barriers to litigation identified, it has had to consider: what legislative proposals would realistically be accepted, how

[119] A first Directive proposed by the Commission in 2009 was based on Art 103 TFEU and would have excluded the Parliament from the legislative procedure. In the end the Directive was adopted under Arts 103 and 114, so requiring use of the co-decision procedure.

[120] In some Member States, eg Germany, there has been resistance to the introduction of disclosure rules on the basis that litigation proceeds on the basis that it is for the claimant to prove its case, see A Howard, 'Too Little, Too Late? The European Commission's Legislative Proposals on Anti-Trust Damages Actions' (2013) 4 *Journal of European Competition Law & Practice* 455, 460. The author is suspicious that the extent of compromises in the Directive and

it should balance the potential deterrent, compensatory and other functions of private actions; how it should balance private and public enforcement; whether it should adopt a more holistic, all-encompassing, or a more gradual, sequential approach; and how to encompass lessons emerging from the US experience and to safeguard against an unleashing of some of the excesses connected with the litigation culture developed there.[121] It has therefore had to exercise caution to ensure that, in seeking to bolster and encourage private enforcement in the EU, rules are not made so claimant friendly that antitrust litigation gets out of control and encourages undeserving claims to be commenced (creating the risk of false positives).[122] Were that to occur, courts might become inclined to adopt narrow constructions of substantive and procedural rules, making it harder for public enforcement agencies,[123] as well as private litigants, to establish violations.

A brief examination of the package of EU measures illustrates how the Commission and the legislature have resolved some of these difficult issues presented. A first point is that the Commission has taken the view that legislation governing damages action was required to clarify and harmonise certain issues. Although therefore some matters have been dealt with primarily through soft recommendations and guidance, others have been dealt with through harmonising legislation, the Directive, which has to be transplanted into national law by the end of 2016.

Second, the Directive has generally embraced the compensatory approach,[124] reflecting the Commission's articulated view that, public and private enforcement should pursue different, albeit complementary, objectives and that *all* victims of antitrust violations, including small and medium-sized enterprises (SMEs) and consumers, direct and indirect purchasers, should be able to obtain full compensation (but *not* over-compensation). The Directive clarifies that:

— it 'sets out certain rules necessary to ensure that anyone who has suffered harm caused by an infringement of competition law by an undertaking ... can effectively exercise the right to claim full compensation for that harm from that undertaking...';[125]

— national courts 'shall ensure that any natural or legal person who has suffered harm caused by an infringement of competition law is able to claim and to obtain full compensation for that harm';[126]

the rather timid selection of the procedural issues are linked to political concerns regarding the sanctity of national procedural autonomy, ibid 464.

[121] See eg, the responses to the Commission's Green Paper (n 12).

[122] A choice may have to be made as to whether false positives or negatives are worse.

[123] See eg, WE Kovacic, 'Private Participation in the Enforcement of Public Competition Laws', London, 15 May 2003, available at www.ftc.gov/public-statements/2003/05/private-participation-enforcement-public-competition-laws.

[124] But see also nn 140 and 141 and text.

[125] Directive 2014/104/EU (n 15) Art 1(1).

[126] ibid Art 3(1).

- full compensation shall 'cover the right to compensation for actual loss and for loss of profit, plus the payment of interest'[127] but 'shall not lead to overcompensation, whether by means of punitive, multiple or other types of damages';[128]
- indirect, as well as direct, purchasers can sue (and indeed in some cases overcharges are presumed to be passed on to them by direct purchasers);[129] and
- as overcompensation must not ensue, national courts must ensure the passing-on defence is available to defendants.[130] Recognising the complexity that is likely to follow for national courts in applying a passing-on defence, the Directive provides that '[t]he Commission shall issue guidelines for national courts on how to estimate the share of the overcharge which was passed on to the indirect purchaser'.[131]

Third, the Directive has sought to tackle some (but not all) of the practical difficulties which have been confronting victims of EU antitrust infringements, to encourage damages actions and to establish certain minimum standards for litigation throughout the EU. It addresses the problem of information asymmetry and that disclosure is not widely available in some Member States by providing that, subject to certain conditions, national courts must be able to order a defendant (or claimant) to disclose relevant evidence under its control where a request is accompanied by a reasoned justification sufficient to support its plausibility.[132] National courts must however limit disclosure of evidence to that which is proportionate and must protect confidential information and give full effect to legal professional privilege.

The Directive also clarifies that: a finding of an infringement by a NCA or a review court should be irrefutably established for the purposes of damages' claims based on it before a national court in that state (so in these follow-on actions a claimant will have to establish only causation, loss and the quantum of damages,[133] not the existence of the breach);[134] national

[127] ibid Art 3(2). The basis is tortious—to ensure that the compensation puts the person who suffered harm in the position that it would have been had the infringement of competition law not been committed, ibid.

[128] ibid Art 3(3).

[129] ibid Arts 12 and 14.

[130] ibid Art 13.

[131] ibid Art 16.

[132] ibid Art 5. It also provides for disclosure from third parties and competition agencies.

[133] Although these are formidable obstacles to overcome.

[134] Directive 2014/104/EU (n 15) Art 9 (although currently in some Member States the decisions of their NCAs bind their national courts, in a majority of states NCA decisions do not have any binding effect). The Commission's original proposal that decisions of NCAs were to constitute full proof before any EU Civil Court that an infringement occurred provoked considerable debate and was not adopted in the final Directive. Final decisions of an NCA may, however, be presented before the national courts of another Member State as at least prima facie evidence of a competition law infringement.

limitation periods must not be less than five years and cannot commence to run before the infringement has ceased and the claimant knows, or can reasonably be expected to know of it (it must also be suspended or interrupted until public enforcement proceedings are terminated);[135] and undertakings responsible for an infringement through joint behaviour, should (except for certain SMEs and immunity recipients) be jointly and severally liable for the infringement.[136] Further, it establishes a rebuttable evidential presumption of harm in cartel cases[137] and empowers national courts to estimate the amount of harm in cases where precise quantification is impossible or excessively difficult.[138] The Commission's practical guide on the quantification of harm for damages is specifically designed to assist national courts in this sphere.[139]

Fourth, in order to ensure that such actions do not disrupt public enforcement, the Directive overrides the case law of the ECJ[140] and limits national rules governing disclosure by providing an absolute bar on the disclosure of leniency statements and settlement submissions.[141] Finally, the Directive incorporates provisions relating to consensual dispute resolution.

This brief summary (see also the table set out in the Annex below) indicates that over-enforcement cannot be anticipated as a consequent of the current reforms. The US 'toxic cocktail', consisting of, in particular, class actions, contingency fee arrangements, favourable attorneys' fees rules, treble damages, broad discovery, jury trials and the rule of joint and several liability, with no right of contribution, are not provided for in the Directive.[142] Rather, it prohibits punitive damages, seeks to avoid fishing exercises by restricting disclosure to scenarios where a request for evidence is plausible, provides for joint and several liability (but with some limits and a general right to

[135] ibid Art 10 (this means in practice that proceedings may commence many years after an infringement has ended).

[136] ibid Art 11.

[137] ibid Art 17(2), pushing the burden onto the defendant to rebut the presumption by providing evidence to establish there was in fact no overcharge.

[138] ibid Art 17(1). The Directive also incorporates provisions on consensual dispute resolution.

[139] SWD(2013) 205 (n 14). See also, an external study prepared for the Commission, Oxera, 'Quantifying Antitrust Damages. Towards Non-Binding Guidance for Courts. Study Prepared for the European Commission' (EU Publications Office, 2010); and Commission, 'Draft Guidance Paper—Quantifying Harm in Actions for Damages based on Breaches of Article 101 or 102 of the Treaty on the Functioning of the European Union (June 2011), available at ec.europa.eu/competition/consultations/2011_actions_damages/draft_guidance_paper_en.pdf.

[140] In both *Pfleiderer* (n 110) paras 23–24 and *Donau Chemie* (n 116) paras 25–27, the ECJ recognised that national courts could only apply, subject to EU law and particularly the principle of effectiveness, their national rules on the right of access to documents if no binding regulation under EU law on the subject applied.

[141] Directive 2014/104/EU (n 15) Art 6(6).

[142] See eg, Gavil (n 2).

contribution from other infringers) and does not deal with attorney fees, jury trials or class actions (the latter being dealt with only by a recommendation). Although one concern could be that as substantive EU antitrust laws are interpreted more broadly than their US counterparts in some areas, such as vertical restraints and unilateral conduct, there is a danger that greater volumes of private action will create a risk of false positives, the EU package, does not provide huge additional incentives to the launch of these types of claim. Rather, many of its more detailed provisions focus on measures designed to stimulate actions in cartel damages cases; indeed, its provisions seem likely to have the greatest impact in follow-on cases. Further, it could be argued that these are areas where litigation *should* be encouraged, as few competition agencies have sufficient resources to dedicate towards enforcement in these spheres.

Greater concern may thus centre on the question raised at the beginning of this chapter as to whether the reforms have done enough to overcome the impediments to litigation and to achieve the Commission's objectives of increasing, and harmonising, private damages actions across the EU. Three core problems seem potentially to exist. First, because the Commission has not adopted a holistic approach, attempting to introduce a completely harmonised framework,[143] a number of significant obstacles to national actions and areas of legal ambiguity appear to remain. For example, the Directive does not contain provisions dealing with the admissibility of economic evidence, causation, remoteness and quantification of damages (dealt with only in the form of a non-binding practical guide). These rules will consequently continue to be governed by national law, subject to their compliance with the principles of effectiveness and equivalence. Further, although the Commission hopes that the introduction of a set of common principles in the field of collective redress will help to ensure that effective compensation is obtained by final consumers and SMEs in mass harm situations, its ability to bolster the position of such consumers is uncertain. Not only does the Recommendation on collective redress take the form of 'soft law', but the recommendation is simply that collective redress systems should, as a general rule, be based on the 'opt-in' principle (under which claimant parties are formed through the directly expressed consent of their members).

[143] Howard (n 120) 456. ('At first glance, the proposed Directive appears to be a random selection of minimum procedural requirements that lack coherence or structure. This is not a blueprint set of procedural rules that govern damages actions from start to finish.') Although the Directive is based on both Arts 103 and 114 TFEU (n 119) (to ensure that the differences in the liability regimes applicable in the Member States do not negatively affect both competition and the proper functioning of the internal market), arguably it simply provides a guarantee that a minimum set of rules will govern actions across the EU rather than providing a set of harmonised rules.

A valid concern may therefore be that such classes will encompass only a small percentage of antitrust victims.[144]

Second, even where harmonising rules have been adopted, there still seems to be significant scope for divergence in national rules in some areas. For example, given diverse national approaches to disclosure, it seems possible that different interpretations will be adopted to the Directive's requirements relating to the plausibility and proportionality of a request for disclosure. Further, the Directive leaves Member States the opportunity to introduce more favourable national rules in some situations. It seems likely that, a number of Member States will take opportunities to facilitate private actions, for example, by adopting more generous rules relating to disclosure, limitation periods and class actions. The existence of national differences is therefore likely to continue to affect where litigants choose to commence their actions and to result in forum-shopping.

Third, a legitimate anxiety may be that the working of a number of the Directive's provisions will introduce considerable complexities into national proceedings (for example, as the courts grapple with the complex rules applicable to limitation, joint and several liability and passing-on) so detracting from its goal of facilitating them.

The details of the package, and the issues and concerns that they raise, are further explored in subsequent chapters. It is clear, however, that the Commission and the EU legislature have taken a courageous and innovative first step in the journey towards encouraging damages claims throughout the EU and the development of a coherent EU system governing them. The Commission has worked hard to avoid the pitfalls experienced in the US and the new framework lays the foundations for the law in this area to develop sequentially as the EU and national courts interpret and assess the full implications of the provisions in cases arising before them. Whether the package of reforms will be a success, and/or whether further measures will be required, remains to be seen.

[144] See Lande (n 7) 6 (recovery in the EU will also be severely limited if lawyers are not allowed to receive contingency fees; 'the vast majority of consumer-victims and small business-victims' may therefore 'continue to be uncompensated').

Annex: Factors Impacting on Antitrust Litigation in the US and EU Respectively

	United States	**European Union (current)**	**European Union (once the Directive is implemented)**
Statutory provision governing private rights of action?	Statutory provisions governing damages and injunction (Clayton Act, §§ 4 and 16)	Principles developed by the ECJ. Essentially EU right to compensation/injunction governed by national law *subject to it being compatible with EU principles of equivalence and effectiveness (in particular rules must not render exercise of rights practically impossible or excessively difficult)*	Directive: requires Member States to set out rules necessary to ensure that anyone who has suffered harm caused by a competition law infringement can obtain full compensation (Art 1) Directive does not deal with right to an injunction
Compensatory principle? Punitive or multiple damages?	Treble Damages (Clayton Act, § 4)	Governed by national law *subject to EU principles of equivalence and effectiveness* (punitive damages must be available if available in equivalent situations under national law, *Manfredi*)	Compensation for action loss and loss of profit, plus interest. Punitive and multiple damages prohibited (Art 3)
Standing and remoteness	Vigorous rules governing antitrust injury, standing and remoteness	Governed by national law *subject to EU principles of equivalence and effectiveness*	Compensation for any person that has suffered harm but no provision as to how rules of remoteness to be applied
Passing-on and indirect purchasers	Neither passing-on defence nor claims by indirect purchasers generally permitted under federal law	Governed by national law *subject to EU principles of equivalence and effectiveness*	Indirect purchaser actions expressly permitted and passing-on defence mandated (Arts 12&14)
In *pari delicto* doctrine	Not a defence to an antitrust action (unless perhaps a plaintiff equally and voluntarily participated in the challenged misconduct)	Governed by national law but principle of effectiveness requires damages unless claimant bears significant responsibility for the breach (*Crehan*)	

(*continued*)

Annex: (*Continued*)

	United States	**European Union (current)**	**European Union (once the Directive is implemented)**
Follow-on cases: weight of public law finding	Judgment—prima-facie evidence (Clayton Act, § 5(a))	Commission decisions binding but impact of NCA decisions governed by national law (Reg 1/2003, Art 16)	Commission decisions binding and decisions of NCA or review court binding on national courts in that Member State (Art 9)
Causation, harm and quantification	After injury and causation shown tendency is to apply favourable burden of proof and allow estimation of damage	Governed by national law *subject to EU principles of equivalence and effectiveness*	Evidential presumption of harm in cartel cases—national courts to estimate harm (Art 17)
Limitation periods	Four years from when the cause of action accrues but tolling in certain circumstances (eg during government action or for fraudulent concealment) (Clayton Act §§ 4B and 5(i))	Governed by national law *subject to EU principles of equivalence and effectiveness*—much litigation in some Member States (eg UK) as to when limitation periods start to run	Limitation periods must not be less than five years—stipulation of when periods can start to run (Art 10)
Availability of class actions	Opt-out class actions	Governed by national law *subject to EU principles of equivalence and effectiveness* but Recommendation for Member States to adopt opt-in class actions	
Legal Costs	Successful plaintiff gets costs and reasonable attorney fees—otherwise each pay own (Clayton Act, § 4)	Governed by national law—some Member States apply loser pays principle	
Disclosure of evidence	Broad discovery rules	Governed by national law—disclosure not widely available in civil systems although recognised by common law systems (eg UK/Ireland)	Subject to some exceptions, provision for disclosure of evidence supported by plausible claim (Art 5)

(*continued*)

Annex: (*Continued*)

	United States	European Union (current)	European Union (once the Directive is implemented)
Impact on leniency	Damages for leniency applicants reduced to single damages	National court must balance competing interests of claimant and defendant when deciding when to order disclosure of leniency documents—no absolute rule against or in favour of disclosure permitted	Absolute bar on disclosure of leniency documents and settlement decisions (Art 6) Modification of rules governing joint and several liability for leniency applicants
Joint and Several Liability	Joint and several liability for co-infringers with no right of contribution	Governed by national law *subject to EU principles of equivalence and effectiveness*	Joint and several liability for co-infringers with exceptions for certain SMEs and leniency applicants
Admissibility of expert evidence	Admissibility of expert evidence	Governed by national law *subject to EU principles of equivalence and effectiveness*	
Motions to dismiss and summary judgment	Courts now more willing to reject claim and/or grant summary judgment (*Matsushita* and *Twombly*)	Governed by national law *subject to EU principles of equivalence and effectiveness*	
Impact of substantive rules	Since end of 1970s reach of substantive law narrowed and shift away from reliance on per se rules—significantly impacted on ability of plaintiffs to win antitrust cases outside of cartel cases	Broader scope to rely on presumptions of illegality under both Article 101 and 102 (than under Sherman Act, ss 1 and 2).	

3

Welfare Effects of Right to Damages—A Practical Approach and the Swedish Perspective

LARS HENRIKSSON*

1. INTRODUCTION: WELFARE-ENHANCING EFFECTS ARISING FROM THE RIGHT TO DAMAGES

THE NEW DIRECTIVE on antitrust damages actions[1] will essentially establish the right for anybody who has suffered harm from infringements of EU competition law to claim and obtain full compensation for that harm. Such a right already exists. For instance in Sweden, the right to full compensation for aggrieved natural and legal persons is enshrined in Chapter 3, section 25 of the Swedish Competition Act. Although much of the debate has been concentrated on issues regarding whether such a right should exist in the first place, and, if so, who should be entitled to compensation, little attention has been devoted in the legal literature to what the likely effects will be in the economy in general of this legal instrument and what challenges and caveats need to be addressed in order to make it efficient both in theory and in practice.[2]

* Professor of Law, Antitrust & Competition Law, LLD, MSc Econ & BA. This chapter is based on a presentation at the conference 'EU Competition Law and the Emerging Harmonization of Private Enforcement: The Upcoming Directive and Beyond' organised by the Swedish Network for European Legal Studies in Uppsala, May 2014, and my contribution to a research project funded by the Arts and Humanities Research Council (AHRC) 'Comparative Competition Law Private Enforcement and Consumer Redress in the EU 1999–2009'. See also the results of that project in B Rodger (ed), *Competition Law—Comparative Private Enforcement and Collective Redress Across the EU* (Kluwer, Law International, Alphen aan den Rijn 2014).

[1] Directive 2014/104/EU of the European Parliament and of the Council of 26 November 2014 on certain rules governing actions for damages under national law for infringements of the competition law provisions of the Member States and of the European Union [2014] OJ L349/1 ('the Directive').

[2] The exception is the comprehensive Antitrust damages impact study: A Renda et al, *Making Antitrust Damages Actions more Effective in the EU: Welfare Impact and Potential Scenarios, Final Report for the European Commission* (21 December 2007) DG COMP/2006/A3/012.

Although the right to damages under Swedish law primarily addresses the issue of ensuring compensation for an injured party, the legal instrument still exists in an economic and a legal context where this issue is definitely in focus, but it also supports the overall legislative objective of making undertakings comply with competition law in the first place. At the outset, it is important to bear in mind that outside common law countries damages are traditionally and first and foremost not punitive in nature, but rather compensatory. As such, you might argue that the right to damages per se, is not much of a deterrent *ex ante* to the behaviour of firms (or rather executives) in the market place.

The overall aim of this chapter is to investigate whether the right to damages may have positive welfare effects and for whom: is it primarily to the benefit of consumers, or producers? To that end, the welfare effects that are likely to follow from the rights in the Directive are explored in general and what other important legal factors will influence such welfare effects is examined. The Swedish experience to date of actions for damages is presented.

In order to address this quandary properly, there are a number of important factors that need to be analysed. Establishing a right to damages is perhaps the easy part, but practical application and efficiency is still fraught with difficulties.

2. WELFARE EFFECTS OF DAMAGES IN GENERAL

2.1 The Concept of Welfare in Economic Theory

When assessing a legislative measure such as the Directive, it is necessary to establish what is meant by welfare. In order to understand the effects in theory, you need to understand a basic microeconomic model. Introducing a practically workable definition of the concepts welfare and welfare effect may seem a cumbersome task and far too theoretical to be able to lead in evidence in a practical case. At this stage of the analysis it is, however, not the task at hand. We are not interested in exactly pinpointing the actual harm, but rather in understanding what general effects will follow from legal instruments and government intervention in the market place. This will at least present a good understanding of the direction in which the effects are likely to move.

In general, a welfare effect refers to gains and forfeitures of both producers and consumers viewed together. The main question related to state intervention in markets is normally not whether an individual consumer is worse or better off, but rather how the consumers, viewed collectively, are affected by such measures (consumer welfare). The consumer interest is undoubtedly also only one side of the market and in order to establish how markets function as a whole, it is also essential to address the question of *total welfare*, ie what effects will arise for consumers and producers taken together.[3]

To settle the problem of measuring welfare effects we normally use consumers' and producers' surplus. For individuals, the consumer surplus is defined as the difference between the maximum price the consumer is willing to pay for a good and the actual price paid. Thus taken as a group, the consumers' surplus will be the total sum of such individual surpluses. Analogously, the producer surplus is defined as the difference between the market price of a good and the marginal cost of production times the sum of all units produced by a firm. Another way of defining producer surplus would be to view it as the difference between the firm's revenue and its total variable cost. These concepts therefore reflect the aggregate net benefits of consumers and producers respectively.

The equilibrium market volume and price is dependent on both the nature of demand and supply, which in turn are determined by factors like underlying cost structure, technology, consumer preferences, income, etc. Government intervention may have essentially three major effects on the market:

— Consumer surplus may change by making some consumers better off than others, eg, price control measures may benefit consumers as a whole even though some consumers are not able to buy a product due to a reduction in output. Depending on the elasticity of demand, this is, however, not a guarantee for an increase in consumers' surplus, and if demand is very inelastic (demand quality does not change much when prices do), consumers may even be worse off compared to when demand is very elastic;
— Producer surplus may also change in terms of lower profitability; lower overall profits as a result of a reduction in output and some producers may even exit the market. Hence, price control measures normally implies that the producers' surplus is reduced;
— If total surplus is reduced, this means that there is a net loss in total surplus, which is called a *deadweight loss*, which can be explained by the fact that the loss in producer surplus is greater than the gain in consumer surplus.

To ascertain whether a measure in the market place is favourable, desirable or motivated is usually related to the question of whether it enhances *economic efficiency*, which is essentially the maximisation of aggregated consumer *and* producer surplus. If a particular measure leads to total welfare

[3] For an introduction to microeconomics and the welfare effects, see generally RS Pindyck, DL Rubinfeld, *Microeconomics*, 8th edn (Upper Saddle River, New Jersey, Prentice Hall, 2012) and A Goolsbee, S Levitt and C Syverson, *Microeconomics* (New York, Worth Publishers, 2013).

(sum of consumer and producer surplus) being offset by the deadweight loss, it means that an economic inefficiency occurs.[4]

In a simplified model, an unregulated competitive market would achieve economic efficiency in terms of no deadweight loss and a market price that equals marginal cost. This is what we would call a perfectly competitive market. Equally simplified, in a perfect monopoly, where all consumers are price takers, this would mean that the market price was set by the monopolist, who in turn would maximise profits at the point where marginal revenue equalled marginal cost. Typically, this would lead to a lower output than under perfect competition and also a higher price.

The resulting deadweight loss of monopolies are traditionally the main concern due to the combination of inefficiency and the market power of the producer; not only is the market less efficient but consumers are also forced to pay the maximum price they are willing to pay. This in turn relates to the concepts of productive and allocative efficiency. A market is considered to be productively efficient when all resources are used efficiently. A monopoly can normally earn additional profits by charging different prices according to the elasticity of demand of different customer groups; this would make that market more efficient. If the monopoly were able to identify the customers' marginal propensity to pay this could in theory, under such perfect price discrimination, make the market efficient in terms of *productive efficiency*. However, the consumers' surplus would in such a case be reduced to a minimum, thereby reducing the *allocative efficiency* correspondingly. Under perfect competition, allocative efficiency would be maximised, mirroring the fact that demand would be satisfied both in terms of quality and price, whereas producers would earn zero profits.

In reality, most markets are somewhere in between these extreme theoretical scenarios. The underlying theory of how markets work still applies but whether a measure will have the desired effects in reality can arguably be a cumbersome task to ascertain. The main problem is to decide what weight shall be attributed to productive and allocative efficiency. Is the legislation designed to only take into account the interest of consumers or is it also concerned with the interests of the producers? In extreme scenarios, where fixed costs are exceptionally high, an extreme consumer focus would even—paradoxically, it may seem—favour monopolies because this would be the only way of minimising the price, as more than one producer would not achieve the minimum scale necessary to supply the product or service in question. Conversely, an extreme producer focus would imply that consumers are worse off.

[4] Note that whether this is viewed positively depends on the objective of the measure. Sometimes the legislator has an interest in making markets less efficient because certain goods and services are less desirable or have unwanted side effects. This motivates, for instance, the existence of the retail monopoly for alcoholic beverages in Sweden.

However, taking a practical view on markets, it seems obvious that there is a constant interplay between producers and consumers. It appears unrealistic to regard either supply or demand as exogenous static factors, which means that an extreme consumer focus could sometimes lead to undesired effects in the market. Legislative measures that are designed only to accommodate and enhance consumer welfare may therefore seem to take a rather myopic approach.

When making an assessment of the welfare effects of possible damages, it may seem self-evident that an individual consumer who has suffered antitrust harm would certainly experience positive welfare effects. After all the alternative to damages, ie having no right to recourse from an infringer of antitrust law for harm suffered, would leave that particular consumer worse off than the one who would have such a right. Therefore, for the individual the right to damages should be regarded as a welfare-enhancing measure.

This conclusion should remain the same for consumers as a group; at least as long as 'consumers' does not regard end consumers, and as long as consumer welfare is of prime concern. Why is that? Antitrust harm does not always have an immediate impact on the end consumer. In many cases, the directly aggrieved party could be an up or downstream intermediary, a competitor or a supplier and thereby the harm caused by the infringer may have indirect effects on end consumers. Since the actual effects in such cases vary depending on the structure and nature of the market, it is not necessarily true that the right to damages for all aggrieved parties leads to unambiguously positive effects in the market. Also, if you were to assume that consumer welfare was the only concern of EU competition law, the analysis would be rather straightforward. A relevant question here is therefore what is the legal instrument designed for and what might be a proper welfare standard (benchmark) for competition law?

2.2 Aims and Objectives of the Directive

The essence of the Directive is set out in Chapter I, Article 1. From the Article it follows, *first,* that *anyone* who has suffered harm resulting from a competition law infringement by an undertaking or association of undertakings shall *effectively* be able to exercise the right to claim *full compensation* for such harm from the infringer. This is the main objective of the Directive, although the scope is wider. Hence, *secondly* (and seemingly equally importantly), the rules are designed to foster undistorted competition in the internal market and to remove obstacles to the proper functioning of the internal market by ensuring that there is *equal protection* throughout the Union for any aggrieved party. This secondary objective is twofold in nature. To begin with, it is designed to ensure that there are no procedural and/or practical obstacles for cross-border disputes within the EU, thereby supporting private law litigation for damages. The Directive recognises the uneven playing field that exists today between the Member States, which also works as a disincentive to exercise the right to the establishment and provision of goods and services to such Member States where the rights to damages are better catered for. Therefore, an approximation of the laws of the Member States is necessary.

Also, and in accordance with the *Courage* ruling, the rights that follow from the Directive support the full effectiveness of Article 101 TFEU. In particular, the *practical effect* of the prohibition laid down in Article 101(1) TFEU would, in the absence of the right, be put at risk if it were not possible for any individual to claim damages for loss caused to him/her by a contract or by conduct restricting or distorting competition. The ECJ has underlined that the existence of a right to damages strengthens the working of EU competition rules and discourages the illegal restriction or distortion of competition.[5]

It follows from Article 3 of the Directive that damages shall be compensatory in nature, thereby ruling out the possibility of overcompensation, whether by means of punitive, multiple or other types of damages. The aggrieved party should therefore be placed in the position in which that person would have been had the infringement not been committed. The right to full compensation includes actual loss, loss of profit and interest.

These are the overarching rights vested on the aggrieved parties and thereby set the boundaries for and state the objectives of the Directive.

2.3 The Objectives of EU Competition Law

Although determining the overall objective of EU competition law may seem obvious at first glance, it is nonetheless a more complex issue than meets the eye. At the outset, it should be noted that EU competition rules have remained unchanged since 1957, whereas economic theory has advanced considerably over the last few decades. Naturally, the application of the rules is now also more in line with economic theory, and an ongoing debate on competition policy concerns how to bring the application and enforcement of the rules, which are worded in rather general terms, in line with the advancements in economic theory.[6]

[5] Case C-453/99 *Courage Ltd v Bernard Crehan and Bernard Crehan v Courage Ltd and Others* [2001] ECR I-6297, paras 26–27.

[6] On the objectives of EU competition law see D Geradin, A Layne-Farrar and N Petit, *EU Competition Law and Economics* (Oxford, Oxford University Press, 2012) 19. See also I Kokkoris and H Shelanski, *EU Merger Control—A Legal and Economic Analysis* (Oxford, Oxford University Press, 2014) 32; R O'Donoghue and J Padilla, *The Law and Economics of Article 102 TFEU*, 2nd edn (Oxford, Oxford University Press, 2013) 5; J Faull and A Nikpay (eds) *The EC Law of Competition*, 2nd edn (Oxford, Oxford University Press, 2007) 3; and L Henriksson, *Konkurrensrättsöverträdelser—Ekonomisk analys i den juridiska processen* (Stockholm, Norstedts Juridik, 2013) 21.

According to Article 3(3) TEU, the Union shall inter alia establish an internal market. It shall work for the sustainable development of Europe based on balanced economic growth and price stability, a highly *competitive social market economy*, aiming at full employment and social progress, a high level of protection and the improvement of the quality of the environment. It shall promote scientific and technological advances. Although the notion of social market economy appears to include more than the attainment of economic efficiency to the benefit of consumers, it still stresses that the rules on competition exist within a context of other rules that are not all aimed at achieving unregulated market freedom.[7] Although the Union is highly concerned with the functioning of the market as such, there are still limitations on the commercial freedom of undertakings, but a liberal market economy is the main scenario.[8]

The rules on competition also play an important role in achieving the objective of the realisation of the internal market, which does not necessarily lead to economic efficiency in the individual cases in which the rules are applied. Although the internal market, as a whole, removes national barriers to interstate trade, this does not automatically translate into economic efficiency, especially in cases where demand characteristics are national. Therefore, the single market imperative must be considered when applying the rules on competition.[9]

It is also true that one of the top priorities of EU competition law is to achieve effective competition within the internal market, as seen already in early case law.[10] The realisation of an internal market characterised by free movement and free competition are the hallmarks of an open market economy. The efficient allocation of resources also governs how competition enforcement should be conducted under the rules. It thus becomes rather clear that the interests of the consumer are of prime concern.[11] Looking at

[7] Regarding the concept of social market economy, see D Tarschys, 'Det sociala Europa—ett komplext begrepp' in G Bertola et al (eds), *Är EU en social marknadsekonomi? Sociala Europa—en antologi* (Stockholm, Svenska Institutet för Europapolitiska Studier (SIEPS), 2011:2op) 8–20. See also J Hettne, 'Kan Lissabonfördraget minska EU:s sociala underskott?' in G Bertola et al (eds), ibid, 21–39. See also FW Scharpf, *Governing in Europe: Effective and Democratic?* (Oxford, Oxford University Press, 1999) Ch 2.

[8] See FW Scharpf, 'Socio-ekonomiska assymmetrier i den europeiska integrationsprocessen' in G Bertola et al (eds), ibid, 40–55. See also FW Scharpf, *The Socio-Economic Asymmetries of European Integration* (Stockholm, SIEPS, 2010:10epa).

[9] See generally E Deards and S Hargreaves, *European Union Law* (Oxford, Oxford University Press, 2004). On the issue of the artificial partitioning of the internal see in particular the Joined Cases C-501/06 P, C-513/06 P, C-515/06 P and C-519/06 P *GlaxoSmithKline Services and Others v Commission and Others* [2009] ECR I-9291 and Joined Cases C-468/06 to C-478/06 *Sot. Lelos kai Sia EE and others v GlaxoSmithKline AEVE Farmakeftikon Proionton* [2008] ECR I-7139.

[10] Case 6-72 *Europemballage Corporation and Continental Can Company Inc v Commission* [1973] ECR 215, paras 24–25.

[11] *cf* U Bernitz, *Svensk och europeisk marknadsrätt 1—konkurrensrätten och marknadsekonomins rättsliga grundvalar*, 3rd edn (Stockholm, Norstedts Juridik, 2011) 24.

Sweden it becomes even clearer that the consumer interest constitutes a very important factor to consider when applying competition law.[12]

It is important to bear in mind that EU competition law has an ordoliberal heritage, which emphasises the importance of the notion of *Ordnungspolitik*, as outlined by the Freiburg economists W Eucken, F Böhm, H Grossmann-Doerth and L Miksch. According to that school of thought, there is a considerable degree of, if not distrust then at least genuine scepticism, against private economic power, which inter alia entails the concept of competition on merits/performance competition (*Leistungswettbewerb*) as opposed to the obstruction or foreclosure of competition (*Behinderungswettbewerb*). Essentially this means that competition policy should be designed so as to force undertakings with market power to act as if (*als ob*) they have competition, thereby not taking advantage of the powerful position they enjoy in the market, all to the benefit of consumers.[13]

It appears that consumer welfare is of greatest interest in analysing the effects and impacts of legislative instruments. Notwithstanding this prime concern, it cannot be ruled out that other concerns need to be addressed as well. The ECJ has underlined that not only are the interests of competitors and consumers protected, but also the *structure of the market* and thereby *competition as such*. This implies that an infringement of competition law does not necessitate the demonstration of final consumers being deprived of the advantages of effective competition in terms of supply or price.[14]

In relation to the possibility of obtaining damages it may seem contradictory that an infringement appears to encompass other effects than actual harm, the latter being the substance of the Directive. It is, nonetheless,

[12] See the preparatory works of the Swedish Competition Act, Government Bill, 1992/93:56, *Ny konkurrenslagstiftning* 66; Government Bill 2007/08:135, *Ny konkurrenslag* 67; and Government Bill 1999/2000, *Konkurrenspolitik för förnyelse och mångfald* 153. In Norway, s 1 of the Norwegian Competition Act explicitly states that the objective of the law is to foster competition in order to achieve an efficient use of society's resources, whereby the consumer interest shall be taken into special account. See also O Kolstad, 'Konkurranseloven som virkemiddel til å fremme "forbrukernes interesser"' (2005) 118ER:102 *Tidskrift for Rettsvitenskap* 2.

[13] For an excellent overview and in-depth analysis of the ordoliberal approach, see DJ Gerber, *Law and Economics in Twentieth Century Europe: Protecting Prometheus* (Oxford, Oxford University Press, 2003) 250. More specifically on the main issues of *Ordnungspolitik*, see C Dümchen, *Zur kartellrechtlichen Konzeption Franz Böhms*, vol 4 of Wirtschaftsrecht und Wirtschaftsverfassung (Franfurt am Main, Lang, 1980); L Miksch, *Wettbewerb als Aufgabe: Grundsätze einer Wettbewerbsordnung*, 2nd edn (Godesberg, 1947) and L Miksch, 'Die Wirtschaftspolitik des Als Ob' (1949) 105 *Zeitschrift für die gesamte Staatswissenschaft* 310; HC Nipperdey, 'Wettbewerb und Existenzvernichtung' (1930) 28 *Kartell-Rundschau* 127; and F Böhm, *Wettbewerb und Monopolkampf: Eine Untersuchung zur Frage des wirtschaftlichen Kampfrechts und zur Frage der rechtlichen Struktur der geltenden Wirtschaftsordnung* (Berlin, 1933).

[14] See *GlaxoSmithKline* (n 9) paras 62–64. See also Case C-8/08 *T-Mobile Netherlands BV, KPN Mobile NV, Orange Nederland NV and Vodafone Libertel NV v Raad van bestuur van de Nederlandse Mededingingsautoriteit* [2009] ECR I-4529, paras 38–39, where the ECJ held that there does not need to be a direct link between market conduct that is restrictive by object and consumer prices.

logical that the prohibition also covers conduct and agreements that have a potential effect, since the idea underpinning competition law is to force undertakings not to engage in the forbidden dealings and conduct in the first place.

The fact still remains that although consumers are of prime interest there are also the interests of competitors, the structure of the market and competition as such. The applicable welfare standard therefore appears to be adjusted so that it will also consider producer welfare to some extent, although it is rather unclear how much. In any case, a full focus on consumer interests alone would appear not to be in line with applicable law. The appropriate welfare standard would therefore need to—at least to some extent—include the producers' surplus. However, in this balancing act a considerably greater amount of weight is given to the consumers' interest. It is therefore safe to conduct an assessment, such as this one, on the basis of whether consumers will be better or worse off as a result of the legal instrument at hand.

2.4 Welfare Effects in a Simplified Market Setting

In a simplified market setting, where there is one or more sellers and no intermediaries (eg, wholesalers and retailers), analysing welfare effects seems straightforward. For the sake of argument we can presume that the producer (seller) has infringed competition law and that this has led to an increase in prices that would not have taken place without the infringement.

Absent the right to compensation, consumers would suffer the consequences of the infringement. Paradoxically, administrative fines could even exacerbate the harm, as it would be likely that an infringer who has been forced to pay fines needs to compensate that cost, which ultimately will affect consumers. In a worst-case scenario the consumers would have to pay the overcharge in period 1 and suffer from an indirect effect of the administrative fine in period 2. Naturally, the latter could potentially amount to a new infringement and should not take place in practice. However, the passing-on of such costs and the possibility for an infringer to reap the rewards of illegal conduct would at least be a serious risk that trading partners would have to take into account. Consequently, the welfare effects for consumers would be negative and would increase the producers' surplus at the expense of the consumers' surplus.

Introducing a right to damages, whereby illegal overcharges or the combined effect of output and price need to be compensated by giving consumers the right to recourse, would in theory outweigh the effects of the illegal behaviour, but would not go beyond that. Compared to the situation that would have prevailed in the absence of such an infringement, consumers would not have gained anything through damages, but rather avoided the negative effects of the infringement. The welfare effects are therefore at best neutral. Conversely, the welfare effects for the producer who is in breach of competition law would naturally not be more than the illegal gains emanating from the infringement, and the introduction of a duty to pay compensatory damages would take away the illegal profits earned. Paying damages would have correspondingly negative welfare effects on the producer, which is the general idea behind the prohibition.

Arguably, this creates disincentives for producers to engage in illegal behaviour; there should be no gains resulting from prohibited conduct. The fact that damages do not go beyond compensation does, however, mean that they constitute per se a rather small deterrent effect. In the producer's worst-case scenario, the remedies for consumers would only entail the repayment of the profits that should not have been earned in the first place. This is why the compensatory damages need to be combined with sanctions in order for competition law to have any deterrent effect. Naturally, any flaws or shortcomings related to the rights of obtaining damages will influence the welfare effects negatively for the consumers and, vice versa, positively for producers. I will revert to that issue below.

2.5 Welfare Effects in Complex Market Settings

Essentially there are different welfare effects depending on which market player is entitled to damages. Awarding damages to an undertaking active at the wholesale level of the distribution chain does not necessarily yield the same welfare effects as awarding damages to end consumers. The more complex the market setting, the more difficult it may be to measure the actual and final effects and/or harm in the market.

Although the findings above apply generally, the analysis becomes increasingly complex when a more real-world scenario is assessed. Markets are typically not designed in such a way that there is only one direct producer-consumer relationship. Antitrust injury usually affects direct trading parties and competitors to the producer. Primary line antitrust injury, ie such harm that is caused to the producer's direct competitors (eg, predatory pricing, price squeezing, loyalty schemes, etc), is arguably the most common and the EU Commission has prioritised combatting such foreclosing actions. Also, conduct that affects a producer's downstream trading parties in the distribution chain may also cause antitrust harm. Discriminatory actions may, eg, raise prices for some wholesalers/retailers but not others. Insofar as such behaviour can be regarded as, eg, abusive under Article 102 TFEU, the parties discriminated against may have suffered such secondary line antitrust harm.

In cartel cases, the negative effects of the illegal behaviour may naturally have a direct effect on consumers, but more commonly, the effects are more indirect in the sense that they are primarily being experienced by trading parties to the cartel whereby consumers will only feel the effects if the harm is passed on to them. If the trading parties are public entities, the indirect effect on consumers will be even more remote and in fact much more difficult to measure. In the Swedish asphalt cartel case the illegal actions resulted inter alia in overcharges vis-à-vis the buyers (local authorities and the former Swedish Road Administration) and thereby the antitrust harm did not have a direct impact on consumers, but rather on the taxpayers.[15] The effects, which the cartel actually had on consumer welfare more specifically, are at best hard to calculate.

From a strict consumer welfare point of view, it is far from clear that any harm caused upstream in the distribution chain will actually filter down to end consumers and reduce the consumers' surplus, eg, in terms of higher prices, lower output and/or inferior quality. In fact, the actual effects are to a large extent dependent on the same factors as when assessing the impact of countervailing the buyer power of intermediaries.

Essentially, such power may at least to some extent offset the selling power exercised by a producer with market power. The comparison with an assessment of countervailing buyer power does not, however, do the instrument of damages justice as it refers to another assessment, namely whether an infringement has occurred or whether a merger should be deemed to significantly obstruct effective competition in the relevant market. Damages are only awarded in cases of actual infringement, with the addition that somebody has suffered actual antitrust harm. In cases where the legal instruments based on the Directive will be applied, it presupposes that there is actual harm somewhere in the distribution chain. The key question is whether this harm is done directly to consumers or whether they suffer such harm indirectly.

Therefore, it cannot be ruled out that if a wholesaler/retailer suffers actual harm, it must be presumed that the illegal behaviour on the part of the infringer has had a negative impact on the trading party. This harm will certainly, to some extent, either be passed on to consumers, whose welfare will be negatively affected, or it will result in a reduction in profitability. Even if consumers do not experience higher prices or a reduction in output, the inefficiency caused in the distribution chain implies that the benefits gained from the level of efficiency that would have been in place in the absence of the infringement and antitrust harm are foregone. The consumers might have been even better off without the damage caused upstream.

Consequently, even in more complex market settings, it must be presumed that the right to damages cannot be seen as a welfare-reducing measure—this

[15] MD 2009:11, *NCC Aktiebolag, Peab Asfalt AB, Peab Sverige AB, Peab Asfalt Syd AB (appellant only)*, S *Grus & Asfalt Aktiebolag (appellant only), Svenska Väg Aktiebolag (endast klagande) v Konkurrensverket et vice versa.*

would entail that a finding of infringement were materially wrong and based on bad economics. The sound enforcement and application of competition law, which is in line with economic theory, would subsequently single out conduct that is detrimental to efficiency and consumers. A legal instrument that awards the aggrieved party the right to claim compensation for harm caused by economically harmful behaviour would therefore be a welfare-enhancing measure, at least if the actual harm is done. Without actual harm, it would still have positive welfare effects, as it would *ex ante* send a message to potential infringers that any illegal gains must be paid back.

Again, the counterfactual scenario appears to be most unacceptable; if the aggrieved party lacked the possibility of obtaining damages, European competition law would subsequently indirectly accept that abusers of a dominant market position or cartel members were entitled to keep the illegal gains of their wrongdoings and that their—illegal—surplus were reduced only by the administrative fines. Based on the leniency programme this might even in some cases be reduced to zero.

Although the actual effects of a duty to compensate aggrieved parties for illegal acts may not always filter down to consumers directly, this does not mean that the consumers' surplus is unaffected. Ultimately someone will have to bear the consequences of the wrongful actions and therefore even indirect harm to consumers must be considered as welfare-improving in general. Despite the fact that there may be cases in which this will not materialise, the opposite situation would definitely reduce consumers' surplus, even *ex ante*.

It follows, therefore, that the Directive as a legal instrument per se should be regarded as welfare-enhancing. It appears most unrealistic to have rules on competition without an instrument ensuring that illegal gains are repaid to those who have suffered harm from illegal actions. Although the Directive is of a compensatory nature and thereby has less of a deterrent effect, it still has obvious and indispensable merits.

This part of the analysis was devoted to the general effects of the Directive as such. The next step is to analyse the challenges that lie ahead to ensure its effective application. Despite its merits, applying the Directive under national law is still sprinkled with caveats. The experience from almost 22 years of EU-based competition law in Sweden serves as an illustration of the pitfalls that can arise and the supplementary measures that could be needed in order to safeguard the rights that are enshrined in the Directive in practice.

3. WELFARE EFFECTS OF THE RIGHT TO DAMAGES IN SWEDEN

3.1 Damages for Antitrust Injury in Sweden over 22 Years

The importance of the private enforcement of competition law was already acknowledged in the Government Bill of the first EU-adapted Competition

Act that entered into force on 1 January 1993. A revised Competition Act entered into force on 1 November 2008. Chapter 3, sections 25–26 of the Competition Act cover rules on damages. At the outset, the legislator held that it was crucial that the enforcement of the rules on competition in Sweden should as far as possible not be entirely dependent on public enforcement, ie cases brought by the Swedish Competition Authority (*Konkurrensverket*, KKV). An explicit rule on the right to damages caused by antitrust injury was therefore introduced in order to encourage undertakings to act against anticompetitive behaviour and it was designed to function as an instrument for compensation for aggrieved parties and as a deterrence for infringers of the rules on competition.[16]

Damages can be awarded if an undertaking intentionally or negligently infringes any of the prohibitions in Articles 101 and 102 TFEU or the corresponding Swedish national rules. The existence of the explicit rule is motivated by the fact that antitrust trust damages are not covered by the Damages Act (SFS 1972:207),[17] as damages for pure economic loss for third parties cannot generally be awarded under Swedish law unless the damage is caused by behaviour subject to penal sanctions. The Damages Act and general principles for damages in Sweden complement the Competition Act, inter alia, the rules on joint and severable liability where more than one undertaking has infringed the prohibitions and also the requirement to show adequate causality between the tortious act and the damage incurred.

The liability for joint behaviour will need to be adjusted for antitrust harm in Sweden in relation to the wrongdoings of small and medium-sized enterprises (SMEs) following Article 11(2) of the Directive. This could be viewed as limiting consumer welfare, as it potentially reduces welfare for consumers, however, it seemingly reflects the multiple objectives of competition law; limiting the scope of damages liability may safeguard competitor viability and thereby also competition as such. In turn, this could be a benefit to consumer welfare in the long run.

Furthermore, the right to damages is dependent on the fact that somebody has incurred injury that can be compensated. The amount to be compensated shall correspond to the injury caused, not more. In some areas of Swedish law other principles for compensation apply. The Patents Act, section 58[18] stipulates, for example, that any person who, intentionally or through gross negligence, commits patent infringement shall pay *reasonable compensation* for use of the invention as well as compensation for the *additional loss* resulting from the infringement. When determining the amount of compensation due to patent infringements, particular consideration shall be taken of lost profits, profits realised by the party committing the infringement, damage to the reputation of the invention, non-pecuniary

[16] Government Bill (1992/93:56) *Ny konkurrenslagstiftning* 34.

[17] Damages Act (1972:207).

[18] Patents Act (SFS 1967:837).

loss; the interest of the patent holder in preventing infringement from taking place. There are no such corresponding rules on how to quantify the damages under the Competition Act. However, the general principle is that *full compensation* shall be awarded to the suffering party.

Regarding the issue of definition of the kind of antitrust harm in question, the existing National Swedish rules on damages appear to be well in line with the Directive.

3.2 Swedish Forum Rules

Effective access to a judicial system is a prerequisite for positive welfare effects. In Sweden, cases on competition law are handled by the general courts or by arbitration, the latter arguably more common in commercial litigation. According to Chapter 10 of the Swedish Code of Judicial Procedure (SFS 1942:70), private litigation through open court procedures related to damages (in Sweden) is handled by the general courts comprising 48 District Courts, six Courts of Appeal and the Supreme Court. However, as regards antitrust damages, the Stockholm City Court is always competent to deal with such cases. The Stockholm City Court is also the special forum for public enforcement and the only competent court to deal with cases involving, for example, administrative fines for a violation of the Competition Act. In public enforcement, the Stockholm City Court's judgments can be appealed to the Market Court as the final instance for such cases. This allows for a limited extent of forum shopping.

The national Swedish rules on arbitration explicitly allow any arbitral tribunal to consider the civil consequences of competition law between the parties,[19] which also serves as a limitation regarding the matters of competition law that can be examined by an arbitral tribunal. In *Coinstar*, a dispute arose in connection with a grant-back clause where the question was whether arbitrators were competent to deal with competition law questions related to patent ownership and applications. The Court of Appeal, in agreement with the Malmö District Court, held that an arbitral tribunal is in fact authorised to examine such cases. Referring to the Supreme Court judgment in NJA 2008 s 120, it was established that it is not contrary to EU law for such tribunals to deal with competition law matters. Although national courts, following the ECJ ruling in *Eco Swiss*, are authorised to consider the consistency of arbitration awards with Article 101 TFEU in cassation procedures, this presupposes, according to the Supreme Court, that arbitral tribunals are authorised to deal with cases related to competition law.[20]

[19] Arbitration Proceedings Act (1999:116) s 1.

[20] See Court of Appeal (*Hovrätten över Skåne och Blekinge*) Case T-2520-08 *Coinstar Inc v Scan Coin Industries AB*. See also, NJA 2008 s 120, *Ystad Hamn Logistik AB v Bornholmstrafikken* and Case C-126/97 *Eco Swiss China Time Ltd v Benetton International NV* [1999] ECR I-3055.

3.3 Quantification of Harm

One of the more difficult issues related to whether damages will have positive welfare effects is whether it would be possible to quantify damages under national law in practice. In cases where this will prove difficult, once adequate causality has been established, the actual compensation may otherwise be reduced to an ostensible right. This dilemma naturally applies in many damages cases, so courts and tribunals should already have sufficient experience of handling this issue.

However, in addressing this difficulty the Directive provides, inter alia, that courts (as defined under Article 267 TFEU) shall be empowered to estimate the amount of harm. This possibility is already in place through the provision in Chapter 35, section 5 of the Swedish Code of Judicial Procedure. Furthermore, the Directive requires the introduction in national law of a rebuttable presumption that cartel infringements cause harm and that the competition authority should be able to assist national courts in the quantification of harm. From a welfare perspective, these instruments are designed to combat some important practical obstacles that would otherwise reduce consumer welfare.

3.4 Persons Entitled to Damages

The current Swedish rule on damages does not provide any limitations as to *who* is entitled to damages, which means that it is well in line with the Directive. This implies that both contracting parties and any aggrieved third party (indirect purchasers) are entitled to damages. Originally, however, only 'other undertakings or a contracting party' were entitled to damages. The 1993 Competition Act defined undertakings as legal or natural persons engaged in economic or commercial activity, which ruled out activities carried out by authorities that were of a non-economic or non-commercial nature. Undertakings also encompassed associations of undertakings. In the *Broform* case, the former *Vägverket* (the former National Road Administration, now the Swedish Transport Administration) had allegedly abused its dominant position in the market for the procurement of bridges. The claimant argued that the abuse consisted of the creation and application of a system for controlling the receipt of construction design documents which potential suppliers were forced to use. This particular task vested on the administration was, according to the Stockholm District Court, not of a commercial or economic nature, but rather a part of the administrative obligations that rested with the authority in the administration of national roads. The ruling was upheld on appeal.[21]

[21] Court of Appeal (*Svea Hovrätt*) Case T-2452-01 *Broform aktiebolag v State of Sweden / Vägverket*.

The difficulties in determining which party could be held liable for damages under the old rule were illustrated by the intermediate judgment in *Skånska*[22] by the Stockholm District Court. Two companies were party to a bid-rigging cartel against two local authorities during a public procurement process. The company NCC was awarded the contract and the question raised in the case was whether the other cartel member, although not a direct party to the contract, could also be held liable for damages. The District Court acknowledged that the wording of the law allowed undertakings not party to the contract to simply escape liability, but that such an interpretation would be too strict and that the parties which suffered losses as a result of the cartel behaviour were in a position to seek damages from any of the cartel members regardless of whether they were contracting parties or not.

Although the previous wording did not contain any limitations regarding the number of undertakings entitled to damages, the preparatory works of the Act indicate that the damages rules in the Competition Act were designed to primarily protect competitors, but also undertakings up or downstream in the distribution chain. However, in practice it was deemed unclear which companies other than the contractual parties really were entitled to compensation. It was clear, however, that an undetermined or abstract group of consumers (primarily consumers not party to a contract with the infringing undertaking) were not entitled to damages. This was explained by the argument that the Competition Act was directed at the terms and conditions in business relationships. Seemingly, consumers other than those in a contractual relationship with an undertaking were not considered worthy of protection or concerned by the subject matter of the law.

A public inquiry did not find this explanation entirely convincing, as effective competition was just as much a concern for consumers in general as for undertakings. In hindsight, this finding also appears to be more in line with the welfare analysis above. Accordingly, it was later decided that there should be no limitations regarding who should be entitled to damages, which would also make the rule more in line with general rules on damages. The new rules on damages entered into force on 1 August 2005 and the subject matter of the rule remained unchanged after the introduction of the new Competition Act in 2008. Thus, the existing rules should in principle be well in line with the requirements of the Directive related to persons entitled to sue for damages. An effective damages regime should not exclude any directly or indirectly aggrieved party and both the Directive and the existing rules in Sweden meet this basic requirement.

[22] Intermediate judgment by the Stockholm District Court (*Linköpings kommun*) Cases T-6580-03, T-8371-03, T-14898-03 *Tranås kommun v NCC AB and Skånska Sverige AB*. Upheld on appeal by the Court of Appeal (*Svea Hovrätt*) in Case T-9597-04.

3.5 The Passing-On of Overcharges and Indirect Customers

As already discussed in more general terms regarding complex market settings above, it may be a cumbersome task to specify exactly where the actual harm has materialised. This difficulty should not be overlooked bearing in mind that the compensatory nature of the rules on damages precludes any overcompensation. Therefore, if the harm caused has been passed on to other parties, the first party cannot claim damages, as it has already been compensated.

The question is, thus, what actual harm has been passed on to indirect purchasers, who are indeed entitled to damages in principle. Article 14 of the Directive provides that when calculating the compensable damage, a claimant needs to take into account that the burden of proof rests with the claimant to show both that the commercial practice has indeed led to overcharges being passed on down the distribution chain and also the scope thereof. Moreover, a claimant may claim reasonable disclosure from the defendant or third parties, who, viewed together with Chapter II of the Directive regarding the disclosure of evidence, will need special attention and require amendments to national Swedish law. Article 14(2) also provides rules on evidence relief and in conjunction with Article 15 that makes it possible for courts to take due account of other pending and decided cases, as well as information in the public domain (seemingly *ex officio*).

Even though consumer welfare may be reduced in individual cases as a result of difficulties in proving actual and passed-on harm, and the fact that it can be hard in general to assess actual consumer harm, consumers would still be even more worse off without these rules. The Directive is designed to relieve the claimant of some of the more difficult tasks and ease the burden of proof. Therefore, the general welfare effects should be considered positive for consumers.

3.6 Prolonged Time Limits for Claims on Antitrust Damages

Concurrently with the widening of the circle of individuals entitled to damages, the Government decided to propose an amendment to the rules regarding the five-year time limit for claims for damages (which is now the minimum period according to the Directive). In addition to doubts over whether such a short time limit was in line with EU law, the interest in harmonising the rule with general rules on time limits for claims—which is 10 years in Sweden calculated from accrual—there were also more practical concerns about such a short time limit. Naturally, too short a limitation period would seriously reduce the possibilities of obtaining damages, and thereby also have negative effects on consumer welfare.

Private litigation involving damages claims are often follow-on lawsuits in the wake of successful cases brought by the KKV and investigations undertaken by it. Since those cases tend to be time consuming and at times overly complex, a 10-year time limit, calculated from the time the damage was caused (which is not necessarily the same time as the infringement causing the damage), was considered more adequate in order to promote private litigation.

The current rules will certainly need to be adjusted under Swedish law and the limitation period according to Article 10 of the Directive shall not begin to run before the infringement has ceased and the claimant knows, or can reasonably be expected to know, of the behaviour and that it constitutes an infringement; that the infringement caused him harm; and the identity of the infringer.

Apart from the rules on when this limitation period starts to run, the Directive also provides for new clock-stoppers connected to competition authority proceedings related to the same infringement that caused the antitrust harm.

3.7 Clarification of Antitrust Liability Under both EU and Swedish Law

Before the amendments in August 2005, it was regarded as implicit that antitrust damages could be awarded in Swedish courts as a result of infringements of EU competition rules. In a Government Bill from 2000, the Government did not deem it absolutely necessary to explicitly spell this out in the Swedish Competition Act. However, following the ruling in *Courage*[23] and in order to ensure its full effect, the Government proposed an amendment to explicitly allow claims for damages not only for violations of the Swedish Competition Act but also of the EU rules. The clarification entered into force on 1 August 2005, with the objective to avoid having less favourable domestic rules regarding rights for individuals derived from EU law than those governing similar domestic actions and to ensure that the rules do not render the exercise of rights conferred by EU law practically impossible or excessively difficult, thereby satisfying the principles of equivalence and effectiveness.[24]

3.8 Pre-Trial Discovery v Duty of Disclosure

During the public inquiry on the award of damages under the Competition Act, it was initially discussed whether the modernisation of the competition

[23] *Courage* (n 5).

[24] See Case C-261/95 *Rosalba Palmisani v Istituto nazionale della previdenza sociale* (INPS) [1997] ECR I-4025, para 27.

rules and especially the direct applicability of Article 101(3) TFEU would actually lead to more private litigation. Although the modernisation of the rules has certainly made it easier for a judge or arbitrator, an increase in private litigation has been considered doubtful.[25] The public inquiry found that EU competition law in general and Swedish law in particular lacked the key legal instruments in order to give private parties *incentives* for litigation. Therefore, the introduction of treble damages, one-way fee shifting (as opposed to losing parties paying all the fees), overseeing the legality of contingency fee arrangements, access to pre-trial discovery, access to juries consisting of laypersons (creating uncertainty for the defendant about the judicial outcome) and a relaxed view on how to calculate the antitrust damages, were all considered. None of these elements have any counterpart in the Swedish legal system.[26] One key element has, however, been introduced in Sweden, namely the possibility of class action.

In acknowledging the difficulties for private parties to obtain evidence in litigation for antitrust damages and bearing in mind the advantages of the American *discovery* procedure, the public inquiry considered that some similar instrument of law should be introduced in Sweden, although not including the overseas procedures of depositions and interrogatories. The American discovery process was deemed too difficult to reconcile with Swedish law. At the same time, the prevailing provisions on the *duty of disclosure* under Chapter 38, section 2 of the Swedish Code of Judicial Procedure was considered ill-suited and inadequate for antitrust damages litigation. Essentially, the provisions make it possible to force a party to submit specified documents that are assumed important as evidence, but the rule requires the claimant to be precise as to which documents are sought after and what the claimant intends to prove with those documents. Disclosure cannot be used as a tool for investigating the existence of possible evidence of infringements of competition law, ie 'fishing expeditions' are not allowed. In addition, disclosure may be a blunt instrument if the defendant knows which documents should be submitted at the same time as the destruction of the document in question is not sanctioned.[27] The public inquiry concluded that a system similar to the one used in intellectual property law should be used as a model for antitrust private litigation; namely the introduction of an *infringement investigation* procedure modelled after the duties enshrined

[25] See Public inquiry (*Rätten till skadestånd enligt konkurrenslagen*), SOU 2004:10, 97. See also CD Ehlerman and I Atanasiu (eds), *European Competition Law Annual 2000: The Modernisation of EC Antitrust Policy* (Oxford, Hart Publishing, 2001) 72–80.

[26] SOU 2004:10, 98. The public inquiry made references to JS Venit, 'Brave New World: The Modernization and Decentralization of Enforcement under Articles 81 and 82 of the Treaty' (2003) 40 *Common Market Law Review* 545 and W Wils, *The Modernisation of the Enforcement of Articles 81 and 82 EC: A Legal and Economic Analysis of the Commission's Proposal for a New Council Regulation Replacing Regulation No. 17* (New York, Fordham, 2000).

[27] SOU 2004:10, 100.

in the Agreement on Trade-Related Aspects of Intellectual Property Rights (TRIPS Agreement) and Intellectual Property Rights Enforcement Directive (IPRED).[28]

Notwithstanding the advantages of a discovery procedure, the Government found, however, that even the rules on the duty of disclosure are limited only to those documents that are not subject to trade secrets (Chapter 36, section 6 of the Swedish Code of Judicial Procedure). An undesirable side effect of the introduction of an infringement investigation might be the disclosure of trade secrets between competitors and other parties or the unwarranted exploitation of the knowhow of other undertakings and that such a rule, on balance, could do more harm than good. At least, it would be difficult to demonstrate the exceptional reasons that are normally required to surrender such information. Furthermore, an infringement investigation could interfere with ongoing investigations by the Commission and Competition Authorities. All in all, the Government found that the argument for a new system did not carry enough weight to be introduced.[29]

3.9 A Collective Redress Scheme

The Group Proceedings Act[30] entered into force on 1 January 2003. Individuals, organisations (acting on behalf of a member) and authorities (public class action) can bring class actions on behalf of the members of the particular class action. The Government decides which authorities are competent to bring public class actions and for what matters.

The class action mechanism appears to be well-suited for antitrust damages and it is possible to use both individual class actions as well as organisational class actions. The latter is especially suitable when the damages sought relate to a commodity, service or any other utility that an undertaking has offered directly to consumers. It was discussed in the preparatory documents whether it was suitable for the KKV to act on behalf of consumers (public class action). The purpose of class action is mainly twofold; the obvious motivation is naturally to provide individuals with the possibility to gain compensation that they could not have obtained alone. The instrument does, however, serve another purpose as well, namely to set a precedent or legal standard and thereby achieve or promote the interests of society at large.[31] The KKV was considered to be well-equipped for the latter task. Representing individuals seeking compensation is not one of the main tasks

[28] Directive 2004/48/EC of the European Parliament and of the Council of 29 April 2004 on the enforcement of intellectual property rights [2004] OJ L157.

[29] Government Bill (2004/05:117) 41.

[30] Group Proceedings Act (SFS 2002:599).

[31] Government Bill (2001/02:107) 37.

of the KKV and this fact could, in some cases, lead to a conflict of interests for the authority. As the authority is primarily concerned with the functioning of the market, deterring undertakings from infringing competition law and bringing such violations of the law swiftly to an end, the overall conclusion was that it was not appropriate to assign the task of heading public class actions to the KKV.[32]

Although the class action mechanism has been viewed as well-suited for competition law infringements, there have been no class actions based upon competition law infringements raised either on behalf of smaller companies or consumers seeking redress.

3.10 Private Litigation and Claims for Antitrust Damages in General in Sweden

In the 1990s there were very few cases related to competition law private litigation. This could at least in part be explained by the fact that there have been few cases on competition law that directly involved consumers.

Moreover, there is a low propensity to go to court in Sweden, which was acknowledged in the preparatory documents. In comparison with the United States, there are significant cultural differences involving a reluctance to bring lawsuits in general and also a less competitive business climate, perhaps in part explained by and inherited from the old competition rules dating back to 1946 that did in fact, to some extent, allow anticompetitive agreements and cartels, at least as long as they were made public in the national cartel register.[33] The new rules from 1993 marked a dramatic change in the approach to competition and it is only natural to believe that the transition is still ongoing. That said, in the 2000s, firms have been more inclined to seek redress through court procedures and arbitration based on competition.

Claims for damages under Article 101 and 102 TFEU and the Competition Act have experienced a slow start in Sweden. Indemnity liability claims (third party claims) are still quite scarce in Swedish case law and contractual liability is likely to be subject to arbitration in most cases. Only a few third party claims have resulted in judgments, whereas the majority of cases have been settled out of court, although several of these cases started as formal lawsuits. The follow-on cases in relation to serious cartels have

[32] Government Bill (n 29) 32–33.

[33] Between 1946 and 1993 the national cartel register covered in total 1250 anticompetitive agreements and 4777 cartel agreements. The register was closed in 1993, following the introduction of the new EU-based competition rules. The register is now only available at the National Archives and encompasses some 340 volumes. See KKV Memo, *Kartellregistret—Kartellregistrets historia, 1946-1993*, 2004-08-27 Dnr 811/2004.

mostly been open court cases (although settled) and they have involved both indemnity and contractual liability. Although arbitration cannot be ruled out for indemnity liability cases, they are most commonly dealt with by the general courts, which is the normal procedure for cases involving public procurement.

We have still not seen any consumer redress cases in Sweden. This can be explained by the fact that consumers were not entitled to sue for damages before the modernisation of the rules in 2004, unless the consumers were contracting parties. More importantly, however, the almost decade-old provisions for class actions have so far not been used in any competition law case.

4. SUMMARY

In this article, I have analysed the welfare effects of the new Directive. From a theoretical point of view the legal instrument must be viewed as welfare-enhancing for consumers, which is the prime concern of EU competition law. Not only will the rights to damages improve the welfare of individual consumers, it is also likely to lead to welfare improvements *ex ante* for consumers as a group and support the overall objectives of competition law.

That being said, it does not rule out the fact that the welfare effects may be difficult to assess in practice. Although aggrieved parties have the right to obtain compensation, the burden of proof is on them to show actual damage and demonstrate adequate causality of this damage. This alone is a challenge for claimants. Furthermore, the right to damages presupposes that the defendant has infringed competition law. A stand-alone finding thereof may prove insurmountable and will in practice imply that damages claims will be follow-on suits from public enforcement, although somewhat eased by the relaxation of the evidence rules contained in the Directive. The willingness to bring lawsuits in general is also of utmost importance. Therefore, there are a number of caveats to whether there will be positive welfare effects for consumers ex post.

4

Challenges for Swedish Courts: Will the New Directive on Competition Damages Actions Help?

INGEBORG SIMONSSON*

1. CAN WE EXPECT ANY CHALLENGES?

1.1 Challenges for Swedish Courts

THE MOST IMPORTANT challenge for Swedish courts is that too few antitrust damages cases are brought. Out of the less than 10 competition law cases initiated annually at first instance (public and private enforcement plus cases on dawn-raids and related issues, plus cases brought directly before the Market Court),[1] on average only two are actions for damages. Of the cases brought, many settle before trial. This means that Swedish courts have limited chances of accumulating a critical mass of cases and establishing legal principles pertaining to quantification of harm. In addition, there is presently no exclusive forum for antitrust damages cases, even though Stockholm City Court is always competent to hear those cases at first instance.

This chapter addresses whether the forthcoming Directive on Competition Damages Actions can be expected to generate more litigation in Swedish courts.[2] It is submitted that the level of compensation, seen in relation to the

* Judge at Stockholm City Court, LL D, Associate Professor of European Law at Stockholm University.

[1] Volumes according to the recent Ds 2014:2 *Patent- och marknadsdomstol* (Swedish Governmental Committee Report on a Patent and Market Court), 145–48.

[2] Directive 2014/104/EU of the European Parliament and of the Council of 26 November 2014 on certain rules governing actions for damages under national law for infringements of the competition law provisions of the Member States and of the European Union [2014] OJ L349/1. The text of the Directive was agreed between the European Parliament and the Council on 17 April 2014 in the ordinary legislative procedure, and was based on the Commission, 'Proposal for a Directive of the European Parliament and of the Council on certain rules governing actions for damages under national law for infringements of the competition law provisions of the Member States and of the European Union' COM(2013) 404 final (11 June 2013).

risks of litigation, may be different if one compares harm caused by local, regional or cross-border antitrust infringements respectively. This means that the frequency of litigation can be expected to be higher in relation to large scale infringements and vice versa. On the whole, it may be optimistic to believe that litigation will increase more than marginally in smaller Member States such as Sweden.

1.2 Some Basic Features of the Directive

The Directive on Competition Damages Actions will provide plaintiffs with incentives to bring actions for damages based on EU competition law, through harmonisation of procedural remedies.[3] The Directive seeks to introduce a level playing field.[4]

There are certain provisions in the Directive which will have an influence on the economic incentives to bring claims. The combined right to full compensation and ban on overcompensation in Article 3 is one such provision.[5]

Save for the rules on interest, which will be addressed below, Article 3 of the Directive on Competition Damages Actions corresponds to what must be considered the present state of Swedish law.

2. THE STARTING POINT FOR AN ANALYSIS OF THE IMPACT OF THE DIRECTIVE IN SWEDEN

2.1 Examples of Litigation on Damages in Swedish Courts

I have compiled a list of antitrust damages cases brought in the last 12 years before Stockholm City Court. The City Court has jurisdiction to hear antitrust damages cases as a first instance court, although its jurisdiction is not exclusive. This means there are other cases before Swedish courts not accounted for here. Another reservation is that I have excluded cases on nullity of contracts where no damages calculations were at issue. Furthermore, antitrust damages can be brought before arbitration panels, and such cases

See also the Corrigendum to the position of the European Parliament adopted at the first reading on 17 April 2014 with a view to the adoption of Directive 2014/104/EU of the European Parliament and of the Council on certain rules governing actions for damages under national law for infringements of the competition law provisions of the Member States and of the European Union P7_TA-PROV(2014)0451, (COM(2013)0404—C7-0170/2013—2013/0185(COD)), (10 September 2014), available at www.europarl.europa.eu/plenary/en/texts-adopted.html.

[3] See in particular Directive 2014/104/EU, rec 4.
[4] See in particular ibid recs 6–10.
[5] See Appendix for the full text of ibid Art 3.

remain outside of the list. Nevertheless, the compilation may be seen as a good illustration of the frequency of national antitrust damages litigation.

While the list may at first sight give the impression that litigation is rather frequent, one should keep in mind that these cases have been brought over a period of 12 years, which means on average two or three cases per annum. Furthermore, numbers are made up to a great extent by one single bulk of follow-on cases related to a road construction cartel case. If those follow-on cases are discounted, litigation remains modest.

Out of the 28 cases reported above, 13 were follow-on cases brought in the wake of a road construction cartel. Two were follow-on cases brought in connection with the *TeliaSonera* margin squeeze case (see the judgment of the EUCJ in Case C-52/09).[6] The remaining 13 cases were various types of stand-alone claims. At least 17 of the cases were settled amicably. Three cases failed after full trial in open court because the plaintiffs could not demonstrate the alleged infringements.

2.2 Cases Where Swedish Courts Quantified Antitrust Damages

At present, there is no case law from the Swedish Supreme Court (*Högsta domstolen*) which specifically addresses the principles applicable for compensation of antitrust damages.

Cases where Swedish courts have been called upon to quantify antitrust harm through calculation of damages are very rare. Damages quantification was carried out in the joined cases *OÜ E-Direct and Europe Investor Direct Aktiebolag v VPC Aktiebolag*.[7] A brief account of the cases will be given here.

Three claimants brought actions against the Central Securities Depository VPC. It was common ground that the claimants for several years in their businesses used address information relating to shareholders in Swedish companies. For many years they had obtained that information through copies of share ledgers, which VPC administered. In late 1998 or early 1999 the claimants no longer received share ledgers from VPC. In October 2000, VPC informed them that the price for paper copies of the information in the share register (instead of the DVDs previously provided) would amount to SEK 1 185 615. This was much higher than the price paid previously (SEK 26 000). Stockholm City Court found that VPC had abused its dominant position by refusing to supply the information, and ordered VPC to pay damages of a total of SEK 3 900 000 plus interest. The claimants had

[6] T 10956-05 *Tele2 Sverige AB v TeliaSonera Aktiebolag (publ)* and T 15382-06 *Yarps Network Services AB v TeliaSonera Aktiebolag (publ)*.

[7] Judgment of 20 November, 2008, in Joined Cases T 32799-05 and T 34227-05 *OÜ E-Direct and Europe Investor Direct Aktiebolag v VPC Aktiebolag* (Stockholm City Court).

Table 1: List of Antitrust Damages Cases Brought in Last 12 Years

Case no	Filed	Subject matter	Status	Parties	Outcome
T 20621-10	2010-12-17	Restitution and damages; abuse of dominance	Closed 2014-02-07	*Verizon Sweden AB v Tele2 Sverige Aktiebolag*	Dismissed on the merits following full trial
T 5995-09	2009-04-17	Damages, abuse of dominance	Closed 2012-05-31	*Preem Aktiebolag v Gävle Hamn AB*	Dismissed on the merits following full trial
T 5289-09	2009-04-02	Damages, request for a negative declaratory judgment	Closed 2009-04-27	*Akzo Nobel NV v CDC Cartel Damage Claims Hydrogen Peroxide SA*	Case withdrawn
T 5285-09	2009-04-02	Damages, request for a negative declaratory judgment	Closed 2009-04-27	*Akzo Nobel Chemicals Holding Aktiebolag v CDC Cartel Damage Claims Hydrogen Peroxide SA*	Case withdrawn
T 5284-09	2009-04-02	Damages, request for a negative declaratory judgment	Closed 2009-04-27	*Eka Chemicals Aktiebolag v CDC Cartel Damage Claims Hydrogen Peroxide SA*	Case withdrawn
T 1385-09 T 8728-08	2009-01-30	Payment for goods/services contract, counter argument on nullity of contract clause or adjustment of the price because of abuse of dominance (overpricing)	Closed 2009-11-13	*AB Fortum Värme samägt med Stockholms stad v Farsta Strand Business Center AB*	Settled during trial
T 2679-08	2008-02-22	No information available	Closed 2008-05-02	*Solna Bilteknik AB v Kontrollerad Bilverkstad i Sverige AB*	Case withdrawn
T 21129-07	2007-10-19	Nullity of anticompetitive contract clauses and related issues	Closed 2008-11-17	*Skånemejerier ek för v Arla Foods amba*	Settled

(continued)

Table 1: (*Continued*)

Case no	Filed	Subject matter	Status	Parties	Outcome
T 15382-06	2006-06-29	Damages; infringement of the Competition Act and Art 102 TFEU (follow-on, see Case C-52/09 *TeliaSonera* before the EUCJ)	Pending 2011-02-23	*Yarps Network Services AB v TeliaSonera Aktiebolag (publ)*	Pending
T 34227-05	2005-12-23	Damages; abuse of dominance	Closed 2008-11-20	*OÜ E-Direct v VPC Aktiebolag*	Plaintiff won; part of damages awarded
T 32799-05	2005-12-07	Damages; abuse of dominance	Closed 2008-11-20	*Europe Investor Direct Aktiebolag mfl v VPC Aktiebolag*	Plaintiff won; part of damages awarded
T 14900-05	2005-05-17	Damages; cartel overcharges (follow-on)	Closed 2010-09-01	*Linköpings kommun v NCC Aktiebolag mfl*	Settled
T 11686-05	2005-04-11	Damages; cartel overcharges (follow-on)	Closed 2010-07-13	*Ulricehamns kommun v Skanska Sverige Aktiebolag*	Settled
T 11529-05	2005-04-08	Damages; breach of contract and abuse of dominance	Closed 2007-11-09	*Primeur Vin Aktiebolag v Systembolaget Aktiebolag*	Dismissed on the merits following full trial
T 10969-05	2005-04-04	Damages; Competition Act	Closed 2005-09-30	*Verisec AB v Pointsec Sweden AB*	Settled
T 10956-05	2005-04-01	Damages; infringement of the Competition Act and Art 102 TFEU (follow-on, see Case C-52/09 *TeliaSonera* before the EUCJ)	Pending	*Tele2 Sverige AB v TeliaSonera Aktiebolag (publ)*	Pending

(*continued*)

Table 1: (*Continued*)

Case no	Filed	Subject matter	Status	Parties	Outcome
T 31609-04	2004-12-15	Damages; cartel overcharges	Closed 2010-07-13	*Vaggeryds kommun v Skanska Sverige Aktiebolag*	Settled
T 9744-04	2004-06-18	Damages; cartel overcharges	Closed 2010-07-13	*Kristianstads kommun v NCC Aktiebolag and others*	Settled
T 9740-04	2004-06-18	Damages; cartel overcharges	Closed 2010-07-13	*Bromölla kommun v NCC Aktiebolag and others*	Settled
T 6160-04	2004-04-16	Damages; cartel overcharges	Closed 2010-07-13	*Götene kommun v NCC Aktiebolag and others*	Settled
T 6158-04	2004-04-16	Damages; cartel overcharges	Closed 2010-07-13	*Ulricehamns kommun v NCC Aktiebolag*	Settled
T 6155-04	2004-04-16	Damages; cartel overcharges	Closed 2010-07-13	*Vaggeryds kommun v NCC Aktiebolag*	Settled
T 6145-04	2004-04-16	Damages; cartel overcharges	Closed 2010-07-13	*Klippans kommun v NCC Aktiebolag and others*	Settled
T 6141-04	2004-04-16	Damages; cartel overcharges	Closed 2010-07-13	*Värnamo kommun v NCC Aktiebolag and others*	Settled
T 14898-03	2003-09-05	Damages; cartel overcharges	Closed 2010-09-01	*Linköpings kommun v NCC Aktiebolag and others*	Settled
T 8371-03	2003-05-09	Damages; cartel overcharges	Closed 2010-07-13	*Tranås Kommun v NCC Aktiebolag and others*	Settled
T 6580-03	2003-04-08	Damages; cartel overcharges	Closed 2010-09-01	*Linköpings kommun v NCC Aktiebolag and others*	Settled
T 7896-02	2002-05-15	Restitution of fees, damages for breach of Art 102 TFEU	Closed 2008-12-15	*Hydro Aluminium Sverige AB, Energi E2 A/S v Staten genom affärsverket svenska kraftnät*	Settled

calculated damages as lost gross revenues, minus the costs that were saved as a result of the infringement. The City Court rejected this approach and accepted only that the damage should equal the lost profits. The Court applied the rule in the Code of Judicial Procedure, providing that in case it is difficult to prove a loss fully, the court shall estimate the damage to a reasonable amount.

On appeal, the finding of an abuse was upheld, but the abuse was deemed to have been in operation for a shorter period of time. The Court of Appeal awarded half the amounts of damages awarded by the City Court.

Among other cases which are still pending, quantification of harm will be part of the challenges for the courts in *Tele2 Sverige AB v TeliaSonera Aktiebolag* and *Yarps Network Services AB v TeliaSonera Aktiebolag*,[8] which are pending in Stockholm City Court.

3. WILL THE DIRECTIVE'S PROCEDURAL PROVISIONS GIVE CLAIMANTS BETTER INCENTIVES?

Some reflections will be made here on whether the procedural provisions of the Directive will give potential claimants a better position or not, seen in relation to the presently applicable Swedish legislation.

3.1 Rules on Disclosure

The rules on disclosure of evidence in Chapter II of the Directive on Competition Damages Actions,[9] once implemented, will represent a move from a relatively straightforward set of generally applicable rules in Chapter 38 of the Swedish Code of Judicial Procedure to a much more complex and sophisticated set of rules. Whether claimants will be in a better or worse position, as a result of the introduction of the rules in the Directive, is difficult to estimate in advance and it might well depend on case to case. Either way, increased litigations costs on disclosure can be expected, given the complexity.

3.2 Binding Effect of a Finding of an Infringement

It would seem that the introduction of a binding effect of a finding of an infringement in a public enforcement case, for the purpose of a private

[8] Cases T 10956-05 and T 15382-06 *Tele2 Sverige AB v TeliaSonera Aktiebolag* and *Yarps Network Services AB v TeliaSonera Aktiebolag*.

[9] See Appendix for the full text of Directive 2014/104/EU, Arts 5–8.

enforcement case, would greatly help claimants. Presently, the experiences from the follow-on damages cases related to the road construction cartel and the *TeliaSonera* margin squeeze case is that of systematic re-litigation to establish, again, whether there has been an infringement (or indeed several infringements). A binding effect of the finding of an infringement in a national public enforcement case, as set out in Article 9 (1-2) of the Directive on Competition Damages Actions, would put claimants in a better position.[10]

The binding effect of a Commission decision applying Articles 101 or 102 TFEU is already established according to case law. When national courts rule on agreements or practices which are already the subject of a Commission decision they cannot take decisions running counter to that of the Commission, even if the latter's decision conflicts with a decision given by a national court of first instance.[11] This case law is codified in Article 16 of Regulation No 1/2003.[12] Its relevance for damages cases was confirmed by the EUCJ in *Otis*.[13] The rules in Article 9 (1-2) will not put national decisions on an equal footing with Commission decisions, but will greatly reduce the need for re-litigation about the existence of infringements.

3.3 Limitation Periods

The provisions on limitation periods in the Directive on Competition Damages Actions are more sophisticated than the present 10-year limitation period applicable under Chapter 3, section 25 of the Swedish Competition Act, and seem more generous towards claimants.[14] Claimants will be able to benefit from the fact that limitation periods do not start to run until the infringement has ceased and the claimant becomes aware of the infringement and its consequences (or can be expected to know). At present under Swedish law, action must be brought within 10 years from when the harm occurred. It goes without saying that claimants are often made aware of harm caused by secret infringements only several years after they occurred. By then the now applicable limitation period may already have expired. Implementation of Article 10 of the Directive would consequently provide better incentives for claimants.

[10] See Appendix for the full text of Directive 2014/104/EU, Art 9(1)-(2).

[11] Case C-344/98 *Masterfoods v HB Ice Cream* [2000] ECR I-11369, para 52.

[12] Council Regulation (EC) No 1/2003 of 16 December 2002 on the implementation of the rules on competition laid down in Articles 81 and 82 of the Treaty [2003] OJ L1/1.

[13] Case C-199/11 Otis and Others EU:C:2012:684, para 51.

[14] See Appendix for the full text of Directive 2014/104/EU, Art 10.

3.4 Summary; Whether the Procedural Provisions can be Expected to Generate More Litigation in Swedish Courts

As set out above, it is ambiguous whether the introduction of the Directive's rules on disclosure will work for the benefit of claimants or defendants. The rules on disclosure can be expected to increase litigation costs. On the other hand, the introduction of a binding effect of the finding of an infringement in a national public enforcement case will put claimants in a better position. And the forthcoming rules on limitation periods are much more generous towards claimants than existing Swedish rules.

On balance, it must be considered uncertain whether the draft procedural provisions will benefit claimants to such an extent that antitrust private enforcement litigation will increase in Swedish courts. The next step in the analysis is to see whether the Directive will provide claimants with better economic incentives.

4. WILL THE DIRECTIVE PROVIDE CLAIMANTS WITH BETTER ECONOMIC INCENTIVES?

4.1 Can Approximations or Rules of Thumb be Used in the Quantification of Damages Before National Courts?

Pursuant to the Directive on Competition Damages Actions, the rules for the quantification of antitrust harm remain a matter for national legislation.[15]

It can be assumed that a claimant will only bring an antitrust damages claim if chances to obtain compensation equal or exceed a level which justifies the costs and risks associated with litigation. In this context it is of particular interest to consider appropriate levels of compensation. Whether damages can be approximated or (in the extreme) must be proved euro by euro, is a major issue in antitrust damages litigation. It must be considered well-known that a claimant will not be able to determine, based on the proceedings in a public enforcement case, the quantum of antitrust harm.[16] National competition authorities will seldom set fines in relation to actual harm caused.[17] Competition authorities will often work with proxies in the calculation of fines, and not with actual overcharges.[18] If antitrust harm

[15] Directive 2014/104/EU, rec 46 and Arts 16–17.

[16] Organisation for Economic Co-operation and Development (OECD), 'Report on the Nature and Impact of Hard Core Cartels and Sanctions against Cartels under National Competition Laws (OECD, DAFFE/COMP(2002)7) 16.

[17] ICN Working Group on Cartels, 'Defining Hard Core Cartel Conduct, Effective Institutions, Effective Penalties' (International Competition Network, European Communities, 2005) 54 and 59.

[18] Commission, 'Staff Working Paper Accompanying the White Paper on Damages Actions for Breach of the EC Antitrust Rules' SEC(2008) 404, 29.

could be approximated, it would ease the burden on claimants. Such proxies should not constitute an upper limit of damages. Proxies might be useful for harm that is notoriously difficult to quantify, such as harm caused by bid-rigging or market sharing.

The Commission has previously suggested that average overcharges in price-fixing cases could serve as guidance for courts in determining the quantum of damages.[19]

Studies of overcharges are limited to cartels, a type of exploitative infringement. I am not aware of similar studies for abuse of dominance. Exclusionary infringements can of course lead to overcharges, if the cartel or the dominant undertaking is able to overcharge once competition has been oppressed or eliminated. Nevertheless, studies on overcharges will not be helpful for the determination of harm suffered by those that are the direct targets of exclusions or boycotts.

Proxies of cartel overcharges will probably not work as a basis for calculation of harm caused by most forms of vertical infringements.

In the 2013 quantification paper, the Commission takes a cautious stance as regards proxies for damages. It is stated that the insights into the effects of cartels do not replace the quantification of the specific harm suffered by claimants in a particular case. However, the Commission also notes how national courts have, on the basis of such empirical knowledge, asserted that it is likely that cartels normally do lead to an overcharge and that the longer and more sustainable a cartel was, the more difficult it would be for a defendant to argue that no adverse impact on price did take place in a concrete case. Such inferences, however, are a matter for the applicable legal rules.[20]

According to Article 17(1) of the Directive on Competition Damages Actions, Member States shall ensure that the national courts are empowered, in accordance with national procedures, to estimate the amount of harm if it is established that a claimant suffered harm but it is practically impossible or excessively difficult to precisely quantify the harm suffered on the basis of the evidence available. Furthermore, Article 17(2) provides that it shall be presumed that cartel infringements cause harm. The infringer shall have the right to rebut this presumption. Cartels in particular are addressed in the preamble, where it is said that it is appropriate to presume that in the case of a cartel infringement, such infringement resulted in harm, in particular via an effect on prices. Depending on the facts of the case, cartels result in a rise in prices, or prevent a lowering of prices which would otherwise have

[19] ibid 209.

[20] Commission, 'Staff Working Document—Practical Guide Quantifying Harm in Actions for Damages based on Breaches of Article 101 or 102 of the Treaty on the Functioning of the European Union' SWD(2013) 205, para 145.

occurred but for the cartel. This presumption should not cover the concrete amount of harm. Infringers should be allowed to rebut the presumption. It is appropriate to limit this rebuttable presumption to cartels.[21]

There is an opening for approximating harm under applicable Swedish rules. According to Chapter 35, section 5 of the Code of Judicial Procedure, Swedish courts are allowed to estimate the harm caused if full evidence of the extent of such harm cannot be brought at all or only with great difficulty. In the preparatory works of the Competition Act of 1993, this possibility is highlighted for antitrust damages.[22] It is generally accepted that it is very difficult for the claimant to provide evidence of antitrust harm.[23] Application of Chapter 35, section 5 of the Code of Judicial Procedure has been suggested in academic writing as a basis for alleviating the standard of proof as regards the quantum of harm.[24]

Evidently, no national court will be in a position to quantify damages unless the claimant has demonstrated that the defendant has infringed competition law. Furthermore, the claimant must belong to the circle of actors which typically or specifically can be said to be eligible for compensation. This latter question entails an assessment of causality between the infringement and any harm suffered by the plaintiff.[25] Only then will the court be called upon to quantify damages.

I will refer to some well-known studies published in the US and in Europe on cartel overcharges, and discuss how those studies have been understood in the Swedish context. A well-known study, often referred to, is the one made by Connor and Lande.[26] The authors found mean cartel overcharges of 25 per cent. It appears that cartel overcharges are decreasing over time, possibly as a result of intensified supervision and enforcement. During the years 1991 through 2004, estimated overcharges were between 17 and 19 per cent for national cartels and 25 per cent for international cartels. The lowest overcharges, 17 per cent, could be observed among national cartels which only operated in one country. The explanation for the tendency for international cartels to generate higher overcharges was, according to the authors, the lesser threat that outsiders enter the market, as compared to cartels that

[21] Directive 2014/104/EU, rec 47.

[22] Prop 1992/93:56 *Ny konkurrenslagstiftning* (Swedish Government Bill on New Competition Legislation) 96.

[23] Commission, 'White Paper on Damages Actions for Breach of the EC Antitrust Rules' COM(2008) 165 final, 5.

[24] N Wahl, *Konkurrensskada* (Stockholm, JureCLN AB, 2000) 379.

[25] Prop 2004/05:117 *Skadestånd enligt konkurrenslagen m.m.* (Swedish Government Bill on Competition Damages Actions) 23.

[26] JM Connor and RH Lande, 'How High do Cartels Raise Prices? Implications for Reform of the Antitrust Sentencing Guidelines Thinking Creatively About Remedies' (2005) 80 *Tulane Law Review* 513, JM Connor and RH Lande, 'The Size of Cartel Overcharges: Implications for US and EU Fining Policies' (2006) 51 *The Antitrust Bulletin* 983.

are more limited geographically. In other words, higher overcharges can be expected for cartels with a larger geographic footprint and vice versa. Only seven per cent of the cartels did not generate any overcharges at all.

In a subsequent external study prepared for the European Commission and published in 2009 (the Oxera Report),[27] the study by Connor and Lande was tested through a sort of filtering process. Oxera excluded numerous sources used by Connor and Lande, limiting its own study to 114 sources which, according to Oxera's own criteria, were considered most reliable. Just like Connor and Lande, Oxera found that 93 per cent of cartels generated overcharges. According to the study, average cartel overcharges in recent years amounted to 26 per cent for international and 16 per cent for national cartels. No specific conclusions could be made by comparing European cartels and cartels elsewhere in the world.

The Swedish Competition Authority's present method for the calculation of fines was adopted in late 2009.[28] As regards the seriousness of the infringement, the basic amount of the fine is set at 10 per cent of the infringer's turnover on the relevant market, as a maximum level. This can be compared to the Commission's level of up to 30 per cent of the value of sales.[29] In other words, proportionally lower fines have been considered deterrent by the Swedish Competition Authority as compared to the levels set by the Commission. This seems logical in relation to the studies just mentioned. Cartels have different impact depending on their geographic footprint. The empirical knowledge available suggests that a worldwide cartel will on average generate higher overcharges than a national cartel and vice versa.

The Swedish Competition Authority's 10 per cent basic amount of fines has been accepted in principle in a judgment by Stockholm City Court. The Court referred to the research made by Connor and Lande and by Oxera.[30]

Fines reflect the deterrence model and aim at confiscating the unlawful gains. The 10 per cent level applied by the Swedish Competition Authority can, for the time being, be seen as an approximation of average overcharges caused by Swedish cartels. It is not unthinkable that we might see a similar level, if damages for cartels are to be approximated by Swedish courts. Of course, further studies and insights into overcharges may change our perceptions of appropriate levels.

[27] Oxera, 'Quantifying Antitrust Damages—Towards Non-Binding Guidance for Courts—Study Prepared for the European Commission (2009) 89, available at http://ec.europa.eu/competition/antitrust/actionsdamages/quantification_study.pdf.

[28] Konkurrensverket, 'Metod för att fastställa konkurrensskadeavgift' (Dnr 394/2009) www.konkurrensverket.se/globalassets/konkurrens/pm/metod-for-att-faststalla-konkurrensskadeavgift-160-kb.pdf.

[29] Commission, 'Guidelines on the Method of Setting Fines Imposed Pursuant to Article 23(2)(a) of Regulation No 1/2003' [2006] OJ C210/02, para 21.

[30] Judgment of 24 February 2012 in Case T 19974-10 *Konkurrensverket v Scandorama and Ölvemarks* (Stockholm City Court).

If, hypothetically, an overcharge is 10 per cent, and that harm is distributed over more than one level of trade and over many different customers or trading partners within each level of trade, the harm is pulverised and each potential claimant has only a small claim. Such small claims, seen in isolation, may not justify the bringing of an action in court. It may be necessary to bring those claims together through collective redress. Another option is for a claimant to bring the claims together by purchasing such claims from those that suffered a loss.

If a proxy for cartel overcharges of, say, 10 per cent is applied, that would only form the basis of the calculation. As explained, deductions for passing-on would have to be made in accordance with the provisions in the Directive. I find it difficult to see how such levels would provide a real incentive for claimants, unless they can establish in the case at hand that the overcharge was actually higher.

In summary, claimants will in all likelihood have to make detailed calculations based on the data they can accumulate, to convince the courts that antitrust harm can be quantified at a certain level. This equals the situation today and does not bring about any real change in terms of incentives to bring claims.

4.2 The Payment of Interest from the Time the Harm Occurred until Compensation is Paid

According to Article 3(2) of the Directive on Competition Damages Actions, full compensation shall cover the right to compensation for actual loss and for loss of profit, plus payment of interest. Payment of interest from the time the harm occurred until compensation is paid would improve the position of claimants, at least in those Member States where compensation from such an early date is presently not available.

Although Article 3(2) is not clear with respect to the point in time from which interest is due, it is clarified in recital 12 of the Directive that interest 'should be due from the time when the harm occurred until the time when compensation is paid'.[31] Such a principle could be compared to the present default rule applicable under Swedish law,[32] according to which payment of interest is due from one month after the statement of a claim. The claim must often be accompanied by a statement of the facts which make up the claim.

The time lag between discovery of a competition law infringement and the bringing of an action for damages is often considerable, and the right

[31] See Appendix for the full text of Directive 2014/104/EU, rec 12.

[32] Swedish Act on Interest (*räntelagen*) (1975:635) s 4.

to interest from when the harm occurred could make a major difference for potential claimants. The provision in Article 3(2) of the Directive thus seems like a step forward.

4.3 Deadweight Loss

The Commission suggests in the 2013 working document that deadweight loss should be compensated. The Commission refers to volume effects, which is caused by the fact that fewer of the products in question are bought due to the rise in prices.[33] Deadweight loss is however intrinsically difficult to measure.[34] In a study preceding the Directive, it was pointed out with reference to US law that customers suffering deadweight loss have generally been denied standing.[35] The Commission nevertheless envisages litigation to encompass such losses. If, indeed, deadweight loss can be quantified and compensated, this would provide claimants with better economic incentives to bring claims.

4.4 Provisions on Passing-On of Overcharges

Another set of provisions in the Directive on Competition Damages Actions which will have an influence on the economic incentives to bring claims are the provisions on passing-on. These rules will limit individual claims and provide indirect purchasers with a right to compensation. This is because claimants will not be allowed compensation for overcharges that were passed on. On the other hand, indirect purchasers will be able to claim damages.[36]

There is presently no legislation on passing-on under Swedish law, and (at least to this author's knowledge) no case law either. Provisions on passing-on will bring about some legal certainty by introducing principles for the assessment. Whether this can be expected to increase litigation is much more uncertain. Claimants have been known to sue for full damages without reduction for passing-on (see for instance *Verizon Sweden AB v Tele2 Sverige Aktiebolag*, above). The other side of the coin is that indirect purchasers will obtain a much stronger position once it is made clear that they can claim damages.

[33] SWD(2013) 205 (n 20).

[34] CR Leslie, 'Antitrust Damages and Deadweight Loss' (2006) 51 *The Antitrust Bulletin* 521.

[35] Ashurst, 'Study on the Conditions of Claims for Damages in Case of Infringement of EC Competition Rules' (2004) 12, available at ec.europa.eu/comm/competition/antitrust/others/actions_for_damages/study.html.

[36] Directive 2014/104/EU, Arts 12–16.

4.5 Summary on Economic Incentives

The possibility hinted at in soft law of approximating antitrust damages is an interesting route. However, the present Swedish view on overcharges approximations (a 10 per cent proxy for public enforcement cases) is probably insufficient to give claimants better economic incentives. On the other hand, payment of interest from the time the harm occurred until compensation is paid would improve chances for claimants. Compensation of deadweight loss (also referred to as volume effects) would seem like a step forward, but may remain largely hypothetical as a result of the considerable difficulties in calculating such damages. Finally, provisions on passing-on will bring about some legal certainty by introducing principles for the assessment. Whether implementation of the Directive can be expected to increase litigation is on balance uncertain. The most important change lies in improved substantive rules on right to pre-trial interest.

5. COLLECTIVE REDRESS

The Directive on Competition Damages Actions will not harmonise the Member States' law on collective redress. It should however be seen in conjunction with the Commission Recommendation on Collective Redress.[37] According to the Recommendation, all Member States should have collective redress mechanisms at national level for both injunctive and compensatory relief, which respect the basic principles set out in the Recommendation. These principles should be common across the Union, while respecting the different legal traditions of the Member States. Member States should ensure that the collective redress procedures are fair, equitable, timely and not prohibitively expensive.

Legislation on collective redress was adopted in Sweden in 2002 and entered into force on 1 January 2003.[38] As set out in preparatory works, collective redress has been available in Sweden in competition law cases for several years.[39] However, no actual cases have been brought, at least not to this author's knowledge. There is presently some confusion as to which court is competent to hear such cases. The default rule is for collective

[37] Commission Recommendation of 11 June 2013 on common principles for injunctive and compensatory collective redress mechanisms in the Member States concerning violations of rights granted under Union Law [2013] OJ L201/60.

[38] Swedish Act on Collective Actions (*lag om grupprättegång*) (2002:599).

[39] Prop 1992/93:56 (n 19) 28 and 31–32, and Ds 2008:74 *Utvärdering av lagen om grupprättegång* (Swedish Governmental committee report evaluating the Act on collective Actions) 182–84.

actions to be brought in Nacka District Court.[40] At the same time, Stockholm City Court is always competent to hear cases on damages pursuant to Chapter 3, section 26 of the Competition Act. However, the absence of collective antitrust damages cases is unlikely to stem from this conflict of rules. It seems far more likely that the absence of cases is the result of the combined effect of an opt-in rule in the Group Proceedings Act, the ban on ambulance chasing and the very restrictive view on contingency fees applicable to members of the Swedish Bar Association.

6. SUMMARY AND CONCLUSIONS

If the Directive on Competition Damages Actions is to generate more litigation in Swedish courts, the Directive must provide better incentives for claimants procedurally or economically. Whether the incentives on points of procedure are better is unclear. At least the binding effect of the outcome in a public enforcement case should make litigation somewhat more attractive for claimants. Limitation periods will also be more generous towards claimants and allow litigation in cases that are otherwise time barred. As regards economic incentives, the real difference would be in improved chances of obtaining pre-trial interest, from the day the harm occurred rather than from the day when the claim was presented. Collective redress already exists but has not generated any antitrust damages litigation so far. Prospects for collective redress may improve once the passing-on rules have been implemented, since those rules will provide indirect purchasers with better opportunities to bring antitrust claims. Then again, direct purchasers will know for sure that they cannot be compensated for overcharges that were passed on.

[40] Swedish Regulation (2002:814) on the competence for first instance general courts to handle cases on collective actions (*Förordning* (2002:814) *om behörighet för tingsrätter att handlägga mål enligt lagen* (2002:599) *om grupprättegång, m.m*).

Part II

Private Enforcement and the New Directive in Context

5

The Damages Directive and Other Enforcement Measures in EU Competition Law

VLADIMIR BASTIDAS VENEGAS*

1. INTRODUCTION

THE DAMAGES DIRECTIVE was adopted in November 2014.[1] The main aim of this measure is to strengthen the private enforcement of competition rules by facilitating damage actions by individuals.

This chapter aims to put the Damages Directive in the broader context of other measures enforcing EU competition law, in particular measures of public enforcement. The purpose is to evaluate the Damages Directive from a macro-perspective. The intention is not to make an in-depth analysis of specific provisions in the Directive as such analyses are made in other chapters in this book. Accordingly, this chapter first describes the aims, incentives and measures relating to both public as well as private enforcement in Sections two and three. Section four addresses how the two methods of enforcement complement each other and Section five identifies areas of friction. Section six discusses the purpose of the Damages Directive and how it affects the interplay between private and public enforcement. Finally, in Section seven, some conclusions are made.

2. AIMS AND MEASURES OF PUBLIC ENFORCEMENT

Public enforcement has been the main way of enforcing EU Competition Law, ever since the first regulation on competition law enforcement,

* Senior lecturer, Uppsala University.

[1] Directive 2014/104/EU of the European Parliament and of the Council of 26 November 2014 on certain rules governing actions for damages under national law for infringements of the competition law provisions of the Member States and of the European Union ('Damages Directive') [2014] OJ L349/1.

Regulation 17, was adopted.[2] Although the introduction of the current regime under Regulation 1/2003 was aimed at increasing private enforcement in the Member States, it primarily regulates public enforcement by the Commission and national competition authorities.[3] This subsection describes the aims of public enforcement as well as existing measures and remedies under that regime, in order to clarify the scope and role of private enforcement discussed in the following subsection.

As regards the aims of public enforcement, it firstly purports to stop ongoing infringements. The current regime for public enforcement under Regulation 1/2003 lays down a number of measures in order to detect, investigate and stop ongoing infringements. As concerns the detection of competition law infringements, the Commission and the national competition authorities are empowered to initiate investigations on their own initiative as well as to investigate complaints from third parties.[4] In addition, the Commission may conduct sector enquiries.[5] In the investigation of possible competition law infringements, the Commission has powers to make requests for information,[6] dawn raids,[7] and impose penalty payments.[8] In cases where the Commission and national competition authorities detect breaches of competition law, they may stop such infringements through prohibition decisions or by adopting commitments made by the undertakings.[9] To facilitate detection the Commission may also reduce fines under the Leniency Notice for companies that provide the Commission with information that help to establish a breach.[10] Similarly, leniency is also available in almost all Member States. Moreover, the Commission may also facilitate the final conclusion of competition cases by making cartel settlements.[11]

A second aim of public enforcement is to prevent undertakings from engaging in prohibited conduct in the future. This can be achieved in two different ways. First, the content of competition law may be clarified. This raises the awareness of undertakings on the state of the law and thus allows them to avoid competition law infringements. Second, undertakings may

[2] Council Regulation 17, First Regulation implementing Articles 85 and 86 of the Treaty [1959–62] OJ Spec Ed 87 (Reg 17/62).

[3] Council Regulation 1/2003 of 16 December 2002 on the implementation of the rules on competition laid down in Articles 81 and 82 of the Treaty [2003] OJ L1/1 (Reg 1/2003).

[4] ibid, Arts 7(1) and 5.

[5] ibid, Art 17.

[6] ibid, Art 18.

[7] ibid, Art 20.

[8] ibid, Art 23(1).

[9] ibid, Arts 7, 9 and 5.

[10] Commission Notice on immunity from fines and reduction of fines in cartel cases ('Leniency Notice') [2006] OJ C298/17.

[11] Commission Regulation 622/2008 of 30 June 2008 amending Regulation 773/2004, as regards the conduct of settlement procedures in cartel cases ('Cartel Settlement Regulation') [2008] OJ L171/3.

be deterred from breaching competition law through sanctions imposed on them.[12]

Concerning the clarification and development of the rules, this is an important aim of the public enforcement of competition law. This occurs through case law from the Union Courts, binding legal acts and decisions made by the Commission as well as the publishing of soft law, such as notices and guidelines.[13]

As regards deterrence, the main measure is the imposition of fines. Article 23 of Regulation 1/2003 permits the Commission to impose fines amounting to a maximum of 10 per cent of the company's turnover of the preceding year.[14] Similarly, national competition authorities may impose fines through national law.[15] According to the optimal deterrence model, a risk-neutral undertaking is not likely to engage in illegal cartel behaviour if the expected costs of being caught exceed the profits that could be made through the cartel agreement, including the probability of detection.[16] The effects of fines may also be increased through leniency.[17] The Leniency Notice provides the possibility for undertakings to completely avoid fines, or to reduce them, if they cooperate with the Commission.[18] Leniency is expected to increase the incentives for cartel participants to cooperate with competition authorities by providing them with information about existing cartels. Thus, leniency should increase the probability of detection.

An important issue, which is also pertinent to the role of private enforcement, is whether the current system of public enforcement, in particular the level of fines, is effective in deterring undertakings from engaging in competition law infringements. A first observation is that the literature indicates that the imposition of fines has not reached an adequate deterrence level. In a study made by Combe and Monnier, it was found that the level of fines was suboptimal.[19] This conclusion was drawn even though the authors calculated the deterrence effect with a probability of detection of 100 per cent (which is not realistic). In real markets, it seems as the probability of detection of clandestine cartels may be less than 30 per cent.[20] Thus, cartel participants were not even imposed fines that would amount to the profits

[12] WPJ Wils, 'The Relationship between Public Antitrust Enforcement and Private Actions for Damages' (2009) 32 *World Competition* 3, 7.

[13] ibid, 5.

[14] Reg 1/2003.

[15] ibid, Art 5.

[16] E Combe and C Monnier, 'Fines Against Hard Core Cartels in Europe: The Myth of Overenforcement' (2011) 56 *The Antitrust Bulletin* 235, 245–46; Wils (n 12) 7.

[17] Wils (n 12) 7.

[18] Leniency Notice (n 10).

[19] Combe and Monnier (n 16) 245–46.

[20] JM Connor, 'Recidivism Revealed: Private International Cartels 1990–2009' (2010) 6 *Competition Policy International* 101, 109.

made through the anticompetitive behaviour.[21] The study seems also to support the results of previous studies on antitrust fines and deterrence.[22] In addition, studies have shown the existence of repeat offenders (recidivism), indicating that undertakings that have already been subject to sanctions are still not deterred from breaking the rules.[23]

The alleged insufficiency of fines in the current public enforcement regime has sometimes induced calls for alternative or additional measures of enforcement, in particular criminal sanctions imposed on those individuals that engage companies in cartel arrangements.[24] This is expected to increase the deterrence effect at least for the individuals involved in the actual cartel cooperation. Although this topic is not relevant to the subject of this chapter and therefore not further explored here, the discussion on the inadequacies of the current regime may indicate that there is room for additional and complementary measures aimed at increasing the deterrence effect, including private actions for damages.

3. PRIVATE ENFORCEMENT—AIMS, MEASURES AND INCENTIVES

Private enforcement of the EU competition rules has been possible ever since the Court established that Articles 101(1) and 102 TFEU (then Articles 85 and 86 EEC) have direct effect.[25] However, private enforcement has not occurred in practice to the desired level. The introduction of Regulation 1/2003 aimed at decentralising the enforcement of EU competition law and thus to encourage private parties to use national courts.[26] Although decentralisation seems to have induced more private enforcement, it is still claimed that the level of private enforcement is inadequate. As regards civil actions for damages, the amount of litigation has been too low.[27] It is in this context that the Commission pushed through the Damages Directive.

[21] Combe and Monnier (n 16) 269.

[22] GJ Werden, SD Hammond, and BA Barnett, 'Deterrence and Detection of Cartels: Using all the Tools and Sanctions' (2011) 56 *The Antitrust Bulletin* 207, 214; C Veljanovski, 'Cartel Fines in Europe—Law, Practice and Deterrence' (2007) 30 *World Competition* 65.

[23] C Harding, 'Cartel Deterrence: The Search for Evidence and Argument' (2011) 56 *The Antitrust Bulletin* 345, 368–74; Connor (n 20).

[24] WPJ Wils, 'Should Private Antitrust Enforcement be Encouraged in Europe' (2003) 26 *World Competition* 473, 481; Combe and Monnier (n 16) 269.

[25] Case 127/73 *Belgische Radio en Televisie and société belge des auteurs, compositeurs et éditeurs v SV SABAM and NV Fonior* [1974] ECR 51, para 16.

[26] Reg 1/2003.

[27] The Commission stated in its Impact Assessment Report that follow-on actions had only occurred in 15 out of 52 cases where the Commission had established a competition law infringement in the period 2006–12: Commission Staff Working Document, Impact Assessment Report, 'Damages Actions for Breach of the EU Antitrust Rules, SWD(2013) 203 Final (Impact Assessment Report), para 52. See also S Wisking and K Dietzel, 'European Commission Finally Publishes Measures to Facilitate Competition Law Private Actions in the European Union' (2014) 35 *European Competition Law Review* 185, 186.

Three aims can be attributed to private enforcement. A first aim of private enforcement is to terminate ongoing infringements. In this context, Articles 101(2) and 102 TFEU function as remedies achieving this aim.[28] Regulation 1/2003 has also facilitated the use of this remedy as national courts were empowered to apply the whole of Article 101 TFEU. In this context, it is important to underline that private actions may decrease the so-called enforcement gap, meaning the cases that are not pursued through public enforcement because of either limited resources or lack of interest.[29] The Commission has discretion in prioritising which cases to pursue. Thus, it is not obliged to pursue every case where there is a potential competition law infringement.[30] In this context, it should be noted that the purpose of introducing Regulation 1/2003 was also to free resources to focus on serious infringements such as price-fixing cartels.[31] It may also be more difficult for the Commission to detect breaches of competition law in vertical agreements or abuse of dominance. Clearly, parties to an agreement or customers to a dominant undertaking may be better placed to discover infringements. Consequently, there are a number of breaches of competition law that may be 'uninteresting' or not a priority to pursue or too costly to detect. Here, arguably, private enforcement has a complementary role to play by taking these cases to national courts.

A second aim of private enforcement is corrective justice, to compensate individuals for harm caused to them by a competition law infringement.[32] It is a well-known fact that the possibility to claim compensation was established as an EU law-based remedy in *Courage*.[33] Importantly, as remedies in public enforcement do not have the aim of compensating victims, private enforcement has an important complementary role in achieving this aim.

[28] E Hjelmeng, 'Competition Law Remedies: Striving for Coherence or Finding New Ways?' (2013) 50 *Common Market Law Review* 1007, 1015.

[29] AP Komninos, 'New Prospects for Private Enforcement of EC Competition Law: Courage v. Crehan and the Community Right to Damages' (2002) 39 *Common Market Law Review* 447, 458.

[30] Case T-24/90 *Automec Srl v Commission of the European Communities* [1992] ECR II-2223. This is more apparent after the Commission's guidance on enforcement priorities in the area of Article 102 TFEU: Communication from the Commission—Guidance on the Commission's enforcement priorities in applying Article 82 of the EC Treaty to abusive exclusionary conduct by dominant undertakings [2009] OJ C45/7 (Guidance Paper).

[31] See Reg 1/2003, rec 3; Commission, 'White Paper on the Modernisation of the Rules Implementing Articles 85 and 86 of the EC Treaty', COM(99) 101 final, para 10.

[32] Hjelmeng (n 28) 1010; Komninos (n 29) 458; K Cseres and J Mendes, 'Consumers' Access to EU Competition Law Procedures: Outer and Inner Limits' (2014) 51 *Common Market Law Review* 483, 496; A Ezrachi and M Ioannidou, 'Public Compensation as a Complementary Mechanism to Damages Actions: From Policy Justifications to Formal Implementation' (2012) 3 *Journal of European Competition Law & Practice* 536, 538; Wils (n 12) 12.

[33] Case C-453/99 *Courage Ltd v Bernard Crehan and Bernard Crehan v Courage Ltd and others* [2001] ECR I-6297.

According to the Commission, compensation for harm caused is also part of the right to effective judicial protection.[34]

A third aim of private enforcement is that it may increase the deterrence effect of competition law on potential infringers.[35] As compensation for harm will add up to the fines imposed through public enforcement, it increases the 'punishment' effect on cartel participants. Whether private enforcement is effective in promoting deterrence could be questioned. As described below, there are a number of difficulties for private litigants which may decrease their incentives to take action. In addition, the incentives for private litigants also depend on the amount of damages that may be awarded in such actions. In particular, damages limited to actual loss without consideration to the probability of detection are insufficient to act as a deterrent.

It follows that the aims of private enforcement more or less duplicate the aims of public enforcement of terminating infringements and promoting deterrence. The main differences between the two types of enforcement are that the aim of private enforcement is not (at least from the individual's point of view) to clarify and develop the rules,[36] even though stand-alone actions may contribute to that goal, and that public enforcement is not aimed at compensating victims of competition law infringements.[37]

As regards the incentives for individuals to engage in private enforcement, the relevant factors are simply the costs and benefits of private litigation.[38] Clearly, if the costs outweigh the benefits for potential litigants, there will be no private enforcement. In this context, it should be noted that deterrence, as such, is probably not a factor that increases the incentives for private parties to litigate.[39] Moreover, even if benefits as a whole are higher than costs, pursuing damages actions to recover smaller losses caused by competition law infringements may not provide sufficient incentives for individuals to litigate as the net benefits of litigating are simply too small.[40] This is the reason why collective redress may be necessary to induce litigation regarding harm caused at the consumer level.[41] The Commission has therefore issued a recommendation on common principles on collective redress.[42] In addition, the incentive to litigate is also decreased because of a free-rider

[34] Impact Assessment Report, 27.

[35] Hjelmeng (n 28) 1010; Komninos (n 29) 458; Cseres and Mendes (n 32) 484 and 496. Ezrachi and Ioannidou (n 32) 537.

[36] Wils (n 12) 5.

[37] ibid, 5.

[38] Wils (n 12) 9.

[39] Cseres and Mendes (n 32) 498.

[40] ibid.

[41] Cseres and Mendes (n 32) 499.

[42] Commission Recommendation of 11 June 2013 on common principles for injunctive and compensatory collective redress mechanisms in the Member States concerning violations of rights granted under Union Law ('Collective Redress Recommendation') [2013] OJ L201/60.

problem, as potential litigants may wait for others to litigate first before engaging in follow-on actions.[43]

On the cost side, there are several factors that increase costs and which probably explain the disincentives and the lack of actual private enforcement taking place.[44] A first factor is the cost for establishing a breach. Establishing a breach may require complex and sophisticated economic reasoning, the use of economic experts and a great deal of information.[45] This, in turn, requires access to documents in the hands of the defendants that may be difficult for private parties to get hold of, unlike the situation for competition authorities that have coercive powers, such as the possibility to conduct dawn raids in order to extract necessary information from alleged infringers. In addition, as explained above, competition authorities may increase the instability of cartel agreements through measures such as leniency that ultimately induce cartel members to offer the information required to find a breach voluntarily.[46] The problem of establishing a breach becomes pertinent not only for self-standing actions but also if national rules require re-litigation of the breach of competition rules in follow-on actions. Ultimately, in the absence of rules at the EU level, the practical possibilities for private litigants to enforce competition law depend on national rules, which are only subject to the EU principles of equivalence and effectiveness.

Moreover, even if the breach may be established, the claimant must still show causation and quantify the harm.[47] It seems that these are quite difficult for private litigants to prove, as they require access to specific information as well as complex economic calculations. The quantification of harm requires a comparison with the hypothetical situation where the competition law infringement has not occurred in the market.[48] As concerns price-fixing cartels, establishing the level of a supra-competitive charge may be indicative of the harm caused. However, as regards the harm caused by market-sharing cartels or exclusionary abuse, it is clearly much more difficult to quantify the harm caused. Likewise, the harm inflicted on consumers because of the reduction of output (the deadweight loss), is difficult to prove.[49]

In sum, it seems that the costs faced by private litigants are substantial. Moreover, in the absence of EU rules, conditions under national law for establishing a breach and quantifying the harm may vary substantially

[43] Cseres and Mendes (n 32) 496.
[44] ibid, 498.
[45] ibid.
[46] Cseres and Mendes (n 32) 500.
[47] Komninos (n 29) 478.
[48] Commission, 'White Paper on Damages Actions for Breach of the EC Antitrust Rules, COM2008/0165 final ('White Paper'), 2.5.
[49] C Leslie, 'Antitrust Damages and Deadweight Loss' (2006) 51 *The Antitrust Bulletin* 521, in particular 542; Wils (n 24) 481.

between different Member States.[50] As discussed below, the main purpose of the Damages Directive is to lower these costs for private litigants as well as to partly harmonise national rules on compensation.

4. PRIVATE ENFORCEMENT AS A COMPLEMENT TO PUBLIC ENFORCEMENT

Private enforcement is generally viewed as a complement to public enforcement.[51] As stated above, public and private enforcement share the common aims of terminating ongoing and deterring future infringements. However, considering the low number of private actions for damages, it would seem that private enforcement has only a complementary role in deterring competition law infringements. As regards the termination of infringements, private enforcement may result in the detection and termination of infringements that are not targeted by public enforcement. In addition, the main role of private enforcement is to compensate victims for harm caused by competition law breaches, which is not considered in public enforcement. Consequently, looking at the aims of the two types of enforcement, they have different functions and complement one another.

In addition, public and private enforcement interact. Public enforcement facilitates private enforcement through follow-on actions. The existence of violations of the competition rules are established by public enforcement. Under the condition that a final decision from public enforcers is recognised in damages actions, the follow-on actions of claimants only need to establish the harm suffered as well as a causal link between the breach and the harm.[52] This allows private claimants to benefit from the enhanced resources, as well as stronger methods of coercion, in the hands of the authorities dealing with public enforcement. At the same time, facilitating damages action, public enforcement promotes one of its own aims; namely the deterrence effect as infringers of competition law will also have to compensate individuals for harm.

5. FRICTION BETWEEN PUBLIC AND PRIVATE ENFORCEMENT

It would seem that friction between public and private enforcement may in particular occur in three areas. First, follow-on damage actions in addition

[50] Impact Assessment Report, paras 49–54.

[51] Editorial Comment, '"One Bird in the Hand..." The Directive on Damages Actions for Breach of the Competition Rules' (2014) 51 *Common Market Law Review* 1333, 1334; R Gamble, 'The European Embrace of Private Enforcement: This Time with Feeling' (2014) 35 *European Competition Law Review* 469, 479.

[52] Wils (n 12) 16.

to fines set by competition authorities may result in over-deterrence. Second, follow-on actions may decrease the incentives for participating in leniency programmes. Third, access to documents submitted in connection with leniency programmes may discourage defendants from participating in these programmes.

The first potential friction between private and public enforcement is that the accumulation of fines and damages awarded may result in the over-enforcement of the competition rules. However, there are strong indications that this is not the current situation. As discussed above, existing studies tend to show that the main problem in the current system is under-enforcement. In fact, it seems that the Commission needs to increase fines substantially in order to reach an optimal deterrence level. Therefore, considering the low level of damage claims being pursued, it seems unlikely that such a negative effect constitutes an immediate concern. Naturally, the situation may change with time and the application of the Damages Directive.

As regards the second potential friction, the imposition of fines due to private litigation may decrease the incentives for cartel members to participate in leniency programmes. The very purpose of leniency is for the cartel members to decrease fines, or to obtain immunity. Opening up and facilitating private damages actions may to a certain extent decrease the gains made from avoiding fines imposed by competition authorities. Again, because of the low level of current damage actions, this potential friction seems unproblematic at the moment.

The most obvious friction between public and private enforcement concerns the access to documents of public enforcement cases for follow-on cases driven by private litigants.[53] On the one hand, these cases concern securing the effectiveness of the leniency programme and on the other the facilitation of damage claims. The Court has held that a balancing exercise must be carried out in the specific case.

The landmark case in this area is *Pfleiderer*.[54] In 2008 the German Competition Authority fined three companies for breach of Article 101 TFEU. Pfleiderer, a customer of the fined cartel participants, started to prepare a civil action for damages. During the course of the preparations for that civil action, the company applied to the German Competition Authority for access to the case file, including documents related to the leniency application (according to German rules) made by the cartel members. The German Competition Authority partly rejected the application, in particular with regard to documents related to leniency. The case was subsequently brought before the national court, which requested a preliminary ruling from the Court of Justice.

[53] Case C-360/09 *Pfleiderer AG v Bundeskartellamt* [2011] ECR I-5161; Case C-536/11 *Bundeswettbewerbsbehörde v Donau Chemie AG and others* EU:C:2013:366.

[54] *Pfleiderer* (n 53).

The Court found that in the absence of common rules, it is up to the Member States to adopt rules regarding access to documents related to leniency applications made by cartel members in civil actions on damages. Member States are bound by the principle of effectiveness and cannot undermine the 'effet utile' of Articles 101 and 102 TFEU. Moreover, the Court pointed out the importance of the leniency programmes for uncovering breaches of Articles 101 TFEU and how access to documents for persons seeking damages could undermine the application of leniency programmes. Cartel members could be discouraged from participating in these programmes, especially bearing in mind that competition authorities may exchange information and documents under Regulation 1/2003. On the other hand, the Court underlined the right of individuals to claim damages in the earlier cases, *Courage* and *Manfredi*.[55] The Court stated that the principles of equivalence and effectiveness apply to national rules on access to leniency documents, requiring a balance to be struck between the interests of securing compensation for individuals and the protection of the information submitted from applicants for leniency.[56] According to the Court, this assessment could only be made on a case-by-case basis, taking account of all relevant factors.[57]

This standpoint was clarified in *Donau Chemie*, a case concerning national rules subjecting access to a competition case file, including leniency documents, to the approval of all the parties to the case.[58] Thus, *any* of the companies had the possibility to reject access to the leniency documents. The Court stated that it was necessary to balance the interests in the given case as an absolute rule either refusing or granting access to leniency documents could undermine the effectiveness of Article 101 TFEU.[59] The Court explained that in cases where access to documents was necessary for the civil action, in the absence of other alternatives, an absolute rule refusing access would make the right of compensation impossible or excessively difficult.[60] On the other hand, for a number of reasons, an absolute rule granting access would either not be necessary or be in breach of Union law. First, such a rule could deter cartel members from cooperating with the competition authorities. Second, it would be unlikely that the requesting party would need to have access to all the documents in the preparations for civil action. Third, granting access could breach the rules on professional secrecy, the protection of business secrets, as well as the protection of personal data.[61]

[55] *Courage* (n 33); Joined Cases C-295/04 to C-298/04 *Vincenzo Manfredi v Lloyd Adriatico Assicurazioni SpA* (C-295/04), *Antonio Cannito v Fondiaria Sai SpA* (C-296/04) *and Nicolò Tricarico* (C-297/04) *and Pasqualina Murgolo* (C-298/04) *v Assitalia SpA* [2006] ECR I-6619.

[56] *Courage* (n 33) para 30.

[57] ibid, para 31.

[58] *Donau Chemie* (n 53).

[59] ibid, para 31.

[60] ibid, para 32.

[61] ibid, para 33.

The Court furthermore emphasised the requirement that national courts must be able to balance interests, which would not be the case with a national rule that permitted any of the cartel members to refuse access.[62] Accordingly, national courts should make the analysis in two steps. First, the national court needs to explore the interests of the requesting party, in particular the existence of other options to obtain the documents in question. Second, the national court needs to assess the negative effects of granting access on the public interest or the interests of other parties.[63] In this context, the Court rejected the general argument that access to the documents submitted to the national competition authority under the leniency programme would risk the potential participation of cartel members. Instead, the national court should make this balancing of interests for each document that has been requested by the claimant.[64]

What follows from *Pfleiderer* and *Donau Chemie* in particular is that absolute rules, either granting or barring access, are in breach of EU Law. In addition, the assessment must be made in the context of other national rules regarding access to documents. The consequence is that rulings on granting access may vary between different Member States. Moreover, and importantly, the Court has opened up the possibility of granting access to leniency documents at national competition authorities. This may threaten national leniency programmes and thus weaken a crucial tool in public enforcement.

All in all, it follows that although the number of damages claims may in theory result in over-enforcement or a decrease in the incentive to participate in leniency programmes, the most serious friction between public and private enforcement concerns the disclosure of leniency documents to private litigants. It also seems clear that the Court has opened up the possibility for leniency documents to be released to private claimants in damage actions, even if interests must be weighed in every individual case.

6. THE EFFECTS OF THE DAMAGES DIRECTIVE ON THE INTERPLAY BETWEEN PUBLIC AND PRIVATE ENFORCEMENT

Three points can be made regarding the Damages Directive as concerns the effects on private and public enforcement. First, the aim of the Directive is to increase the incentives for individuals to engage in private enforcement. Second, the Damages Directive reinforces the complementarity between public and private enforcement. Thirdly, the Damages Directive aims at a balance between facilitating private enforcement and protecting public enforcement.

[62] ibid, paras 34–38.
[63] ibid, paras 44–45.
[64] ibid, paras 47–48.

As concerns the first point, it is obvious that the main aim of the Directive is to increase the incentive mechanism for civil actions. Arguably, the Directive achieves this aim in two different ways: by specifying the content of the right to damages, and decreasing the costs for private litigants.

As regards the content of the right to damages, the Damages Directive states that *any* individuals that are harmed by competition law infringements are entitled to full compensation, including the loss of profits and the payment of interest.[65] Although, this follows already from *Courage* and *Manfredi*, the Damages Directive specifically determines the scope of the right to damages in more detail, which would otherwise be regulated by national rules subject to the principles of effectiveness and equivalence.[66] In particular, the rules on the right of indirect purchasers and the passing-on defence in Articles 12–15 of the Damages Directive seem to have this purpose. Importantly, the Directive also limits over-compensation and multiple damages in Articles 2 and 15.

The extent to which the Directive clarifies all aspects of the rights granted to claimants could be debated. For instance, as regards access to national courts for indirect purchasers to make damage claims, it has been contested whether the Directive truly changes the state of the law as follows from the Court's case law.[67] It could, moreover, be debated whether the Directive will actually result in an enhanced incentive effect for damage actions. The several limitations to damage actions with the aim of avoiding over-compensation may decrease the incentives for private litigants as well as decrease the deterrence effect of damage awards. This clearly shows that the main underlying policy of the Directive is to promote corrective justice, and not to promote deterrence.

As regards the purpose of decreasing costs for private litigants, it is clear that the main bulk of the provisions in the Damages Directive address this particular problem. As discussed above, private claimants face substantial costs in terms of gathering evidence to prove the harm caused which may discourage damage actions. Several measures have the aim of decreasing costs while balancing against the protection of the effectiveness of public enforcement and the general principles of law, including the protection of business secrets. The rules on regulating the disclosure of documents from the defendants (cartel members) in Article 5 of the Damages Directive are essential for claimants to establish either the existence of a breach (in independent actions) or to quantify damages. As concerns information in the hands of the competition authorities, this is regulated in particular by Article 6 of the Damage Directive. In addition, it is also stated in Article 17(1)

[65] Damages Directive, Art 3.

[66] *Courage* (n 33) para 26; *Manfredi* (n 55) paras 90 and 95.

[67] M Strand, 'Indirect Purchasers, Passing-on and the New Directive on Competition Law Damages' (2014) 10 *European Competition Journal* 361, 372–74.

of the Damages Directive that the national courts should be able to estimate the harm caused. Arguably, this facilitates the possibility of obtaining damages also in cases where quantification is difficult or not possible. In addition, Article 17(2) of the Damages Directive states that cartels are presumed to cause harm, although this presumption may be rebutted.

However, it should also be emphasised that a number of factors that seem to be problematic have not been explicitly addressed by the Directive. This may limit the positive effects of the Directive on the incentives for private litigants to engage in actions for damages. As regards the problem of numerous claimants with small losses, collective redress was left outside the scope of the Directive and is instead dealt with in a Commission Recommendation.[68] Moreover, the Directive does not harmonise rules on causation or standing which may limit the practical possibilities of private litigants being awarded damages in the Member States.

Regarding the second point, the aim of reinforcing the complementarity of public and private enforcement, the Directive increases the value of decisions made by national competition authorities in follow-on actions for damages. As stated above, Decisions by the Commission are already sufficient to establish a breach of competition rules in civil damage actions, as national courts cannot make decisions that are contrary to Commission Decisions.[69] As regards the decision by national competition authorities or a review court, the Directive establishes that such final decisions made in the same Member State where the civil action takes place establishes a breach under Article 9(1) of the Damages Directive. According to Article 9(2) of the Damages Directive, the final decision made by a review court or national competition authority in another Member State constitutes prima facie evidence of a competition law breach. Obviously, the purpose of these rules is to increase the value of public enforcement decisions for follow-on actions on damages. As explained above, public authorities have more far-reaching measures to investigate and establish competition law infringements than private litigants. The interplay between public and private enforcement avoids or decreases the costs for the claimant. Re-litigating competition law infringements may prove costly considering the complexity of competition law cases and the amount of evidence needed. This may be in particular the case for customers of cartels, as cartels are secret by nature. Re-litigating cases where a breach of competition law has already been established by the public authorities is simply inefficient.

As concerns the third point, the balance made between private and public enforcement, there are in particular two rules in the Damages Directive that address this issue. According to Article 6(6) of the Damages Directive, leniency statements and settlement submissions are not to be disclosed by

[68] Collective Redress Recommendation (n 42).
[69] Reg 1/2003, Art 16(1).

order from national courts. National courts only have the right to control that documents in the hands of the competition authority are actually part of leniency statements.[70] As explained above, the main friction between private and public enforcement concerns the disclosure of statements made in leniency applications. While access to those documents would benefit civil actions, it would also create disincentives for undertakings to cooperate with competition authorities, thus decreasing the effectiveness of public enforcement. Leniency is, perhaps, the most successful tool in antitrust enforcement and it does not seem likely that private enforcement could compensate the loss of successful cases through leniency.

The issue that has been raised is whether the rule in the Damages Directive rejecting all access to leniency statements and settlement submission, without a balance of interests made by the national court, is in breach of the principle of effectiveness.[71] On the other hand, it has been claimed that under *Pfleiderer* and *Donau Chemie* the case-by-case analysis that needs to be carried out by the national courts regarding the access to leniency documents applies under the condition that there are no common EU rules.[72] Thus, it could be argued that the existence of the Damages Directive precludes the application of the principle of effectiveness. Such a conclusion seems premature. The principle of effectiveness applied to national rules is an expression of the principle of effective judicial protection which also applies to secondary legislation. It would seem that the adopted common rules cannot make the rules so restrictive that individuals have no chance of being awarded compensation in cases where the cartel members have participated in a leniency programme or settlement procedure.[73] That seems, however, not to be the case. As emphasised by the Court in *Pfleiderer* and *Donau Chemie*, the national courts had to take into account in their case-by-case analysis the possibility of obtaining information through other means than access to the leniency documents. In this regard, the rule in Article 6(6) of the Damages Directive, read in conjunction with the definition of leniency statements under Article 2(16) of the Damages Directive, only limits the non-disclosure of documents to those statements where the undertaking in question acknowledges the existence of the cartel and explains its role in it. Moreover, the Damages Directive includes a number of other measures that facilitate civil claims for damage actions, such as re-enforcing the evidential value of decisions made by national competition authorities, the facilitation

[70] Damages Directive, Art 6(7).

[71] C Kersting, 'Removing the Tension between Public and Private Enforcement: Disclosure and Privileges for Successful Leniency Applicants' (2014) 5 *Journal of European Competition Law and Practice* 2; Wisking and Dietzel (n 27) 188.

[72] I Vandenborre and T Goetz, 'EU Competition Law Procedural Issues' (2014) 5 *Journal of European Competition Law & Practice* 648, 650.

[73] Kersting (n 71) 3.

of the disclosure of documents other than leniency statements, as well as the disclosure of other information in the hands of competition authorities. In the balancing exercise under *Pfleiderer* and *Donau Chemie*, it seems that the existence of these other measures makes it unlikely that the non-disclosure of leniency statements would make it impossible or excessively difficult to gain access to relevant documents in order to establish a breach or to quantify damages. Therefore, it is not evident that there is a conflict between the Damages Directive and the Court's case law.

The second rule that addresses the balance between private and public enforcement is Article 11(4) of the Damages Directive. According to that provision, parties that have participated in the leniency programmes or a settlement procedure are, as a rule, only liable to their direct or indirect purchasers. Such parties are only liable to other claimants if the latter cannot obtain compensation from others. It follows that the rules attempt to limit the liability and alleviate the problem addressed above, that damages together with fines may undermine the purpose of participating in leniency programmes by decreasing liability.

7. CONCLUSIONS

The promotion of private enforcement and litigation on damages faces two main challenges. First, there are substantial costs in the discovery of evidence for establishing a breach and causation. Second, there is a potential friction with public enforcement as regards the leniency programmes.

The Damages Directive addresses both these issues. Several provisions in the Damages Directive purport to decrease the costs for private litigants in civil actions for damages, in particular by facilitating the establishment of a breach in follow-on actions as well as the disclosure of evidence. By doing so, the Damages Directive also reinforces the interplay between public and private enforcement. Arguably, this may in turn increase the deterrence effect of competition law remedies as a whole. Whether the measures are sufficient to provide adequate incentives for private litigants may be debated, as it seems that several problematic issues are not included in the Directive, which may still limit the practical possibilities of starting damage actions.

As regards the second issue, the Damages Directive protects public enforcement by limiting access to documents related to leniency programmes and settlement procedures. The Directive aims, in particular, at closing the door to access the documents which was opened by the Court's judgments in *Pfleiderer* and *Donau Chemie*. This indicates that public enforcement remains the main priority and that private enforcement is mainly an instrument to promote corrective justice and effective judicial protection rather than deterrence.

6

Embedding Procedural Autonomy: The Directive and National Procedural Rules

PIETER VAN CLEYNENBREUGEL*

1. INTRODUCTION

THE DIRECTIVE ON damages actions[1] builds on and extends the case law of the Court of Justice, effectively embedding the Court's peculiar 'national procedural autonomy' focus within an instrument of EU secondary legislation. This chapter illustrates the Directive's continued procedural autonomy focus and additionally forecasts the impact that focus will have on the design and review of national procedural choices within the Directive's enforcement scheme.

Section two conceptualises the traditional procedural autonomy modus operandi on the basis of which the Court of Justice has promoted EU private damages actions. While that modus operandi has offered a toolkit to streamline and restructure national remedial and procedural systems, it in itself has been unable to provide sufficiently sound foundations for the development of a coherent private enforcement system.

The Directive aims to address those shortcomings by imposing more general procedural obligations on Member States. Section three asserts that the direct incorporation of general procedural obligations in an instrument of EU secondary legislation paves the way for more intense interventions by the Court of Justice, without however fully addressing the undesirable

* Assistant Professor of European and Competition Law, Europa Institute, Leiden Law School, Leiden University, the Netherlands; PhD (KU Leuven), LLM (Harvard), LLM, LLB (KU Leuven).

[1] Directive 2014/104/EU of the European Parliament and of the Council of 26 November 2014 on certain rules governing actions for damages under national law for infringements of the competition law provisions of the Member States and of the European Union ('Damages Directive') [2014] OJ L349/1.

side effects of the procedural autonomy focus. In order to alleviate those effects, more structured *substantive law* harmonisation initiatives should be envisaged. The scope and nature of the obligations in the present Directive highlight that such initiatives are unlikely to be developed in the near future.

2. PRIVATE ENFORCEMENT AND THE 'NATIONAL PROCEDURAL AUTONOMY' FOCUS

Despite early policy initiatives to promote the private enforcement of Articles 101 and 102 TFEU[2] and judicial proclamations establishing the direct effect of those provisions,[3] the Court's judgment in *Courage v Crehan* is generally considered to be the starting point for the development of EU antitrust private damages actions. In that judgment, the Court explicitly acknowledged for the first time a *right* for competitors and individuals to claim damages[4] on the basis of the direct effect of Article 101(1) and Article 102 TFEU.[5] In order to effectuate that right, the Member States' legal orders were to make private enforcement claims possible on the basis of national remedial and procedural rules. The Court's well-known principle of national procedural autonomy—translated into its even better-known principles of equivalence and effectiveness—provided a basis for doing so. This section revisits the key features and ensuing operationalisation of the national procedural autonomy focus in relation to private damages claims (2.1). It will be submitted that the national procedural autonomy focus fosters a piecemeal design mechanism to establish and maintain an EU-focused private enforcement regime. Formally addressing national procedural issues, those obligations equally have repercussions for the application of national substantive rules. Since those obligations are imposed on all Member States by means of judgments addressing very specific questions and problems encountered by only one national judge, vague, open-ended or case specific proclamations made by the Court constituted a rather weak legal basis for the EU's damages actions system to be founded on. The *Manfredi*, *Pfleiderer*, *Donau Chemie* and *Kone*[6] judgments particularly

[2] The Commission had already published a study in 1966 outlining the possibilities of and limits encountered by private damages actions across the Member States, see European Commission, 'La réparation des conséquences dommageables d'une violation des articles 85 et 86 du Traité instituant la CEE' (1966) 1 série concurrence. See also AP Komninos, *EC Private Antitrust Enforcement: Decentralised Application of EC Competition Law by National Courts* (Oxford, Hart Publishing, 2008) 163.

[3] See to that extent above all Case 127/73 *BRT v Sabam* [1974] ECR 51.

[4] V Milutinovic, *The 'Right to Damages' under EU Competition Law: From Courage v. Crehan to the White Paper and Beyond* (The Hague, Wolters Kluwer, 2010).

[5] Case C-453/99 *Courage v Crehan* [2001] ECR I-6297.

[6] Joined Cases C-295/04 to C-298/04 *Manfredi and Others* [2006] ECR I–6619; Case C-360/09 *Pfleiderer* [2011] ECR I-5161; Case C-536/11 *Donau Chemie* EU:C:2013:366; and Case C-557/12 *Kone* EU:C:2014:1317.

exemplify those weaknesses. It should thus come as no surprise that those judgments contributed to calls for more enhanced legislative action (2.2).

2.1 Right through Remedies and Procedures: The National Procedural Autonomy Focus and its Limits

In *Courage*, the Court of Justice explicitly held for the first time that the practical effect of the prohibition laid down in Article 101(1) TFEU would be put at risk if it were not open to any individual to claim damages for loss caused to him/her by a contract or by conduct liable to restrict or distort competition.[7] Such a right would strengthen the working of the EU competition rules and discourage agreements or practices, which are frequently covert, and which are liable to restrict or distort competition.[8] It is well known that the Court immediately nuanced the scope of the right identified by reiterating that in the absence of EU law on the matter,

> it is for the domestic legal system of each Member State to designate the courts and tribunals having jurisdiction and to lay down the detailed procedural rules governing actions for safeguarding rights which individuals derive directly from [EU] law, provided that such rules are not less favourable than those governing similar domestic actions (principle of equivalence) and that they do not render practically impossible or excessively difficult the exercise of rights conferred by [EU] law (principle of effectiveness).[9]

As a result, it fell upon national legal orders to ensure that national remedies and procedural rules did not impede the successful initiation of damages claims before national judges on the basis of Article 101 TFEU.

The Court's reasoning in *Courage* was hardly surprising and reflected the classical 'national procedural autonomy' approach to EU law enforcement.[10] According to that approach, Member States have to adopt a 'hit-or-miss' approach as to the compatibility of their existing remedial and procedural systems with EU law. Rules that patently obstruct the initiation of damages claims would in that constellation have to be abolished, and above all to be disapplied by a judge in a particular dispute. National judges as such are responsible for deciding whether or not national remedial or procedural rules comply with the EU requirements of equivalence and effectiveness and thus fall within the scope of EU-sanctioned procedural autonomy. Although

[7] *Courage* (n 5) para 26.
[8] ibid para 27.
[9] ibid para 29.
[10] For a summary of the classical perspective, see P Van Cleynenbreugel, 'National Procedural Choices before the Court of Justice of the European Union' in L Gruszczynski and W Werner (eds), *Deference in International Courts and Tribunals: Standard of Review and Margin of Appreciation* (Oxford, Oxford University Press, 2014) 176–78.

both requirements are open-ended and prone to changes over time, the Court of Justice ultimately maintains the final authority to interpret the scope of those principles and the extent of the compatibility of national remedial and procedural rules with EU law. This is all the more the case since the Court of Justice consistently relies on the principle of procedural autonomy to intervene in and to regulate national substantive law choices that would otherwise completely escape the scope of EU law.[11] Thus, the procedural autonomy focus relied on in *Courage* essentially invited the Court to wait for questions from national judges on how national rules governing damages actions were to be construed as a matter of EU law and to respond to the questions received by interpreting the principles of equivalence and effectiveness as a matter of EU law.

In practice, a procedural autonomy focus enables the Court to impose either negative or positive obligations on national legal orders through a reference for a preliminary ruling mechanism.[12] While such obligations are in principle only addressed to the referring judge and binding on the latter,[13] they also serve as benchmarks for other judges in the same and other jurisdictions.[14] From that perspective, reliance on the principle of national procedural autonomy implies that the Court of Justice will—depending on the ways in which questions to it have been phrased or on the extent to which it decides to rephrase the questions from the national judge—*de facto* review the substantive law choices made by a Member State and the procedural rules accompanying those choices. The Court will either leave in place national procedural rules or mandate their disapplication. To the extent that disapplication is ordered, the Court will do so implicitly, generally holding that EU law precludes particular national choices.[15] In doing so, the Court effectively imposes on Member States an obligation to refrain from applying specific procedural rules, ie a negative procedural obligation or an obligation not to do something. Since domestic rules would not apply to the case at hand, a national judge will subsequently be tasked to resolve the case on the basis of the remaining and EU-compatible national procedural rules.

[11] For the explicit acknowledgement of that framework, see K Havu, 'Horizontal Liability for Damages in EU Law—The Changing Relationship of EU and National Law' (2012) 18 *European Law Journal* 407–26 and also S Drake, 'Scope of Courage and the Principle of "Individual Liability" for Damages: Further Development of the Principle of Effective Judicial Protection by the Court of Justice' (2006) 31 *European Law Review* 841.

[12] Formally interpreting EU law in accordance with the mechanism laid down in Art 267 TFEU.

[13] See Case 29/68 *Milch-, Fett- und Eierkontor GmbH v Hauptzollamt Saarbrücken* [1969] ECR 165, para 3.

[14] See in that regard Case 28/67 *Firma Molkerei-Zentrale Westfalen/Lippe GmbH v Hauptzollamt Paderborn* [1968] ECR 154.

[15] See eg Case C–312/93 *Peterbroeck* [1995] ECR I–4599, para 21 for a well-known example in relation to rules of civil procedure.

Although the Court generally only holds that EU law precludes particular national choices, at times it nevertheless crosses a fine line between calling for the disapplication of specific national rules and proposing an alternative that better corresponds to the requirement of effectiveness as mandated by EU law. As such, the Court has not shied away from imposing so-called positive procedural obligations as a matter of EU law.[16] Positive obligations impose on national judges and/or legislators a specific obligation to act in a certain way, ie to replace an incompatible national provision or gap in a national legal system with an EU-tailored alternative. In that situation, the Court itself determines which actions are the appropriate ones for a national judge or a national legislator to take. In most circumstances, the Court of Justice relies on the *principle of effective judicial protection*, rather than on the principle of effectiveness, to impose such positive obligations.[17] The identification and imposition of a remedy for Member State liability resulting from an infringement of EU law directly exemplifies this approach,[18] as does the Court's ruling in *Vebic*, where national law was to enable—at least theoretically—the participation of the national competition authority (NCA) in review proceedings against decisions adopted by the latter.[19] In both cases, a direct result of the Court's proclamation was that Member States' legal orders had a particular obligation to act rather than merely to work out a particular solution themselves by refraining from applying their national rules.

The interplay between negative and positive procedural obligations—read into the principles of equivalence and effectiveness/effective judicial protection as core elements of national procedural autonomy—has proven a most useful tool for the shaping of a judicially steered private enforcement environment in areas where the EU legislator did not (wish to) intervene. However, the method used for doing so has two main disadvantages.

Firstly, the scope of the obligations imposed and even the distinction between negative and positive obligations is difficult to define clearly. Negative and positive procedural obligations are essentially two sides of the same coin. The procedural autonomy focus does not, however, make clear in itself when and why positive obligations should or could be imposed. As a result, the precedent value of procedural autonomy judgments beyond the confines of very specific cases can genuinely be questioned.

Secondly, the approach fails to offer sufficiently strong systemic design building blocks to develop and sustain an EU-managed enforcement system.

[16] For a nuanced distinction in that regard, W Van Gerven, 'Of Rights, Remedies and Procedures' (2000) 37 *Common Market Law Review* 501.

[17] S Prechal and R Widdershoven, 'Redefining the Relationship between 'Rewe-effectiveness' and Effective Judicial Protection' (2011) 4 *Review of European Administrative Law* 31–50.

[18] Joined Cases C-6/90 and C-9/90 *Francovich* [1991] ECR I-5357.

[19] Case C-439/08 *Vebic* [2010] ECR I-12471, para 63.

The Court will generally respond to the questions as phrased by national judges or will rephrase those questions to provide as accurate an answer as possible. Since those questions essentially determine the answer of the Court, the Court does not have an incentive to provide a clear distinction between both types of obligations and to consider whether and to what extent those obligations are necessary to construct a private enforcement system rather than to address a particular question asked by a particular national judge.

2.2 Procedural Autonomy in Practice: Negative and Positive Procedural Obligations in the Court's Private Enforcement Case Law

A direct result of the piecemeal and case-dependent nature of a national procedural autonomy focus has been that the full-fledged design of a private enforcement system could only be realised imperfectly by the Court of Justice. Since Court judgments do not constitute general proclamations on the future state of EU law, they cannot be considered as guiding benchmarks for all national judges. In addition, the confusing combined application of negative and positive obligations that persists in this approach—as will be illustrated in this section—makes it difficult for national judges to infer sufficiently specific and useful principles from the Court's judgment. This section analyses the scope of negative and positive obligations found in the Court's quintessential private enforcement judgments and identifies the negative and positive obligations appearing in those judgments. Doing so will demonstrate that—almost 15 years after *Courage*—the procedural autonomy focus has not succeeded in developing a clear, coherent and predictable private enforcement system across Member States' legal orders.

In *Courage*, the Court clearly opted to impose additional negative obligations on Member States. After having identified a right to damages, the Court continued that EU law *precludes* a rule of national law under which a party to a contract liable to restrict or distort competition within the meaning of that provision is barred from claiming damages for loss caused by performance of that contract, on the sole ground that the claimant is a party to that contract.[20] Such rules—notwithstanding exceptions relating to unjust enrichment and own contribution to competition law

[20] *Courage* (n 5) para 36 (emphasis added). In Case C-199/11 *Europese Gemeenschap v Otis et al* EU:C:2012:684, the Court extended this reasoning to situations where a public authority—in this case the European Commission—wished to claim damages from an undertaking with which it concluded a contract. The fact that the Commission also acted as the primary public enforcement body in the cartel case at hand did not as such affect the right conferred on everyone to claim damages under Art 101 TFEU; some safeguards needed to be in

infringements[21]—ought to be disapplied in order to enable damages claims to be initiated. The phrasing of this obligation evokes confusion, at least from the point of view of designing an operational private enforcement system.

The Court clearly phrases the obligation imposed on the English legal order as a negative obligation, ie an obligation not to maintain particular rules in force. At the same time, however, that obligation essentially imposes a positive obligation on all national legal orders to ensure that parties to a contract would still be able to initiate damages actions on the basis of Article 101 TFEU. As a result, the disapplication of a national rule in one legal system triggers the imposition of a positive obligation on all other Member States to adapt and fine-tune their national legal systems. The problem with this approach lies in the fact that the scope of this positive obligation is left particularly unclear. Of course, it could be inferred that national legal orders now have to allow for damages actions on the basis of Article 101 TFEU to be lodged by parties to an anticompetitive—and therefore void—agreement. At the same time, however, the scope and extent of unjust enrichment rules remaining in place and the role of remaining claims concerning the claimant's own contribution to the anticompetitive agreement continue to be governed by national law, provided that the conditions of equivalence and effectiveness are fulfilled.[22] In practice, this meant that Member States remained able to regulate those aspects and the remedial and procedural rules surrounding them, at least as long as the Court deemed such regulation to fit the EU enforcement scheme. As a result, the positive obligations imposed were only vague and hardly sufficiently helpful to guide Member States' legal orders in tailoring their procedural systems to the specific needs of a newly recognised right to damages.

Manfredi addressed some of those concerns by directly imposing more generally applicable positive procedural obligations on the different Member States. In addition to confirming that the right to damages also related to Article 102 TFEU,[23] the Court particularly held that it is for the national court to determine whether a national rule which provides that the limitation period for seeking compensation for harm caused by an agreement or practice prohibited under Article 101 TFEU begins to run from the day on which that prohibited agreement or practice was adopted, particularly where it also imposes a short limitation period that cannot be suspended,

place, however, in order to guarantee the equality of arms between claimant and defendant in private enforcement proceedings, see paras 75–76 of the judgment. See also M Botta, 'Commission Acting as Plaintiff in Cases of Private Enforcement of EU Competition Law: Otis' (2013) 50 *Common Market Law Review* 1105–17.

[21] *Courage* (n 5) para 29.

[22] ibid para 31.

[23] *Manfredi* (n 6) para 39.

renders it practically impossible or excessively difficult to exercise the right to seek compensation for the harm suffered.[24] As such, the Court essentially imposed a very open-ended obligation to reconsider the scope and format of limitation periods, without, however, being able or willing to prescribe a specific or reasonable limitation period as a matter of EU law itself.[25]

In addition, the Court in a similar fashion stated that it must be possible to award particular damages, such as exemplary or punitive damages, pursuant to actions founded on the EU competition rules, if such damages may be awarded pursuant to similar actions founded on domestic law.[26] The Court did not impose a full-fledged obligation, but merely left the matter to be determined on the basis of domestic law in each Member State individually. In relation to interests payable on awarded damages, the Court proved more straightforward. It held that it follows from the principle of effectiveness and the right of any individual to seek compensation for loss caused by a contract or by conduct liable to restrict or distort competition that injured persons must be able to seek compensation not only for actual loss (*damnum emergens*) but also for loss of profit (*lucrum cessans*) plus interest.[27] As a result, all Member States' legal orders are obliged to allow for remedies also covering loss of profit and interest.

The different obligations included in this judgment are all phrased in a similar way. In all cases, the Court first of all formulated general positive obligations imposed on Member States' legal orders, prior to translating those obligations into essentially negative obligations for the particular legal order under scrutiny in the Court's assessment. In doing so, the Court indirectly limited the scope of the procedural obligations imposed to the particularities of a single legal order, even though it could safely be assumed that those obligations would apply to and regulate proceedings in any Member State's legal order. The judgment did not, however, clarify whether and to what extent this would be the case.

The *Pfleiderer* judgment continued the mixed negative-positive obligations approach identified in both *Courage* and *Manfredi*. The case concerned the interplay between public and private enforcement and the granting of access for private claimants to self-incriminating documents retained by an NCA. In its judgment, the Court deemed it necessary for a national judge to weigh the respective interests in favour of the disclosure of the information and in favour of the protection of that information provided voluntarily by the applicant for leniency.[28] Weighing should take place on a case-by-case

[24] ibid para 82.
[25] ibid paras 78–80.
[26] ibid para 93.
[27] ibid para 95.
[28] *Pfleiderer* (n 6) para 30.

basis, taking into account all the relevant factors of the case.[29] From that point of view, EU law as such did not preclude a person who had been adversely affected by an infringement of EU competition law and was seeking to obtain damages from being granted access to documents relating to a leniency procedure involving the perpetrator of that infringement. It was nevertheless for the courts and tribunals of the Member States, on the basis of their national law, to determine the conditions under which such access must be permitted or refused by weighing the interests protected by EU law.[30] In its assessment, the Court continued to rely on a classical procedural autonomy argument to make its claim. It stated that national rule governing access to information in private actions based on Article 101 TFEU should be no less favourable than those governing similar domestic claims and should not be applied in such a way as to render the obtaining of such information impossible or excessively difficult.[31]

As such, it would appear that national courts are merely prohibited from disallowing information to be accessed in cases where such access would be possible as a matter of national law. To the extent that national legal orders did not establish a leniency programme or did not foresee any access to documents in national cases, access would not be a matter of concern.[32] That approach is nevertheless difficult to reconcile with the Court's claim that national courts apply Articles 101 and 102 TFEU in the general interest defined by EU competition law.[33] In doing so, national courts are obliged to give shape to a particular understanding of EU access to leniency documents in the national legal orders. It would seem that the Court considers itself competent to determine the scope of EU general interests and to guide national courts in that regard. As such, the Court imposes an essentially positive obligation on national courts to balance different interests, without providing clear guidance on how to proceed in performing the balancing exercise.

In *Donau Chemie*, the Court once again maintained that national law must not be developed in such a way as to preclude any possibility for the national courts to conduct that balancing exercise on a case-by-case basis.[34] The same judgment also posited that courts, which are empowered only to take due note of the consent or refusal expressed by the parties to

[29] ibid para 31.

[30] ibid para 32. The German judge ultimately refused access to the requested documents in the national case, see Amtsgericht Bonn, *Pfleiderer/Bundeskartellamt*, judgment of 18 January 2012, 51 Gs 53/09 AG Bonn.

[31] *Pfleiderer* (n 6) para 30.

[32] ibid para 23. See also SB Völcker, 'Case C-360/09, Pfleiderer AG v. Bundeskartellamt, Judgment of the Court of Justice (Grand Chamber) of 14 June 2011, nyr' (2012) 49 *Common Market Law Review* 695, 699.

[33] *Pfleiderer* (n 6) para 19.

[34] *Donau Chemie* (n 6) para 35.

the proceedings concerning the disclosure of the evidence in the file, cannot sufficiently intervene in order to protect overriding public interests or the legitimate overriding interests of other parties, including that of allowing the disclosure of the documents requested.[35] A negative obligation to disapply rules categorically prohibiting access to certain documents was once again accompanied by the positive obligation to balance the EU's interests with those of a private claimant. The Court did not, however, clarify what factors were to be taken into account in the balancing exercise and left it to each national judge to define the scope of those obligations. National courts had to be able to determine, on a case-by-case basis, whether access to leniency documents could be granted. As such, an obligation to allow for such balancing at all times in national procedural rules could clearly be read in the judgment.

Kone offers yet another reconfirmation of the limited systemic design abilities of a national procedural autonomy focus. This case concerned the question of whether so-called umbrella pricing effects would qualify for compensation on the basis of Article 101 TFEU. Umbrella pricing practices relate to damages incurred by economic operators which did not deal with members of a cartel, but which had paid higher prices for goods or services provided by the cartelists' competitors. As those higher prices result from the cartel restricting competition in the market, economic operators dealing with the cartelists' competitors could equally suffer damages.[36] According to Austrian law, compensatory claims relating to such damages were prohibited by national law. In this setting, the Court of Justice, using its traditional phrasing, ruled that EU law precludes the interpretation and application of domestic legislation enacted by a Member State which categorically excludes, for legal reasons, any civil liability of undertakings belonging to a cartel for loss resulting from the fact that an undertaking not party to the cartel, having regard to the practices of the cartel, set its prices higher than would otherwise have been expected under competitive conditions.[37] In phrasing this negative obligation, the Court clearly states that national law cannot categorically exclude claims on the basis of umbrella pricing. At the same time, however, this means that Member States have an obligation to allow such claims to be developed across all domestic legal systems. The precise conditions and specific limits for such claims—that could still fall within the ambit of the more general obligation—are not accounted for in the judgment.

[35] ibid para 37.

[36] *Kone* (n 6) para 34. On umbrella pricing, see also D Hansberry et al, 'Umbrella Effect: Damages Claimed by Customers of Non-Cartelist Competitors' (2014) 5 *Journal of European Competition Law & Practice* 196–205.

[37] *Kone* (n 6) para 33.

The assessment of the scope of procedural obligations identified in the Court's private enforcement cases is instructive from two different points of view. Firstly, the broad-brush overview offered here allows us to identify a parallel in the scope of obligations imposed on domestic legal orders by the Court of Justice. The Court consistently formulates its obligations in a negative way, but adds positive procedural obligation dicta to its negatively formulated operative parts. As a result, all obligations imposed on specific legal orders here could in fact also be read as positive obligations imposed on all Member States to facilitate private enforcement claims in accordance with the requirements identified in the case law. As mentioned above, however, both the identification and scope of those positive obligations often remain unclear, resulting in uncertainty for national legal orders as to what EU law is particularly required of them.

Secondly, the obligations identified only touched upon a very limited number of issues associated with private damages claims. Those issues were obviously highly dependent on the questions referred to by national courts and have therefore not enabled the Court of Justice to design a more complete and coherent private enforcement system. As a result, the national procedural autonomy focus as applied to EU competition law private enforcement offered some, yet hardly sufficient guidelines for domestic legal orders on how to proceed facilitating private enforcement claims as a matter of EU competition law. Issues such as standards and burden of proof of harm, fault requirements, causality and the quantification of damages remained the province of diversified national procedural regimes, without the Court having been able to offer concrete guidance or to impose specific obligations in that regard. It is therefore not surprising at all that EU legislative intervention was considered necessary to structure and steer developments in this area.[38]

3. EMBEDDING PROCEDURAL OBLIGATIONS IN THE DIRECTIVE

The EU Damages Directive[39] directly responds to the specific shortcomings of the national procedural autonomy focus identified in the previous section. It includes a clearer set of predominantly positive procedural obligations (obligations to include particular procedural rules in the national legal order) that have to be implemented in all Member States (see Section 3.1 below). At the same time, however, the positive obligations imposed do not—and cannot—deviate from the key features offered by a 'national

[38] The August 2004 Ashurst Report already reached that conclusion, available at ec.europa.eu/competition/antitrust/actionsdamages/economic_clean_en.pdf (last accessed 6 August 2015).

[39] Directive 2014/104/EU (n 1).

procedural autonomy' focus. As a result, the Directive essentially reconfirms and keeps in place the national procedural autonomy focus grounded in negative procedural obligations imposed on Member States. By embedding this approach within the framework of a Directive, however, the intensity with which the Court will continue its assessment of national procedural rules can be expected to increase in both number and focus (see Section 3.2 below).

3.1 More Clearly Established Procedural Obligations ...

The Directive's main aim is to set out

> certain rules necessary to ensure that anyone who has suffered harm caused by an infringement of competition by an undertaking or by an association of undertakings, can effectively exercise the right to claim full compensation for that harm from that undertaking or association.[40]

In doing so, it particularly aims to ensure equivalent protection throughout the Union for anyone having suffered harm, removing national law obstacles impeding such protection.[41] As such, it essentially contains a set of clear obligations imposed on national legal orders (see Section 3.1.1 below) and above all rules regulating the disclosure of evidence in national court proceedings (see Section 3.1.2 below). Those obligations and rules complement, yet do not replace, the procedural autonomy focus relied on by the Court. Article 4 of the Directive clearly reiterates that general framework, imposing the general obligations on Member States to ensure that rules and procedures are designed to comply with the principles of effectiveness and equivalence.[42]

3.1.1 Clearly Formulated Positive Procedural Obligations

Although Article 4 of the Directive refers to both equivalence and effectiveness, the EU institutions paid particular attention to outlining conditions that would enable national legal systems and national courts to comply with the principle of effectiveness.[43] As a result, six clear positive obligations imposed on Member States and national courts pervade the Directive.

[40] Directive 2014/104/EU, Art 1.

[41] ibid rec 3. An essential component of this commitment to facilitating private enforcement consists of including actions on the basis of infringements of national competition law, which had been applied in parallel with EU competition law provisions by national actors, within the scope of EU private enforcement, see Directive 2014/104/EU, rec 10.

[42] ibid Art 4.

[43] See particularly ibid recs 3–4.

At times, those obligations touch upon national substantive law provisions,[44] but primarily they seek to harmonise national procedural rules.

Firstly, Article 9(1) of the Directive requires procedural rules to be in place which allow a national judge to deem an infringement proven if an infringement has been adopted by the NCA of the same Member State. The same goes for decisions adopted by NCAs in other Member States, which, however, must only be acknowledged as *prima facie* evidence of an infringement of competition law.[45] In reality, this minimum obligation nevertheless requires Member States at the very least to allow claims on the basis of NCA decisions from other Member States to be brought within the jurisdiction of the former.

Secondly, the Directive imposes clear obligations in relation to time limits. Those limits should be at least five years,[46] and may only begin to run once the infringement has ceased and the claimant knows or can reasonably be expected to know of the behaviour and the harm caused by the infringer.[47] In addition, the Directive outlines particular situations and rules concerning the interruption or suspension of the limitation period: if a competition authority takes action for the purpose of an investigation or more formal proceedings, limitation periods shall be suspended at least until one year after the infringement decision has become final or after proceedings have otherwise been terminated.[48] Limitation periods will also be suspended for the duration of any consensual dispute resolution process.[49] Interestingly, the Directive does not clarify whether suspension or interruption is to occur when a competition authority in another Member State initiates proceedings for the same kind of anticompetitive behaviour, applying EU law to the situation at hand. At present, the Directive does not make a clear distinction between public enforcement proceedings initiated in the same or in another Member State and their effect on the suspension of national limitation periods for the purpose of private enforcement. In the light of the distinction in evidentiary value of infringement decisions posited in Article 9, it could be assumed that the limitation period rules also only relate to authority proceedings initiated in the same Member State. If that proves to be the case, the effectiveness of limitation periods and the coordination between public

[44] eg, the inclusion of interests in damages awards and the prohibition to allow for punitive or multiple damages claims (Art 3(2)) or the presumption of cartel harm (Art 17(2)). This showcases an interesting general tension between EU and national law, where the EU's perception of 'procedural law' does not necessarily align with diversified national conceptions of substantive and procedural law.

[45] Directive 2014/104/EU, Art 9(2).

[46] ibid Art 10(3). This also means that Member States may continue to rely on limitation periods of general duration or application, as long as they fall within the confines set out by the Directive, see also rec 36 for that point.

[47] Directive 2014/104/EU, Art 10(2).

[48] ibid Art 10(4).

[49] ibid Art 18(3).

enforcement actions in one Member State and private damages claims in another can be seriously questioned. The Directive, however, does not offer a definitive answer in this respect.

Thirdly, the Directive mandates and develops rules relating to the joint and several liability of multiple infringers. Article 11 of the Directive clearly sets out the principle of joint and several liability, exempts small and medium-sized enterprises from its application and offers particular guarantees for a leniency immunity recipient.[50] To that extent, national procedural rules have to enable one of the infringers to recover a contribution from any other infringer.[51]

Fourthly, in order to allow the defence of passing-on and to enable indirect purchasers to lodge a damages action, Article 12 of the Directive mandates Member States to develop additional procedural rules. In essence, Member States lay down procedural rules which are appropriate to ensure that compensation for actual loss at any level of the supply chain does not exceed the overcharge harm suffered at that level. National courts have in particular to be able to estimate the share of any overcharge that has been passed on.[52] With a view to facilitating claims by indirect purchasers, the Directive additionally obliges national courts to presume that passing-on occurred if the defendant committed an infringement of competition law, which resulted in an overcharge for the direct purchaser and the indirect purchaser purchased those goods or services that were the direct or indirect object of the infringement.[53] That presumption is rebuttable, yet has to be incorporated into national law. To facilitate the assessment made by domestic courts, the procedural rules of the Member States should enable the courts to access information from other damages actions relating to other actors and to use relevant information in the public domain resulting from the public enforcement of competition law.[54]

Fifthly, if an infringer chooses to settle a claim for damages,[55] the settling party can only claim damages for the remaining part of damages suffered, excluding the share of damages inflicted on it by the settling infringer.[56] Non-settling infringers cannot recover the damages paid from a settling infringer. In cases where non-settling infringers cannot pay the claim for

[50] ibid Art 11(2).
[51] ibid Art 11(5).
[52] ibid Art 12(5).
[53] ibid Art 14(2).
[54] ibid Art 15.
[55] It should be mentioned that the Directive seemingly promotes amicable solutions such as settlements, as Art 18(3) now determines that a competition authority may consider paid consensual dispute compensation as a mitigating factor in determining the amount of a fine it would be called upon to impose after the settlement procedure. This provision somehow relates to the public enforcement stage of antitrust infringement proceedings and therefore appears to be out of place within this Directive.
[56] Directive 2014/104/EU, Art 19(1)

damages, however, the injured party may claim the rest of the damages suffered from that settling infringer, unless this has expressly been excluded in the consensual settlement.[57] National courts have to determine, on a case-by-case-basis, whether and to what extent those conditions are applicable. National procedural rules at the very least have to enable national courts to make such assessments and to take the effects of consensual settlements into account when deciding on damages claims within the scope of the Directive.

Sixthly, national courts have to be able to quantify the amount of harm suffered. National law should in that regard allow for estimates to be made in instances where such quantification appears difficult or impossible in practice. An NCA should also be able to intervene in damages proceedings to assist a national court; in that situation, the national court should explicitly request such assistance and the competition authority should be at liberty to consider the appropriateness of its intervention in any particular case.[58]

3.1.2 A Nuanced Disclosure of Evidence Regime

In addition to the abovementioned specific obligations, the Directive obliges Member States in a very detailed way to develop a procedural regime for the disclosure of evidence. This regime, which resembles the discovery procedure relied on in common law jurisdictions,[59] enables national courts to obtain relevant information from defendants, third parties and public authorities. Such information may be necessary or even indispensable for the claimant to make a sufficiently developed claim or for the defendant to rebut a *prima facie* strong damages request. According to Article 5 of the Directive, national courts should at least be able to order the claimant, defendant or a third party to disclose relevant evidence which lies under their control.[60] National procedural law has to draw up requirements for a disclosure request to be completed. A request should at all times include a reasoned justification with reasonably available facts and sufficient evidence to support the plausibility of a claim for damages.[61] More specifically, national courts have to be able to order the disclosure of either specified items of evidence or particular relevant categories of evidence.[62] Those categories have

[57] ibid Art 19(2)–(3).

[58] ibid Art 17(1) and (3).

[59] Rule 26 of the US Federal Rules of Civil Procedure on the Duty to Disclose and on Discovery serves as an obvious example in this respect. The Rules can be consulted at www.uscourts.gov/uscourts/rules/civil-procedure.pdf.

[60] Directive 2014/104/EU, Art 5(8) underlines that Member States can maintain or introduce rules leading to a wider disclosure. Documents maintained by NCAs cannot always be covered by such wider extensions, see Art 6 and the discussion below.

[61] Directive 2014/104/EU, Art 5(1).

[62] ibid Art 5(2).

to be described as precisely and as narrowly as possible on the basis of the reasonably available facts in the reasoned justification provided by the parties. In any case, the national courts have to assess whether or not disclosure can be deemed proportionate. In ways similar to the *Pfleiderer* test, national courts have to consider the legitimate interests of all parties concerned, prior to determining whether disclosure is indeed proportionate. The Directive therefore additionally posits three benchmarks national courts always have to assess and on the basis of which disclosure has to be reasoned: (1) the extent to which available facts and evidence support a claim; (2) the scope and cost of disclosure and the prevention of non-specific searches of little relevance to parties in the judicial proceedings; and (3) the confidentiality and means of protecting such confidential information in place when disclosure should be ordered.[63] The parties, against whom disclosure is sought, must be provided with an opportunity to be heard prior to any disclosure decision.[64] At the same time, national courts should have effective means available to them to protect such confidential information. The Member States remain at liberty to design their systems to take those considerations into account.[65]

In addition to the general disclosure regime, the Directive further develops and refines disclosure obligations in relation to evidence included in the file of a competition authority. As a basic principle, national procedural rules should ensure that national courts only order the disclosure of NCA documents if no party or third party is reasonably able to provide that evidence on the basis of the general disclosure regime.[66] Prior to ordering the disclosure of such documents, national courts have to address two additional proportionality elements: (1) the request has to relate to specific documents held by the competition authority and (2) the request will not put the effectiveness of public competition law enforcement at risk.[67]

In relation to the second condition, and answering directly to the balancing test developed in *Pfleiderer*, the Directive further clarifies the scope of information that can be disclosed by an NCA. Firstly, leniency statements and settlement submissions cannot at any time be disclosed, contrary to what the Court had suggested in *Pfleiderer*.[68] In that situation, national courts should nevertheless be able to access the evidence to check whether it effectively qualifies in one of both categories.[69] Secondly, information that

[63] ibid Art 5(3). In doing so, (EU) rules on legal professional privilege have to be respected, see Art 5(6).

[64] ibid Art 5(7).

[65] ibid Art 5(4). It should be stressed, however, that the interest of undertakings to avoid actions for damages cannot be protected in national law, see Art 5(5).

[66] ibid Art 6(10).

[67] ibid Art 6(4).

[68] Directive 2014/104/EU, Art 6(6).

[69] ibid Art 6(7); the competent NCA involved may assist the court in doing so, as may the authors of the evidence.

may be disclosed on the basis of the enhanced proportionality test relates to: (1) information that was prepared by a natural or legal person specifically for the proceedings of a competition authority; (2) information that the competition authority has drawn up and sent to the parties in the course of its public enforcement proceedings; and (3) settlement submissions that have been withdrawn.[70] Those documents can in principle only be disclosed once the competition authority has closed its own proceedings.[71] Other NCA documents can be disclosed on the basis of the more lenient general disclosure test in Article 5 of the Directive, without, however, interfering with the rules and practices concerning the protection of internal documents and exchange of information by competition authorities.[72] A national authority should always be able to submit observations to the national court which is to rule on the disclosure of NCA documents.[73]

In the event of failure to comply with disclosure orders or when evidence is destroyed, penalties must be imposed by national courts. The Directive lists two penalties that have to be included in national law in that regard: (1) the possibility to draw adverse inferences, such as presuming the relevant issue to be proven or dismissing claims and defences in whole or in part; and (2) the possibility to order the payment of costs.[74]

The nuanced and complicated system of disclosure raises two additional questions. On the one hand, the Directive does not restrict the ordering of the disclosure of documents held by an NCA in one Member State to courts from the same Member State. As a result, it would not seem implausible that a court in Member State A orders the disclosure of documents from an NCA in Member State B. This would mean that the national procedural systems have to ensure that such exchanges are in fact possible and that mechanisms are provided at Member State level to coordinate or facilitate such exchanges. The Directive remains remarkably silent about the need for and the development of such mechanisms. Recital 17 clarifies that requests for evidence taken directly in another Member State are to be governed by the generally applicable regime in Regulation 1206/2001 on cooperation between courts in civil and commercial matters. No specific transnational information exchange mechanisms have thus been provided for.

Secondly, there are situations where a party, due to its participation or involvement in public enforcement proceedings, was able to obtain access to documents falling under the more stringent disclosure rules outlined here. As a result, leniency statements or individual documents relating to an on-

[70] ibid Art 6(5).

[71] ibid. See also Art 7(2); if a party to the public enforcement proceedings obtained the evidence, national law should establish sufficiently protective mechanisms to ensure that the full effect of the limits on disclosure are maintained.

[72] ibid Art 6(9) *juncto* 6(3).

[73] ibid Art 6(11).

[74] ibid Art 8.

going (non-closed) public enforcement procedure, could be made available by that party in a private enforcement action. The Directive partially addresses that situation by requiring national courts to order the inadmissibility of such evidence or at least to ensure that it is otherwise protected under applicable national rules so that the full effect of the limits on disclosure as provided for in Article 6 of the Directive can be maintained.[75] To the extent that a private party had access to leniency statements or settlement submissions, those documents can be deemed admissible, if a Member State chooses to allow this, and on condition that sufficient confidentiality or other protective guarantees are offered to protect the interests of the leniency or settlement applicant concerned.[76] In any case, the Directive clearly states that the limits on disclosure—both the prohibitions in Article 6(6) and the conditional disclosure regime in Article 6(5)—should be maintained as minimum protective standards across all legal orders.

3.1.3 Interim Conclusion

The abovementioned cursory overview of specific procedural obligations incorporated in the Directive results in two preliminary conclusions. Firstly, the Directive remains loyal to the national procedural autonomy focus. Rather than regulating the requirements of fault, the amount of damages and the causal link between both, it proceeds in mainly focusing on the regime concerning the disclosure of evidence and on the introduction of particular presumptions aimed at facilitating private enforcement claims, such as the presumption of harm and the binding force of an NCA decision. Some exceptions notwithstanding, such as the prohibition to allow for punitive damages in relation to damages actions covered by the Directive, national private law regimes will continue to determine the scope and successful initiation of damages actions grounded on the basis of Articles 101/102 TFEU. It can thus be submitted that EU law harmonises only national procedural provisions as a means to change or restructure the scope and format of actions based on national private law.

Secondly, the procedural obligations included in the Directive mainly aim to provide minimum standards, still allowing for a competition between national procedural systems and the accompanying room for forum shopping to remain in place. The continued reliance on more or less open-ended proportionality criteria when assessing the permissibility and scope of the

[75] ibid also states that evidence obtained can only be traded in a limited way. It is only to be used by the natural or legal person requesting its disclosure or any person succeeding to those persons. This may include situations where a third party acquired someone's disclosure claim. Evidence falling within the Art 6(5) or 6(6) categories could only be used by the natural or legal person who obtained this information, see Art 7(3) *a contrario*.

[76] ibid Art 7(2) *juncto* Arts 7(1) and 6(6).

disclosure of evidence provides a clear example of this. As a consequence, national courts will be more likely to seek guidance, either from NCAs when possible[77] or from the Court of Justice to determine the exact scope of those obligations, especially in relation to the proportionality assessments required from them.

3.2 Enabling more Focused Future National Procedural Assessments?

The Directive overwhelmingly highlights that the Commission, Council and European Parliament chose to rely on procedural law harmonisation and on the imposition of procedural obligations to approximate national private law systems. In practice, this will also mean that the Court will continue to rely on its procedural harmonisation toolkit—comprising the principles of equivalence, effectiveness and effective judicial protection—to fine-tune such harmonisation. In light of the Directive's provisions, this section briefly looks forward to two potential future evolutions in that regard. Firstly, the Court will be enticed more consistently to rely on the principle of effective judicial protection as a means to interpret and even extend the scope of application of the provisions and presumptions covered by the Directive. Secondly, this approach will create new gaps and problems, resulting in a review of the Directive, which will most likely have to include more substantive law harmonisation elements. The envisaged review provision in Article 20 of the Directive is likely to facilitate or at least enable that process.

It has been clear from earlier procedural harmonisation fields in areas as disparate as environmental and asylum law,[78] that once the EU legislator allows for national procedures to be harmonised, the Court of Justice feels more comfortable to intervene directly in national legal orders on the basis of the principle of effective judicial protection.[79] It can therefore safely be expected that this principle will once again be invoked to shape the operation of different presumptions. In the context of the Directive, it could particularly be envisaged that the actual operationalisation of the proportionality assessments in disclosure proceedings or the extent to which passing-on presumptions and damages estimations have to be made could be prone to interpretations in the name of effective judicial protection. In those

[77] eg, in relation to NCA document disclosure, see ibid Art 6(11).

[78] See, eg, Joined Cases C-128/09, C-129/09, C-130/09, C-131/09, C-134/09 and C-135/09 *Boxus* [2011] ECR I-9711 (environmental law) and case C-69/10 *Samba Diouf* [2011] ECR I-7151 (asylum law).

[79] See in that regard, P Van Cleynenbreugel, 'The Confusing Constitutional Status of Positive Procedural Obligations in EU law' (2012) 5 *Review of European Administrative Law* 81, 100.

instances, as case law in other sectors clearly indicates, the Court will not shy away from imposing additional or complementary obligations on Member States' legal orders. Contrary to similar activities in the absence of EU procedural harmonisation, newly imposed judicial obligations will be more detailed and tailored to the specificities of the harmonised procedural rules. It can be expected that the Court will not only interpret the Directive's provisions, but also expound on additional or more nuanced obligations that complement the presumptions and assessment benchmarks of the Directive.

The most surprising side effect of the Directive in that regard will be that procedural and substantive law rules not directly regulated by the Directive, will nevertheless now be considered to fall within the scope of application of EU law, as those rules may impede the effective application and enforcement of EU presumptions and assessment schemes. Recital 11 is illustrative in this regard, clearly stating that 'other conditions for compensation under national law, such as imputability, adequacy and culpability' are to be assessed on the basis of the principles of effectiveness and equivalence, as well as the Directive. In so maintaining, it clearly presages that the inherently national law conceptions equally fall within the ambit of EU law—at least when relied on in private damages actions relating to EU competition law infringements—and that they should be interpreted in light of the Directive, which in itself will be interpreted in light of the procedural autonomy principles. The Directive thus allows the Court's procedural autonomy focus to continue with more vigour in the future.

To the extent that a truly harmonised private enforcement culture with limited opportunities for forum shopping remains desirable from a political point of view, it is not entirely unlikely that more substantive law reforms will have to be pushed for, either indirectly by the Court or directly during the review stages of the Directive. Article 20 of the Directive explicitly prescribes that a report on the application of the Directive will have to be drawn up, which could be accompanied by a legislative proposal. At the same time, however, the report has to focus particularly on specific issues (financial constraints on undertakings to pay private damages after public enforcement fines have been imposed, proof of infringement on the basis of NCA decisions and the application of passing-on), which are not likely to elicit substantive law harmonisation. It would thus be safe to conclude that at this stage of the harmonisation of EU private damages actions, the EU legislator wishes to stick to its procedural harmonisation approach rather than develop a truly substantively harmonised private enforcement area. As a consequence, the Court of Justice will have the opportunity to continue its procedural autonomy focus, albeit against a background of more clearly established and harmonised assessment benchmarks that have to be applied across all Member States. Procedural autonomy and effective judicial protection will therefore continue to provide the EU law backbone for the continued and step-by-step creation of an integrated EU competition law private enforcement framework.

4. CONCLUSION

This chapter has argued that the Directive on damages actions directly responds to, but also confirms and sustains the piecemeal 'national procedural autonomy' approach that set regulatory developments in the private enforcement of EU competition law in motion. It has identified the key features and shortcomings of this approach and the ways in which the Directive responds to those features. It has been submitted that the Directive directly confirms and regulates different topics (punitive damages, access to leniency documents, room for indirect purchaser standing) which had previously been touched upon by the Court of Justice. In doing so, the Directive transforms judicially formulated 'negative procedural obligations with a positive obligation twist' into clear positive obligations requiring legislative or judicial action in the Member States. From that point of view, the Directive is likely to result in more intensified and focused judicial scrutiny over those rules in the name of effective judicial protection in the EU.

7

Private Enforcement of Competition Law in Intellectual Property Cases

PAUL LC TORREMANS*

1. INTRODUCTION

1.1 Intellectual Property as a Special Case

SUFFICE IT TO say that in the light of the apparent paradox between intellectual property rights as exclusive rights that exclude direct competition on the one hand and the 'dogma' of free competition in our market economy on the other (hand), intellectual property experts have been used to dealing with aspects of competition law for a long time. Moreover, competition law arguments have been raised in private litigation for several decades. It may, therefore, not come as a surprise to find a chapter on intellectual property in a volume that deals with the Directive on competition damages actions.[1]

But, and this is unlikely to surprise competition lawyers, intellectual property is also in this respect (yet again) different. The Directive takes as a starting point that private enforcement of competition law has as its aim to claim compensation and if one reads on in the Directive, compensation is seen very much, or even exclusively, as damages. The standard scenario is one where the party that suffered damage as a result of the breach of competition law sues the party responsible for the breach and seeks compensation for the damage. In other words, there is anti-competitive behaviour by one party and the aggrieved party seeks redress by way of a lawsuit aiming

* Professor of Intellectual Property Law, University of Nottingham.

[1] Directive 2014/104/EU of the European Parliament and of the Council of 26 November 2014 on certain rules governing actions for damages under national law for infringements of the competition law provisions of the Member States and of the European Union [2014] OJ L349/1.

at compensation by way of damages. The Directive aims to facilitate this scenario.

This scenario is possible in an intellectual property context, but it is rare. The key difference in relation to intellectual property is that there is an exclusive right. The party that is allegedly in breach of competition law has an exclusive right that involves by definition a restriction on competition. More importantly, this is a private right that is primarily giving its owner the opportunity to stop others from doing certain things. This 'negative' right is also private in the enforcement sense. Rightholders need to bring legal action themselves to enforce their right. The standard intellectual property scenario is therefore one where the party that allegedly abuses competition law sues for alleged infringement of its exclusive intellectual property right. The defendant, the alleged infringer, can then raise competition law by way of defence. Liability as a result of the infringement of the intellectual property right is denied and the right should not be enforced in the particular circumstances because its exercise amounts to an abuse of competition law. Such a defence effectively amounts to a type of private enforcement of competition law, but it is very different from the type the Directive takes as its starting point.

1.2 Injunctive Relief and Defences

In addition, damages are often not the main remedy sought in intellectual property cases. Injunctive relief plays instead the most important role. One is primarily interested in stopping the abuse of competition law. Raising competition law as a defence has, as its aim, to stop the infringement action from being successful and to exclude any liability, but equally important, it aims at stopping the allegations (also shared with partners, clients and financial institutions) that the defendant is liable. Much more than compensation for what went before, the aim is to unblock the road for the future. In any case, any damage suffered by the exercise of the rightholder's right to enforce his/her intellectual property right will be hard to calculate. It is therefore rare that damages are sought from the holder of an intellectual property right. Courts have even held that any claim that has as its real aim to stop the holder of an intellectual property right from enforcing that right, whatever legal tool is used by the party that would have been the alleged infringer in an infringement lawsuit, amounts to an abuse of procedure.[2] One has a right to enforce one's intellectual property right and the alleged infringers in such cases often have no obvious right or ground of action of their own to bring a case before they are sued for infringement. In these circumstances one is often better advised not to try to privately enforce

[2] Court of First Instance Brussels, 19 September 2003 [2004] *Auteurs & Media* 38.

competition law oneself. With courts starting from the perspective that a patent entitles its proprietor to the exclusive right to prevent others from exploiting the invention, that securing that right by preventing manufacture or sale without consent could not be an abuse[3] and that enforcement of patent rights can only be considered abusive if the patent was obviously not infringed or invalid,[4] proving that the way in which the exclusive right is exercised was always going to be an uphill struggle for any claimant.

1.3 Private Competition Law Claims and Damages

That is not to say that competition law is, in the context of intellectual property rights, always raised as a defence and enforced privately in that way. Occasionally a claim is made, primarily in interlocutory proceedings, with the direct support of competition law provisions. A typical example occurs in the context of a refusal to licence an intellectual property right, where the party to whom the licence is refused goes to court in interlocutory proceedings to obtain a (compulsory) licence on the basis of the argument that the refusal to licence amounts to an abuse of a dominant position. But again, damages are not the (main) objective in these proceedings. There are, however, also cases where damages are the objective, even if they are rare. One could think, eg, of a patent pool that forms a cartel and where the party that is excluded from participation in the patent pool and that suffers damage as a result brings proceedings against the patent pool on the basis that their conduct amounts to an abuse of a dominant position and that the excluded party is entitled to compensation. In such a scenario damages play the dominant role and the Directive would be directly applicable.

1.4 Disclosure

The Directive will not be applicable though in most intellectual property scenarios, because as we have seen, there will not simply be a claim for damages when an action for the private enforcement of competition law is brought. However, national procedural rules do in general allow the defendant to raise a competition law-based defence and the fact that the Directive merely focuses on private enforcement to an action for damages as a remedy does not cause an undue amount of problems. The second part of the Directive may in this respect turn out to be far more problematic. Admittedly, the

3 *Philips Electronics NV v Ingman Ltd* [1998] 2 CMLR 839; [1999] FSR 112.

4 *SanDisk Corp v Koninklijke Philips Electronics NV* [2007] EWHC 332 (Ch); [2007] FSR 22.

Enforcement Directive[5] already provides in its Articles 6 and 7 for measures related to evidence in the context of intellectual property enforcement proceedings, but they are intended to benefit primarily the claimant in infringement proceedings. We have seen above though that in terms of the private enforcement of competition law, the party that needs the evidence is mainly the defendant in the intellectual property infringement proceedings. Here the Directive's provisions on disclosure[6] come in very handy. However, these apply, as the title of the Directive already indicates, to actions for damages. One can therefore expect that, even if this is not the main aim of the party invoking the competition rules, that the party will in the future also start to make an ancillary claim for damages, however small the amount may be. This would subsequently bring the proceedings within the scope of the Directive and the party would then be able to benefit from the disclosure rules. Whilst this seems perfectly workable at first glance, there are grounds for criticism. An ancillary claim for damages, merely to get the benefit of the disclosure rules, is clearly a burdensome and potentially costly addition to the proceedings. Secondly, there is a real risk that the courts may throw out the damages claim as an abuse of procedure if it is obvious that it was brought merely to benefit from the disclosure rules to which the party was normally not entitled since its real case did not involve a claim for compensation and damages.

In the following two sections of the chapter, I will look at the scenario in which competition law is raised as a defence and at the scenario in which a FRAND[7] licensor allegedly abuses its dominant position by seeking injunction relief against a potential licensor that expressed the willingness to take out a licence respectively.

2. COMPETITION LAW AS A DEFENCE IN INTELLECTUAL PROPERTY INFRINGEMENT CASES

2.1 The Lead-In

The typical intellectual property infringement case in which competition law is raised as a defence is an Article 102 case. The defendant will argue that the claimant occupies a dominant position and that the way in which he or she proposes to exercise the intellectual property right amounts to an abuse of that dominant position. Not only should the claimant be sanctioned for the abuse of his or her dominant position (this might involve

[5] Directive 2004/48/EC of the European Parliament and of the Council of 29 April 2004 on the enforcement of intellectual property rights [2004] OJ L195/13, Ch 2, s 2.

[6] Ch 2 of Directive 2014/104/EU.

[7] Fair, reasonable, and non-discriminatory terms.

the compulsory grant of a licence to the defendant), the infringement claim should also be dismissed, as the court can never be asked to sanction what amounts to an abuse of a dominant position.

The presence of a dominant position is not unusual in an intellectual property context. By definition an intellectual property right is an exclusive right and whilst this does not automatically follow, the granting of such an exclusive right can contribute to or result in the creation of a dominant position. It is equally clear though that there is a difference between the existence of a dominant position, which does not create a problem at all under Article 102, on the one hand and the abuse of a dominant position, which Article 102 prohibits, on the other. The existence of the intellectual property right as such is not at issue in an Article 102 context, as intellectual property rights are restrictions on competition in the furtherance of competition.[8] And an exclusive right that is in essence a negative right to prevent others from carrying out certain acts, such as, eg, making the patented product whilst the patent is in force, must be used and exercised in order for it to function. There is, in other words, no problem at the structural level, but abuse may well arise at the behavioural level, depending on how the intellectual property right is exercised. There will, in other words, be ways in which the right is exercised that amount to the mere use of the right and there will be ways in which the right is exercised that amount to an abuse of the right.[9] The latter will be caught by Article 102.[10] Striking that balance is a delicate exercise, which came to the fore in the *Magill* case. We will therefore look at that case in some detail, even if it is not a case of private enforcement (by means of a defence) of competition law. Magill merely asked the competition authorities to enforce Article 102. The *Magill* case is needed though in the run up to the *IMS* case, which did involve the private enforcement of the competition rules that were invoked as a defence in an intellectual property infringement case. What preceded this was on top of that a refusal to licence, which makes the case even more interesting for our analysis. IMS refused to grant a licence on its copyright and the defendant decided to go ahead with its planned activity, despite the absence of a licence. It was then sued for copyright infringement and invoked an abuse of a dominant position by IMS as a defence.

[8] See P Torremans, *Holyoak and Torremans Intellectual Property Law*, 7th edn (Oxford, Oxford University Press, 2013) 13–17 and M Lehmann, 'Property and Intellectual Property: Property Rights as Restrictions on Competition in Furtherance of Competition' (1989) *International Journal of Industrial Property and Copyright* 1, 12.

[9] Refusing to license on reasonable terms (at least outside a standards / FRAND context) or refusing to license at all are as such not abuses; see *Philips Electronics* (n 3).

[10] For a detailed analysis see Torremans (n 8) Chs 5 and 18.

2.2 *Magill*

In the *Magill* cases,[11] the issue whether or not there was an actionable abuse of a dominant position under Article 102 arose when Magill wished to publish the listings of programmes of the British Broadcasting Corporation (BBC), Independent Television (ITV), and Radio Telefís Éireann (RTE) in a single weekly publication. The three companies refused to supply those listings and invoked their copyright in the listings to do so. It should be noted that they published their own guides, which thus enjoyed a form of monopoly, and supplied, free of charge, the weekly listings to foreign publications; they also supplied daily listings to the press. The Commission[12] ruled that the three companies abused their dominant position in exercising their copyright in such a way and required that advance information be supplied to Magill and eventually the case made its way up to the CJEU.[13]

The CJEU easily agreed that the broadcasters occupied a dominant position in the relevant market. Even so, the question remained whether the refusal to license amounted to an abuse of that dominant position. The existing case law pointed towards the fact that the mere existence of the intellectual property right and a use that stays within the specific subject matter of the right cannot amount to an abuse. If the possession of the immaterial right is to have any value, its owner must be free to decide under which circumstances and under which financial conditions he or she is prepared to grant a licence. A right to refuse to grant a licence must be part of such a system and must therefore come within the specific subject matter of the right. In normal circumstances, such a refusal can therefore not be in breach of Article 102. There may, however, be circumstances in which the intellectual property right is used improperly, to serve purposes that have nothing to do with the real purpose and essential function of the right. If the right is abused, the refusal to grant a licence is no longer used to implement the essential function of the right and, just as anything else in relation to an exclusive or monopoly intellectual property right, exposes itself to the sanction of Article 102.

This approach is endorsed by the Court's judgment. The Court argued that a refusal might, in exceptional circumstances, constitute an abuse.[14] These exceptional circumstances involved the following in this case: the

[11] Case T-69/89 *Radio Telefis Eireann v Commissions of the European Communities (Magill TV Guide Ltd intervening)* [1991] ECR II-485; Case T-70/89 *British Broadcasting Corp & BBC Enterprises Ltd v Commission (Magill TV Guide Ltd intervening)* [1991] ECR II-535; Case T-76/89 *Independent Television Publications Ltd v Commission (Magill TV Guide Ltd intervening)* [1991] ECR II-575.

[12] Decision *Magill TV Guide/ITP, BBC & RTE* [1989] OJ L78/43.

[13] Joined Cases C-241/91 P and C-242/91 P *Radio Telefis C-241/91 Independent Television Publications Ltd v Commission* [1995] ECR I-743.

[14] ibid at paras 54 and 57 respectively.

broadcaster's main activity is broadcasting; the television guides market is only a secondary market for the broadcaster. By refusing to provide the basic programme listing information, of which they were the only source, the broadcasters prevented the appearance of new products that they did not offer and for which there was a consumer demand. The refusal could not be justified by virtue of their normal activities and by denying access to the basic information that was required to make the new product the broadcasters were effectively reserving the secondary market for weekly television guides to themselves. The use of copyright to block the appearance of a new product for which the copyright information is essential, and to reserve a secondary market to oneself, is an abuse and cannot be said to be necessary to fulfil the essential function—that is, the reward and encouragement of the author—of copyright. This is especially the case if one is the only source of the copyright information or material, and the latter element is of particular importance. It may not be part of the abuse, but the availability of other sources for the material would take away the element of dominance. And without dominance, there can simply be no abuse of a dominant position.

2.3 *IMS Health*: Facts and Issues

It has become clear from the discussion above that it is at least arguable that Magill had left open several issues.[15] These issues were primarily open to argument, because it was not clear whether the decision on that point in *Magill* depended entirely on the facts of the case—that is, on whether other facts could receive a different treatment—or whether they were a necessary element from a legal point of view. One of the issues left open is the question of whether a finding of exceptional circumstances required, cumulatively, that the intellectual property right was linked to essential inputs for secondary markets, on the one hand, and that a new product had to be introduced in that market for which there was significant and unmet demand, on the other. Do the conditions in Magill apply cumulatively—as was the case in *Magill*—or are they alternative conditions? The latter option would see the essential facilities doctrine apply to many more cases, because there would be more exceptional circumstances. *Magill* also stresses the need for the monopolisation of a secondary market—but how secondary should that market be? Is it simply a separate or derivative market? And could the essential facilities doctrine apply if the competitor that was refused a licence

[15] See the discussion in paras 88–105 and the conclusion in para 106 that there is '*a very serious dispute*' concerning these in the Order of the President of the Court of First Instance of 26 October 2001 in Case T-184/01 *R* [2001] ECR II-3193. This Order was upheld by the Order of the President of the Court of Justice of 11 April 2002 in Case C-481/01 *P(R)* EU:C:2002:223. See also *Intel Corp v Via Technologies Inc* [2003] FSR 574 (CA).

wanted to compete in the rightholder's main market? In other words, how close to the core business of the rightholder can one come?

The IMS Health saga provided an opportunity to answer some of these questions. IMS Health developed along two parallel tracks on the basis of the following facts. IMS Health is a major supplier of marketing data to pharmaceutical and other healthcare companies. In the German market, it has established a structure of in total 1,860 local geographic segments called 'bricks', each containing a comparable number of pharmacies, in order to collect standardised data without violating data protection laws, which do not allow for the identification of individual pharmacies' data. That structure is protected by copyright under German copyright law. That point as such is not in dispute, but there is more to it than pure copyright.

From the user or consumer perspective, there is a high demand for the data collected through the use of the brick structure, which has become an impressive success in the market. The brick structure has de facto become the industry standard and its competitors asked for it to be licensed to them in order for them to be able to compete. The user is, indeed, only interested in data that is presented in a comparable fashion. When IMS Health's competitors, NDC Health and AzyX Deutschland GmbH Geopharma Information Services, applied for a licence covering the brick structure at various stages during the complex timeline and developments of the case, the details of which are not necessary for our present purposes, the granting of such a licence was refused by IMS Health and in the end it resulted in a complaint by NDC and AzyX to the European Commission for an abuse of a dominant position. In due course, the Commission issued its Decision, in which it went against IMS at a first stage, but without reaching a final conclusion. Interim measures were imposed. The Commission Decision was appealed and, as a result, two Orders of the President of the Court of First Instance[16] and one Order from the President of the European Court of Justice,[17] which suspended the interim measures, followed. In the light of that suspension and of the sceptical attitude that the Presidents of the two courts took towards the Commission's approach, the Commission withdrew its Decision ordering interim measures.[18]

At the same time, however, IMS Health's competitors had decided to make use of the brick structure anyway, without waiting for the granting of the licence. IMS Health therefore brought copyright proceedings against them in the German courts. In the course of these copyright proceedings,

[16] Order of the President of the Court of First Instance of 10 August 2001 in Case T-184/01 *R* [2001] ECR II-2349; Order of the President of the Court of First Instance of 26 October 2001 in Case T-184/01 (n 15).

[17] Order of the President of the Court of Justice of 11 April 2002 in Case C-481/01 *P(R)* EU:C:2002:223.

[18] Commission Decision of 13 August 2003 [2003] OJ L268/59.

the German court referred the case to the European Court of Justice for a preliminary ruling.[19] This is, in other words, the standard intellectual property scenario for the private enforcement of competition law by way of raising competition law concerns as a defence. The fact that there was also a complaint lodged with the European competition authorities at the same time is also an example of what Recital 5 of the Directive calls complementary systems of enforcing competition law in the following words:

> Actions for damages are only one element of an effective system of private enforcement of infringements of competition law and are complemented by alternative avenues of redress, such as consensual dispute resolution or public enforcement decisions that give parties an incentive to provide compensation.[20]

2.4 *IMS Health* in the European Court of Justice

The scepticism towards the broad interpretation of the essential facilities doctrine proposed by the Commission that has been expressed in the foregoing analysis was also reflected in the Orders of the President of the Court of First Instance and the President of the Court of Justice. It is therefore welcoming to see that the European Court of Justice adopted a much more careful and sensible approach in its judgment in *IMS Health v NDC Health*.[21]

The Court, first of all, turned its attention to the vital question of when, in a copyright context, a facility has become an essential facility. The Court held that, in order to determine whether a product or service is indispensable for the purposes of enabling an undertaking to carry on business in a particular market, it must be determined whether there are products or services that constitute alternative solutions. It does not matter in that respect that these alternative solutions are less advantageous, or whether there are technical, legal, or economic obstacles capable of making it impossible—or at least unreasonably difficult—for any undertaking seeking to operate in the market to create—possibly in cooperation with other operators—the alternative products or services. The existence of economic obstacles will only be able to rule out an alternative solution if it is established, at the very least, that the creation of those products or services is not economically viable for production on a scale that is comparable to that of the undertaking in control of the existing product or service. This is a very strict interpretation of the essential facility point and, because the existence of an essential facility is a prerequisite that must be met before even the issue of abuse can be addressed, this will severely limit the number of cases in which the exercise of copyright will be interfered with.

[19] Case C-418/01 *IMS Health v NDC Health* EU:C:2004:257.
[20] Directive on antitrust damages actions (n 1) rec 5 (emphasis added).
[21] *IMS* (n 19).

In the *IMS* case, the Court advised the German Court that, in applying the test, account must be taken of the fact that a high level of participation by the pharmaceutical laboratories in the improvement of the 1,860-brick structure protected by copyright has created a dependency by users in relation to that structure, particularly at a technical level. The Court went on to say that:

> In such circumstances, it is likely that those laboratories would have to make exceptional organisational and financial efforts in order to acquire the studies on regional sales of pharmaceutical products presented on the basis of a structure other than that protected by copyright. The supplier of that alternative structure might therefore be obliged to offer terms which are such as to rule out any economic viability of business on a scale comparable to that of the undertaking which controls the protected structure.[22]

The strong suggestion to the German Court is therefore no doubt that these additional circumstances have turned the block structure into an essential facility.

Once it has been established that the facility—in this case, the block structure, as protected by copyright—is an essential facility, the second step—that is, the issue of whether there has been an abuse of a dominant position, in this case, by refusing to license the block structure—can be addressed. The Court ruled on this point that three conditions have to be met cumulatively for there to be an abuse:

- the refusal is preventing the emergence of a new product for which there is a potential consumer demand;
- there is no objective justification for this refusal;
- the refusal is such as to exclude any competition in a secondary market.[23]

In this way, the Court clearly adopts a very restrictive interpretation of its earlier dicta in *Magill*[24] and *Bronner*.[25] The Commission's suggestions that the criteria could be applied alternatively, rather than cumulatively, and, in particular, that the existence of separate markets was not required, has been straightforwardly rejected. The point is now clear: all three requirements apply cumulatively if there is to be a finding of abuse.

The Court then went on to clarify each of the three requirements and their application in the *IMS Health* case. The third condition—relating to the likelihood of excluding all competition in a secondary market—requires that it is possible to distinguish an upstream market, constituted by the

[22] ibid, 1577.
[23] ibid, 1579.
[24] *Radio Telefis* (n 13).
[25] Case C-7/97 *Oscar Bronner GmbH and Co KG v Mediaprint Zeitungs- und Zeitschriftenverlag GmbH and Co KG* [1988] ECR I-7791.

product or service that forms the essential facility (for example, in *Bronner*, the market for home delivery of daily newspapers, and in *IMS Health*, the market for brick structures) and a (secondary) downstream market, on which the product or service in question—that is, the essential facility—is used for the production of another product or the supply of another service (for example, in *Bronner*, the market for daily newspapers themselves, and in *IMS Health*, the market for the supply of sales data).[26] The fact that the essential facility is not marketed separately is not regarded as precluding, from the outset, the possibility of identifying a separate market. It is indeed sufficient that a potential market, or even a hypothetical market, can be identified.[27] One of the positive aspects of this approach is that an abuse can also be found in those circumstances in which the rightholder's behaviour does not simply hinder competition, but acts to exclude competition completely to such an extent that, in reality, no downstream market exists.

Secondly, it is now clear that a secondary market does not have to be of secondary importance to the rightholder, as was the case on the facts in *Magill*. All that is required is the existence of two markets—or, in the words of the Court:

> Accordingly, it is determinative that two different stages of production may be identified and that they are interconnected, the upstream product is indispensable inasmuch as for supply of the downstream product.[28]

It is therefore possible that the applicant for the licence that is refused wanted to compete head on with the rightholder in the same market.

In practical business terms, it will be relatively easy to determine the markets involved in those cases in which there is a real existing market for the goods or services that allegedly amount to an essential facility, but things get more difficult when one is looking at the potential or hypothetical markets that the Court mentions and which are likely to represent the majority of cases. Indeed, the abuse complained of prevents the existence of a real market in business terms. The Court's approach is to argue that there is a potential or a hypothetical market if two conditions are met:

- the products or services must be indispensable in order to carry on a particular business;
- there is an actual demand for them on the part of undertakings, which seek to carry on the business for which they are indispensable.

In terms of the *IMS Health* case, this means asking whether the 1,860-brick structure constitutes, upstream, an indispensable factor in the downstream

26 *IMS* (n 19) *1580.*
27 See V-L Bénabou, 'Chroniques: Transversales' [2004] *Propriétés Intellectuelles* 807, 825.
28 *IMS* (n 19) 1580.

supply of German regional sales data for pharmaceutical products, coupled with the demand on the part of the competitors of IMS.[29]

The approach adopted by the Court refers back to the criteria used to determine whether or not a facility is indeed an essential facility. One could allege that it is therefore a circular reasoning. More importantly, however, this may well be a workable solution. Admittedly, copyright itself is narrowly associated with its exploitation: for example, IMS only created the brick structure in order to be able to supply the sales data, and the brick structure and the copyright in it have little, or no, value outside the sales data business. The distinction between two markets for the creation of the copyright work, and the right and the work, on the one hand, and for the exploitation of the work on the sales data market, on the other, may therefore seem artificial. But this is a peculiarity of copyright and one should resist the temptation to argue that the creation of two, somewhat artificial, markets in this way opens the door for the application of the essential facilities doctrine in a vast number of cases to the detriment of copyright.[30] It should indeed be remembered that two additional requirements must be met before the essential facilities doctrine can be applied.

It is to these two other requirements that we now turn. The first condition relates to the emergence of a new product. The Court clarified, in this respect, that in the balancing of the interest in protection of copyright and the economic freedom of its owner against the interest in protection of free competition, the latter interest can only prevail over the copyright interest if refusal to grant a licence prevents the development of the secondary market to the detriment of consumers. The applicant, therefore, needs a licence to be able to offer a new and different product, and to show consumer demand for such a product. The consumer interest point is therefore of vital importance. Copyright is indeed not granted to stop the emergence of new and different products for which there is a demand; any use of copyright to that end must amount to an abuse of a right.

The final requirement is that the refusal to license must be unjustified. This means simply that the court is to examine whether the refusal of the request for a licence is justified according to objective considerations.

In conclusion, a lot of points have been clarified in relation to the essential facilities doctrine and its application in relation to copyright (and intellectual property rights in general).[31] It is submitted that the Court's restrictive approach is to be applauded, because it does justice to the pro-competitive role of copyright (and other intellectual property rights), on the one hand, and because it allows, on the other, competition law to stop any abuse for

[29] ibid.

[30] See Bénabou (n 27) 825.

[31] For a UK application of the *Magill–IMS* case law, see *Attheraces Ltd v British Horse Racing Board Ltd* [2006] FSR 20, rev'd on appeal [2007] ECC 7.

undue purposes of copyright (or other intellectual property rights). Those cases in which copyright (or intellectual property rights in general) will be interfered with will be limited to a small number and this may well be rightly so. The Court may not have ruled out all difficulties in applying the test in practice and further difficult cases will no doubt arise, but it did at least get the balance right in theory.

Returning to the main topic of this chapter, private enforcement of competition law, the *Magill–IMS* case law demonstrates that it is possible to raise competition law successfully as a defence in intellectual property infringement cases and to successfully proceed to the private enforcement of Article 102. However, it is also clear that the balance between use and abuse is a delicate one and that that makes any of these cases complex ones, with an important burden of proof resting on the shoulders of the party that raises the competition law concerns. Hence also the important value of the disclosure rules that are contained in the Directive and that were referred to above. Taking advantage of them will require the introduction of a claim for damages in the case though, even if it is ancillary and the primary aim is the granting of a licence.

3. THE FRAND DEBATE ON INJUNCTIVE RELIEF

3.1 How Does the Issue Arise?

This issue arises in the context of standard setting. The telecommunications industry offers probably the best example, with its 3G and 4G standards, but standards exist in a wide variety of industries. Typically, standardisation bodies and the companies of the sector sit together to establish a (technical) standard to which the whole industry will adhere, allowing for worldwide, or at least regional, compatibility between the equipment of the various manufacturers. Companies have to declare the patents they own when they want to see the underlying technology included in the standard and they then have to declare their willingness to license these patents, which subsequently become standard essential patents, or SEPs, on fair, reasonable and non-discriminatory terms, or FRAND terms, to all companies that want to adopt the standard. It is important to note though that the exact terms of each licence and in particular the licence fee, form the object of individual negotiations between the licensor and each (potential) licensee.[32] Therefore, it is of course possible that the licensee objects to what is offered by the licensor and feels that what is on offer does not correspond to FRAND terms in the sense that, whilst a licence will not be bluntly refused in most cases, the

[32] P Debré and S Corbineau-Picci, 'Brevets essentiels et redevances Frand' (2014) 51 *Propriétés Intellectuelles* 126, 126–27.

terms of the licence are not non-discriminatory. This is, however, not the possibility we are concerned with here. We are concerned with the option that the potential licensee is unwilling to enter into a licence agreement and in particular with the situation where that unwillingness is expressed by a de facto dragging on indefinitely of the contractual negotiations. The potential licensor may then be tempted to sue for infringement of the patent and ask the court for injunctive relief. The question then arises whether such a move constitutes an abuse of a dominant position, which is forbidden according to Article 102.

3.2 The Starting Points

A very first requirement is the existence of a dominant position. The European Commission has consistently taken the view that the combination of an exclusive right, in the form of a patent, and the fact that as part of a standard the patent turns into a standard essential patent, gives rise to the existence of a dominant position,[33] but as Advocate General Wathelet correctly stated in his conclusion in the *Huawei* case, this does not follow automatically in all cases and will need to be established by the national judge dealing with the case or by the Commission, depending on the enforcement scenario.[34] Anyone wishing to operate the standard and make his/her own equipment compatible with it has after all no choice but to enter into a licence agreement for the patent concerned. That, rather easily, puts the rightholder and potential licensor in a position of dominance.[35]

Injunctive relief, as part of patent infringement proceedings, is on the other hand a key remedy in intellectual property law and, taken on its own, there is nothing wrong with seeking injunctive relief in a situation where the potential licensee carries out allegedly infringing activities whilst a licence is not (yet) in place.[36] The FRAND context may change that conclusion though. In particular, whilst retaining the option to seek injunctive relief, the landmark *Orange-Book-Standard* decision of the German Federal Court of Justice[37] has confirmed that in FRAND circumstances the defendant in

[33] See Case No COMP/M.6381—*Google/ Motorola Mobility*, Commission Decision of 13 February 2012, available at ec.europa.eu/competition/mergers/cases/decisions/m6381_20120213_20310_2277480_EN.pdf and Case COMP/38.636—Rambus, Commission Decision of 9 December 2009, available at ec.europa.eu/competition/antitrust/cases/dec_docs/38636/38636_1203_1.pdf.

[34] Opinion of Advocate General Wathelet in Case C-170/13 *Huawei v ZTE* EU:C:2014:2391, para 57.

[35] See also Debré and Corbineau-Picci (n 32) 126–27.

[36] J Vesala and K Havu, 'Is EU Competition Law Undermined by Injunctions against Essential Patent Infringers? National Courts and the Principle of Sincere Cooperation' (2014) 5 *Journal of European Competition Law & Practice* 6.

[37] 6 May 2009, KZR 39/06.

patent infringement proceedings for a SEP can rely on a FRAND competition law defence against a claim for injunctive relief if the claimant refuses to licence the SEP on FRAND terms. That may therefore create a situation where the dominant position that is held as a result of the ownership of the SEP is abused.[38] The key question will then of course be to determine under which circumstances there will be an abuse, leading to the conclusion that the defendant can again use competition law as a defence in this situation where competition law is enforced privately.

3.3 The Orange-Book-Standard Approach

The German Federal Court of Justice set very stringent requirements for the FRAND competition law defence to apply.[39] The defendant should first of all have made an offer to enter into a licence agreement, but that offer must be concrete, binding and unconditional. The offer must be made completely in good faith. It cannot even be subject to a condition that the courts find the patent valid and infringed.[40] The offer can merely leave the royalty rate to the reasonable discretion of the patentee/licensor, with a potential role for the court to scrutinise such a royalty rate if it is deemed to be unreasonably high. In a scenario where the defendant in the infringement case made use of the SEP before its offer was accepted, it should have acted as if its offer had been accepted if it is to rely on the FRAND defence. Hence, royalties should be paid into an escrow account to which the patentee has access and accounts should be made available. Finally, the right to reclaim royalties should have been waived. All this amounts to a very strict set of conditions, which involve almost a complete and unconditional surrender on the part of the (potential) licensee and it makes the FRAND defence a rather unattractive proposition.

3.4 The Commission's Approach

The European Commission on the other hand seems to operate a more flexible set of criteria. Its starting point is that in a SEP context in which the licensor has committed itself to license on FRAND terms, it is anticompetitive and an abuse of dominant position to exclude competitors from the market by seeking injunctive relief on the basis of the SEP or SEPs. The only condition to which this starting point is subject is that the (potential)

[38] Vesala and Havu (n 36) 6.

[39] KZR (n 37).

[40] These two points were, in contrast, the very first points considered by the English High Court of Justice before that Court was willing to turn its attention to the rate of the royalty in a FRAND licence. *Vringo Infrastructure Inc v ZTE(UK) & Another* [2013] EWHC 1591 (Pat).

licensee is willing to take a licence on FRAND terms.[41] It is obvious that this approach is utterly incompatible with the German approach and that the CJEU will eventually have to determine the correct approach.

3.5 *Huawei*

That opportunity to determine the correct approach arose rather quickly in the *Huawei* case.[42] The *Landgericht* in Dusseldorf was asked to apply a FRAND defence in this case[43] and it referred the matter to the CJEU.[44] The Court was particularly concerned about the clash between the two approaches, as under the Orange-Book-Standard approach the defendant's FRAND defence would fail, where it would succeed under the Commission's approach. And if it were to apply the Commission's approach, the Court was not clear as to how the defendant should prove his/her willingness to take a licence.

Advocate General Wathelet put his conclusion in the case to the Court on 20 November 2014.[45] In this conclusion he tries to reconcile the various points of view in a creative way. On the one hand he sees a weakened position of the patent owner due to the FRAND licence obligation. It is in his view therefore essential that the rightholder retains in principle the right to seek injunctive relief and to exercise its fundamental right to have access to a court.[46] The potential licensee on the other hand needs to use the patent to be able to compete. It can therefore, in the Advocate General's view, make a start with the use of the patent and only later on seek a licence.[47] The speed and complexity of the telecoms market re-enforce that point in this particular case. It is then up to the rightholder to alert the potential licensee to the alleged infringement (unless it is clear that the potential infringer is fully aware of the patent and of the fact that its activity is infringing) and to make an offer to take a licence.

[41] See European Commission, (2014) 8 *Competition Policy Brief*, with reference to Case AT.39985—Motorola, Commission Decision of 29 April 2014, available at ec.europa.eu/competition/antitrust/cases/dec_docs/39985/39985_928_16.pdf and Case AT.39939—Samsung, Commission Decision of 29 April 2014, available at ec.europa.eu/competition/antitrust/cases/dec_docs/39939/39939_1501_5.pdf.

[42] *Huawei v ZTE*, Landgericht Düsseldorf, 4b O 104/12, 21 March 2013, available at www.justiz.nrw.de/nrwe/lgs/duesseldorf/lg_duesseldorf/j2013/4b_O_104_12_Beschluss_20130321.html.

[43] See A Jones, 'Standard-Essential Patents: FRAND Commitments, Injunctions and the Smartphone Wars' (2014) 10 *European Competition Journal* 1.

[44] Case C-170/13 *Huawei Technologies* (pending at the time of writing, see judgment of the fifth chamber dated 16 July 2015).

[45] Opinion of Advocate General Wathelet in *Huawei v ZTE* (n 34).

[46] ibid, para 77.

[47] ibid, para 82.

That offer has to include all conditions of the proposed licence.[48] The potential licensee is not obliged to accept the proposal, but it is under an obligation to reply to it in a detailed and serious way and to make a counterproposal. Only a reply that is merely aimed at delaying matters and that is not serious would avoid the conclusion that at this stage the seeking of injunctive relief amounts to an abuse of a dominant position.[49]

If no negotiations are started or if they are not completed successfully, the potential licensee can ask the court or an arbitral tribunal to establish FRAND conditions, but the rightholder can then ask for a bank warrantee to cover the ongoing alleged infringement.[50] The potential licensee also retains the right to apply for the invalidity of the patent at a later stage or to argue later that the patent is not essential for the standard.[51] The rightholder on the other hand can seek access to the books of the potential licensee without abusing its dominant position.[52] And it can institute a claim for damages with regard to infringing activities that have already been carried out, once again without this amounting to an abuse of its dominant position.[53]

What emerges is an approach that attempts to facilitate the conclusion of a FRAND licence and that reserves the right to seek injunctive relief in those cases where the infringement is blatant, ie the alleged infringer is aware of the matter and makes no attempt to seek a licence, or where no serious attempt has been made to agree a FRAND licence.[54] The one question that remained wide open at the time of writing was whether the Court of Justice of the EU would eventually follow the approach suggested by its Advocate General. It did so on 16 July 2015 when the fifth chamber ruled that:

1. Article 102 TFEU must be interpreted as meaning that the proprietor of a patent essential to a standard established by a standardisation body, which has given an irrevocable undertaking to that body to grant a licence to third parties on fair, reasonable and non-discriminatory ('FRAND') terms, does not abuse its dominant position, within the meaning of that article, by bringing an action for infringement seeking an injunction prohibiting the infringement of its patent or seeking the recall of products for the manufacture of which that patent has been used, as long as:
   — prior to bringing that action, the proprietor has, first, alerted the alleged infringer of the infringement complained about by designating that patent

[48] ibid, paras 84–85.
[49] ibid, para 88.
[50] ibid, paras 93 and 98.
[51] ibid, paras 94 and 96.
[52] ibid, para 101.
[53] ibid, para 102.
[54] ibid, para 103. The approach relies more on the view of the Advocate General in Case C-238/87 *Volvo v Veng* [1988] ECR 6211) and Case C-53/87 *Renault v Maxicar* [1988] ECR 6039 than on *Magill* (n 11). The latter is based on a somewhat different factual scenario in his view.

and specifying the way in which it has been infringed, and, secondly, after the alleged infringer has expressed its willingness to conclude a licensing agreement on FRAND terms, presented to that infringer a specific, written offer for a licence on such terms, specifying, in particular, the royalty and the way in which it is to be calculated, and

— where the alleged infringer continues to use the patent in question, the alleged infringer has not diligently responded to that offer, in accordance with recognised commercial practices in the field and in good faith, this being a matter which must be established on the basis of objective factors and which implies, in particular, that there are no delaying tactics.

2. Article 102 TFEU must be interpreted as not prohibiting, in circumstances such as those in the main proceedings, an undertaking in a dominant position and holding a patent essential to a standard established by a standardisation body, which has given an undertaking to the standardisation body to grant licences for that patent on FRAND terms, from bringing an action for infringement against the alleged infringer of its patent and seeking the rendering of accounts in relation to past acts of use of that patent or an award of damages in respect of those acts of use.

And to conclude with a brief reference to the Directive, here again there is no prominent place for damages. One can therefore again ask whether the real value of the Directive will not be the recourse to the discovery rules. Bringing an ancillary claim for damages to get inside the scope of the Directive will be even more difficult in these cases.

3.6 A Brief Caveat

We have taken it for granted above that an SEP necessarily, or at least in the majority of cases, leads to a dominant position. One may of course encounter a difficult situation where the owner of a patent (aggressively) tries to licence that patent under FRAND conditions, even in circumstances where the proposed activity of the (potential) licensee does not fall within the scope of the patent. We are then in the presence of a standard, but it is not essential or an essential facility for the (potential) licensee. The conduct is clearly abusive, but the question needs to be asked whether one is here in the presence of a dominant position. Is it the SEP standard of the patent that objectively gives rise to a dominant position or could one argue that there is no position of dominance because the (potential) licensee has an alternative to taking the licence? With the proposed activity not covered by the licence, the (potential) licensee is not bound to accept the FRAND licence and has another way out. In other words, does the position of the (potential) licensee have an impact on the determination of the dominant position? Maybe a better way of looking at it is to argue that in these circumstances the market is defined in a wider way and that in that wider market the owner of the SEP does not hold a dominant position.

4. CONCLUSION

This chapter set out to demonstrate that private enforcement of competition law works in the area of intellectual property. This is clearly the case, but it operates in a rather different way than the one that the Directive has in mind. Even though the discovery provisions of the Directive might be useful and improve the situation, the focus on damages will mean that the Directive will be of limited use to the private enforcement cases in the area of intellectual property.

Part III

Transparency, Leniency Programmes, and Human Rights

8

Transparency and Liability in Leniency Programmes: A Question of Balancing?

XAVIER GROUSSOT* AND JUSTIN PIERCE**

1. INTRODUCTION

THE LENIENCY PROGRAMME is a programme developed by the Commission, through its Notice on Immunity from fines and reduction of fines in cartel cases.[1] Though the leniency programme has no legislative force and is not binding on Member States, it serves the objective of being an effective application of Articles 101 and 102 TFEU and thus can be viewed as a useful tool to uncover and bring infringements of competition rules to an end. In that sense, it forms part of the public enforcement of competition law. Another tool for ensuring the effective application of competition rules is through the use of private liability claims, the so-called private enforcement of competition law. The aim of this chapter is to clarify the relationship between private enforcement actions and the leniency programme, viewed through the rules on the protection or disclosure of information from one process to another. The question of whether the lack of transparency in the disclosure rules and the manner in which information access is granted to private litigants contained in EU leniency applications may potentially undermine the leniency programme. The case law of the ECJ on balancing the obligation of transparency with the need to protect the leniency applicant will be carefully scrutinised. This situation of weighing occurs when claimants in 'follow-on' actions in damages seek access to the files of the national competition authorities or the Commission. As a preliminary point, it is also important to keep in mind that

* Professor Lund University.
** Doctoral Candidate Lund University.

[1] Commission Notice on the non-imposition or reduction of fines in cartel cases ('1996 Notice') [1996] OJ C207/4.

leniency applications hardly ever mention the causation or the extent of the price increase resulting from the cartel. Therefore, a national court or the ECJ may in practice have to balance the ease of disclosing the application against the time and cost of proving the same facts by other means.[2] This chapter will explore, first, the rationalisation for and the roots of the current EU leniency framework. The potentiality for a decrease in the applications for leniency given the lack of clarity of sharing information and the rules surrounding confidential material that has been disclosed in liability claims are discussed in Section two. Secondly, the chapter raises the question whether the case law of the Union courts is eroding the effectiveness of the leniency programme through judicial balancing that is less than clear on the applicability of disclosure obligations and in some way runs counter to the principle of transparency (Section three). Finally, the last part of this chapter assesses the impact of the new Damages Directive on the issue of balancing. What is left of the case law on balancing after the adoption of the Directive governing actions for damages under national law for infringements of European and national competition law?

2. THE UNCERTAINTY OF LENIENCY AND LIABILITY

At the EU level, considerable responsibility for market regulation falls under the watchful eye of the European Commission, DG Comp. Within their array of duties, the regulation and stabilisation of the EU market is a central function. Most competition lawyers and regulators would agree with the contention that one of the more directly harmful practices resulting from market freedom is the formation and operation of cartels. Cartels have been described as 'cancers on the open market economy', and as such, the Commission has prioritised the rooting out, investigating and punishing of cartelists.[3] Over the years, the Commission has begun to use more sophisticated and enhanced market surveillance techniques to identify and quash this type of anti-competitive behaviour and it has been a priority of

[2] See J Temple Lang, 'The Duty of Cooperation of National Courts in EU Competition Law' (2014) 17 *Irish Journal of European Law* 27, 32–34. According to the author, '[e]ssentially, these factors concern whether the same information is available to the claimant from other sources, and the relevance of the leniency material to the issues before the national court. If many documents that existed before leniency was sought are anyway being disclosed, the leniency application is less necessary. If the leniency application (or a similar application to another competition authority) had been disclosed elsewhere, there would be little point in withholding it.'

[3] See speech by M Monti, 'Fighting Cartels Why and How? Why Should We Be Concerned with Cartels and Collusive Behaviour?' 3rd Nordic Competition Policy Conference, Stockholm, 11–12 September 2000, available at europa.eu/rapid/press-release_SPEECH-00-295_en.htm (last accessed 27 October 2014).

the past/previous Commissions.[4] However, as with most illegal activities the more refined the policing becomes, the greater the sophistication of the mechanisms of those wishing to avoid detection becomes. As such cartels are not only difficult to detect, sometimes due to their international flavour, but they are epitomised by complex, costly and lengthy investigations.[5] Of course, the easiest way for an enforcement authority to prove their case is to allow the perpetrator to 'confess' and supply the evidence to support their statement.

The US has taken this position for a long time, viewing its Antitrust Division's Leniency Program as their 'most important investigative tool for detecting cartel activity'.[6] Spurred on by the success enjoyed by their American counterparts, many national jurisdictions within the EU have implemented a leniency programme.[7] This type of programme offer companies an incentive to 'blow the whistle' on cartels, making cartel participation riskier and creating a 'race to confess' in order to obtain full immunity.[8] DG Comp decided to introduce a leniency programme and in 1996, the first of the EU leniency documents came into force.[9] As always with systems that are tainted with rewarding bad behaviour, an inherent danger lurks in the shadows. If the reward outweighs or at least is heavily mitigated, the deterrent effect of punishment is diminished. Put another way, if a leniency programme operates too effectively, companies can simply enter into anti-competitive agreements and the remaining danger will be an internal one, insofar as who is granted leniency first. It is at least arguable that there needs to be a certain degree of uncertainty and subjectivity in favour of the decision maker to operate this type of programme without detracting from the danger of punishment.

This lack of transparency and certainty needs to be balanced. The Commission's first attempt in 1996 was on the receiving end of some severe criticism.[10] Much of it surrounded the perceived lack of transparency and

[4] The modernisation and sophistication is often credited to the Kroes Commission having cartel busting as its priority, for life after Kroes see, A Riley, 'The Modernisation of EU Anti-Cartel Enforcement: Will the Commission Grasp the Opportunity?' CEPS Special Report (7 January 2010).

[5] For an empirical analysis see K Hüschelrath, 'Determinants of the Duration of European Appellate Court Proceedings in Cartel Cases', available at ftp.zew.de/pub/zew-docs/dp/dp14062.pdf.

[6] For further information on the US leniency program see www.justice.gov/atr/public/criminal/leniency.html (last accessed 27 October 2014).

[7] L Ortiz Blanco (ed), *EU Competition Procedure*, 3rd edn (Oxford, Oxford University Press, 2013). See Ch 6 generally and p 250 specifically.

[8] Some have questioned this as an effective enforcement mechanism: A Stephan, 'An Empirical Assessment of the European Leniency Notice' (2009) 5 *Journal of Competition Law and Economics* 537.

[9] Commission Notice on the non-imposition or reduction of fines in cartel cases ('1996 Notice') [1996] OJ C207/4.

[10] See, for example, N Levy and R O'Donoghue, 'The EU Leniency Programme Comes of Age' (2004) 27 *World Competition: Law & Economics Review* 75.

certainty inherent in the programme, one of the principle criticisms being the uncertainty of what level of information was required to meet the hurdle of leniency. The Commission required applicants, who wished to have the full effect of leniency, to provide 'decisive evidence',[11] coupled with the fact that companies were forced to wait until the end of the investigations in order to know whether and to what extent leniency had been granted.[12] Whilst a certain level of discretion for the Commission has to be accepted, an overly burdensome system has the opposite result of pro-market protection, which lies at the heart of good regulation.

This type of uncertainty and wide discretion has potentially greater negative market effects. It is true to say that this type of criticism of a lack of certainty and transparency was not only restricted to leniency applications. You only have to go a stone's throw back in the competition history books to see this very criticism being made of the previously reformed application of what is now Article 101 Treaty of the Functioning of the European Union (TFEU). The negative clearance system in place from 1962 meant that undertakings had great difficulty in making a self-analysis of whether a certain course of action would bring them into the scope of Article 101(1), essentially by applying to the Commission for an evaluation of the satisfaction of Article 101(3) the Commission had a wide discretion to give a broad and overly purposive interpretation of the type of behaviour captured by Article 101(1). The varying degrees of application by the Commission lacked any certainty or transparency of the underlying rationale for an agreement to be captured by the provision. As Jones points out, this led to a system whereby agreements were treated in a categorical way leading to different sets of rules for agreements producing similar economic effects.[13] Such uncertainty in the market is not conducive to stability or growth.

Moreover, the applicable legal rules are capable of having considerable influence on market activities and outcomes.[14] The application of the rules, the consequences of their application, ie restriction of business practices or the imposition of fines or other remedial decisions, sends signals to the market causing adjustments in market processes and behaviour. Given the far-reaching effects of Commission practice and decisions, it is fundamental

[11] See B (b) of the 1996 Notice that states 'is the first to adduce decisive evidence of the cartel's existence'.

[12] See ibid E (2) that states: 'Only on its adoption of a decision will the Commission determine whether or not the conditions set out in Sections B, C and D are met, and thus whether or not to grant any reduction in the fine, or even waive its imposition altogether. It would not be appropriate to grant such a reduction or waiver before the end of the administrative procedure, as those conditions apply throughout such period.'

[13] A Jones, 'Left Behind by Modernisation? Restrictions by Object under Article 101(1)' (2010) 649 *European Competition Journal* 649.

[14] Although related to emissions trading see, S Bogojević, *Emissions Trading Schemes: Markets, States and Law* (Oxford, Hart Publishing, 2013).

to the stability of the market that the legal rules, remedies, practices and enforcement priorities are applied efficiently, with certainty and transparency. Certainly, since the 2004 modernisation project, there has been an increase in the amount of information released by DG Comp to the market.[15] The leniency programme has at the same time undergone a modernisation and updating process. In 2002, the Commission responded to the criticisms and uncertainties inherent in both the wording and the practice of the 1996 Notice and introduced a revised 2002 Notice.[16] Under the revisions, the Notice brought greater clarity to the correlation between information and leniency and the assessment thereof.[17] Moreover, the 2002 Notice actively addressed the manner of evidence. The Notice, which sets out the conditions under which an undertaking—on account of its cooperation with the Commission—may be granted an exemption from fines or a reduction of the fines imposed, is governed by an overriding objective to ensure that such exemptions or reductions were granted in conditions of increased transparency and certainty.[18] Nonetheless, the 2002 Notice did not clarify or remedy all the points of issue that companies had with the leniency programme. In *Masco Corp*, a challenge was brought on the basis of a lack of clarity on how the Commission had arrived at a final decision having given an indication that leniency would be granted, albeit in varying degrees.[19] Despite the dashing of expectations, the Court expressed that there was necessarily a wide margin of appreciation on which the Commission could and should rely. This in itself is a non-contentious and necessary support for the Commission from the courts. As already stated, it is vital that a balance is struck between leniency, transparency and certainty.

Whilst there are mechanisms in place to obtain an indication from the Commission, such as the hypothetical conversations and ability to give oral evidence, it is important not to lose sight of the underlying rationale for the

[15] In 1996, the European Commission embarked on a long and ambitious journey to reform the interpretation and application of the EU competition law rules. It commenced with the review and overhauling of the working of Art 101 TFEU, before moving on to review the functioning of the EU Merger Regulation (Council Regulation (EC) No 139/2004 on the control of concentrations between undertakings, Official Journal L 24, [2004] p 1–22) and its approach to abusive exclusionary conduct by dominant undertakings under Art 102 TFEU. The core objectives of each set of reforms was to ensure that there was a shift from rules based on form to the utilisation of rules focused on the economic effects of the conduct at issue and to reinforce the Commission's growing view that the central goal of the EU competition rules should be the protection of competition on the market as a means of enhancing consumer welfare.

[16] Commission notice on immunity from fines and reduction of fines in cartel cases Official Journal C 45, 1 [2002] p 3–5.

[17] See, for example, A Kayhko 'European Commission's 2006 Leniency Notice—for Better or for Worse' (2008) 2 *Competition Law International* 4; and DJ Arp and CRA Swaak, 'A Tempting Offer: Immunity from Fines for Cartel Conduct under the European Commission's New Leniency Notice' (2003) *European Competition Law Review* 9.

[18] Case C-510/11 *Kone Oyj and Others v European Commission* EU:C:2013:696, para 83.

[19] Case T-378/10 *Masco Corp and Others v European Commission* EU:T:2013:469.

leniency programme. As the Court stated in *Schindler*, the information disclosed by the Commission both in its practice of setting fine levels and the granting of leniency is sufficient for a prudent trader, by taking legal advice if need be, to foresee in a sufficiently precise manner the likely outcome.[20] Despite there being judicial support through a considerable margin of appreciation, the Commission has made further changes, again this can be said to be driven by the need to furnish companies with some clarity and certainty.

The 2006 Leniency Notice introduced a mechanism through which Leniency Notice applicants are able to establish their status as the first 'whistle-blower', it also clarifies the protection given to corporate statements made by companies in their application for leniency from being made available to claimants in civil damages proceedings to some extent, as discussed below. The progression of revisions to the Notices has to a large extent been driven by refinement, experience and answers to the calls for more transparency and certainty. This underlying focus of the Commission on establishing a strong leniency programme comes, potentially, at a high cost. Namely, that an over protection of information received under the leniency programme can potentially cause further uncertainty in the realm of private damages. The remainder of this chapter looks at the case law of the Union courts in this respect and the potential impact it has on the operation of the private damages.

3. ACCESS TO LENIENCY DOCUMENTS AND THE WEIGHING OF INTERESTS

One of the more pressing issues in relation to the success of the leniency programme is the control of access to the information disclosed. This is an especially thorny issue insofar as it intersects the interests of at least three parties. On the one hand, there is the leniency participant, which for reputation and commercial stability requires that the information provided to support its position be kept confidential as far as permitted. The second is the Commission itself; for if it is viewed by the market as having insufficient authority to adequately ensure a certain level of confidentiality regarding the information provided, its credibility is shot and with it falls the effectiveness of the leniency programme. Finally, there are the interests of private litigants who may have suffered a loss resulting from cartel behaviour. It is a priori that Article 101 TFEU is directly effective, in other words, it bestows rights on individuals especially where they are adversely affected

[20] Case C-501/11 *Schindler Holding Ltd and Others v European Commission* EU:C:2013:522. See also Case C-266/06 P *Evonik Degussa v Commission and Council* EU:C:2008:295, paras 50–55, in the context of the certainty of fines.

by a breach of the Article. These individuals have a particular interest in accessing the information, in order to substantiate a claim.

As Ortiz Blanco points out, these claims for access will usually involve one or more of three predominant categories of information held by the Commission. The first is the leniency or immunity statement itself or a transcript thereof. Second, pre-existing supporting documents submitted voluntarily by the applicant together with their leniency/immunity application. Thirdly, pre-existing documents investigated by the Commission in an inspection or pursuant to an information request on the basis of the knowledge obtained through the leniency application.[21] To date, the Commission has been reluctant in this regard and has strongly resisted applications for access to any of these categories of information.[22] However, the position taken by the Commission can hardly be described as resting on solid ground, as will be discussed below.[23] Following the draft Directive on private damages and the progressive line of case law encouraging and facilitating the right of injured parties to pursue a claim for damages, the question of access to leniency-related documents is likely to be subjected to further tests in the future.

In this discussion of access to documentation and information, a point of consideration is the administrative system of enforcement within the EU. The principle requiring that EU institutions, including the Commission, make decisions in a transparent way has a role to play in the discussion as a result of the presentation of one the principle routes for a potential challenge. Whilst this is not the space to be filled by a definitive discussion over the role and scope of the transparency principle, if such a thing exists, it is necessary to understand the interplay between transparency and competition law enforcement of the Commission. As a starting point, the popular definition of transparency rests with the opinion of Advocate General Colomer, according to which, transparency is concerned with being clear, obvious and understandable without doubt or ambiguity.[24] Outside this all-encompassing definition, the precise meaning of transparency depends on the context in which it is used and the function that it is expected to fulfil.

[21] Ortiz Blanco (n 7) para 6.54.

[22] See, as an example, the inclusion of oral evidence in leniency applications and restrictions on disclosure of the transcribed contents thereof even after disclosure under the access to file rules: 2006 Notice [2006] OJ C298/19, para 33. One of the difficulties associated with the Commission's desire to protect leniency information is the applicability of Regulation (EC) No 1049/2001 of the European Parliament and of the Council of 30 May 2001 regarding public access to European Parliament, Council and Commission documents [2001] OJ L 145 on transparency and access to documents to the Commission and the extent to which this impacts on the Commission's desire not to disclose information, see A Caruso, 'Leniency Programmes and Protection of Confidentiality: The Experience of the European Commission' (2010) 1 *Journal of European Competition Law & Practice* 453.

[23] See as an example Case T-437/08 *CDC Hydrogene Peroxide v Commission* EU:T:2011:752, para 49.

[24] Opinion of AG R-J Colomer in C-110/03 *Belgium v Commission* [2005] ECR I-2801, para 44.

Furthermore, the application of the principle is contoured by the legitimate aim that is pursued by the decision maker.[25] In particular, transparency applies only insofar as respecting it does not cause the fettering of the discretion of a decision maker pursuing a Union objective. The greater landscape, in which transparency functions, relates to the legitimacy of the Union institutions and actions. For some, transparency is a multifaceted principle that serves a number of functions depending on the context of its application.[26] The Union has sought to clarify this in respect of the rights of individuals to information and documentation of institutional decision makers. The enactment of Regulation No 1049/2001 is an example, although transparency and access to documents stemming from the Commission exercising its administrative duties in competition matters through this legislation is restricted.

Recently, in *EnBW Energie*, the Court found that the exceptions to the right of access to documents set out, in particular, in Article 4 of Regulation 1049/2001, where the documents covered by the request for disclosure fall within a particular area of EU law, cannot, in the present case, which is proceeding under Article 81 EC (new Article 101 TFEU), be interpreted without taking account of the specific rules governing access to those documents, which are laid down in this instance by Regulations 1/2003 and 773/2004.[27] Those two regulations pursue different objectives from those of Regulation 1049/2001, since they are designed to ensure that the rights of defence of the parties concerned are respected and that complaints are dealt with diligently, while at the same time ensuring compliance with the duty of professional secrecy in proceedings under Article 81 EC (new Article 101 TFEU), and not to facilitate as far as possible the exercise of the right of access to documents or to promote good administrative practice by guaranteeing the greatest possible transparency in the decision-making process of public authorities and the information on which they base their decisions.[28]

It is apparent that as a starting point under this Regulation there is a right to access to documents, by any natural or legal person residing or having its registered office in a Member State. The question that this raises is whether this right is taken to include those submitted under the Leniency Notice.

[25] See S Prechal and ME De Leeuw, 'Transparency: A General Principle of EU Law?' in U Bernitz, J Nergelius and C Cardner (eds), *General Principles of EC Law in a Process of Development* (London, Kluwer Law International, 2008).

[26] A Buijze 'The Six Faces of Transparency' (2013) 9 *Utrecht Law Review* 3.

[27] Council Regulation (EC) No 1/2003 of 16 December 2002 on the implementation of the rules on competition laid down in Articles 81 and 82 of the Treaty Official Journal L 1, [2003] p 1–25. Council Regulation (EC) No 139/2004 on the control of concentrations between undertakings, Official Journal L 24, [2004] p 1–22.

[28] Discussion on the distinction between investigations and decisions is acknowledged but due to space constraints the point is not elaborated on: see Case C-404/10 *Commission v Éditions Odile Jacob* EU:C:2012:393, para 109 and Case C-477/10 *Commission v Agrofert Holding* EU:C:2012:394, para 51.

According to the Commission, the answer to this is clearly in the negative, the Commission relies on the interpretation of Article 4(2) and (3) of the Regulation that permits the refusal to grant access to a document where disclosure would undermine the protection of (a) the commercial interests of a natural or legal person, including intellectual property;[29] (b) court proceedings and legal advice; and (c) for the purpose of inspections, investigations, and audits. Moreover, Article 4(3) limits the obligation placed on the Commission on the grounds that disclosure would seriously undermine the decision-making processes.[30] However, the Union courts have been more reluctant to this strict approach of the Commission. Some of this scepticism is surely based on the competing interests at stake, discussed above.

In *CDC Hydrogene Peroxide*, the Court responded to the Commission's arguments by refusing to accept the Commission's interpretation finding that the absoluteness of the Commission's interpretation with the application of Regulation 1049/2001 without any limit in time, would be tantamount to the exclusion of any document in a competition case merely by reference to a possible future adverse impact on its leniency programme.[31] Moreover, the Court was critical of what it considered an illustration of the broad application of Commission policy not to release information even where such information related to a document which was not itself submitted by an applicant for leniency and contained no information likely in itself to damage the interests of the companies which applied for leniency. The Court finding that such a broad interpretation of the concept of investigation activities is incompatible with the principle that, by reason of the purpose of Regulation 1049/2001, set out in Recital 4, namely, 'to give the fullest possible effect to the right of public access to documents', the exceptions laid down in Article 4 of that Regulation must be interpreted and applied strictly.[32]

What we see here is that the balance of the transparency requirement, insofar as the right to access of documentation goes, requires that the Commission clearly justifies why access should not be given. However, the situation becomes clearer and directed more in favour of the Commission's

[29] The Court has specified that it is not possible to regard all information concerning a company and its business relations as requiring the protection which must be guaranteed to commercial interests under the first indent of Art 4(2) of Reg 1049/2001 if application of the general principle of giving the public the widest possible access to documents held by the institutions is not to be frustrated, see further Case T-380/04 *Terezakis v Commission* EU:T:2008:19, para 93.

[30] Interpreted restrictively [The Commission considers that the interdependence of, on the one hand, the protection of the commercial interests of the undertakings in question and, on the other hand, of the public interest in preventing anti-competitive practices justifies the fact that it relied on the protection of the commercial interests of undertakings in the context of the assessment under the third indent of Article 4(2) of Reg 1049/2001].

[31] *Hydrogene Peroxide* (n 23) paras 60–62.

[32] ibid, para 63.

stance when the provisions of the competition and merger regulations are brought into the mix. Regulations 1/2003 and 773/2004 deal directly in a restrictive way with the right of access to documents in the file relating to a proceeding under Article 101 TFEU. There is a clear intention from the legislature to place restrictive conditions on access and not to provide a right of access to a file for third parties other than complainants.[33] Moreover, it seems that the same rules are equally applicable to certain documents provided to the Commission voluntarily with a view to obtaining immunity or a reduction in the amount of the fines imposed.

In *EnBW*, the Court, on appeal from the General Court, found that it is common that the disclosure of such documents (leniency), regardless of whether they have been provided to that institution on a voluntary basis or under compulsion, are in any event strictly governed by Regulations 1/2003 and 773/2004.[34] In contrast to the absoluteness of the Commission's interpretation, the approach of the ECJ in *EnBW* is marked by a strong rhetoric of balancing the competing interest in the context of claimants seeking to obtain leniency documents by making requests to the Commission under Regulation No 1049/2001.[35] In order to ensure the effective protection of the right to compensation enjoyed by a claimant, there is no need for every document to be disclosed to that claimant on the ground that that party is intending to bring an action for damages, as it is highly unlikely that the action for damages will need to be based on all the evidence in the file relating to that proceeding.[36] Any person seeking compensation for the loss caused by a breach of Article 101 TFEU must establish that it is necessary for that person to be granted access to documents in the Commission's file, in order to enable the latter to *weigh up*, on a case-by-case basis, the respective interests in favour of the disclosure and the protection of those documents, taking into account all the relevant factors in the case.[37]

Moreover, in *EnBW*, the ECJ arguably took a narrow view regarding the situations in which enabling private actions should be prioritised over protecting the integrity of the leniency programme. In that sense, where there are countervailing interests against disclosure, the test is one of necessity of access. In the absence of any such necessity, the interest in obtaining compensation for the loss suffered as a result of a breach of Article 101 TFEU cannot constitute an overriding public interest, within the meaning of Article 4(2) of the Transparency Regulation.

[33] See *Éditions Odile Jacob* (n 28) para 118 and *Agrofert* (n 28) para 59.

[34] Case C-365/12 P *European Commission v EnBW Energie Baden-Württemberg AG* EU:C:2014:112, para 93.

[35] This approach is founded on Case C-536/11 *Donau Chemie and Others* [2013] EU:C:2013:366, paras 30–33.

[36] *EnBW Energie* (n 34) para 107.

[37] ibid, para 108.

However, even taking these supporting provisions into account a number of uncertainties still exist that have to be taken into consideration. For example, whether statements or information given voluntarily fall under the competition regulations and whether the protection of a category of information from disclosure is a possibility. It seems that it is likely given the application of Regulation 773/2004. Although whether and to what extent this is possible under Regulation 1/2003 is unclear at best. It is evident that a tension exists between the Union courts and the Commission when it comes to the disclosure of materials under the leniency programme.

A common stance through the case law surrounding these issues is the Commission and the court finding themselves at loggerheads. The Commission sees leniency as an important tool at its disposal to dismantle cartels, whilst it views private enforcement as a form of compensation for injury suffered. The courts, on the other hand, seem to adopt the view that the granting of rights to a person entitled to claim compensation for the loss caused to him/her by a breach of Article 101 strengthens the working of the EU competition rules, thereby making a significant contribution to the maintenance of effective competition in the European Union.[38] As such there is a clear balance to be reached to ensure that the protection of the leniency information does not overstretch so as to diminish the additional avenue of enforcement for private actions. In *Donau Chemie,* the Court states that in order to ensure the effective protection of the right to compensation enjoyed by a claimant, there is no need for every document to be disclosed to that claimant on the ground that that party is intending to bring an action for damages, as it is highly unlikely that the action for damages will need to be based on all the evidence in the file relating to that proceeding.[39] This indicates the clear balancing that the courts are undertaking to ensure that the floodgates are not opened or that they are narrowed to the point of locking out private enforcement. The newfound impetus and focus on private enforcement poses additional questions, namely how far should the courts go in order to achieve this balance. This is especially pertinent given the proposed new directive in this area and the role of the national courts.

The new Directive on damages actions[40] is the result of the cryptic case law of the ECJ as to the relationship between the leniency programme and private liability in competition cases and the difficult role given to national courts in balancing the many interests at issue in claims related to access

38 See Case C-453/99 *Courage and Crehan* [2001] ECR I-6297, paras 26–27; Joined Cases C-295/04 to C-298/04 *Manfredi and Others* [2006] ECR I-6619, para 91; Case C-360/09 *Pfleiderer* [2011] ECR I-5161, para 28; and *Donau Chemie* (n 35) para 23.

39 *Donau Chemie* (n 35).

40 Directive 2014/104/EU of the European Parliament and of the Council of 26 November 2014 on certain rules governing actions for damages under national law for infringements of the competition law provisions of the Member States and of the European Union [2014] OJ L349/1.

to evidence.[41] As a preliminary point, it is worth remarking that both the leniency programmes and claims for damages serve the objective of the effective application of competition law. It is, therefore, impossible to maximise its full effectiveness when a balancing has to be realised between the interests of the various participants involved in infringements of Article 101 TFEU and facing the consequences.

The *Pfleiderer* case offers a prime example of the uncertainty created for the national courts to deal with disputes concerning access to leniency documents in the files of the competition authorities.[42] In *Pfleiderer*, the German competition authority had fined different wallpaper manufacturers for having infringed Article 101 TFEU. An industrial purchaser of such paper, Pfleiderer claimed to have sustained serious harm resulting from the cartel and requested full access to the file of the national competition authority. The latter refused to grant access and the refusal was challenged before the national court, which made a reference to the ECJ. At issue in this case was the balancing between, on the one hand, the interests of a leniency applicant not to disclose its evidence before the competition authorities and, on the other, the interests of other private parties to claim damages that may strongly depend on such evidence. Before weighing the different interests at stake, the ECJ give us interesting guidelines as to the nature of the leniency programmes in the context of EU law and the scope of the right of access to documents. As emphasised by the ECJ, the leniency programmes are useful tools if efforts to uncover and bring infringements of competition rules to an end are to be effective. They thus serve the objective of the effective application of Article 101 TFEU. Nevertheless, the effectiveness of the programmes could be undermined if documents relating to a leniency procedure were disclosed to persons wishing to bring an action for damages, even if the national competition authorities were to grant the application for leniency, exemption in whole or in part from the fine, which they might have imposed. In the absence of binding regulations under European Union law on the subject, it is for Member States to establish and apply national rules on the right of access, by persons adversely affected by a cartel, to documents relating to leniency procedures subject of course to the procedural requirements of equivalence and effectiveness.[43]

[41] P Lowe and M Marquis (eds), *Integrating Public and Private Enforcement of Competition Law—Implications for Courts and Agencies* (Oxford, Hart Publishing, 2014) 13–81. According to them (p 64) '[t]he uncertainty resulting from *Pfleiderer* might have played a role in prompting the European Commission to finally, after a long period of deliberation introduce a legislative proposal for a directive on private damages actions for infringements of national and EU competition rules'.

[42] *Pfleiderer* (n 38) paras 23–26.

[43] In particular, the Member States may not render the implementation of EU law impossible or excessively difficult (see, to that effect, Case C-298/96 *Oelmühle and Schmidt Söhne* [1998] ECR I-4767, paras 23–24 and the case law cited) and, specifically, in the area of competition law, they must ensure that the rules which they establish or apply do not jeopardise the effective application of Arts 101 and 102 TFEU (see, to that effect, Case C-439/08 *VEBIC* [2010] ECR I-12471, para 57).

As to the specific issue of weighing, the Court puts the burden of balancing between public (leniency programmes) and private (damages) enforcement on the national courts. The ECJ is really careful here in assessing the competing interests at the same 'hierarchical' level of importance. In that sense, it is stated that the existence of the right to damages strengthens the working of the EU competition rules by discouraging agreements or practices, frequently covert, which are liable to restrict or distort competition. From that point of view, actions for damages before national courts can make a significant contribution to the maintenance of effective competition in the EU.[44] This position differs from the Opinion of Advocate General Mazák, who highlighted the restricted practical importance of private damages actions in the cartel area, to the extent of questioning whether the term 'private enforcement' is even proper.[45] For the ECJ, EU law does not preclude a person, who has been adversely affected by an infringement of EU competition law and who is seeking to obtain damages, from being granted access to documents relating to a leniency procedure involving the perpetrator of that infringement. It is 'for the courts of the Member States, on the basis for their national law, to determine the conditions under which such access must be permitted or refused by weighing the interests protected by European Union law'.[46]

4. BALANCING AND THE DAMAGES DIRECTIVE

June 2013 marked the date on which the Commission adopted a proposal for a Directive on certain rules governing actions for damages under national law for infringements of European and national competition law.[47] With this proposal, the Commission is clearly driving an agenda in attempting to carve out leniency materials from undue disclosure requests.[48] The Commission makes the case strongly by including in the Directive a statement, stating that leniency programmes and settlement procedures are important tools for the public enforcement of Union competition law as they contribute to the detection, the efficient prosecution and the imposition of penalties for the most serious competition law infringements. Therefore, undue disclosure of self-incriminating statements such as leniency statements and settlement

[44] *Pfleiderer* (n 38) para 29.

[45] ibid, para 40 of the Opinion.

[46] ibid, para 32.

[47] COM(2013) 404 final. See A Schwab, 'Finding the Right Balance—the Deliberations of the European Parliament on the Draft Legislation Regarding Damage Claims' (2014) 5 *Journal of European Competition Law & Practice* 65.

[48] Rec 22 states: 'This Directive does not affect the right of the court to consider under national or Union law the interest of effective public enforcement of competition law when ordering disclosure of any type of evidence with the exception of leniency statements and settlement submissions.'

submissions, which are solely produced for the purpose of such cooperation, may deter undertakings from cooperating, especially if disclosure poses a risk of exposing cooperating undertakings or their managing staff to civil or criminal liability under worse conditions than the co-infringers that do not cooperate with competition authorities. The solution to which, according to the Directive, is that leniency statements or settlement submission and such documents should be exempt from the disclosure of evidence. The Commission elaborates on this further by stating that the exception from disclosure should also apply to literal quotations of a leniency statement or a settlement submission in other documents.[49]

However, on the same point, the Commission considers that in order to ensure that this complete exception from disclosure does not unduly interfere with the injured parties' right to compensation, it should be limited to these voluntary and self-incriminating leniency statements and settlement submissions. It is difficult to see how these two objectives can be aligned in this way. In one breath the Commission is calling for an almost blanket protection of the leniency programmes and permitting disclosure so as to ensure private enforcement is not compromised. Moreover, on a reading of Article 6 of the Directive there is a clear attempt by the Commission to restrict the jurisdiction of national courts to call for or allow for the disclosure of leniency documentation or settlements. Without a shadow of a doubt the inclusion of this type of restraint on disclosure runs contrary to the current judicial opinion reflected in the case law of the Union courts. Article 6 states:

> Member States shall ensure that, for the purpose of actions for damages, national courts cannot at any time order a party or a third party to disclose any of the following categories of evidence: (a) leniency statements; and (b) settlement submissions.

With a further restriction in Article 7 that states:

> A claimant may present a justified request that a national court access the documents contained in the above paragraph for the sole purpose of ensuring that their contents fulfil the definitions given in Article 4(1)(16) and 4(1)(18). In that assessment, national courts may request assistance from the competent competition authority. The authors of the concerned documents may also have the possibility to be heard. In any case, the Court shall not provide access to those documents to the other parties or third parties.

It is true to say that there has not been complete clarification from the courts as to the scope and the conditions for access to files and to the leniency documents. As discussed above, the balancing of non-disclosure whilst ensuring the effectiveness of private enforcement is something that the courts have as yet not definitively explained. We can, however, by looking at recent

[49] See rec 24.

opinion and cases, see that there is a judicial trend towards ensuring that the individual right to damages is not rendered ineffective as a result of non-access. A recent opinion of AG Kokott suggests that the appropriate manner in dealing with the issue is to require that any person seeking compensation for the loss caused by a breach of Article 101 must establish that it is necessary for that person to be granted access to documents.[50]

This approach suggests a balancing or a weighing up. In the context of her opinion, AG Kokott is advocating this as a way to ensure that the Commission simply adopts a blanket policy of non-disclosure. That the Commission, in order to fulfil its obligations as an institution, where there is a 'necessity' should weigh up, on a case-by-case basis, the respective interests in favour of disclosure of such documents and in favour of the protection of those documents, taking into account all the relevant factors in the case.[51] This is, at least on first blush, a practical way in which to approach the question. Clearly, a rule that renders access to any document as absolute is likely to result in making it, if not impossible, then certainly excessively difficult to be successful in an action for private damages.

This raises the question as to the legal traditions and national rules within the Member States and the effect that these will have on cases brought at a national level against cartel members who have participated at a Union level but may have been subject to national leniency programmes or where the national competition authority has acted through the European Competition Network. The disparities in national procedural and substantive rules of evidence and the role of the national courts in particular types of procedures may be cause for concern. After all, when only access to the documents relating to the proceedings enables those parties to obtain the evidence needed to establish their claim for damages and there is no other way of obtaining that evidence, a refusal to grant them access to the file renders the right to compensation, which they derive directly from EU law, useless.

Equally, a restrictive approach by the national courts will lead to a reluctance of injured parties to risk the time and cost of enforcing their rights. A point that remains largely unexamined in the discussion and how this is squared with the obligations of the Member States under Article 19 TFEU remains a question in flux. However, the Grand Chamber in *Pfleiderer* had an opportunity to address the role of the national courts and the scope of the protection of leniency materials. The Court begins by reiterating that the competition authorities' courts of Member States are required to apply

[50] Case C-557/12 *Kone AG and Others v ÖBB-Infrastruktur AG* EU:C:2014:1317. See N Dunne, 'It Never Rains but it Pours? Liability for "Umbrella Effects" under EU Competition Law in *Kone* Case C-557/12, *Kone AG and Others* vs. *ÖBB-Infrastruktur AG*, Judgment of the Court of Justice (Fifth Chamber) of 5 June 2014, NYR' (2014) 51 *Common Market Law Review* 1813, 1828.

[51] See, by analogy, Case C-28/08 P *Commission v Bavarian Lager* EU:C:2010:378, paras 77–78 and *Donau Chemie* (n 35) paras 30 and 34.

Articles 101 TFEU and 102 TFEU, where the facts come within the scope of European Union law, and to ensure that those Articles are applied effectively in the general interest.[52] Following which it establishes that no common applicable rules apply to leniency or in fact to the access to documents related to leniency programmes, which have been voluntarily submitted, especially when these documents have been made available to the national competition authority.[53] In essence, the Court takes the point of view that the lack of harmonisation in the area means that Member States are free to establish and apply national rules on the right of access, by persons adversely affected by a cartel, to documents relating to leniency procedures. Although the Court adds a catch by stating that national courts must nonetheless exercise that competence in accordance with EU law. Specifically, they must ensure that the rules, which they establish or apply, do not jeopardise the effective application of Articles 101 and 102 TFEU.

This subsequently leads to the rather difficult situation that raises the issue of transparency and certainty. Insofar as the legal traditions and substantive enforcement rules across the Member States are far from harmonised, and if we accept that the Commission's position on their leniency documents is non-disclosure, undertakings may still find that information is released at a national level through private claims. In this regard and as discussed previously, the Court has tried to ensure some form of continuity and certainty by requiring that national courts treat leniency programmes as useful tools to uncover and bring infringements of competition rules to an end and that the effectiveness of those programmes could be compromised if documents relating to a leniency procedure were disclosed to persons wishing to bring an action for damages.

Nevertheless, this acknowledgment must not be to the detriment of an individual who has the right to claim damages for loss caused to him by conduct that is liable to restrict or distort competition. Moreover, it is the view of the Court that the existence of such a right strengthens the working of the competition rules and discourages agreements or practices, frequently covert, which are liable to restrict or distort competition. It is hardly surprising that the Court points at the need for the national court to weigh the competing interests and to arrive at a decision of disclosure either in favour of or against an applicant in private damages. Nonetheless, the national courts are provided with little direction as to how to achieve this balancing or what factors form the spine of any such consideration. The Court in a particularly short judgment ends by stating that the weighing exercise can be conducted by the national courts and tribunals only on a case-by-case basis, according to national law, and taking into account all the relevant factors in each case.

[52] See also, *VEBIC* (n 43) para 56.

[53] A point that exists in a number of cases especially given the European Competition Network and the obligations of national competition authorities under Reg 1/2003.

The concept of balancing is also reflected in the newly adopted Directive (26 November 2014) where the Commission seeks to solidify this by requiring national courts to undertake a proportionality test. Recital 16 of this Directive puts it in these terms:

> National courts should be able, under their strict control, especially as regards the necessity and proportionality of disclosure measures, to order the disclosure of specified items of evidence or categories of evidence upon request of a party. It follows from the requirement of proportionality that disclosure can be ordered only where a claimant has made a plausible assertion, on the basis of facts which are reasonably available to that claimant, that the claimant has suffered harm that was caused by the defendant. Where a request for disclosure aims to obtain a category of evidence, that category should be identified by reference to common features of its constitutive elements such as the nature, object or content of the documents the disclosure of which is requested, the time during which they were drawn up, or other criteria, provided that the evidence falling within the category is relevant within the meaning of this Directive. Such categories should be defined as precisely and narrowly as possible on the basis of reasonably available facts.

This clearly requires that the applicant offers sufficient grounds to establish that the national court should consider the making of an order. It is hardly surprising to arrive at the conclusion that the likelihood of 28 national legal systems all meeting the same standards and having the same approaches is improbable. It is simply food for the growth of inconsistencies and opaqueness of the application of the competition rules in a growing area of enforcement, private damages. Considering that the Directive does not propose any provision that would relieve undertakings from liability on grounds of absence of fault, in other words the matter is left open for national courts to decide. The ECJ confirmed in *Schenker* that it is acceptable for Member States to establish conditions of intention or negligence for the imposition of a fine.[54] Such rules must at least be equal to those in Article 23 of Regulation 1/2003. The Court further held that the reliance of an undertaking on a previous national competition authority decision that its conduct was not contrary to EU competition law is not sufficient to show that an infringement was not committed intentionally or negligently. To avoid a finding that an infringement was committed intentionally or negligently, an undertaking must show that it could not have been aware of the anti-competitive nature of its conduct. The difficulty here being that the overlap between enforcement at a national level in private damages actions and a leniency application would or could be evidence at a national level of intent. Does this mean immediate guilt? How then can an undertaking participate in a leniency programme where the EU allows for a parallel and stricter system of enforcement in a way that leads to such a finding?

[54] Case C-681/11 *Schenker* [2013] 5 CMLR 831.

We see already from the *Kone* case the difficulties that national courts are likely to have with private enforcement cases. Here the disparity to the causal link at a national level to an EU level and the establishment of the attribution of blame for damage was subject to a reference from the Belgian courts. Where the Court of Justice responded by finding that it is, in principle, for the domestic legal system of each Member State to lay down the detailed rules governing the application of the concept of the 'causal link'. However, it is clear from the case law of the Court[55] that national legislation must ensure that European Union competition law is fully effective. Those rules must, therefore, specifically take into account the objective pursued in Article 101 TFEU, which aims to guarantee effective and undistorted competition in the internal market, and, accordingly, prices set on the basis of free competition. Under those circumstances, national legislation must recognise the right of any individual to claim compensation for loss sustained. The full effectiveness of Article 101 TFEU would be put at risk if the right of any individual to claim compensation for harm suffered were subjected by national law, categorically and regardless of the particular circumstances of the case, to the existence of a direct causal link while excluding that right because the individual concerned had no contractual connections with a member of the cartel, but with an undertaking not party thereto, whose pricing policy, however, was the result of the cartel that contributed to the distortion of price formation mechanisms governing competitive markets.[56]

The *Kone* judgment reinforces the position of private applicants as victims of cartels. Building on its rulings in *Courage* and *Manfredi*, the ECJ considered that with respect to the amount of damage, the verifiable causal damage resulting due to the excessive prices of companies, which were specifically *not* involved in the cartel, is also to be taken into consideration. The language of balancing used in *Pfleiderer* and *Donau* is thus abandoned. Priority seems to be given to the right to obtain damages. It is made clear by the ECJ that the leniency programme is a programme developed by the Commission, through its Notice on Immunity from fines and reduction of fines in cartel cases (which has no legislative force and is not binding on Member States). Consequently, that leniency programme cannot deprive individuals of the right to obtain compensation before the national courts for loss sustained as a result of an infringement of Article 101 TFEU.[57] This prioritisation of the right to compensation is now also enshrined in the very text of the new Directive. According to recital 18:

> *While relevant evidence containing business secrets or otherwise confidential information should, in principle, be available in actions for damages, such confidential*

[55] See Case C-375/09 *Prezes Urzędu Ochrony Konkurencji i Konsumentów v Tele2 Polska sp. z o.o* [2011] ECR I-3055; and Case 14/68 *Walt Wilhelm and others v Bundeskartellamt* EU:C:1969:4.

[56] *Kone* (n 18) paras 32–33.

[57] ibid, para 36.

> *information needs to be protected appropriately. National courts should therefore have at their disposal a range of measures to protect such confidential information from being disclosed during the proceedings. Those measures could include the possibility of redacting sensitive passages in documents, conducting hearings in camera, restricting the persons allowed to see the evidence, and instructing experts to produce summaries of the information in an aggregated or otherwise non-confidential form.* Measures protecting business secrets and other confidential information should, nevertheless, not impede the exercise of the right to compensation.[58]

This prioritisation of the right to obtain damage is also coupled with a reduction of the use of balancing by national courts. This minimisation of balancing is reflected in Article 6 of the new Directive. This provision provides for three types of solutions (lists) in relation to access to a competition file depending on the nature of the documents: we find now a black list, a grey list and a white list. The black-listed documents cannot be disclosed. The grey-listed documents may be disclosed after temporary protection. The white-listed documents may, in principle, always be disclosed. Concerning the black list (Article 6(3)), the protection for the leniency applicant is absolute and covers corporate statements and settlement submissions. So in relation to corporate statements and settlement submissions, it may be said that the new Directive gives no discretion for the national court to exercise the so-called balancing exercise enshrined in *Pfleiderer*.[59] Though leniency documents and settlement submissions cannot be disclosed, a claimant may, however, ask for a document to be checked to see whether it really does fall within the black list.[60]

In respect of the grey list (Article 6(4)), it specifies the criteria to be applied by the national courts when assessing the proportionality of an order for disclosure after the end of the (absolute) temporary protection.[61] These documents are prepared for the purpose of the investigation, such as: replies to requests for information, statements of objections and preliminary assessments (under Article 9 of Regulation 1/2003). Accordingly, when the request for disclosure concerns documents on the grey list, the national court must take into consideration 'the need to safeguard the effectiveness of the public enforcement of competition law'. As rightly put by Bentley and Henry, '[t]hese words echo the reasoning in *Pfleiderer*. It follows, … that the

[58] Emphasis added.

[59] P Bentley and D Henry, 'Antitrust Damages Actions: Obtaining Probative Evidence in the Hands of Another Party' (2014) 37 *World Competition* 271, 281.

[60] A claimant may present a justified request that a national court access the documents contained in [Art 6(6)] for the sole purpose of ensuring that their contents fulfill the definitions of [leniency statement] and [settlement submission]. In that assessment, national courts may request assistance from the competent competition authority. The authors of the concerned documents may also have the possibility to be heard. In any case, the Court shall not provide access to those documents to the other parties or third parties: Art 6(7).

[61] They are disclosable by court order only after the authority in question takes a decision in the case or closes its file.

Pfleiderer principle is applicable to requests for disclosure of documents on the grey list, whether in the hands of a competition authority or a private party'.[62] Finally, regarding the white list (Article 6(5)),[63] there is no explicit indication in Article 6 as to whether the national court may undertake a balancing of interests in relation to white-listed documents. Nevertheless, Recital 22 of the new Directive states that,

> This Directive does not affect the right of the court to consider under national or Union law the interest of effective public enforcement of competition law when ordering disclosure of any type of evidence with the exception of leniency statements and settlement submissions.

Therefore, it is argued that white-listed documents may be submitted to a *Pfleiderer* balancing exercise in certain limited occasions where the effectiveness of the public enforcement of competition rules is at stake.[64] In the end, the balancing of interest required by the *Pfleiderer* ruling is now quite limited by the new Directive albeit not fully excluded. This new stance will, hopefully, bring more certainty as to litigations relating to the disclosure of documents in private claims for damages. This should be seen as a good thing.

5. CONCLUDING REMARKS

As discussed in detail above, claims for access to files related to leniency programmes will usually involve one or more of three predominant categories of information held by the Commission or the national competition authorities. The first is the leniency or immunity statement itself or a transcript thereof. Second, pre-existing supporting documents submitted voluntarily by the applicant together with leniency/immunity application in question. Third, pre-existing documents investigated by the Commission in an inspection or pursuant to an information request on the basis of the knowledge obtained through the leniency application.[65] The Commission has been reluctant in this regard and has strongly resisted applications for access to any of these categories of information.[66] In addition, the case law of the ECJ on access to competition files held by the Commission is very restrictive as exemplified by the *EnBW Energie* judgment. The new Directive governing actions for damages under national law is, however, opening up the possibility of access to grey-listed and white-listed information held by national

[62] Bentley and Henry (n 59) 281.

[63] The white list includes pre-existing materials not prepared in connection with the investigation, such as: written agreements; texts of e-mails; and minutes of meetings.

[64] ibid.

[65] Ortiz Blanco (n 7) para 6.54.

[66] See above n 22.

competition authorities. Is the case law of the ECJ on Regulation 1049/2001 in line with the recent legislative developments? One of the related questions at issue here is the extent to which the Commission's belief that the risk of disclosure of leniency information to private actions is, indeed, a deterrent for leniency. As it stands, the stance by the Commission of strict non-disclosure or the protection of the participating undertakings seems to be at one end of the scale. Moreover, it also runs contrary to the Commission's agenda regarding the encouragement of private enforcement. The contradictory stance that exists is bringing with it a certain lack of clarity and certainty, dare we say a lack of transparency?

Moreover, what is left of the case law on balancing after the adoption of the Damages Directive? Our analysis has shown that the *Pfleiderer* balancing can still be relied upon in relation to the grey-listed and white-listed information. Nevertheless, the black-listed information, ie corporate statements and settlement submission, offers an absolute protection to leniency applicants. In that sense, the new Directive gives no discretion for the national court to exercise the so-called balancing exercise enshrined in *Pfleiderer* and ensures an effective protection for the leniency applicants. On the other hand, the essence of the new Damages Directive arguably gives priority to the private enforcement of competition law by making clear that measures protecting business secrets and other confidential information should, nevertheless, not impede the exercise of the right to compensation. This prioritisation of private enforcement is also visible in the most recent case law of the ECJ on leniency programmes. This 'clarification of priority' may play a role in future litigations involving the balancing of interests. In the end, both the limitation of balancing and the 'clarification of priority' bring more certainty to this complex field of law.

9

Access to Documents for Cartel Victims and Cartel Members—Is the System Coherent?

BJÖRN LUNDQVIST* AND HELENE ANDERSSON**

1. INTRODUCTION

ANTITRUST LITIGATION IS characterised by information asymmetry—the evidence necessary to prove a damage claim is often in the hands of the authority that actually conducted the cartel investigation. Cartel members will obviously also be in possession of some evidence, although it is unlikely that one firm holds evidence showing the entire extent of the cartel and its costs. The Directive on Competition Damages Actions addresses this problem, introducing a set of rules on access to documents, empowering national courts, on request from cartel victims, to order the disclosure of relevant documents from competition authorities and defendants. At the same time the Directive imposes something close to a blanket ban on the disclosure of leniency statements and settlement submissions. Not only are national courts prevented from ordering the disclosure of such documents, they may not allow parties to rely on such evidence in damages proceedings. These documents will thus *de facto* become inadmissible in the national courts of the EU.

In this chapter we will analyse the right to access documents for cartel victims and cartel members.[1] We start with an analysis of the case law from the European Court of Justice (ECJ or the Court) and the General Court (GC). The effects of the new Directive will thereafter be scrutinised. These two sections are divided so that we analyse the requestors: (i) individuals and (ii) national courts, and the recipients of these requests: (iii) potential or real defendants, (iv) national competition authorities, and (v) the European

* LL D (EUI), LL M (Michigan).
** Doctoral Candidate in European Law at Stockholm University.

[1] In this chapter, we do not discuss whether the rule in the Directive on the inadmissibility of documents before a national court is in strict violation of a fundamental principle in certain Member States concerning the judge's prerogative to freely assess evidence.

Commission ('the Commission'), separately. Different legal systems are triggered depending on who makes a request and who is the receiver of such a request, and the potential success of obtaining the documents varies considerably. Thereafter, we discuss the rights to the defence and access to documents while being subject to a cartel investigation by the Commission. We conclude with some suggestions for the Member States on how to transpose the Directive so as to maximise private actions without thereby dismantling the leniency programmes.

2. BACKGROUND

In 2001, the ECJ delivered its ruling in *Courage* establishing the right for all victims of antitrust infringements to receive compensation in full.[2] The ruling was already considered seminal then, but few could imagine the forces that were actually set in motion. *Courage* was soon to be endorsed and followed by the ECJ in *Manfredi*.[3]

Following *Courage*, the Commission immediately launched a study on the possibilities of being compensated, and in 2005, it published a Green Paper declaring that the area of private enforcement presented a picture of 'total under development' throughout the EU Member States.[4] This was not acceptable. Achieving vigorous private enforcement became the only way forward. Public and private enforcement were considered as going hand in hand, and a truly effective competition law regime could not be achieved without well- functioning private enforcement. The Commission appeared to be on a mission. A White Paper followed in 2008,[5] actually proposing certain rather inventive tools to boost private enforcement in the EU, eg, scrapping the losing party pay principle for cartel damages cases. The White Paper took inspiration from the Intellectual Property Rights Enforcement Directive (IPRED) concerning enforcement rules for possible intellectual property law infringements.[6] Unfortunately, the White Paper seemed to have met steep resistance at the European Parliament and most, if not all, inventive tools were later scrapped and not included in the Directive.[7]

[2] Case C-453/99 *Courage Ltd v Bernard Crehan and Bernard Crehan v Courage Ltd and Others* EU:C:2001:465.

[3] Case C-295/04 *Manfredi* EU:C:2006:461.

[4] Commission, 'Green Paper on Damages Actions for Breach of the EC Antitrust Rules' COM(2005) 672 final.

[5] Commission, 'White Paper on Damages Actions for Breach of the EC Antitrust Rules' COM(2008) 165 final.

[6] Directive 2004/48/EC of the European Parliament and of the Council of 29 April 2004 on the enforcement of intellectual property rights [2004] OJ L157/32.

[7] The right to obtain evidence in the Private Enforcement Directive, ie Directive 2014/104/EU of the European Parliament and of the Council of 26 November 2014 on certain rules governing actions for damages under national law for infringements of the competition law provisions of the Member States and of the European Union [2014] OJ L349/1, is less strong than the corresponding right to access evidence and information for right holders in the IPRED.

Then came the Court's ruling in *Pfleiderer*,[8] and part of the enthusiasm vanished into thin air. Having fended off US litigants requesting the disclosure of EU leniency documents for quite some time, the problem had now been brought home.

With the *Pfleiderer* ruling, the Court opened up the possibility for national courts to order the disclosure of leniency documents. Private actions could now be perceived to pose a real threat to leniency programmes as national courts were no longer allowed to impose blanket bans on the access to leniency documents. Instead, the courts would have to weigh the interest of achieving a well-functioning private enforcement system against the interest of safeguarding the attractiveness of EU and national leniency programmes. National courts had to decide on a case-by-case basis whether the disclosure of leniency documents would seriously undermine the attractiveness and functioning of leniency programmes. Indeed, a daunting task for a national court.

Something had to be done to protect the attractiveness of the leniency programmes. A proposal for a Directive on Competition Damages Actions was presented by the Commission in June 2013[9] without many of the inventive steps provided in the White Paper, and after much negotiation and several amendments, the Directive was adopted in November 2014.[10]

The Directive on Competition Damages Actions attempts to achieve the dual goal of facilitating private enforcement actions while at the same time protecting national and EU leniency programmes. Below is a presentation of the current law on access to documents in damages proceedings, followed by a presentation of the new rules and the implications they will have on current national and EU rules on access to documents.

3. ACCESS TO DOCUMENTS ACCORDING TO THE ECJ

Trying to prove not only the existence of a cartel, but also a causal link between such a cartel and any loss sustained is not easy. Add to that the task of quantifying the harm sustained and it is easy to see why the area of private enforcement has been an area of 'total underdevelopment' throughout the EU. Cartel cases today are fact-intensive and often very complex.

If a plaintiff in a damages action is able to rely on the work done and the evidence gathered by a competition authority, this will definitely make things easier. Most litigation cases are so called follow-on actions where the

[8] Case C-360/09 *Pfleiderer AG v Bundeskartellamt* EU:C:2011:389.

[9] COM(2013) 404 final.

[10] Directive 2014/104/EU of the European Parliament and of the Council of 26 November 2014 on certain rules governing actions for damages under national law for infringements of the competition law provisions of the Member States and of the European Union [2014] OJ L349/1. For further information on the history and adoption of the Directive, see ec.europa.eu/competition/antitrust/actionsdamages/documents.html.

existence and scope of the cartel has already been established. Furthermore, there is by now a series of cases concerning the right of (alleged) cartel victims to gain access to evidence held by competition authorities, national as well as DG COMP. As will be discussed below, the Court's willingness to allow the disclosure of evidence appears to vary depending on whether (i) it is the file of a national competition authority or DG COMP, (ii) whether the requestor is a national court, a potential cartel victim or an alleged cartel member.

3.1 A Court or an Individual's Access to a File of a National Competition Authority or a Court

First out in a series of cases dealing with access to documents was *Pfleiderer*. In January 2008, the German competition authority imposed fines on a number of décor paper manufacturers for breach of Article 101 TFEU. Pfleiderer was one of their customers. During the three years preceding the decision in the cartel case, Pfleiderer estimated that it had purchased goods to a value exceeding EUR 60 million from the cartel participants. It now considered the possibilities of bringing damages actions against the cartelists, and requested access to all the material in the file of the German competition authority. Access was denied, and Pfleiderer turned to the court. The German court actually ruled in favour of Pfleiderer's claim, but before enforcing the ruling it made a request for a preliminary ruling to the ECJ. What the national court wished to know was whether the provisions of EU competition law—especially Articles 11 and 12 of Regulation 1/2003[11]—prevented a national court from granting access to leniency applications and documents voluntarily submitted by a leniency applicant in that connection.[12]

Advocate General Mazák was the first to have his say on the matter. AG Mazák took the view that there should be a division between different kinds of documents. The disclosure of voluntary self-incriminating statements by leniency applicants could substantially reduce the attractiveness and thus the effectiveness of leniency programmes. According to AG Mazák, the interference of the cartel victims' right to an effective remedy was justified by the legitimate aim of ensuring an effective (public) enforcement of Article 101 TFEU. Hence, such documents should at all times be kept out of the reach of civil litigants. As regards all the other pre-existing documents, however, they should be accessible to civil litigants.[13]

[11] Council Regulation (EC) No 1/2003 of 16 December 2002 on the implementation of the rules on competition laid down in Arts 81 and 82 of the Treaty [2003] OJ L 1/1.

[12] *Pfleiderer* (n 8) para 18.

[13] Opinion of AG Mazák, *Pfleiderer* (n 8) para 47.

The Court did not follow the reasoning of AG Mazák. Instead, it chose to lay this decision in the hands of the national courts, declaring that in the absence of any EU regulations in this field, national courts have to turn to national regulations to determine the conditions under which such access must be permitted or refused, by weighing the interest in favour of disclosure against the interest of protecting information provided voluntarily by the leniency applicant. That balancing exercise, the Court declared, could only be conducted by national courts on a case-by-case basis, according to national law and taking into account all the relevant factors in the case.[14]

Likewise, in the case of *Donau Chemie*, the ECJ rejected the Austrian legislation allowing defendants in cartel cases to veto any disclosure of documents in the Austrian Cartel Court's file. Again, the Court declared that although the effectiveness of leniency programmes could be compromised if documents relating to leniency proceedings were disclosed to cartel victims, a systematic refusal to grant access to such documents was unacceptable. Instead, such an assessment must be made on a case-by-case basis, taking into account all the relevant factors in the case.[15]

The Court's view in relation to national proceedings has thus been clear. If a case concerns a request for access to a file the national court may not refuse such access without first having carried out a balancing exercise taking into account all the relevant factors in the case.

3.2 Access to the Commission's Files by Individuals

The principle of transparency is set out in Article 15(3) TFEU, but the modalities governing third parties' access to Commission files are laid down in Regulation 1049/2001 ('the Transparency Regulation').[16] The Transparency Regulation is designed to ensure that decisions made by the EU institutions should be subject to greater transparency. The Regulation provides citizens and legal persons of the Union with the right of access to the documents of the institutions. This right does not only cover documents that are drawn up by the institutions themselves, but also documents that fall into their possession.

However, this right of access is not absolute. Article 4 of the Transparency Regulation provides for a number of exceptions, among which we find the protection of commercial interests of natural and legal persons, court

[14] *Pfleiderer* (n 8) para 31.

[15] Case C-536/11 *Bundeswettbewerbsbehörde v Donau Chemie et al* EU:C:2013:366, para 43.

[16] Regulation 1049/2001/EC regarding public access to European Parliament, Council and Commission documents ('Transparency Regulation') [2001] OJ L145/43.

proceedings and legal advice as well as protecting the purpose of inspections, investigations and audits.[17]

As we shall see, although the GC and the ECJ have taken opposing views on the matter, these exceptions have eventually served to prevent private litigants from gaining access to the Commission's files in cartel cases.

In the *CDC Hydrogen Peroxide* case, the applicant—CDC Hydrogene Peroxide Cartel Damage Claims ('CDC')—requested full access to the statement of contents of the Commission's case file in the Hydrogen Peroxide Decision.[18] The Commission denied access to the statement, declaring that it did not constitute a document within the meaning of Article 3(a) of the Transparency Regulation. CDC brought action against the Commission Decision, seeking its annulment. Before the GC, the Commission argued that the disclosure of the statement of contents would undermine the protection of the commercial interests of the cartel companies as well as the purpose of the cartel investigation.[19] The GC did not accept the arguments made by the Commission.

According to the GC, denying access to the statement of contents did not protect any other commercial interest than the interest of the cartel companies to avoid damage claims, an interest not protected by the Transparency Regulation. Nor did it accept the claim that a denial of access would protect the interests of the investigation as the investigation had been closed two years earlier and the appeals did not concern the issue of guilt but rather the calculation of fines.

Given the above, the GC annulled the Commission Decision and allowed full access to the statement of contents. This is not the only time that the GC has ruled in favour of the party seeking access to the Commission's files. However, it may be that the GC holds a more favourable view of giving access than the ECJ. The recent *EnBW* case shows the division between the GC and the ECJ on this issue.[20]

In 2007, the Commission imposed fines on a number of companies for taking part in a cartel related to Gas Insulated Switchgear (GIS), a power substation device. Following the decision, EnBW, an energy distribution company, claimed to have been harmed by the GIS cartel. In order to gather evidence regarding the cartel, EnBW made a request to the Commission for access to the Commission's entire case file. Access was denied on the basis that all the documents were covered by the exceptions set forth in Article 4 of the Transparency Regulation. Their disclosure would undermine not only the protection of the purpose of the Commission's investigations, but also

[17] ibid Art 4(2).

[18] Case COMP/F/38.620—Hydrogen peroxide and perborate.

[19] Case T-437/08 *CDC Hydrogene Peroxide Cartel Damage Claims v Commission* EU:T:2011:752, paras 29 and 55.

[20] Case C-365/12P *Commission v EnBW Energie Baden-Württemberg AG* EU:C:2014:112.

the protection of the commercial interest of the companies involved in cartel proceedings, as well as the Commission's decision-making process.

The GC annulled the Commission Decision to refuse access to the entire case file, contending that the Commission could not rely on a general presumption that all of the documents fell under the exceptions listed in Article 4 of the Transparency Regulation.

Once again, the General Court considered that the Transparency Regulation gave as wide a right of access as possible and, accordingly, the exceptions against disclosure should be interpreted strictly and narrowly. Therefore, the Commission should have carried out a concrete review to establish whether the conditions for refusing disclosure were effectively met in relation to each document in its administrative file.

The Commission could not come to terms with the ruling of the GC. Referring to the specific rules governing access to administrative files in competition matters (in particular, Regulations 1/2003 and 773/2004,[21] hereafter the Antitrust Regulations), the Commission appealed the ruling before the ECJ.

The ECJ reasoned that the Antitrust Regulations and the Transparency Regulation are on the same footing in the EU legal order. Accordingly, they should be applied consistently. If the purpose of the Transparency Regulation is to confer a right of access to the EU institutions' documents, the extent of such access should depend on the activities of the institution. According to the ECJ, the Commission's activity in antitrust proceedings does not require the same level of disclosure as compared to the legislative activities of the EU. Moreover, the exceptions set forth in Article 4 of the Transparency Regulation cannot be interpreted without taking account of the Antitrust Regulations' specific rules on access to the file.

Here, the ECJ noted that, according to the Antitrust Regulations, in principle it is only the parties to cartel proceedings that have a right to access the Commission's files. The ECJ thus found that if third parties, such as EnBW, were able to access the Commission's files through the Transparency Regulation, the specific system put in place by the Antitrust Regulations would be jeopardised. The Commission's investigative powers, which mostly rely on the information given by companies, would be undermined by the lack of guarantee that the documents submitted (voluntarily or not) by investigated companies would be treated with the highest degree of confidentiality.

Consequently, the ECJ concluded that the Commission was entitled to rely on a general presumption, stemming from the Antitrust Regulations, that the documents in a cartel file fell within one or more of the exceptions

[21] Commission Regulation (EC) No 773/2004 of 7 April 2004 relating to the conduct of proceedings by the Commission pursuant to Arts 81 and 82 of the EC Treaty [2004] OJ L 123/18.

in Article 4 of the Transparency Regulation. The Commission could thus apply a blanket approach to a third party's broad and unspecified request, thereby sparing itself a fastidious document-by-document review of its voluminous cartel files.

The *EnBW* case is not the only one where the ECJ has allowed the Commission to rely on such a presumption. In two earlier cases, concerning state aid and concentrations, the ECJ made the same interpretation.[22] Thus, the ECJ seems to limit individuals' right of access to documents held by the Commission.

3.3 Access to the Commission's Files by National Courts

Indeed, individuals seeking access to the Commission's files will face an uphill battle. However, seeking such access through a national court may prove a safer route to follow. Such a procedure is not governed by the Transparency Regulation, but by both national rules on access to documents and Regulation 1/2003.

Regulation 1/2003, Article 15(1) read in conjunction with Article 4(3) TEU regarding the general duty of loyal cooperation, implies a duty on the part of the Commission to provide documents relating to an administrative investigation for use in civil proceedings before national courts.[23] The outer limit of Article 15(1), as an indirect means of obtaining documents from the Commission, is unclear. In general, the Commission may disclose information including business secrets, while the parties may also rely on information in the national court provided to them in the administrative proceedings before the Commission.[24]

When transmitting information to national courts, the Commission has to ensure that the guarantees provided to individuals under Article 339 TFEU (to protect confidential information and business secrets) are upheld (*cf Delimitis*[25] and *Postbank*[26]). However, this does not mean that access to such information should be denied. The national court may create a 'ring of confidentiality' and implement other methods so that the information may still be used by the judge and the parties to the proceedings before the national court as long as the information is not made public outside the court room.

[22] Case C-404/10P *Editions Odile Jacob v European Commission* EU:C:2012:393 and Case T-308/08 *The Netherlands v Commission* EU:T:2009:329.

[23] Case T-353/94 *Postbank v Commission* EU:T:1996:119, paras 64–67.

[24] Bellamy & Child, *European Union Law of Competition*, 7th edn (Oxford, Oxford University Press, 2013) 1187.

[25] Case C-234/89 *Delimitis* EU:C:1991:91.

[26] *Postbank v Commission* (n 23).

In addition to Article 15(1) of Regulation 1/2003, a national court can order the Commission to submit information under the national procedural rules applicable to the court. This might seem somewhat surprising and even at odds with the federal idea of the EU. Nevertheless, Article 15(1) of Regulation 1/2003 does not harmonise national rules regarding access to documents, nor preclude the national courts from using national procedural rules. Moreover, the Commission in its amicus curiae brief to the UK High Court in *National Grid* (for details, see below) admits that it would be likely to follow such an order to disclose evidence produced by a national court under national procedural rules.[27]

An interesting case concerning national courts' access to documents held by the Commission is the English case *National Grid Electricity Transmission v ABB*.[28] Just like in the *EnBW* case discussed above, *National Grid* concerned a follow-on suit originating from the gas insulated switchgear cartel busted by inter alia the Commission.[29] The claimant in this case sought to obtain several documents held by the defendants and/or the Commission. Unlike the *EnBW* case, the plaintiff in *National Grid* did not ask the Commission directly, but had the High Court request documents from both the defendants and the Commission. This seems to have been a much more successful strategy.

First, the High Court dealt with a request concerning documents that the defendants had obtained from the Commission during the course of the cartel investigation. The defendants claimed that access to such documents should be denied under EU law since the Commission's cartel decision was still under appeal. The High Court ordered the defendant to give access to the documents. In order to mitigate the confidentiality issues caused by the ongoing appeal of the Commission Decision, the High Court created a 'confidentiality ring' where only the legal and expert advisers of the parties were granted access to the material. Moreover, the High Court rejected the argument that even though documents could have been obtained from the defendants under English laws, access should instead be sought directly from the Commission under Article 15(1) of Regulation 1/2003. The High Court argued that that would infringe the principles of equivalence under EU law, and that claimants using EU law must not be discriminated against and should have equal access to domestic procedural regulations. The High Court's order excluded any material that had been created for or that included passages from documents prepared for the purpose of any leniency application.

[27] N Khan, 'Observations of the EU Commission Pursuant Article 15(3) of Regulation 1/2003 in National Grid', November 2011, available at ec.europa.eu/competition/court/amicus_curiae_2011_national_grid_en.pdf (last visited 30 November 2014).

[28] *National Grid Electricity Transmission v ABB* [2011] EWHC 1717. See also *National Grid Electricity Transmission v ABB* [2012] EWHC 869.

[29] Case COMP/38.899—Gas Insulated Switchgear.

The claimant also wished to gain access to certain documents *held by the Commission*, asking the High Court to request those documents from the Commission under Article 15 of Regulation 1/2003. The High Court conceded and made a request to the Commission, expressly excluding any leniency material from the request. The Commission agreed to provide the requested material, including copies of the responses to the Statement of Objection (SO) and other documents submitted to the Commission during the course of the cartel investigation. However, before the material was transmitted to the High Court, the defendants challenged the Commission Decision to disclose the documents and sought interim measures. In November 2012, the President of the General Court decided to grant interim relief and suspended the transmission of the documents to the national court pending the outcome in main proceedings.[30] The case before the ECJ is not resolved yet.

It is interesting to note that the case took another turn following the ECJ's ruling in *Pfleiderer*. Until then the door to accessing leniency materials had appeared shut. However, as it now was ajar, the claimant seized the opportunity and amended its request for disclosure. It now sought access to the confidential version of the Commission Decision *from the defendants* as well as the defendants' responses to the SO (including any accompanying material), this time not excluding any leniency material from the request.

The questions subsequently arose as to whether (i) the ruling in *Pfleiderer* applied also to the disclosure of leniency material in the context of a Commission Decision, and (ii) whether the national court had jurisdiction to determine an application for the disclosure of documents held by the defendants containing leniency material submitted to the Commission, or whether such a request had to be made directly to the Commission pursuant to Article 15 of Regulation 1/2003.

It is interesting to note that the National Courts Notice[31] states that the Commission will not transmit to national courts information submitted by a leniency applicant without the consent of the applicant. The English High Court in *National Grid*, however, concluded that national rules, under the weighing principle in *Pfleiderer*, may be used to access such material directly from the defendants.[32] The Commission seems also to agree in its amicus curiae that given the general language of the ECJ in the *Pfleiderer* judgement, the principle is applicable not only to material submitted under national leniency programmes but also to material submitted to the

[30] Case T-164/12 R *Alstom* EU:T:2014:1089.

[31] Commission Notice on the co-operation between the Commission and the courts of the EU Member States in the application of Articles 81 and 82 EC [2004] OJ C101/54:Vol II, App B7, para 25.

[32] *National Grid* (n 28).

Commission within the framework of the EU leniency programme. The ECJ did not make a distinction between national competition authorities and the Commission when reaching its judgment.

Moreover, the High Court and, to some extent, the Commission seem to imply that the prerogative to decide whether certain information or evidence should be submitted to the national court is for the national court to decide, not the Commission, irrespective of whether that information has also been provided under the leniency system.

The High Court did eventually grant access, in a limited way, to leniency material held by the defendants. It reached its decision by weighing interests, determining whether the documents were necessary for the case to dispose fairly and the general aim of upholding the leniency system. First, the High Court discussed whether the leniency applicant, in the case at hand, would be placed in a worse situation in the private enforcement suit in comparison with other cartel members. Second, generally, how to uphold the attractiveness of the leniency system, while still maintaining that firms granted immunity from fines should still, in principle, be exposed to liability under private enforcement to the same extent as the other cartel members. These are the two concerns that must be taken into consideration when applying the *Pfleiderer* test.

Both the High Court and the Commission identified the first issue to be the major reason for not providing information, and the fact that providing access might give the perception that the leniency applicant was worse off and that that might lessen the incentive for cartel members to apply for leniency, was only a secondary concern. The High Court declared that access would have been denied if the civil litigant had sought compensation solely from the firm that had been granted full immunity (and thus not appealed the Commission's decision), and this had been done while the appeal was still pending before the EU Courts.

In the end, the High Court granted only limited access, while referring to the aim of protecting the leniency system. However, the *National Grid* case is interesting as it shows that national courts may in principle obtain access to a great deal of material provided that it can maintain and guarantee confidentiality during the course of the proceedings and is able to perform the *Pfleiderer* test in a responsible way. The Commission will not grant access to leniency documents under the National Courts Notice, while *National Grid* shows that such documents may be obtained from the defendants under national procedural rules. Only in exceptional circumstances will the Commission deny access to, for example, copies of responses to SOs under Article 15(1) of Regulation 1/2003 or the National Courts Notice. This is in sharp contrast to the *EnBW* case (discussed above), where a potential plaintiff addressing the Commission on its own was not able to access the same documents.

3.4 The Law as it now Stands—Concluding Remarks

It is clear, as the law now stands, that there is no uniform approach towards the issue of access to cartel case files. Or rather there is a clear dividing line between different kinds of cases. The ECJ makes a clear distinction between cases concerning requests by cartel victims made to national authorities and courts on the one hand and requests made to the Commission on the other. When it comes to national cases, the Court does seem to consider leniency programmes and private actions to be on an equal footing. National courts should not be allowed to accept blanket bans on disclosure but rather carry out a case-by-case analysis. When it comes to requests made to the Commission, on the other hand, the Commission is allowed to rely on a presumption that all the documents in its file are covered by confidentiality.

Moreover, there is a dichotomy between cartel victims requesting material and national courts making such requests. Making use of national courts, and thus national rules for obtaining evidence alone or in conjunction with Article 15(1) of Regulation 1/2003, greatly increases the possibility of obtaining documents from the Commission. Comparing the two cases *EnBW* and *National Grid*, it seems that the Commission grants access to certain material when a national court requests it, but denies access when an individual requests, possibly, the same information. Moreover, national rules regarding access to evidence are applicable vis-à-vis defendants, national competition authorities and even vis-à-vis the Commission.

4. ACCESS TO DOCUMENTS ACCORDING TO THE DIRECTIVE

One of the explicit aims of the Directive on Competition Damages Actions is to facilitate access to documents. As competition damages litigation is characterised by information asymmetry, claimants should be afforded the right to obtain the disclosure of evidence relevant to their claim, without it being necessary for them to specify individual items of evidence. This is laid down in recital 14 of the Directive. So how should this aim be achieved?

It is important to bear in mind that the Directive is addressed to the Member States and not to the Commission. Thus, the application of the Transparency Regulation will not be affected when the Directive takes effect. It is also important to note that the Directive is not addressed directly to national competition authorities. Instead, the Directive applies to national courts.

4.1 Access to Evidence held by Individuals and Competition Authorities

Articles 5 and 6 of the Directive deal with the question of access to documents. Both Articles deal with the situations where national courts may or may not order the disclosure of evidence. While Article 5 lays down the general rules concerning access to documents, Article 6 regulates the disclosure of evidence included in the file of a competition authority. The main idea behind these two Articles is to deal with the information asymmetry governing antitrust cases and to make it easier for plaintiffs to gather evidence supporting their damages claim.

Article 5 requires the Member States to ensure that national courts are able to order defendants or third parties to disclose relevant evidence where a plaintiff in a damages case has presented a *reasoned justification* sufficient to support the plausibility of the claim.[33] If the plaintiff can provide a justification to support such plausibility, defendants and third parties may thus have to disclose specified documents or *relevant categories* of documents. However, the possibility for a plaintiff to obtain access to evidence is not without limits. The judge handling the request will have to ensure that disclosure orders are *proportionate* and that *confidential information is duly protected*. Now it becomes interesting.

When determining whether disclosure is proportionate, the national court shall consider (i) to what extent the claim or defence is supported by facts, (ii) the scope and cost of the disclosure, and (iii) whether the requested evidence contains any confidential information. As for the scope and cost of disclosure, the national courts are here required to prevent non-specific searches for information that are unlikely to be of relevance to the parties in the procedure.[34] A claimant should not be able to embark on a fishing expedition.

This is also emphasised in Article 6 of the Directive, which stipulates that when carrying out the proportionality assessment, the national court shall consider whether the request has been phrased specifically with regard to the nature, object or contents of the documents held in the competition authority's file or whether the request is non-specific. Furthermore, the court is required to consider the need to safeguard the effectiveness of the public enforcement of competition law. The right of the individual should thus be weighed against the public interest, and *perhaps* this wording will allow for an interpretation along the lines of the ECJ's interpretation of Article 4 of the Transparency Regulation. When the national court assesses a request to access the file of a national competition authority, it shall consider whether the request is specific or non-specific. Will this allow the national court to refuse access when the applicant has requested access to an entire case file?

4.2 Protecting Leniency Programmes Under the Directive

As for the public interest and the need to safeguard an effective public enforcement of the antitrust rules, the Directive specifically addresses

33 Art 5(1) of the Directive on Competition Damages Actions.
34 ibid Art 5(3).

leniency programmes and the importance that they remain attractive to cartel participants. Thus, Article 6(6) of the Directive prohibits national courts to order the disclosure of leniency statements and settlement submissions.[35] Furthermore, national courts, under certain circumstances, are prevented from admitting such evidence. Article 7 limits the use of evidence obtained by individuals or firms through access to the file of a competition authority. According to Article 7(1), Member States shall ensure that leniency statements and settlement submissions, which are obtained by a natural or legal person solely through access to the file of a competition authority, are either deemed inadmissible in actions for damages or otherwise protected under the applicable national rules to ensure full effect of the limits on the use of evidence pursuant to the prohibition stipulated in Article 6. Depending on the interpretation, Article 7(1), in conjunction with Article 6(6), seems to de facto 'blacklist' leniency statements and settlement submissions held by competition authorities or by the defendant. The aim is to protect the leniency programmes, ensuring that cartel members are not discouraged from seeking leniency, thus limiting the perception that a leniency applicant would be worse off in the follow-on private suits than the other cartel members.

While this is a bold first step in the creation of procedural rules on inadmissibility at EU level, the issue is how wide the scope of inadmissibility is. The national court may not ask the competition authorities for leniency statements or settlement submissions, and even if the parties have obtained those documents from a competition authority (including the Commission), they seem to be de facto inadmissible in a national court. Firstly, such a per se rule risks being at odds with the ECJ's idea about proportionality, and weighing the interest of upholding the leniency system vis-à-vis the interest of the cartel victims, in *Pfleiderer*.[36] Secondly, the question is how Article 7 should be interpreted. The provision of inadmissible evidence in the Directive and, generally, under national procedural rules, is the exception to the rule. Normally, a court should be able to access information and a judge should be able to pick up and use evidence freely in order to be able to come to a conclusion that is correct both in fact and in law.

Thus, rules on inadmissibility should presumably be interpreted narrowly. For example, Articles 6(6) and 7(1) identify 'leniency statements and settlement submissions' as inadmissible. That is clearly narrower than the exemption for all leniency documents stipulated in the National Courts Notice.

[35] ibid Art 6(6).

[36] See eg C Kersting 'Removing the Tension Public and Private Enforcement: Disclosure and Privileges for Successful Leniency Applicants' (2014) 5 *Journal of European Competition Law & Practice* 2, 3. Compare with speech by A Italianer, 'Competition Law within a Framework of Rights and the Commission's Proposal for a Directive on Antitrust Damage Actions' 12th Annual Conference of the Association European Competition Law Judges, Luxembourg, 14 June 2013, available at ec.europa.eu/competition/speeches/text/sp2013_06_en.pdf (last visited 1 August 2015).

Under the Directive, a national court would, in principle, be able to grant access and obtain all the evidence submitted by a leniency applicant to the Commission, in certain circumstances under the limitation in Articles 6(5)[37] and 7(2), while not having access to the 'leniency statements and settlement submissions'. In other words, the documents where the leniency applicant or its officers describe the cartel and how it works are not admissible, but other documents, eg, attachments and other hard evidence to such statements may be admissible.[38]

Under the Directive, the Commission would presumably subsequently be able to provide access to more material supplied under the leniency procedure than it is able to do today under the National Court Notice. At least this is the case if the Commission interprets Articles 6(6) and 7(1) in the Directive as *lex specialis* compared to the National Court Notice. What might cause the Commission not to give access to other forms of leniency material is Article 6(3) that stipulates '[t]his Article is without prejudice to the rules and practices under Union or national law on the protection of internal documents of competition authorities and of correspondence between competition authorities'. This issue is whether Article 6(3) applies to the National Court Notice, and whether the National Court Notice is overruled by *Pfleiderer*.

An idea worth pursuing when transposing the Directive into national law is that the firm that was granted full immunity should be allowed to regress any and all damages that that firm was ordered to pay against the other members of the cartel. Thus, the firm that has been granted immunity should not at the end of the day be liable for any costs of the cartel. Should such an extended rule of regress be implemented in the Member States, access can be granted under Articles 5 and 6 of the Directive to other forms of leniency material than 'leniency statements and settlement submissions', while still upholding and even promoting the integrity of the leniency programme. The firm that has been granted immunity would possibly not suffer any costs and this rule would act as an additional incentive to notify cartels under the leniency programmes. Moreover, the fundamental civil law doctrine of the judge's prerogative to freely assess evidence should be upheld and protected in principle. It is a fundamental doctrine, at least in the Scandinavian legal tradition, which has served these Member States well. Also, inventive procedural ideas such as creating a 'confidentiality ring' could be used in order to mitigate the negative ramifications of granting access to leniency material. Business secrets may then be allowed into the cartel damages courts.

[37] Often referred to as the 'grey list'.

[38] See rec 26 of the Directive on Competition Damages Actions, stating that only leniency statements and settlement submissions, which are produced for the sole purpose of cooperating with the competition authorities, are off limits for the court.

4.3 The Law as it will Stand with the Directive—Concluding Remarks

It may come as a surprise that the law as it will stand after the Directive has been transposed will prevent national courts from granting access to documents that are now being disclosed to civil litigants, ie 'leniency statements and settlement submissions'. When the Directive has been transposed, cartel victims will no longer have any possibility of accessing leniency statements or settlement submissions. The Directive stipulates a presumption of harm in Article 17(2), which may lessen the need for evidence concerning causality. However, the cartel victim still needs evidence in order to quantify any damages. The Member States thus need to mitigate the lack of access to evidence by transposing the rules in the right way, giving courts the freedom to grant access to other relevant material. In fact, this also appears to be the legislator's aim as the final version of the Directive now includes a paragraph (Article 6(8)) expressly stating that, to the extent that only parts of the material requested from a competition authority belongs to the categories leniency statements or settlement submissions, the remaining parts shall be released in accordance with the provisions of Article 6.

For example, the replies to the Commission or national competition authorities' SOs by the alleged cartel members may have implications for the cartel victims as well as for the cartel members. These replies may contain valuable information regarding the existence and workings of the alleged cartel. The replies to the SOs will probably increase in importance as evidence or as material for understanding the workings of the cartels. When neither settlement submission nor written or oral leniency statements given by officers working with the alleged cartel companies are accessible or admissible to the national courts, these replies increase in importance. They may contain necessary information in order to connect the decision of the existence of a cartel with the harm it has caused.

5. IS THE SYSTEM COHERENT?

Until now we have discussed access to documents for cartel victims in follow-on suits, but what about the alleged cartel members? What about their right to and possibilities of accessing documents important to their cases before the Commission, the EU Courts or national courts? Accessing documents may be important even for the leniency applicants and the firm that was granted immunity.

The cartel often grows when the Commission starts investigating. Even the leniency applicant does not always know the whole scope of the cartel. Perhaps the leniency applicant only knew of and filed for leniency regarding a national cartel for one product, while in fact the applicant was only part of a national branch of a global multi-product cartel. It seems clear that some cartels have different levels with different participants, ie separate national, regional and even global levels which are all interconnected but where only a few firms actually know about the full magnitude of the cartel. A cartel can thus look very different when comparing the initial leniency application to what the Commission finally decides to fine.

Indeed, there may certainly be several members of national cartels that only knew about the national dimension of the cartel, while in fact they were part of an EU-wide multi-product cartel without knowing the full magnitude of the organisation. These cartel members now need to access documents held by the Commission to limit their liability or to enable them to countersue other cartel members should they be found joint and severally liable for the damages caused by the entire cartel. Thus, these peripheral cartel members may have a similar need for fact and evidence as the cartel victims. In particular, such cartel members that decide not to appeal the cartel decision by the Commission specifically need to obtain evidence so as to limit their liability. They are at risk of being among the first to be sued for damages and are liable under the joint and several rule in the Directive.[39] Only small and medium-sized enterprises (SMEs) may under certain circumstances escape liability for harm caused by other cartel members. Otherwise, they need evidence either to try to limit the liability vis-à-vis the cartel victims, or, at least, to be used when countersuing the other cartel members.

Large cartels covering many markets can therefore create a need for the cartel members, also peripheral members and even the leniency applicant, to follow the Commission investigation closely. They need to influence the Commission to define the cartel and the relevant market accurately. Moreover, they should appeal the decision so not to be the first to get exposed to private action and, even more importantly, so to limit the width, breath and time of the defined cartel. Even though admitting to the collusion, they might need to challenge the Commission's decision on the definition of the relevant market. If the GC or the ECJ does not agree with the Commission on the number of products or the geographic extent of the cartel, the members may save much in the follow-on suits. Moreover, appeals can be attractive so to acquire exculpatory evidence in order to limit future claims for damages, or to at least be able to regress in a proper way against bigger firms that may have been part of the larger, even global cartel, while the participation in the cartel of other firms was only limited. If the firm has only participated in a separate part of the cartel, ie only regarding one product in one national market, it is particularly important for it to access documents that may limit its exposure in the follow-on private damages suits. But it may be difficult to access exculpatory evidence during the Commission's

[39] Art 11 of the Directive. See also that SMEs may escape the joint and several liability under certain circumstances.

cartel investigation. In contrast to private enforcement cases, it seems difficult for firms under investigation to access the replies to the SOs submitted by other alleged cartel members.

The right to access the file after receiving the SO is regulated in Article 27(2) of Regulation 1/2003 and Article 15(1) of Regulation 773/2004. Furthermore, the Commission Notice on access to files[40] sets out who has the right to access files. These rules are derived from the right to the defence, protected both under Article 41(2) of the European Charter of Fundamental Rights (EU Charter) and Article 6(1) of the European Convention for the Protection of Human Rights and Fundamental Freedoms (ECHR).

The landmark cases are *Cement*[41] and *Aalborg Portland*.[42] In these cases, the GC and the ECJ created a special test regarding what documents firms should be allowed to access. The Court concluded that the right to access differs depending on whether the documents sought are (i) incriminating documents or (ii) exculpatory documents.

In the *Aalborg Portland* case,[43] the ECJ stated the general rule that the failure on behalf of the Commission to communicate an incriminating document constitutes a breach of the rights of the defence only if the undertaking concerned shows, first, that the Commission relied on that document to support its objection concerning the existence of an infringement and, second, that the objection could be proved only by reference to that document. On the other hand, where an exculpatory document has not been communicated, the undertaking concerned must only establish that its non-disclosure was able to influence, to its disadvantage, the course of the proceedings and the contents of the decision of the Commission.[44]

The problem seems to be that access is generally not granted to other parties' replies to the Commission's objections (SOs), save where those replies contain new evidence which is potentially incriminating.[45] Exculpatory evidence is not as easily obtained, and the ECJ seldom finds that the Commission violates the right to access documents under the right to the defence when not granting access to exculpatory evidence that was included in the replies to the SO of other alleged members of the cartel. In *Knauf*, the ECJ dismissed the parties' argument that the failure to disclose allegedly exculpatory evidence constituted a violation of its right to the defence, as Knauf

[40] [2005] OJ C325/7.

[41] Case T-25/95 *Cimenteries CBR v Commission* EU:T:2000:77.

[42] Case C-204/00 P *Aalborg Portland and Others v Commission* EU:C:2004:6.

[43] ibid, paras 71 et seq.

[44] See also *Solvay*, where the ECJ recently concluded the general rule: Case C-109/10P *Solvay SA v European Commission* EU:C:2011:686, para 54.

[45] See eg, Calzado and De Stefano, 'Rights of Defence in Cartel Proceedings: Some Ideas for Manageable Improvements' in P Cardonell, A Rosas and N Wahl (eds), *Constitutionalising the EU Judicial System: Essays in Honour of Pernilla Lindh* (Oxford, Hart Publishing, 2012).

had failed to show not only that it did not have access to certain exculpatory evidence, but also that it could have used that evidence for its defence.[46]

In a later case, *Mitsubishi*,[47] the ECJ states:

> ... [I]f a passage in a reply to a statement of objections or in a document annexed to such a reply may be relevant for the defence of an undertaking in that it enables that company to invoke evidence which is not consistent with the inferences made at that stage by the Commission, it constitutes exculpatory evidence. In that case, the undertaking concerned must be authorised to examine the passage or the document concerned and to give its view thereon. However, the mere fact that other undertakings put forward the same arguments as the undertaking concerned and that they may have used more resources for their defence is not sufficient for those arguments to be regarded as exculpatory evidence ...[48]

In fact, *Mitsubishi* is as close as the ECJ has got to overturning a decision by the Commission not to give access to replies to an SO.

However, that seems to be in contrast to the private enforcement actions. In *National Grid*, the English High Court granted access to other parties' replies to SOs and the Commission seems to have agreed that that was both possible and desirable. Under the principles laid down in *National Grid*, you could even argue that a cartel victim should be granted access to the replies to the SOs in a cartel investigation even though the case has been appealed and has not been finally resolved. In contrast, alleged cartel members do not get access to the file during the cartel investigation to the same extent as the cartel victims are granted access after the cartel investigation is concluded, but before the private enforcement case. Perhaps this is a difficult comparison to make. We are in one way comparing apples and pears, but for cartel members that do not plan to appeal the decision by the Commission and later find out exculpatory evidence from, for example, the answers by other alleged cartel members to their SOs, might either feel compelled to challenge the Commission decision or try to use this piece of evidence in the follow-on private suit. In the follow-on suit the cartel victims may also utilise the Directive to access documents held by the Commission in the same way as the cartel victims. In fact, cartel members may possibly under the Directive, and under the principles and logic displayed in *National Grid*, get access to the replies to the SOs which they were denied in the cartel investigation.

Indeed, by not granting access to the alleged cartel members' replies to the SOs while investigating the cartel, the Commission risks that exculpatory evidence will be brought up in the private enforcement follow-on suits.

[46] Case C-407/08P *Knauf Gips KG v European Commission* EU:C:2010:389, paras 24–27.

[47] Case T-110/07 *Siemens v Commission* EU:T:2011:68. Case C-239/11 P *Mitsubishi, Siemens, Toshiba v Commission* EU:C:2013:866, para 43.

[48] ibid, paras 43 and 44.

It may lead to the defendants trying to (informally) reopen the question of whether there was a cartel or the width and scope of such cartel in the follow-on suits.[49] They may claim that no costs were incurred due to the cartel, or that these costs should be set at zero since no harm has been caused. Moreover, by not granting access to the replies, the incentive to appeal the cartel decision delivered by the Commission increases. In fact, the private enforcement system with the rules of joint and several liability under the Directive, together with the rules regarding access to the Commission's file, beg the alleged cartel members to use all means to fight or at least limit the cartel decision.

6. CONCLUSIONS

In this chapter we have dissected the rules regarding access to documents both for victims of cartels and for the alleged perpetrators. Firstly, we have shown that the effect of the Directive is that there might be less access in some jurisdictions. There are cases where the national courts have gone beyond what will be possible after the Directive has been transposed into national regulations. This is an interesting finding in itself. And why is this so? Why has the Commission set out to create a tool for the benefit of cartel victims, in order to increase private action, when the result of that effort is that it in all likelihood will be more difficult to gain access to incriminating documents compared to the situation *ex ante* the Directive? When transposing the Directive, the Member States must therefore interpret the exceptions set out in the Directive regarding access to documents narrowly.

Moreover, the system for granting access must lose some of its 'dysfunctionalities'. The general idea must be to create a transparent investigation where cartels are found judged and where the victims are compensated.

Oddly, the only courts that may request and obtain all leniency material, including leniency statements and settlement submissions, are the EU Courts under the Statute of the Court of Justice of the European Union and the procedural rules of the EU courts. The Directive is not applicable to these courts and they may thus order parties and competition authorities to provide any necessary evidence.

[49] A judgment by the EU Court or a Decision by the Commission on the finding of a violation of Art 101 TFEU is binding on the national court.

Part IV

Private Enforcement Through National Actions

10

Practical Private Enforcement: Perspectives from Portugal

SOFIA OLIVEIRA PAIS*

1. INTRODUCTION

On 26 November 2014, the Directive on competition damages actions was finally signed into law.[1] It is the first act on competition private enforcement adopted in the European Union (EU), arriving at a time when this issue is becoming increasingly relevant in the 28 Member States. Even if we cannot compare developments in the EU to the reality that exists in the United States (US), where antitrust private enforcement represents more than 90 per cent of all antitrust cases,[2] it is a fact that the European context is changing rapidly.[3] In the EU, public enforcement of competition law still holds the priority role, as it should.[4] However, the effectiveness of the laws will increase if private enforcement is also brought into the equation and

* Associate Professor at the Faculty of Law (Portuguese Catholic University), Jean Monnet Chair, Coordinator of the Research Centre for the Future of Law (Porto).

[1] Directive 2014/104/EU of the European Parliament and of the Council of 26 November 2014 on certain rules governing actions for damages under national law for infringements of the competition law provisions of the Member States and of the European Union (Directive on competition damages actions) [2014] OJ L349/1.

[2] See Robert H Lande, 'Benefits of private enforcement: empirical background' in AA Foer and JW Cuneo (eds), *The International Handbook on Private Enforcement of Competition Law* (Cheltenham, Edward Elgar Publishing, 2012) xii, 34

[3] *cf* D Killeen, 'Following in "Uncle Sam's" Footsteps? The Evolution of Private Antitrust Enforcement in the European Union" (2013) 39 *European Competition Law Review* 480, and A Schwab, 'Finding the Right Balance—the Deliberations of the European Parliament on the Draft Legislation Regarding Damage Claims' (2014) 5 *Journal of European Competition Law & Practice* 65. To see the evolution in other contexts such as the Canadian, *cf* D Rosner, 'Private Enforcement of Competition Laws: What Can We Learn from Canada? (2014) 5 *Journal of European Competition Law & Practice* 485.

[4] As referred to by A Stephen, 'Cartels' in I Lianos and D Geradin (eds), *Handbook on European Competition Law Substantive Aspects* (Cheltenham, Edward Elgar Publishing, 2013) 217, 236–38, 'damages have the particular problem of not punishing the individual decision makers responsible'; and, in certain cases, executives responsible for antitrust practices, like price fixing, have even been promoted to the board (see the case involving British Airways, referred to by Stephen).

plays a complementary role,[5] namely by supplying the lack of resources of the European Commission to investigate competition law infringements.[6] In other words, public and private enforcement complement each other, as has been recognised by the European institutions. On the one hand, the Court of Justice clearly stated in *Courage and Crehan*[7] that victim compensation for damages caused by competition violations is essential to their effectiveness and, on the other hand, the EU legislator adopted the Directive. In short, the adoption of the Directive is the culmination of a long process that is far from over as it needs to be transposed by the Member States in the next two years, with the assistance of the Commission.[8] We will address some of the concerns raised by certain solutions established in this Directive, which need to be transposed into Portuguese law.

2. MAIN IMPROVEMENTS OF THE DIRECTIVE ON COMPETITION DAMAGES ACTIONS

The Directive on competition damages actions should be welcomed, as suggested by the Commission, as a significant step towards achieving a more effective enforcement of European competition rules, namely by giving victims easier access to evidence as well as more time to make their claims, and also by preserving the attractiveness of leniency and settlement programmes.[9] Besides the improvements already mentioned, the main

[5] The advantages and disadvantages of antitrust private enforcement have been discussed in the EU for a long time. See, for instance, the excellent article by W Wils, 'Should Private Antitrust Enforcement be Encouraged in Europe' (2003) 26 *World Competition* 473.

[6] Relieving the Commission of some of the 'burden of enforcement', as pointed out by R Whish and D Bailey in *Competition Law*, 7th edn (Oxford, Oxford University Press, 2012) 296–97.

[7] Case C-453/99 *Courage and Crehan* EU:C:2001:465, paras 26–27. Note, however, that national procedural divergences and difficulties often impeded full compensation from antitrust infringements.

[8] It will draft guidelines on the passing on of overcharges. It should be noted that, in the US, the Supreme Court rejected the passing-on defence and, in general, claims by indirect purchasers, even if several state laws allow these kinds of claims; see the case law cited by Whish and Bailey on this topic (n 6) 301. The Commission will also review the Directive and submit a report to the Parliament and the Council six years after its entry into force. Finally, the Commission invites Member States to introduce, by July 2015, collective actions, including actions for damages, in line with the principles set out in the Recommendation on collective redress.

[9] As the EU Commissioner in charge of competition policy, M Vestager, said, 'We need a more robust competition culture in Europe. So I am very glad that the Council has now also formally approved the Directive on antitrust damages actions. I am very pleased that it will be easier for European citizens and companies to receive effective compensation for harm caused by antitrust violations.' The speech is available at europa.eu/rapid/press-release_IP-14-1580_en.htm (last visited 30 December 2014). On the other hand, sustaining that absolute protection of leniency programmes is incompatible with primary law, namely with the principle of effectiveness, and that the best solution would be to grant 'privilege to cartelists who receive immunity from fines in relation to their co-infringers, by giving them the right to full

changes introduced by the Directive include the possibility of the national courts to disclose evidence (which requires facts that support the plausibility of the claim, circumscribe the evidence and apply the proportionality principle), in order to obtain full compensation (not leading to overcompensation),[10] with certain exceptions (leniency statements and settlement submissions, in other words, voluntary self-incriminating statements will be exempted from disclosure)[11] and as long as it respects the principle of proportionality and confidential information (eg, access to files was refused in certain cases because the documents infringed the commercial interests of the undertakings concerned).[12] The final infringement decision of the national authority will constitute proof of that infringement, before courts of the same Member State, in which the infringement occurred, and before the courts of other Member States, it will constitute at least prima facie evidence of the infringement.

Concerning limitation period rules, victims will have five years, from the discovery that they suffered harm, to bring damages claims and one year to claim damages after the final infringement decision of the national competition authority has been issued.

The Directive also establishes a rebuttable presumption that cartels cause harm,[13] accepts and clarifies the consequences of the passing-on defence (establishing a rebuttable presumption that indirect customers suffered

contribution from their co-infringers': cf C Kersting, 'Removing the Tension Between Public and Private Enforcement: Disclosure and Privileges for Successful Leniency Applicants' (2014) 5 *Journal of Competition Law & Practice* 2. See also CF Weidt, 'The Directive on Actions for Antitrust Damages after Passing the European Parliament' (2014) 35 *European Competition Law Review* 438, 438–44.

[10] 'Without prejudice to compensation for loss of opportunity, full compensation under this Directive should not lead to overcompensation, whether by means of punitive, multiple or other damages' (rec 13 of the Directive).

[11] The interaction between the leniency programmes and full compensation through antitrust private enforcement has been discussed in the legal literature for a long time. See, for instance, S Waller, 'Towards a Constructive Public-Private Partnership to Enforce Competition Law' (2006) *World Competition* 367, 367–81; AE Beumer and A Karpetas, 'The Disclosure of Files and Documents in EU Cartel Cases: Fairy Tale or Reality?' (2012) *European Competition Journal* 123; S Oliveira Pais and A Piszcz, 'Package on Actions for Damages Based on Breaches of EU Competition Rules: Can One Size Fit All?' (2014) 7 *Yearbook of Antitrust and Regulatory Studies* 209. Certain literature doubts, however, the compatibility of leniency programmes protection with *Donau*: S Dworschak and L Maritzen, 'Einsicht—der erste Schritt zur Besserung? Zur Akteneinsicht in Kronzeugendokumente nach dem Donau Chemie-Urteil des EuGH' (2013) *Wirtschaft und Wettbewerb* 839.

[12] Case T-181/10 *Reagens SpA v Commission* EU:T:2014:139, para 107.

[13] According to a study prepared for the Commission, available at ec.europa.eu/competition/antitrust/actionsdamages/quantification_study.pdf (last visited 30 December 2014), this presumption is based on the finding that more than 90% of cartels increase prices. This data has, however, been criticised in certain literature, see Weidt (n 9) 438. Presenting some of the difficulties related to the quantification of damages see in addition, E Clark and R Sander, 'Navigating the Quantum Minefield in Cartel Damages Cases' (2014) 23 *Journal of European Competition Law & Practice* (advance access published 23 December 2014) 2.

some level of overcharge) and that consensual settlements are faster and less expensive.[14]

Finally, it also establishes that any participant in an infringement will be responsible vis-à-vis the victims for the whole harm caused by the infringement (joint and several liability) with (a few) exceptions (eg, small and medium-sized businesses (SMEs)).[15] This general solution has been enforced by the recent *Kone* judgement, concerning a follow-on action condemning a cartel.[16] It is a well-known fact that damages claims are normally focused on direct and indirect purchasers in the vertical chain. However, the *Kone* case, concerning umbrella effects, may cause a revolution in this context. The relevant economic question relating to umbrella claims is, as has already been said, 'whether a cartel by the major competitors in an industry had an effect on the price of products which were not expressly subject to the cartel, but were sufficiently close substitutes', benefiting these suppliers from the softening of price competition.[17] Against the recovery of damages, in those cases, it is generally argued that companies outside the cartel are independent and, as cartelists cannot preview the conduct of their competitors, it would be very difficult to prove the causality in competition damages actions,[18] since it would be broken by the action of a third party contributing to the damages.[19] This argument was, however, rejected by Advocate-General Kokkot in *Kone*.[20] In fact, not only did Kokkot argue

[14] Sustaining that in cartel damages claims, procedural interlocutory judgments also encourage the parties to conclude an out of court settlement in addition to a ruling on the merit of the claim and the quantum of the damages, benefiting former cartel members, who can avoid additional reputational damage, and also the claimant and the defendant, concerning legal fees and economic advisors costs, *cf* E Waktare, 'Private Enforcement: Antitrust Damage Settlement Between Claimant CDC and Hydrogen Peroxide Cartellist Kemira (Finland)' (2014) 5 *Journal of European Competition law & Practice* 701.

[15] There is also the possibility of obtaining a contribution from other infringers for their share of responsibility (taking into account their market share or role in the infringement). However, to safeguard the effectiveness of leniency programmes, the Directive establishes that this will not apply to infringers that obtained immunity from fines in return for their cooperation; these immunity recipients will normally be obliged to compensate only their (direct and indirect) customers. Another narrow exception from joint and several liability is foreseen for SMEs that would go bankrupt as a consequence of that liability. SMEs will be liable only to their own purchasers if their market share is under a certain size and their role in the cartel is not essential. Doubting the advantage of special solutions for SMEs in the context of antitrust private enforcement, see D Ridyard, 'BIS Consultation on Private Actions in Competition Law: An Economist's Perspective' (2012) 5 *Global Competition Litigation Review* 152.

[16] Case C-557/12 *Kone* EU:C:2014:1317.

[17] Clark and Sander (n 13) 11.

[18] Arguing that in these cases the solution would be to 'push back on causality and foreseeability tests and consider them automatically met when clear evidence of harm due to a competition law violation has been presented': F Maier-Rigaud, 'Umbrella Effects and the Ubiquity of Damage Resulting from Competition Law Violations' (2014) 5 *Journal of European Competition Law & Practice* 247, 250.

[19] Furthermore, it is said that allowing such recovery would overload the courts and there are no punitive damages in the EU.

[20] Opinion of Advocate-General Kokott in Case C-557/12 *Kone* EU:C:2014:45.

that in umbrella effects cases 'the causal chain traceable back to the cartel is not broken by the intervention of the person not party to the cartel, but is in fact continued if, when determining his prices, that person is (also) guided by the relevant trading conditions and accordingly—and in an entirely foreseeable manner—follows the price initiative taken by the cartel' (no 37), but also that 'the affirmation of the civil liability of cartel members for umbrella pricing is neither more nor less "pro-business" than the categorical exclusion of any obligation to provide compensation' and that it, '[w]ould be eminently unfair to extend unilateral preferential treatment to the cartel members' (no 87). The Court endorsed this broad view, invoking the need to assure the full effectiveness of Article 101 TFEU, and stated that 'the victim of umbrella pricing may obtain compensation for the loss caused by the members of a cartel, even if it did not have contractual links with them, where it is established that the cartel at issue was, in the circumstances of the case and, in particular, the specific aspects of the relevant market, liable to have the effect of umbrella pricing being applied by third parties acting independently, and that those circumstances and specific aspects could not be ignored by the members of that cartel' (no 34). The principle established by the Court, that civil liability of undertakings belonging to a cartel cannot be excluded in umbrella effects cases, although it may have an adverse impact on leniency programmes, it will contribute, along with the new Directive, to the enforcement of antitrust private enforcement, at least in certain markets.

It is not our intention to scrutinise all the improvements presented in the Directive on antitrust damages actions. We will only focus on those solutions that may give rise to certain doubts in the Portuguese context, after a brief introduction to the state of play in that context.

3. ANTITRUST PRIVATE ENFORCEMENT IN THE PORTUGUESE CONTEXT

In Portugal, Rossi and Ferro conducted a survey on competition law cases in Portuguese courts, from 1999 to 2012, and reported more than 30 decisions.[21] Of course, these significant numbers should be considered cautiously as, on the one hand, they include all the cases where Articles 101 and 102 of TFEU and the corresponding national dispositions were pled by any of the parties to the litigation (eg, competition rules are often invoked to challenge the validity of a contractual clause), even if the Court did not consider the issue relevant,[22] while, on the other hand, cases settled prior to

[21] *cf* L Rossi and M Ferro, 'Private Enforcement of Competition Law in Portugal (I): An Overview of Case Law' (2012) 10(Abril/Junho) *Revista de Concorrência e Regulação* 91.

[22] The broad interpretation of 'competition law cases' was the solution followed by the rapporteurs according to B Rodger, in B Rodger (ed), *Competition Law Comparative Private*

a court judgment were not considered. In addition, to our knowledge, with maybe one exception of one controversial case, *Carrefour v Orex Dois*,[23] no follow-on actions have been decided by Portuguese courts,[24] and few collective actions concerning antitrust infringements have been organised so far (in fact, to our knowledge, there is only one case, still pending; on 12 March 2015, the Portuguese Competition Observatory filed a mass damages claim against 'Sport TV', seeking to compensate over 600,000 clients for damages resulting from its anticompetitive practices).[25] However, the Portuguese Supreme Court recently decided the *Toyota* case,[26] concerning a stand-alone action related to a situation of an 'abuse of economic dependency'.[27] In this case, Toyota SC Comércio (Toyota) is the only importer of Toyota's vehicles in Portugal. In 2002, Toyota notified the termination, in 2004, of an exclusive dealership agreement with Auto-AA, an authorised distributor in the north of Portugal. In addition, in 2003, Toyota introduced a selective distribution system for its vehicle sales and did not accept, in 2004, Auto-AA as an authorised dealer (in fact, Toyota intended to replace Auto-AA with another company, which was controlled by Toyota). The Court of First Instance and the Court of Appeal considered that this situation—excluding a company with weak bargaining power, unable to find an equivalent

Enforcement and Collective Redress across the EU (The Netherlands, Wolters Kluwer Law & Business, 2014) 85.

23 *Tribunal da Relação de Lisboa* (Lisbon Court of Appeal), 24 November 2005, proc no 6882/2005-8. In this case, Carrefour charged the defendant for promotional services allegedly rendered; the client argued that those services (eg, opening costs of the products) infringed competition law. The Court considered the contract null and void for infringing the national equivalent to Art 101 and ordered Carrefour to return the payments (€49000) made by the defendant: Rossi and Ferro (n 21) 112–13, considering that case either a 'successful damages claim' or an 'unjust enrichment type of claim'. The possibility, not excluded by the Directive, of bringing other actions for payment instead of an action for damages, such as an action for unjust enrichment, to circumvent the rules on passing-on, has already been addressed by some authors, see M Strand, 'Indirect Purchasers, Passing-on and the New Directive on Competition Law Damages' (2014) *European Competition Law Journal* 361.

24 Follow-on actions could solve many problems, namely reducing the costs of litigation and the calculation of damages could stay with the national competition authorities instead of the national courts. In addition, it has been suggested that in the case of follow-on actions, compensation could be provided from public fines: *cf* Stephen (n 4) 238–39. According to Stephen, this solution would protect the leniency programmes and could also be used as an incentive to compensation (firms should benefit at once from public and private immunity).

25 Lisbon Judicial Court, case no 7074/15.8T8LSB. See M Sousa Ferro, 'Editorial—Collective Redress: Will Portugal Show the Way?' (2015) *Journal of European Competition Law & Practice* (advance access published 7 April 2015) and A Gonçalo, 'Portugal' (2014) *The Private Competition Enforcement Review* (7th edn) 291–92.

26 *Supremo Tribunal de Justiça* (Supreme Court of Justice), *Toyota*, 20 June 2013, proc no 178/07.2TVPRT.P1.S1.

27 Art 12, Law 19/2012, prohibits the abuse of economic dependency consisting of the abusive exploration by one or more undertakings, of a state of economic dependence in which suppliers and customers have no alternative, affecting the functioning of the market or the structure of the competition.

alternative set up with other commercial partners in a reasonable period of time—should be considered an abuse. The Supreme Court of Justice upheld the previous national court decisions, confirmed the existence of an abuse of economic dependency and awarded compensation to Auto-AA amounting to €50,000. The *Toyota* case is the first case in Portugal in which the Supreme Court of Justice awarded compensation for antitrust infringement, strengthening the enforcement of competition law.

It must also be pointed out that there are no specific rules in Portugal for actions for damages from competition infringements. In those cases, besides the Portuguese Competition Law (Law 19/2012, 8 May), the general substantive and procedural rules established in the Civil Code, namely Articles 483 (tort liability)[28] and 562 (damages award), and the Code of Civil Procedure apply.

When there is an infringement, the private party may complain to the Portuguese Competition Authority, and its decision can be reviewed by the Competition, Regulation and Supervision Court[29] (and subsequently the Court of Appeal). Or the private party can complain to the civil courts, and ask for compensation for damages and/or challenge the validity of the agreement, through common declaratory actions, or more rarely through collective actions (the decision can be reviewed by the Court of Appeal and subsequently by the Supreme Court).

Furthermore, there are no specific rules for competition damages actions concerning follow-on actions, settlement procedures[30] or standing to sue for damages. This means that direct and indirect purchasers may have standing, and the courts[31] can request from the parties, opposing parties or third persons the disclosure of documents considered relevant. A refusal to comply could lead to a fine and even reverse the burden of proof.[32]

The judge may also order the production of evidence in order to reach the truth.[33] Expert evidence, in other words an assessment of quantitative damages and a clarification of the economic issues at stake, may be requested by the Court and its probative value is decided by the judge. Recently, in the Portuguese Sport TV case, that kind of request was made and the Portuguese Court of Competition, Regulation and Supervision confirmed, on 4 June 2014, the decision of the Portuguese Competition Authority (PCA) (although reducing the fine), condemning Sport TV for the abuse of

[28] Tort liability, according to Art 483, will depend on the fulfilment of certain conditions: existence of an injury, defendant's fault, damages and the link between injury and damages.

[29] Established by Decree-Law no 67/2012.

[30] According to Portuguese law, parties can, by agreement or conciliation, reach a settlement (which needs to be confirmed by the court), before and during a court proceeding.

[31] Arts 11, 30 and 429–432, Code of Civil Procedure (CPC).

[32] ibid Art 417.

[33] ibid Art 411.

its dominant position in the conditional access market channels with premium sports content.[34]

Concerning the calculation of damages,[35] those awarded are (almost) always compensatory, including actual loss of profits. Punitive damages are (usually) not available in the Portuguese context,[36] nor are contingency fees. In addition, the Portuguese court has a certain amount of discretion; it can decide in accordance with equity (if assessing the damage is impossible or very difficult) and it can reduce or exclude the compensation (if the party contributed to the damages). Furthermore, Portuguese law does not prohibit pass-on defences and there is joint and several liability in actions for damages (and the contribution of each infringer is determined by the court).

On the other hand, legal costs in Portugal are borne by the parties, although at the end of the proceedings the costs of the winning party may be reimbursed by the losing one.[37] The lawyers' fees must compensate the services provided, taking into account the relevance and difficulty of the case. Contingency fees are not allowed, according to Article 101 of the Bar Association Law. However, as it has already been pointed out,[38] there has been a 'dramatic increase in court fees in Portugal as a consequence of the financial crisis of the country', which will certainly limit antitrust damages claims. In this context, alternative funding solutions should be considered.[39]

Finally, concerning settlement, there is no specific judicial settlement procedure available within the scope of competition damages actions. However, Article 22, Law 19/2012, establishes the settlement procedure in the investigation; in other words, during the investigation, the Competition Authority may set a time limit of not less than 10 working days, so the 'undertakings' under investigation express in writing their intention to engage in discussions in order to, eventually, present a settlement draft. On the other hand, competition law issues in Portugal may be, eventually, dealt with through private arbitration. We have already a relevant case in which the Lisbon Court of Appeal confirmed an arbitral decision condemning a company for

[34] Sport TV imposed a discriminatory paying system in the distribution contracts of TV Sport channels: Case no 17384.

[35] Civil Code Art 562.

[36] Although some doubts arose in intellectual property concerning Directive 2004/48/EC of the European Parliament and of the Council of 29 April 2004 on the enforcement of intellectual property rights, [2004] OJ L 195/16. In other words, there are some doubts whether, with its implementation in the Portuguese context, punitive damages were introduced. See HS Antunes, *Da inclusão do lucro ilícito e de efeitos punitivos entre as consequências da responsabilidade civil extracontratual: a sua legitimidade pelo dano* (Coimbra, Coimbra editora, 2011) 432.

[37] Decree-Law 34/2008, 26.2 and Law 72/2014, 2.9.

[38] Gonçalo (n 25) 3.

[39] To see the alternatives available in other countries, such as contingency fees or the possibility of transferring damages claims to a third party see P Buccirossi and M Carpagnano, 'Is it Time for the European Union to Legislate in the Field of Collective Redress in Antitrust (and how)?' (2013) 4 *Journal of European Competition Law & Practice* 6.

abuse of dominant position in the health sector (for excessive prices). The Court considered the contract disposition null and void and significantly reduced the compensation awarded to €887,000.[40]

4. SPECIFIC ISSUES

With the adoption of the Directive on competition damages actions, new rules will have to be implemented in the Member States. We will not address all of them. We will only focus our attention on certain solutions that may raise some difficulties in the Portuguese context, require changes in the Portuguese law or raise some doubts concerning their effectiveness.

4.1 Effects of National Competition Decisions

One of the most relevant issues in the Directive on competition damages actions is the effect of national competition decisions. The final draft of Article 9 of the Directive is quite different from the solution established in the initial proposal presented by the Commission. At the beginning, cartel decisions of national courts and national competition authorities were binding for judges of other Member States. This solution was similar to the one established in Article 16, Regulation 1/2003,[41] concerning the decisions of the Commission under Article 101 or Article 102 TFEU. If the Commission Decision is on appeal, national courts should wait for the final decision and if there are doubts concerning the Commission Decision, the only solution is to make reference to the Court of Justice, according to Article 267 TFEU. However, in the final version of Article 9 of the Directive, final decisions made in another Member State by national competition authorities or review courts are merely prima facie evidence that an infringement of competition law has been established. The solution is different if the cartel decision and the claim for damages occur within one and the same Member State. In that case, the national court is bound by the previous antitrust national decision.

This new solution was introduced in the Directive allegedly to protect the independence of the judges and the Member States. Nevertheless, the same concern or part of it, if relevant, should apply as it has already been pointed out 'for judges in one and the same Member State and Decisions

[40] *Tribunal da Relação de Lisboa* (Lisbon Court of Appeal), *ANF v IMS Health*, 3 April 2014, proc no 672/11.OYRLSB.

[41] Council Regulation (EC) No 1/2003 of 16 December 2002 on the implementation of the rules on competition laid down in Articles 81 and 82 of the Treaty (Text with EEA relevance), [2003] OJ L 1/1.

of the European Commission'.[42] In fact, the decisions adopted by national competition authorities are not binding in all the Member States. While in some countries such decisions only establish a rebuttable presumption (eg, Italy), or it is just an element that the judge can take into consideration (like in Portugal), in other countries (such as Germany) national courts are bound by the decisions made by a foreign national competition authority.[43] Among the various solutions mentioned, the German one seems to be the most effective. Changing Article 9 of the Directive, and setting aside the German solution may not only increase the difficulty of obtaining full compensation, but it may also increase the risk of forum shopping.[44]

4.2 Limitation Period Rules

A further change required by the Directive relates to limitation period rules. Under Portuguese law, the limitation period for tort responsibility is three years, while the Directive establishes five years as the limitation period.

According to Article 498 of the Civil Code, victims in non-contractual liability have three years, from the moment they become aware of their right, to bring damages claims.

On the one hand, the limitation period for the Portuguese competition authority to initiate proceedings for competition infringements, according to Law 19/2012, is five years and there are no special rules regarding suspension or interruption of that period, in order to allow the national courts to delay the proceedings and wait for the decision of the Portuguese competition authority.

According to Article 10 of the Directive, the limitation period shall be at least five years and shall not begin until the infringement of competition law has ceased and the injured party knows or can be expected to know '(a) of the behaviour and the fact that it constitutes an infringement of competition law; (b) of the fact that the infringement of competition law caused harm to it; and (c) the identity of the infringer'. In addition, the limitation period is suspended during the investigations or proceedings of competition authorities.

The new solution established in the Directive will be particularly welcome in the Portuguese context, as it will allow the reconciliation of judicial and administrative proceedings.

On the other hand, the Directive has been criticised for not providing a maximum limitation period. Establishing a limitation period of five years

[42] *cf* Weidt (n 9) 441.

[43] To see the situation in 2013, see Buccirossi and Carpagnano (n 39) 3–5.

[44] On this topic see the pertinent considerations formulated by A Piszcz, in Pais and Piszcz (n 11) 209.

from the moment the victim knows his/her rights and not establishing a maximum limitation period would reward the infringing party for hiding the cartel for years and one should not forget that the older the case, the more difficult it is to prove. Furthermore, and in addition to legal certainty, it has been argued that a maximum limitation period, eg of 10 years, leads to more settlements as infringers will not fear other claims.[45]

4.3 Collective Redress—The Portuguese Opt-Out Model

Another concern of the European institutions, despite not being mentioned in any of the provisions of the Directive, but only in its recital 13 and in the 2013 Commission Recommendation,[46] is collective redress. It is defined as a procedural mechanism that allows 'many similar legal claims to be bundled into a single court action'[47] and referred to in the US as 'class actions', where it has played an essential role in the development of antitrust private enforcement.

One of the main problems, in this context, relates to the legal standing necessary to bring collective action. The Commission favours the opt-in model, where the judgment is only binding for those who opt in, even if experience shows that it is not a very effective solution. In fact, there have been very few antitrust collective redress cases in the Member States and, even those more media-friendly ones, such as *UCF Que Choisir*, were not particularly successful. The former concerns a follow-on action of a French consumer association claiming damages from a cartel involving three mobile operators. Although the cartel could, according to the French Competition Authority, have a negative impact on almost 20 million consumers, only around 12,000 consumers joined the action, receiving in the end some €60. The second case refers to a collective action brought by a UK consumer association (*Which?*), representing only 130 consumers, against JJB Sports, to compensate them for the damages caused by a price-fixing cartel. In the end the amount awarded was £20 per victim.[48] To sum up, in competition

[45] Weidt (n 9) 442.

[46] Commission Recommendation of 11 June 2013 on common principles for injunctive and compensatory collective redress mechanisms in the Member States concerning violations of rights granted under Union Law [2013] OJ L201/60. Sustaining that a legislative intervention on collective redress, through Art 103 TFEU, and considering the regulation to be the most effective method, see Buccirossi and Carpagnano (n 39) 3.

[47] Communication from the Commission to the European Parliament, the Council, the European Economic and Social Committee and the Committee of the Regions, 'Towards a European Horizontal Framework for Collective Redress' COM(2013) 401 final.

[48] These and other cases were referred in detail by Buccirossi and Carpagnano (n 39) 5, who pointed out that consumer associations may not find these actions particularly attractive when victims are dispersed, claims are small and legal expenses are high, like in the French case where the legal expenses amounted to €500,000 while the claim amounted to €750,000.

cases small claims, extensive work and legal expenses discourage both consumer associations and victims to go to court, confirming that an opt-in model is not the most effective solution.

Although the examples above illustrate that the opt-in model is not very effective,[49] and several Member States have established opt-out solutions,[50] the Commission still prefers that solution. In addition, Recital 13 of the Directive declares that '[t]his Directive should not require Member States to introduce collective redress mechanisms for the enforcement of Articles 101 and 102 TFEU'. The combination of section 30 of the Recommendation and Recital 13 of the Directive makes us think that the fears of the excesses of the American experience in the context of class actions, combined with the strong tradition and trust in European antitrust public enforcement, in the end led the European institutions to apparently discourage the use of collective redress. You could say that in the specific context of collective redress, 'the mountain gave birth to a mouse'.

Portugal has an opt-out collective redress system called 'Acção Popular' (PA).[51] It is mentioned in Article 52 (2) of the Portuguese Constitution, which establishes:

> Everyone shall be granted the right of popular actions, to include the right to apply for the adequate compensation for an aggrieved party or parties, in such cases and under such terms as the law may determine, either personally or via associations, that purport to defend the interests in question. That right shall be exercised namely to (...) promote the prevention, cessation or judicial prosecution of offences against public health, consumer rights, the quality of life or the preservation of environment and the cultural heritage.

Damages from competition infringements can be compensated through the PA, as the list of interests mentioned in Article 1 are only examples and the Portuguese Supreme Court in its decision of 7 October 2003 did not refuse that solution.[52]

This right was implemented through Law 83/95 of 31 August 1995 (Popular Action Act/PAA), which establishes special procedural rules

[49] And exceptions should be justified: Communication (n 46) para 1.3. Even if the opt-in model is difficult as damages are low and victims usually fail to opt in, the Commission considers that it is consistent with the legal traditions of the majority of the Member States and the freedom of the victims to take part in the litigation or not.

[50] See the solutions in the Netherlands and Denmark as described in C Lesniken, 'Collective Actions: Rethinking, Funding and National Cost Rules' (2011) 8 *The Competition Law Review* 91, and the Polish opt-in model, even if there has been a drop in the number of group actions, according to Piszcz (n 44) 221, comparing the data from 2010 to 2012.

[51] On this topic, see H Sousa Antunes, 'Class Actions, Group Litigation and Other Forms of Collective Litigation (Portuguese Report)' (2009) 622 *The Annals of the American Academy of Political and Social Science* 161; Rossi and Ferro (n 21), and S Oliveira Pais, 'A união faz a força? Breves reflexões sobre os mecanismos coletivos de reparação no contexto da aplicação privada do direito da concorrência da União' in *Liber Amicorum em Homenagem ao Professor Doutor Mota Campos* (Coimbra, Coimbra editor, 2013) 873.

[52] See Pais and Piszcz (n 11) 215.

concerning this kind of action, namely, 'it is up to the judge's own initiative to collect evidence and [the judge] is not bound by the initiatives of the parties' (Article 17), and even 'if a particular appeal has no suspensive effect, in general terms, the judge may, in a class action, give that effect, to prevent damage irreparable or difficult to repair' (Article 18). Concerning cost expenses, the PAA establishes that the claimant is exempt from the payment of costs if the application is partially granted; if the claim is totally unsuccessful, the claimant will be obliged to pay an amount fixed by the judge amounting to between 10 and 50 per cent of the costs that would be normally payable, taking into account the claimant's financial situation and the formal or substantive reason for the dismissal (Article 20).

The most controversial issues in the PAA are, however, substantive; namely legal standing and compensation, even if the judicial checks available in the PAA might help to reach reasonable solutions.

According to Articles 2, 3 and 16 PAA, standing to initiate a popular action is granted to any citizen, any legally constituted association or foundation (a legal entity whose powers include the interests covered by the PA and is not engaged in any type of professional business competing with companies or liberal professionals), to local authorities in relation to the interests of holders who are resident in the area of their constituency and, finally, to the public prosecutor's office, which may replace the claimants if the contested behaviour endangers the interests involved. SMEs cannot seek compensation directly, but through the claimants referred to in the PAA. If the action is not dismissed by the judge in the preliminary assessment,[53] the claimants will represent all the holders of rights or interests who suffered antitrust damages and did not opt out.

The problem is that the PAA does not fix a minimum number of claimants as in the US with Rule 23 of the Federal Rules of Civil Procedure establishing among other requirements 'numerosity', ie 'the class is so numerous that joinder of all members is impracticable' (usually the benchmark, according to J Douglas Richard, is set at 40 'overcharged purchasers').[54] As popular action may be used by victims to seek compensation for damages caused by antitrust infringements, the issue of the minimum number of claimants assumes increasing relevance.

On the other hand, the court may have to fix compensation for the infringement of interests of holders not individually identified, according to Article 22(2) PAA. Furthermore, the right to damages shall be extinguished within three years from the final judgment that has recognised the damage;

[53] Which the judge might do if the success of the action is considered unlikely (Art 13 PAA).

[54] J Douglas Richards, 'Aggregation of Claims' in *The International Handbook* (n 2) 129. The other requirements of an opt-out class action would be, in addition to numerosity, commonality, typicality, adequacy of representation, predominance and superiority.

the rights corresponding to prescribed amounts shall be delivered to the Ministry of Justice, which will create a special account and allocate the payment of attorney fees and to support access to the courts (Articles 22(4) and (5) PPA). The PAA does not include the possibility of allowing another entity (instead of the court) to distribute the total compensation among the injured parties. Nevertheless, in antitrust cases, consumer associations should be considered the most appropriate entity to fulfil that task, and it has been suggested[55] that Article 31 of the Securities Code may support that solution. In addition, it is important to note that the Portuguese Consumer Association, DECO, has already used the PA successfully to seek compensation for consumers. In the most famous case, *DECO v Portugal Telecom*,[56] the parties arrived at a settlement amounting to €120 million, paid through free national calls for Portugal Telecom's clients during a certain period of time. To sum up, the role of consumer associations, in initiating lawsuits, or being the entity in charge of the receipt and management of the indemnity, should be seriously considered.

5. CONCLUSIONS

Member States have two years to implement the Directive on competition damages actions. Some of the solutions are welcomed by the Member States, while others still raise some doubts.

One of the most relevant issues is the effect of national decisions on judges of other Member States. The Directive puts aside the solutions established in the proposal and establishes that those decisions will only be considered prima facie evidence that an infringement has occurred. This solution does not seem totally coherent with the fact that those decisions are binding for judges in one and the same country. In addition, that solution may not only increase the difficulty of obtaining full compensation, but can also increase the risk of forum shopping.

On the other hand, concerning limitation period rules, the Directive establishes five years, while in Portugal the limitation period for tort responsibility is three. However, the limitation period for the Portuguese Competition Authority to initiate proceedings for competition infringements, according to Law 19/2012, is five years and there are no special rules regarding the

[55] S Rossi and M Sousa Ferro, 'Private Enforcement of Competition Law in Portugal (II): Actio Populari—Facts, Fictions and Dreams' (2013) IV (13) *Revista de Concorrência e Regulação* 35, 78–79.

[56] In this case the telecom incumbent imposed an unlawful 'activation charge' on all clients for all phone calls. The Portuguese courts did not consider the argument of the existence of an abuse of dominant position and condemned Portugal Telecom on other grounds. *Cf* Supreme Court Decision, Case 03A1243, 7.10.2003.

suspension or interruption of that period. The new solution introduced in the Directive, despite not establishing a maximum limitation period, will be particularly welcome in the Portuguese context as it will allow the reconciliation of judicial and administrative proceedings.

Finally, another concern of the European institutions is collective redress; although it is only mentioned in Recital 13 of the Directive and in the Commission Recommendation on common principles for injunctive and compensatory collective redress mechanisms. Using a Recommendation (which is not binding for the Member States) to address the issue of collective redress (instead of approaching it in the Directive) and the fact that the Commission favours an opt-in model (when the experience shows that opt-out models, used in several Member States like Portugal, are more effective) suggest that the fears of the excesses of the American experience in the context of class actions, combined with the strong tradition and trust in public enforcement, apparently led the European institutions to neglect the interests of the victims of competition infringements in this particular context.

In conclusion, even though some of the solutions established in the Directive may raise some doubts, it should be welcomed as a significant step towards achieving a more effective enforcement of competition rules in the EU.

11

Practical Private Enforcement: Perspectives from Poland

ANNA PISZCZ*

1. BACKGROUND

IN POLAND, THE history of competition regulation (in the public interest) began with the Cartel Act (*ustawa o kartelach*) of 28 March 1933, and this in turn was intended to be replaced by the Cartel Agreements Act of 13 July 1939 (*ustawa o porozumieniach kartelowych*). However, the further development of competition law in Poland was prevented by the outbreak of World War II. After the War, Poland experienced the centrally planned economy where almost all the enterprises were state-owned and competition law enforcement did not exist at all before the late eighties.

During the early eighties, the Polish authorities were preparing inter alia the draft Antimonopoly Bill to address some of the problems with the centrally planned economy which was experiencing a depression at the time. The proto-law on competition protection, the Act of 28 January 1987 on counteracting monopolistic practices in the national economy (*ustawa o przeciwdziałaniu praktykom monopolistycznym w gospodarce narodowej*), came into force on 1 January 1988 but the solutions adopted left scholars bewildered. In particular, the Act established the Minister of Finance as an antimonopoly authority which was competent to supervise the state-owned enterprises in respect of their monopolistic practices.

The first mature antimonopoly law (antitrust law, competition law) was the Act of 24 February 1990 on counteracting monopolistic practices and the protection of consumer interests (*ustawa o przeciwdziałaniu praktykom monopolistycznym i ochronie interesów konsumentów*) which came into force on 13 April 1990 (first, under the name of the Act on counteracting monopolistic practices). It came after the inefficient 1987 Act, was suited

* Professor at the Faculty of Law, University of Białystok (Poland), Temporary on Duty of Chairman of the Department of Public Economic Law; member of the Advisory Board to the UOKiK President; piszcz@uwb.edu.pl.

to the needs of a newly adopted market economy and established the new competition authority, the Antimonopoly Office (later renamed the Office of Competition and Consumers Protection). It was in force for over decade, during which time the public enforcement of competition law in Poland was becoming increasingly vigorous.

On 1 April 2001, the 1990 Act was replaced by the Act of 15 December 2000 on competition and consumer protection (*ustawa o ochronie konkurencji i konsumentów*), which was designed to be more compatible with the EC common rules on competition. It was amended considerably as of 1 May 2004, when Poland joined the European Union. This coincided with Council Regulation No 1/2003 of 16 December 2002 on the implementation of the rules on competition laid down in Articles 81 and 82 of the Treaty,[1] coming into force on 1 May 2004 (hereafter: Regulation 1/2003). The challenge for the Polish competition authority (President of the Office of Competition and Consumers Protection *Prezes Urzędu Ochrony Konkurencji i Konsumentów*, hereafter: UOKiK President) was to optimise the public enforcement of national competition law while fulfilling the new role of one of the enforcers of the European common rules on competition.

In 2006, the UOKiK President prepared the new draft Bill which was passed on 16 February 2007—as the Act on competition and consumers protection (*ustawa o ochronie konkurencji i konsumentów*, hereafter: CCPA)—and came into force on 21 April 2007. One of its major characteristics is that it is not possible to initiate proceedings regarding anticompetitive agreements or an abuse of dominance on a complaint anymore; the UOKiK President only does so on his own initiative. Over eight years on,[2] the 2007 Act is still in force; however, it is evolving because of continuing legal challenges. The most important amendment is the Amendment Act of 10 June 2014 (hereafter: the 2014 Amendment Act) which recently came into force on 18 January 2015.

The 2007 Act mainly contains public law provisions (including sanctions), which was the case also of the former antitrust statutes. At the other end of the spectrum are the private law provisions regarding the nullity of anticompetitive agreements and behaviours constituting an abuse of a dominant position. What Polish competition laws lack is a specific legal framework applicable to private enforcement of competition laws (both EU and national competition laws), including damages actions. A specific legal framework applicable to private antitrust enforcement has not been created despite the fact that the concept of group proceedings was developed in the Act of 17 December 2009 on the pursuit of claims in group proceedings (*ustawa o dochodzeniu roszczeń w postępowaniu grupowym*).

[1] [2003] OJ L 1/1.
[2] September 2015.

It is rather remarkable that, so far, public authorities have not established mechanisms that can measure the progress of private antitrust enforcement in Poland. No national statistics on private antitrust enforcement are collected. Private antitrust enforcement cases do not have their own specific case numbers in case registers kept by the courts. Poland still has lessons to learn from, eg, Germany where the national competition authority (*Bundeskartellamt*) has to be informed about all civil litigation concerning competition law infringements, including Articles 101–102 TFEU, and may decide to participate and become involved in civil proceedings.[3] Unfortunately, in Poland the UOKiK President has not collected information on private antitrust enforcement in such or a similar way so far. All of this does not facilitate any scientific analyses intended to involve the measurement of effectiveness of antitrust enforcement in Poland.

2. INSIGHT INTO THE APPROACH OF THE POLISH COURTS

With all the above-mentioned legislation, there has apparently been a very low rate of private antitrust enforcement in Poland. Antitrust has been only sporadically enforced by private claimants.[4] This shows that the system of antitrust enforcement is unbalanced. To fully comprehend the small scale of private antitrust enforcement, you should remember that there are no known cases of antitrust damages actions being brought in the Polish courts by affected third parties.[5] No group actions have been pursued in Poland in respect of antitrust so far; the only group lawsuit in respect of competition protection was on counteracting unfair competition.[6] Stand-alone actions are rare.[7] The most recent Polish study by A Jurkowska-Gomułka

[3] Therefore, the German authority has data on private enforcement; SE Keske, *Group Litigation in European Competition Law* (Antwerp, Intersentia, 2010) 156.

[4] Knowledge gained about other Central and Eastern European states allows us to conclude that they also have proved poor in private competition enforcement so far. See M Brkan and T Bratina, 'Private Enforcement of Competition Law in Slovenia: A New Field to Be Developed by Slovenian Courts' (2013) 6 *Yearbook of Antitrust and Regulatory Studies* 96–105; J Pecotić Kaufman, 'How to Facilitate Damage Claims? Private Enforcement of Competition Rules in Croatia—Domestic and EU Law Perspective' (2012) 5 *Yearbook of Antitrust and Regulatory Studies* 28 ff; K Sein, 'Private Enforcement of Competition Law—the Case of Estonia' (2013) 6 *Yearbook of Antitrust and Regulatory Studies* 135–39; RA Stanikunas and A Burinskas, 'The Impact of EU Competition Rules on Lithuanian Competition Law' (2014) 7 *Yearbook of Antitrust and Regulatory Studies* 102–03.

[5] A Jurkowska-Gomułka, 'Private Enforcement of Competition Law in Polish Courts: The Story of an (Almost) Lost Hope for Development' (2013) 6 *Yearbook of Antitrust and Regulatory Studies* 111.

[6] A Piszcz, 'What Type of Sanctions? Prospects of Private Enforcement of EU Competition Law in Poland' in I Zuģicka (ed), *Proceedings of the 55th International Scientific Conference of Daugavpils University* (Daugavpils, Daugavpils Universitāte Akadēmiskais Apgāds 'Saule', 2014) 602.

[7] Judgment of the Regional Court in Krakow of 8 December 2014 (Case I C 932/14), published at www.orzeczenia.ms.gov.pl.

(of the Centre for Antitrust and Regulatory Studies) did not cause a stir by estimating the number of ongoing private antitrust actions conducted by leading law firms operating in Poland to, in total, three.[8] The survey showed two of them being subject to pre-judicial proceedings at that time.[9]

This will add to the number of antitrust cases identified thanks to the decisions published by the Supreme Court.

By my estimates, collected through public record searches, under all the above-mentioned pieces of antimonopoly legislation there were nine decisions issued by the Supreme Court regarding private antitrust enforcement. Moreover, these were with regard to nullity (and not damages). The actions of nullity used as a sword account for five out of a total of nine cases that reached the Supreme Court.

Most of the anticompetitive practices subject to scrutiny in those nine cases were abuses of a dominant position, in particular in infrastructural markets. Characteristically, none of the nine cases involved consumers as claimants.

Moreover, none of the nine decisions published by the Supreme Court determined that Articles 101 or 102 TFEU were infringed. The European Commission confirmed that between 2008 and 2012, no compensatory follow-on actions followed the cartel decisions in Poland.[10] Only one of the decisions of the Polish Supreme Court (resolution in *TPPD SA v State Treasury*) suggested the possibility of the application of EU competition law in the case scrutinised.[11] The three Supreme Court judges declared that it was possible to decide the case on the basis of not only national competition law, but also EU competition law; however, the lower courts did not examine this question.

Summarising so far, the judgment in *TPPD SA v State Treasury* can be viewed as one single 'episode'. But this one-off episode highlights the difficulties created when infringements of competition law are addressed by private claimants. It has raised, among other things, the issue of the effect of decisions adopted by the national competition authority. Since 1 May 2004, Poland has been bound by Article 16(1) of Regulation 1/2003 stating that when national courts rule on agreements, decisions or practices under the current Articles 101 and 102 TFEU, which are already the subject of a Commission decision, they cannot take decisions running counter to the decision adopted by the Commission. The national courts must also avoid

[8] Jurkowska-Gomułka (n 5) 110.

[9] Ibid.

[10] C Esteva Mosso, *The Commission's Proposal for a Directive on Antitrust Damages Actions* (Brussels, Bruegel, 2013) 7, available at www.bruegel.org/fileadmin/bruegel_files/Events/Presentations/130620_CPL/Carles.pdf (last accessed 16 October 2014).

[11] Case III CZP 52/08 *TPPD SA* (*Toruńskie Przedsiębiorstwo Przemysłu Drzewnego SA*) *v State Treasury* (*Skarb Państwa*), a resolution of the Supreme Court of 23 July 2008, OSP (Jurisprudence of Polish Courts) 2009/7-8/86.

giving decisions which would conflict with a decision contemplated by the Commission in proceedings it has initiated. To that effect, the national court may assess whether it is necessary to suspend its proceedings. Nevertheless, the principle of the binding effect of decisions refers only to decisions adopted by the Commission; there is no such principle embodied in Polish laws in relation to decisions adopted by the UOKiK President (no cross-border effect of decisions) or national competition authorities of other EU Member States (a cross-border effect of decisions), regardless of whether EU competition rules or only national competition laws have been applied.

Before the resolution in *TPPD SA v State Treasury* you could say that thus far the courts have not moved very far towards the principle of the binding effect of national decisions, nor does the Civil Procedure Code (*Kodeks postępowania cywilnego*, hereafter: KPC) allow for such a creativity. Yet this question is central to the future of private antitrust enforcement. First, the Supreme Court advocated the conventional view of the effect of decisions by administrative authorities (in general), according to which such decisions are only evidence (probative effect of national decisions).[12] On the other hand, more surprisingly, in some decisions the Supreme Court established the principle that a decision by the competition authority was the precondition of proceedings before an ordinary court ('prejudiciality').[13] In another series of cases, the Supreme Court held that ordinary courts were free to decide antitrust cases unless antimonopoly proceedings were pending or concluded based on certain types of decisions (the effect of the commencement of national antimonopoly proceedings, the binding effect of national decisions).[14]

Lastly, the Supreme Court argued in favour of the binding effect of final decisions by the UOKiK President.[15] The Court also pointed out that

[12] For example, Case III CZP 46/07 *Danuta K v Commune K (Gmina K) et al*, a resolution of the Supreme Court of 9 October 2007, Biul.SN (Supreme Court Bulletin) 2007/10/7.

[13] For example, Case III CZP 135/95 *Housing Association (Spółdzielnia Mieszkaniowa) in S v Power Plant (Zakład Energetyczny) in Ł et al*, an order of the Supreme Court of 27 October 1995, OSP 1996/6/112; Case III CK 521/02 *PKP SA (Polskie Koleje Państwowe SA) et al v PPH Wilan sp z o.o. (Przedsiębiorstwo Produkcyjno-Handlowe Wilan sp. z o.o.)*, a judgment of the Supreme Court of 28 April 2004, available at www.sn.pl.

[14] eg, Case I CRN 238/93 *Municipal Water and Sewer Utilities sp zoo* (*Miejskie Wodociągi i Kanalizacja sp z oo*) in *K v Brewery in K*), a judgment of the Supreme Court of 22 February 1994, OSNC (Jurisprudence of the Supreme Court Civil Chamber) 1994/10/198; Case I CSK 454/06 *Warsaw Apartments sp z oo v Water and Sewer Utilities SA* (*Przedsiębiorstwo Wodociągów i Kanalizacji SA*) in *W*, a judgment of the Supreme Court of 14 April 2007, published at www.sn.pl; Case III SK 17/06 *Funicular Railway* (*Kolej Gondolowa*) in *K v the UOKiK President*, a judgment of the Supreme Court of 5 January 2007, published at www.sn.pl; these were followed by a judgment of the Appeal Court in Warsaw of 25 November 2009 (Case VI ACa 422/09), available at www.orzeczenia.ms.gov.pl.

[15] Case IV CSK 441/07 *TPPD SA v State Treasury* (n 11); Municipal Heat Supply Company in *O v Housing Association* (*Spółdzielnia Mieszkaniowa*) in *O*, a judgment of the Supreme Court of 4 March 2008, published at www.sn.pl; recently followed by a judgment of the Supreme Court of 21 December 2012 in Case V CSK 9/12 *AB v PGE Mining and Conventional Power SA* (*PGE Górnictwo i Energetyka Konwencjonalna SA*) in *B*, available at www.sn.pl.

ordinary courts should always assess whether it is necessary to suspend proceedings, pursuant to Article 177(1)(3) KPC, awaiting the conclusion of administrative proceedings already underway before the UOKiK President. Already, commentators have voiced concerns that the KPC does not allow the Court to interpret its provisions in such a manner.[16] Article 177(1)(3) KPC provides that the court may (but is not obliged to) stay its proceedings, *ex officio*, where the resolution of the case is dependent on a prior decision by an administrative authority (such as the UOKiK President). There is no doubt that the Supreme Court is wrong regarding the possibility and legal basis for the stay of proceedings, since the KPC contains no provisions which stipulate that the resolution of an antitrust case before an ordinary court is dependent on a prior decision by the UOKiK President. The question of the effect of national antitrust decisions has not yet been resolved satisfactorily in Poland.

All this may raise questions about the scale of public enforcement of EU competition law in Poland. Does the apparent lack of private enforcement correspond with the picture of the public enforcement of EU competition law in Poland? The UOKiK President appears to be enforcing public law sanctions, although the public enforcement of competition law has fallen consistently every year since 2008. In 2009, the UOKiK President completed 107 proceedings with regard to anticompetitive practices, while in 2013 there were 92 such cases (in 2010—103; in 2011—102; in 2012—93). Of the cases which the UOKiK President dealt with in 2009, six regarded infringements which possibly affected trade between Member States within the meaning of Article 101 or 102 TFEU (5.61 per cent). In 2010 there were two such cases (1.94 per cent). In the 2011–13 triennium, the share of cases was even smaller as there was only one case relating to EU law per annum which amounted to about one per cent of the overall score.

All of this gives rise to two questions. The first is how it is possible that such an apparently large number of infringements, which have been investigated and which have taken place in the territory of Poland, do not affect trade between Member States. The second question is whether the figures shown above are considerably influenced by the Commission due to the reallocation of cases. The answer to the second question is that in actual fact cases are not reallocated from the UOKiK President to the Commission. As to the first question, the figures are not as oversimplified as they might first appear. In many of the cases investigated by the UOKiK President, the relevant markets are geographically smaller than the national territory and, therefore the conclusion is that the infringements investigated cannot have an impact on trade between Member States.

[16] A Piszcz, 'Polish Civil Procedure and Antitrust Enforcement—Recent Developments from the Standpoint of Efficiency' in *Recent Trends in Economy and Efficiency of Civil Procedure* (Vilnius, Vilnius University Press, 2013) 282–83.

3. WHY IS PRIVATE ENFORCEMENT NOT BOOMING IN POLAND?

3.1 The Lack of a Specific Legal Framework Applicable to Private Competition Enforcement

Third parties that are affected have a very small appetite for antitrust damages for infringements of both EU competition rules and national competition law. What are the factors that cause difficulties for prospective claimants in the pursuit of their claims and are at the root of the poor condition of private antitrust enforcement? It is not that the enforcement of laws which, on paper, look perfect, is poor. The problem exists partly because of the lack of a specific legal framework applicable to private antitrust enforcement; it seems to prevent affected third parties from engaging in high-risk lawsuits. It is worth comparing the Polish situation with the status quo in Germany where after the introduction of a specific legal framework for private antitrust enforcement the number of actions has grown explosively over a few years.[17]

On the one hand, under Polish civil laws, infringements of EU competition rules and/or national competition law can be classified as torts; therefore, any damages claims from affected third parties must be made within the framework of the general provisions on tort liability contained in Articles 415 et seq of the Civil Code of 23 April 1964 (*Kodeks cywilny*, hereafter: KC). Under the 'general' model of private antitrust enforcement, solutions that address the need to lower barriers to claimants and allow them (in particular consumers) to be treated more favourably than claimants who take part in other categories of civil proceedings, do not exist. These include, among others, such plaintiff-friendly solutions like the reversal of the burden of proof, presumptions (for instance regarding the fault or the extent of the loss), as well as the pre-trial discovery system of the kind that can be found in, for example, the United States. All of these are unknown under the system of private antitrust enforcement in Poland, although the introduction of some of them might provide some value when making decisions in cases, which, in principle, seem legally complex and involve complex factual situations and/or evidence and may be protracted and expensive for claimants who, therefore, need 'hand-holding' by legal counsels.

Furthermore, Polish laws contain no specific legal basis for joint and several liability for co-infringers of competition law. A general legal basis can now be found in Article 441 § 1 KC which stipulates that if several persons are liable for harm caused by tort, their liability shall be joint and several.[18]

[17] www.bundeskartellamt.de/EN/AboutUs/Publications/Activityreports/activityreports_node.html (accessed on 16 October 2014).

[18] See, eg, P Podrecki, 'Civil Law Actions in the Context of Competition Restricting Practices under Polish Law' (2009) 2 *Yearbook of Antitrust and Regulatory Studies* 87.

The concept of 'unity of harm' is a prerequisite for joint and several liability.[19] Such 'unity of harm' exists if it results from the joint operation of harmful factors so that it is impossible to distinguish which factor contributed to what part of the harm. This does not clarify precisely whether the liability of co-infringers in competition law is always joint and several.[20]

Next, Article 63^5 KPC, added as of 18 June 2015, is a general legal basis for amici curiae (friends of the court). However, if the UOKiK President is to fulfil this function with regard to antitrust actions, a specific legal basis needs to be developed. The Polish legislature has just addressed this problem by passing the Amendment Act of 5 August 2015 which will come into force six months after the publication.

Moreover, Polish laws contain no specific provisions on limitation periods with respect to antitrust claims. The time limit for the statute of limitations is three years as of the day when an injured party gains knowledge of the harm and the identity of an infringer, but cannot be longer than 10 years as of the date on which the event causing the damage occurred. More importantly, this time limit is not subject to a suspension or an interruption due to proceedings carried out by the UOKiK President in respect of an infringement. It is further evidence of how the current private antitrust enforcement system in Poland is skewed in a defendant's favour. In practice, many proceedings carried out by the UOKiK President and proceedings in courts which hear appeals against the UOKiK President's decisions last many years. The current construction of the time limit for the statute of limitations is the main reason why such cases are not likely to trigger follow-on lawsuits. The latter also suffer from the second problem, ie jurisprudence that does not provide unambiguous and convergent opinions on the effect of the UOKiK President's decisions which was mentioned above.

Indeed, the Directive on competition damages actions[21] may play a key role in putting these areas of Polish law in order. Its solutions, if implemented in respect of damages actions for infringements of EU competition rules, are at the same time also likely to become embodied in legislation on damages actions for infringements of national competition law.

[19] Case II CKN 859/00 *Knitwear Manufacturing Factory L (Zakłady Przemysłu Dziewiarskiego L) v Alicja G—Foreign Enterprise A (Przedsiębiorstwo Zagraniczne A) et al*, a judgment of the Supreme Court of 20 November 2002, LEX 78881.

[20] See S Oliveira Pais and A Piszcz, 'Package on Actions for Damages Based on Breaches of EU Competition Rules: Can One Size Fit All?' (2014) 7 *Yearbook of Antitrust and Regulatory Studies* 226–27.

[21] Directive 2014/104/EU of the European Parliament and of the Council of 26 November 2014 on certain rules governing actions for damages under national law for infringements of the competition law provisions of the Member States and of the European Union [2014] OJ L 349/1.

3.2 Ambiguous Legal Framework Applicable to Access to Information

The lack of a specific legal framework is not the only factor affecting private antitrust enforcement; it might not even be the most important one. Another factor is that access to the competition authority files is far from unlimited and the legal framework is rather ambiguous but private litigants need accurate information before they sue. The right of access to public information is a flagship principle of the information policy regime in Poland.[22] In principle, Article 5(2) of the Act of 6 September 2001 on the access to public information (*ustawa o dostępie do informacji publicznej*)—in force since 2002 and essentially unchanged since 2002—demonstrates the restrictions concerning this right where the privacy of individuals or business secrets are at stake. Even if they are not, the UOKiK President, as a rule, is unable to share information gathered in the course of proceedings he has carried out. The provisions in Article 73(1) CCPA form a specific framework under which such information may not be used in any other proceedings based on 'separate provisions' (other than provisions of CCPA). However, pursuant to Article 73(2), such 'secrecy' is not offered with regard to inter alia the exchange of information between the UOKiK President and competent bodies if such information may be indicative of the infringement of 'separate provisions'.

It is not entirely clear what the last exception to the principle means. The word 'bodies' can mean so many different things that it is hard to define them all; this includes the problem of classifying courts as 'bodies'. It is fairly certain that under Article 73(2)(5) CCPA the UOKiK President shall disclose information gathered to public prosecutors who carry out proceedings other than those mentioned above (eg, proceedings in cases of infractions). But the question is whether this data is confidential vis-à-vis ordinary courts (dealing with private antitrust litigation) or not? A survey of the academic literature confirmed a lack of consensus concerning this problem. However, in my opinion there are convincing studies that state that under Article 73(2)(5) CCPA, the term 'competent bodies' should be understood as referring to public bodies which are empowered to investigate infringements and institute corresponding proceedings *ex officio*.[23] On that basis, it should be understood that ordinary courts are not 'competent bodies' since they do not have such powers.

There is an interesting difference in the narratives on this position and the opposing one. The latter position is, after the judgments delivered by

[22] See, eg, K Prokop, *Polish Constitutional Law* (Białystok, Temida2, 2011) 60–61.

[23] See, eg, E Rumak and P Sitarek, 'Polish Leniency Programme and its Intersection with Private Enforcement of Competition Law' (2009) 2 *Yearbook of Antitrust and Regulatory Studies* 112.

the CJEU in the *Pfleiderer*[24] and *Donau Chemie*[25] cases, mainly based on the finding that Polish legislation does not give national courts the possibility to conduct the weighing exercise mandated by *Pfleiderer* and *Donau Chemie* and, therefore, is incompatible with EU law.[26] However, the Directive on competition damages actions is 'rolling back' *Pfleiderer* and *Donau Chemie* with regard to discovery and the access of third parties to the competition authority's files. That may help explain why the second interpretation is not necessarily correct. While working on the 2014 Amendment Act, the Polish legislature was reluctant to assume obligations that might result from the *Pfleiderer* and *Donau Chemie* jurisprudence. It opted instead for the strengthening of the level of protection which was criticised in the literature.[27]

Scholars describe a theoretical relationship between Article 73(2)(5) CCPA and the EU jurisprudence, but at the moment no Polish jurisprudence is available which can flesh out vague references in Article 73(2)(5) CCPA. Nor is there any guidance on how to interpret and apply Article 70 CCPA if Polish courts someday would decide to follow the *Pfleiderer* and *Donau Chemie* jurisprudence and appear to perceive themselves as 'bodies' competent enough to require and receive information from the UOKiK President. In the past (before the 2014 Amendment Act), Article 70(1) CCPA provided for the temporary protection of all leniency documents (eg, information and evidence delivered to the UOKiK President 'in return' for immunity from fines or their reduction), as well as the information about the very fact that a leniency application had been submitted (unless the applicant consented in writing to the disclosure).[28] Nevertheless, according to Article 70(2) CCPA, this must have been disclosed to the parties of the given antitrust proceedings before the UOKiK President rendered the final decision.

No one expected dramatic changes to the new Article 70(2) in force as of 18 January 2015; nor is there any explanation given therein now as to the disclosure of information to ordinary courts. The new Article 70 CCPA ascribes protection to settlement documents (the new legal concept which was introduced in Poland on 18 January 2015) as much as leniency documents. Currently, Article 70(4) provides an almost absolute protection of leniency statements and settlement submissions. Pursuant to Article 70(5), a party may take notes of these statements or submissions; the notes must be in writing, either in the party's own handwriting or taken by a person authorised to represent the party. However, parties are only allowed to use

[24] Case C-360/09 *Pfleiderer AG v Bundeskartellamt* [2001] ECR I-05161.

[25] Case C-536/11 *Bundeswettbewerbsbehörde v Donau Chemie AG and others* EU:C:2013:366.

[26] P Sitarek, 'The Impact of EU Law on a National Competition Authority's Leniency Programme—the Case of Poland' (2014) 7 *Yearbook of Antitrust and Regulatory Studies* 204.

[27] Ibid 205–06.

[28] Art 70(3) CCPA.

them for purposes related to proceedings before the UOKiK President or court proceedings resulting from an appeal against a decision adopted by the UOKiK President. The purposes of private antitrust enforcement are not mentioned in Article 70(5).

Furthermore, Article 70(6) CCPA read together with Article 70(1) provides that no leniency/settlement information shall be disclosed under the Act on the access to public information. This raises the question of the interaction between Article 70(1), Article 70(6) and Article 73(2)(5). Do the provisions of Article 70(1) and (6) mean that the disclosure of leniency/settlement information is, in principle, not permitted irrespective of who is applying to the UOKiK President? Or perhaps they only refer to protection from parties (temporary protection) and third parties that might invoke the Act on the access to public information (courts are not such third parties). Another complicated issue is whether the resolution of the problem of ordinary courts as 'competent bodies' has an impact on the interpretation of Article 70. In any case, in this respect the Polish legislature has not done very much to lift the fog of uncertainty that may hold back would-be claimants.

3.3 No Stimuli from the Act on the Pursuit of Claims in Group Proceedings

The Act of 17 December 2009 on the pursuit of claims in group proceedings (hereafter: PCA) came into force on 19 July 2010. Since then no group actions have been pursued in Poland in respect of antitrust. Provisions in the PCA apply to consumer protection, product liability and tort liability claims; it is understood that these include antitrust claims.[29] However, group lawsuits seeking to protect personal rights are barred by Article 1(2) PCA. This strict regulation, intended to rein in group lawsuits, is leading to the creation of an important barrier to access to collective redress. Yet not everyone is convinced that this tool of law enforcement will be efficient.[30]

An opt-in procedure was adopted in the PCA. It is worth remembering that Polish group proceedings have certain clear advantages over other types

[29] See eg, A Jurkowska, 'Antitrust Private Enforcement—Case of Poland' (2008) 1 *Yearbook of Antitrust and Regulatory Studies* 68–69; A Piszcz, 'Still-Unpopular Sanctions: Developments in Private Antitrust Enforcement in Poland After the 2008 White Paper' (2012) 5 *Yearbook of Antitrust and Regulatory Studies* 67.

[30] See eg, T Ereciński and P Grzegorczyk, 'Effective Protection of Diverse Interests in Civil Proceedings on the example of Polish Act on Group Action' in *Recent Trends* (n 16) 47 ff; A Piszcz, '"Class actions" in the Court Culture of Eastern Europe' in L Ervo and A Nylund (eds), *The Future of Civil Litigation* (Heidelberg, Springer, 2014) 366 ff; A Piszcz, 'Has Class-Action Culture Already hit Poland?' in M Etel, I Kraśnicka and A Piszcz (eds), *Court Culture—Conciliation Culture or Litigation Culture?* (Białystok, Temida2, 2014) 140 ff.

of civil proceedings. First, court registration fees are considerably lower (two per cent instead of, in principal, five per cent). Second, the legal basis for contingency fees (up to 20 per cent of the amount awarded in favour of the claimant) was introduced because of the need to make professional lawyers interested in engaging in complex group proceedings. Another advantage of group actions lies in the fact that they fall within the competence of the regional courts (*sądy okręgowe*). As a result, they are judged by a panel of three professional judges instead of a single professional judge at a district court.

However, the positive features of group proceedings seem to be distorted by specific drawbacks. The list includes, first of all, the standardisation of claims in cases concerning monetary relief (Article 2 PCA). Claims can also be standardised into subgroups which can make the standardisation a fiction as the smallest subgroup may comprise only two people. If the standardisation is not approved by all the members of the group, group proceedings will not be allowed by the court. Standardisation is no easy task. The manner in which to standardise claims is questionable as are the possible results thereof in the light of the rule of full compensation.[31] Therefore, lawyers do not work towards standardising claims; declaratory relief is sought instead of monetary relief.[32] They believe defendants to be open to negotiations (which shall end in a settlement) if declaratory relief is granted. But if they are not, it will probably undermine one of the goals of the concept of group action, ie not to multiply actions brought to the courts, as declaratory relief will be followed by massive individual lawsuits against defendants. The difficulty of implementing the standardisation may eventually force group actions to be cut up into hundreds of individual actions after group declaratory relief.

Another drawback stems from the previous one. Given the questions raised about the way in which to standardise claims and the consequential preference for claims for declaratory relief, two phenomena naturally follow. First, contingency fees are not used in practice since they are allowed only in cases concerning monetary relief where the court awards a given sum to claimants. Legal assistance is not rendered on a no-win, no-fee basis where a portion of recoveries goes to the lawyers. Although contingency fees are often associated with funding for collective redress litigation, in practice they do not fulfil this function. Second, lawyers reportedly take upfront fees and if we take them into account we notice that some would-be settlements or individual cases concerning monetary relief must involve relatively modest recoveries.

[31] Piszcz, 'Has Class-Action Culture' (n 30) 143–44.

[32] eg, Case II C 1693/10 *Consumer Ombudsman of Warsaw v BRE Bank*, Regional Court in Łódź.

Another defendant-oriented result derives from the fact that not all the lawyers' fees can be charged to a losing defendant according to the 'loser pays' principle. The court cannot charge more than the maximum fee stipulated in the fees regulations[33] in respect of individual actions.[34] This seems to slightly weaken the assumption that the more members there are in a group of claimants, the easier it is to encourage defendants to resolve the issue outside the judicial process.

Third, group proceedings are very time-consuming. Despite the explanatory notes to the Government's draft of the PCA putting emphasis on increasing efficiency, it will take longer to produce tangible results in group proceedings compared to individual proceedings. After four years with the PCA, of 120 group proceedings initiated between 2010 and 2013, only one case resulted in a final judgment. The proceedings, although very well managed, lasted in two instances over 1200 days.

4. THE FUTURE OF PRIVATE ENFORCEMENT IN POLAND

First, the Polish legislature needs to rethink its approach to collective redress. In 2013, after months of deadlock in its work on collective redress,[35] the Commission issued the Communication 'Towards a European Horizontal Framework for Collective Redress'[36] accompanied by a Commission Recommendation[37] which recommends that all Member States have national collective redress systems based on a number of common European principles. The Member States should implement the principles set out in the Recommendation in national collective redress systems by 26 July 2015 at the latest. The implementation of the Recommendation is not compulsory, but it is possible to follow the Recommendation which is not formally binding for the Member States.

[33] Regulation of the Minister of Justice of 28 September 2002 regulating the issue of fees for advocates' activities and the costs incurred by the State Treasury regarding unpaid pro bono legal aid (*rozporządzenie Ministra Sprawiedliwości z dnia 3 października 2002 roku w sprawie opłat za czynności adwokackie oraz ponoszenia przez Skarb Państwa kosztów nieopłaconej pomocy prawnej udzielonej z urzędu*); Regulation of the Minister of Justice of 28 September 2002 regulating the issue of fees for legal counsels' activities and the costs incurred by the State Treasury regarding unpaid pro bono legal aid (*rozporządzenie Ministra Sprawiedliwości z dnia 28 września 2002 roku w sprawie opłat za czynności radców prawnych oraz ponoszenia przez Skarb Państwa kosztów nieopłaconej pomocy prawnej udzielonej z urzędu*).

[34] Ereciński and Grzegorczyk (n 30) 38; Piszcz, 'Has Class-Action Culture' (n 30) 144.

[35] Piszcz (n 29) 58–60.

[36] Communication from the Commission to the European Parliament, the Council, the European Economic and Social Committee and the Committee of the Regions, 'Towards a European Horizontal Framework for Collective Redress', COM(2013) 401 final.

[37] Commission Recommendation of 11 June 2013 on common principles for injunctive and compensatory collective redress mechanisms in the Member States concerning violations of rights granted under Union Law [2013] OJ L201/60.

Moreover, on 26 November 2014 the Directive on competition damages actions was adopted. Taking collective redress again, it is worth pointing at a discrepancy between what the Directive on competition damages actions suggests and what the Recommendation argues in favour of. Recital 12 of the Preamble of the Directive on competition damages actions declares: '(...) This Directive should not require Member States to introduce collective redress mechanisms for the enforcement of Articles 101 and 102 TFEU (...)'. That seems an odd view, given that Recital 7 of the Preamble of the Recommendation lists competition and consumer protection alongside environmental protection, protection of personal data, financial services legislation and investor protection as areas where supplementary private enforcement of rights granted under EU law in the form of collective redress is of value.

Another general feature of the Directive on competition damages actions that may lead to some debate is that it is slightly misleading to speak of 'the competition law provisions of the Member States' in the title of the Directive. In the definition contained in Article 2(3), national competition law is limited to provisions of national law that are applied to the same case and in parallel to EU competition law pursuant to Article 3(1) of Regulation 1/2003. Moreover, the wording of the last sentence in Recital 10 of the Directive on competition damages actions is as follows: 'This Directive should not affect actions for damages in respect of infringements of national competition law which do not affect trade between Member States within the meaning of Article 101 or 102 TFEU'. This poses a vital question of what meanings are contained in the words 'should not'. The most far-reaching of these would be to the effect that Member States must not model private compensatory enforcement in respect of such infringements of national competition law on the Directive. In any event, it seems unlikely that this interpretation will eventually prove to be correct, since it is inconsistent with the emphasis hitherto placed by the EU institutions on the issue of private antitrust enforcement. Therefore, in my opinion, the words 'should not' were included in Recital 10 to show that for these matters the Directive does not require Member States to model the legal framework on the Directive but they are free to do so. However, it does not seem reasonable for Member States to have 'double' substantive and procedural standards in respect of two types of infringements, as this would make antitrust enforcement even more difficult for ordinary courts.

In particular if the Polish legislature decides to opt for a 'single' standard in respect of two types of infringements, homogenous legal provisions will certainly benefit both ordinary courts and parties to the proceedings. This applies especially to the disclosure of evidence (Articles 5–8 of the Directive on competition damages actions), limitation periods (Article 10), the effect of national final decisions (Article 9), as well as joint and several liability (Article 11).

It is worth highlighting that the EU institutions gave proper consideration to a range of options in respect to the effect of national final decisions. The draft Directive first unveiled a (German-like) cross-border binding effect of national antitrust decisions repeating the scheme of Article 16 of Regulation 1/2003. After the preparatory work in the Council, Article 9 of the draft Directive was transformed in November 2013; the Council's then double standard concerned the no cross-border and cross-border effect of national decisions separately. Emphasis was placed on the probative effect of national decisions instead of their binding effect. Ultimately, Article 9(2) of the Directive states that

> Member States shall where a final decision referred to in paragraph 1 is taken in another Member State, that final decision may, in accordance with national law, be presented before their national courts as at least prima facie evidence that an infringement of competition law has occurred and, as appropriate, may be assessed along with any other evidence adduced by the parties.

Article 9(2) constitutes a minimum harmonisation clause that accounts for an 'at least half-probative' cross-border effect of national antitrust decisions. This gives Member States a choice as to whether they wish their courts to be:

— bound by those decisions;
— governed in their assessments by an irrefutable or rebuttable presumption;
— obliged to treat them as *prima facie* evidence.

Taking into account the jurisprudence referred to in Section two above, it seems that Poland is in a *tabula rasa* situation and free to select one of the above-mentioned competing solutions. However, it would be difficult to choose the minimal solution in the form of *prima facie* evidence, since *prima facie* evidence has not been codified in Polish civil procedure at all and neither judges nor scholars are unanimous regarding what *prima facie* evidence is in Polish legal culture.[38]

Another challenge for the Polish legislature will be to transpose Article 11 of the Directive related to joint and several liability, in particular sections two and three. Referring to the limitations of joint and several liability of small and medium-sized enterprises (SMEs), Article 11(2) constitutes a kind of *de minimis* rule. Member States shall ensure that where the infringer is an SME, it shall be liable only to its own direct and indirect purchasers under certain specified conditions. The above concept (the *de minimis* rule) seems to be an example of a mixture of civil (private) legal provisions and regulatory rules. It is not the first time an EU directive requires national legislatures to intervene in private law for certain EU policy reasons. But is there

[38] See Pais and Piszcz (n 20) 232.

any solid rationale behind the limitations of the civil liability of SMEs? The economic importance of SMEs is unquestionable; on the other hand, one of their main problems is often their lack of knowledge about competition rules. With Article 11(2) of the Directive, the EU institutions are improving the situation for some SMEs. This is certainly praiseworthy and laudable, but it raises an important question. Why, at the same time, do they may make it more difficult for injured persons to obtain fair compensation?[39] The above *de minimis* rule on joint and several liability favours some SMEs. It is worth noting, however, that it will not be easy for SMEs to meet the conditions stipulated in Article 11(2) and, above all, to interpret them.[40]

Article 11(4) of the Directive relates to the limitations of joint and several liability of leniency applicants and, more precisely, immunity recipients. It stipulates that

> '(…) Member States shall ensure that an immunity recipient is jointly and severally liable as follows: (a) to its direct or indirect purchasers or providers; and (b) to other injured parties only where full compensation cannot be obtained from the other undertakings that were involved in the same infringement of competition law (…)'.

This leads to the question of in what circumstances will it be 'impossible' for claimants to obtain compensation from other infringers.[41] It is unclear whether 'cannot' refers to a legal ban (prohibition) or a practical impediment (such as one of the infringers going into liquidation) or both.

What should be the scope of the rule transposing Article 11(4) of the Directive in Poland? The Polish leniency programme refers not only to cartels but also to other agreements, including vertical agreements. It is possible for a participant in a secret vertical agreement covered by Article 101 TFEU (as well as Article 6 CCPA) to report an infringement to the UOKiK President under its leniency programme. Such an applicant shall be granted immunity from antitrust fines but not from normal (regular) joint and several liability. Do 'non-cartel' infringers deserve incentives and privileges similar to those granted to cartel participants? It can be argued that cartel practices (to which the liability privilege is attached) are much more dangerous to market competition than other anticompetitive agreements. However, the possibility of extending the liability privilege to cover non-cartel leniency applicants seems doubtful. Article 11(4) of the Directive seems to be a full harmonisation clause. It does not involve any expressions

[39] See similar concerns in respect of the limitation of civil liability of leniency applicants; C Kersting, 'Removing the Tension Between Public and Private Enforcement: Disclosure and Privileges for Successful Leniency Applicants' (2014) 5 *Journal of European Competition Law & Practice* 4.

[40] See Pais and Piszcz (n 20) 228.

[41] A Howard, 'Too Little, Too Late? The European Commission's Legislative Proposals on Anti-Trust Damages Actions' (2013) 4 *Journal of European Competition Law & Practice* 458.

suggesting that Member States can extend the scope of the liability privilege. Member States are free to do this with respect to competition law infringements of a purely national scope.[42]

Will private mechanisms for antitrust enforcement emerge in Poland alongside the public mechanisms thanks to the Directive on competition damages actions? It seems that the effect of the rules for transposing the Directive might be blunted by the fact that its provisions refer mainly to actions for damages. In Poland, most claims can be categorised as unjust-enrichment claims (claims for ill-gotten gains) resulting from the nullity, and not claims for damages. These may constitute the 'missing middle' in the Polish private antitrust enforcement even after the rules for transposing the Directive are fine-tuned and come into force.

5. CONCLUDING REMARKS

Private enforcement and public enforcement of competition law should be intertwined with and complementary to each other.[43] In Poland it has in practice been proved that they so far hardly even co-exist; private enforcement can be found neither as an alternative to public enforcement nor as a complement thereto.

A review of the Directive on competition damages actions suggests that actions for damages are not the only mechanism in the system of private enforcement of competition law available to victims of infringements, but there are also 'alternative avenues of redress'. Recital 5 of the Preamble implies either that this system involves consensual dispute resolution or, additionally, that it is complemented by public enforcement decisions that give parties an incentive to provide compensation. National competition authorities seem to be seen here as more than routinely engaged in public enforcement. Future policy will determine whether the UOKiK President remains a neutral observer (as has been the case so far) or comes to be seen as a stimulator of compensatory behaviours.

The date of the transposition of the Directive was actually set in Article 21. But the passage of the implementing law should be made as quickly as is practical. Therefore, I recommend that this issue is addressed in the Government's legislative agenda for 2015. Second, training, courses and workshops should be made available to judges to improve their knowledge of competition law and the intricacies of economic analyses.

This is going to be a long-term project (it may take years) aimed at striking a proper balance between the public enforcement and private enforcement of competition law. Antitrust enforcement should be rebalancing in

[42] See Pais and Piszcz (n 20) 229–30.
[43] Piszcz (n 29) 75–76.

a deliberate and sustainable way. I do not believe that this could shift the balance in favour of private enforcement. Public enforcement is here to stay. The strategy for rebalancing antitrust enforcement should focus on 'alternative avenues of redress' in the form of 'decisions that incentivise'. In particular, a greater emphasis should be given to commitment decisions and taking voluntary compensation into account as a mitigating factor when calculating fines. It is worth highlighting that 'settlements', newly introduced into the Polish system of competition law, do not involve compensation as a negotiated remedy.

For academics, such a strategy could be an opportunity to see the sort of policy they have been urging for years in practice.[44]

[44] Ibid.

12

Practical Private Enforcement: Perspectives from Finland—Causal Links, the Principle of Effectiveness and Requirements for National Solutions

KATRI HAVU*

1. INTRODUCTION

THE DIRECTIVE ON antitrust damages actions[1] (the Directive) will clarify and harmonise the law on some aspects of competition restriction-based damages actions. Nevertheless, the entire legislation governing damages claims which are presented before national courts is, in addition to the Directive(-derived) rules, formed by a complex mass of EU and national law. Without any intention of downplaying the Directive and its significance, it should be stressed that the interaction between, on the one hand, EU level case law plus EU principles of law and, on the other, national law, is still of great importance even after the Directive has entered into force and been implemented.

In this contribution, attention is paid to the difficulties of finding correct combinations of EU and national law amongst the many rules and principles that are potentially relevant in the context of damages actions based on EU competition law. Two partially intertwined matters are of special interest here: firstly, causal links and the law on their role and evaluation and, secondly, the EU procedural autonomy principle of effectiveness and

* The author is a Doctor of Laws and works as a Postdoctoral Researcher at the University of Helsinki, Faculty of Law.

[1] Directive 2014/104/EU of the European Parliament and of the Council of 26 November 2014 on certain rules governing actions for damages under national law for infringements of the competition law provisions of the Member States and of the European Union [2014] OJ L349/1.

the outer limits of requirements set by that principle (or of requirements which otherwise appear in the same context). The relevance of both the above-mentioned themes can be noted by observing the current state of EU law[2] or the new Directive with its pointillist and partially vague remarks.[3] Furthermore, the conclusion that the Directive will not resolve all of the difficulties pertaining to these themes is evident.

This contribution seeks to present remarks on causal links and on the outer limits of EU law requirements for national systems from the point of view of EU law, but also mirror the perspective of EU law with actual issues which have already been encountered in Finnish jurisdiction in the context of competition restriction civil litigation. The following sections are organised thematically under the two main topics: *causal links* and *the principle of effectiveness and EU law requirements*. The contribution ends with brief concluding remarks.

2. CAUSAL LINKS: GOVERNING LAW, EVALUATION AND ACCEPTABILITY OF NATIONAL APPROACHES

2.1 Preliminary Remarks

The starting point of EU law has been in accordance with the so-called procedural autonomy that

> [i]n the absence of Community rules governing the matter, it is for the domestic legal system of each Member State to designate the courts and tribunals having jurisdiction and to lay down the detailed procedural rules governing actions … provided that such rules are not less favourable than those governing similar domestic actions (principle of equivalence) and that they do not render practically impossible or excessively difficult the exercise of rights conferred by Community law (principle of effectiveness).[4]

Moreover,

> [i]n the absence of Community rules governing the matter, it is for the domestic legal system of each Member State to prescribe the detailed rules … including those on the application of the concept of 'causal relationship', provided that the principles of equivalence and effectiveness are observed.[5]

[2] See for instance, Case C-453/99 *Courage Ltd v Crehan* [2001] ECR I-6297 (*Courage*), paras 26 and 29; Joined Cases C-295/04 to C-298/04 *Manfredi v Lloyd Adriatico Assicurazioni SpA and others* [2006] ECR I-6619 (*Manfredi*), paras 60–64; Case C–199/11 *Europese Gemeenschap v Otis NV* EU:C:2012:684 (*Otis*), paras 40–43 and 65–66; and Case C–557/12 *Kone AG and others* EU:C:2014:1317 (*Kone*), paras 21–26 and 32–37. See also Case C-439/08 *VEBIC* [2010] ECR I-12471, para 57; Case C-360/09 *Pfleiderer* [2011] ECR I-05161, para 24; and Case C-536/11 *Donau Chemie* EU:C:2013:366, paras 27 and 32–33.

[3] See, for instance, Directive Arts 2–3 and 12–17 and recs 11 and 46.

[4] *Manfredi* (n 2) para 62. See also *Courage* (n 2) paras 26 and 29.

[5] *Manfredi* (n 2) para 64.

A causal link, causal relationship or causal connection constitutes in general one of the most basic conditions for awarding damages. To a great extent it is the basis for a decision concerning whether there is a legally significant connection between an action and the result under evaluation. A legally relevant causal link is also a means of classifying all kinds of unwanted results of actions and omissions into two groups: those which should be compensated for and those which should not (for different reasons). Legally significant connections may thus differ from 'objective' causal connections.[6] It is, moreover, worth underlining that it is relatively difficult to produce an accurate and exhaustive description of what a legally significant causal connection actually entails, and what are, more precisely, the considerations needed to confirm its presence.[7]

The EU concept of a causal link is to all intents and purposes an autonomous concept which should be interpreted as an EU legal term. This is no mean task. In the context of vertical liability, for instance, it has been noted that the Court of Justice of the EU (CJEU) uses the terms 'causal link'[8] and 'direct causal link' or similar expressions without properly explaining or defining what is meant by them. This relates to the fact that in addition to private liability cases it is typical in Member State liability case law that the definition and application of (the conditions of) a causal link are governed by the relevant domestic legal system.[9] Moreover, it has been remarked that

[6] See also, for instance, HLA Hart and T Honoré, *Causation in the Law*, 2nd edn (Oxford, Oxford University Press, 1985) 62–129. As to competition restrictions and causation, see, for example, T Eger and P Weise, 'Harm and Damages as Economic and Legal Categories in Antitrust Law' in J Basedow et al (eds), *Private Enforcement of Competition Law* (Baden-Baden, Nomos Verlagsgesellschaft, 2011); M-O Mackenrodt, 'Private Incentive, Optimal Deterrence and Damages Claims for Abuses of Dominant Positions—The Interaction between the Economic Review of the Prohibition of Abuses of Dominant Positions and Private Enforcement' in Mackenrodt M-O et al (eds), *Abuse of Dominant Position, New Interpretation, New Enforcement Mechanisms?* (Berlin, Springer-Verlag, 2008) 181–88.

[7] See also W Landes and R Posner, *The Economic Structure of Tort Law* (Cambridge, Harvard University Press, 1987) in particular 228–33: the authors suggest that a legally significant causal connection is actually a collective expression for much more complex evaluations.

[8] Or 'relationship'.

[9] As regards discussion see, for instance, N Reich, 'Horizontal Liability in EC Law: Hybridization of Remedies for Compensation in Case of Breaches of EC Rights' (2007) 44 *Common Market Law Review* 705, 726–29; M Weitenberg, 'Terminology' in H Koziol and R Schulze (eds), *Tort Law of the European Community* (Wien, Springer-Verlag, 2008) 335–40; C Van Dam, *European Tort Law*, 2nd edn (Oxford, Oxford University Press, 2013) 321–24. As to case law see, for instance, Case C-352/98 P *Laboratoires Pharmaceutiques Bergaderm* [2000] ECR I-5291, para 42; Case C-472/00 P *Fresh Marine* [2003] ECR I-7541, para 25; Case C-419/08 P *Trubowest Handel GmbH and Makarov* [2010] ECR I-2259, paras 53–64. These cases include references to a 'direct causal link' and other causation related expressions, but the significance of the terms remains vague. In the last mentioned case *Trubowest Handel GmbH and Makarov*, some discussion on the meaning of a direct causal link is included (in the context of the liability of the Community). The Court notes, for instance, that 'the alleged harm must be a sufficiently direct consequence of the conduct complained of without a break in the causal link' (para 57, see also paras 58–59).

the use of the concepts does not seem to correspond to any causation tests used in the legal orders of Member States.[10]

In the context of competition restriction damages actions, the matters highlighted above signify that a central factor of damages liability assessment has been left to be guided by the national laws of Member States. As a result, also diverging decisions as regards to awarding damages in similar situations are at least primarily accepted from the point of view of the relevant EU law.[11] Regardless of the partial limitations set by the principles of effectiveness and equivalence, and regardless of the additions to the state of EU law which have been made in case law and are being made by means of the Directive, the focused way national legislation approaches causal connections has not lost its relevance.

EU case law on competition restriction damages actions is central in evaluating the kind of national rules and solutions that are in accordance with EU requirements and what is directly applicable EU law. But the relevant EU source is not solely law which explicitly mentions causal links or causal connections—laws on many tangential issues are potentially relevant as well. Causal links, as a subject of legal evaluation, overlap with matters such as damage and compensable damage, quantifying losses and potential claimants. Moreover, at least in theory, also EU (case) law which utilises the concept of a causal link or its synonyms could be relevant even though it deals with liability contexts that are different from competition restriction situations.

2.2 Causal Links in Damages Cases Based on Infringements of EU Competition Law

To study the relevant and acceptable law on causal connections in competition restriction cases before national courts, some more in-depth remarks on EU case law and on the Directive are in order. In the competition restriction private liability cases, the CJEU started by discussing a 'loss caused … by a contract or by conduct liable to restrict or distort competition',[12] proceeded to use the term 'causal relationship'[13] and has, more recently, also referred

[10] See Weitenberg, 'Terminology' (n 9) in particular 335 and 337.

[11] These issues have been discussed by this author in, for instance, K Havu, 'Quasi-coherence by Harmonisation of EU Competition Law-related Damages Actions?' in J Smits and P Letto-Vanamo (eds), *Coherence and Fragmentation in European Private Law* (Munich, Sellier European Law Publishers, 2012); K Havu, 'Horizontal Liability for Damages in EU Law—The Changing Relationship of EU and National Law' (2012) 18 *European Law Journal* 407, 414–15. See also D Ashton and D Henry, *Competition Damages Actions in the EU, Law and Practice* (Cheltenham, Edward Elgar, 2013) 102–03.

[12] *Courage* (n 2) para 26.

[13] *Manfredi* (n 2) paras 63–64.

to a 'direct causal link' or 'direct link' in addition to a mere 'causal link'.[14,15] It is not evident what is meant with the addition of the word 'direct' or what the difference between, for instance, a 'direct link' and a 'causal link' is. Simultaneously, discussions on a broad group of potential *claimants or recipients of compensation*[16] emphasise the ambiguity which surrounds the expression a 'direct (causal) link'. The requirement of directness added by the *Otis* case is rather vague if you try to interpret it on the basis of competition restriction damages case law, but also if you try to interpret it with the help of vertical liability case law.[17] Moreover, the relationship between the requirement of directness and other causation-related statements in the umbrella pricing case *Kone and others* remains partially unclear.[18]

The interconnections between the discussions on causal links in CJEU case law—including the references to national law and to the principles of effectiveness and equivalence—and the rules or guidance on potential claimants or recipients of compensation are certainly blurred. This seems to continue to be the case even now, after the adoption of the Directive.[19]

Also, the interrelationships between a causal link and its evaluation and requirements for *full compensation* or compensation for *certain types of losses* are to some extent problematic.[20] You could draw the conclusion that also strict national approaches to causation are acceptable, and not compensating losses which are not causally connected to the competition restriction under the (mainly) national assessment is fine from the point of view of EU law. Playing the devil's advocate, you might claim that the requirement of full compensation, or any requirements on compensation, cannot be relevant in the context of 'losses' or 'damages' that were concluded to be, for instance, too distant or caused by reasons which are separate from the competition restriction.

A national approach to causation which infringes one or both of the principles of effectiveness and equivalence may not be applied to an EU competition law-based damages case before a national court. The principles mentioned above, together with other requirements of principle in EU law, set limits regarding the acceptability of national rules or the results of those rules. Guidance as to the significance of, in particular, the principle of effectiveness is already available even within competition restrictions private

[14] Or 'relationship'.

[15] See *Otis* (n 2) para 65. See also *Kone* (n 2) paras 21–24 and 33–34.

[16] See *Otis* (n 2) paras 40–44; *Kone* (n 2) paras 33–34 and 37. See also the Directive, Arts 2–3 and 12–16.

[17] See, regarding the latter, the discussion on case law above in n 9.

[18] See *Kone* (n 2) paras 21–24, 33–34 and 37.

[19] See for instance *Courage* (n 2) para 26 ('if it were not open to any individual to claim damages for loss caused to him'), which is also frequently referred to in later case law. See also *Manfredi* (n 2) paras 60–64. As to the Directive, see Arts 2–3.

[20] See, for instance, *Manfredi* (n 2) paras 60–64, 90, 95 and 100. As to the Directive, see Art 3 on the right to full compensation. See also Havu, 'Quasi-coherence' (n 11) 34–40.

liability case law.[21] Nevertheless, no exhaustive guidance on acceptable national law or its applications exists. Moreover, some of the conclusions which have been drawn from the principle of effectiveness do not logically follow from the core content of the principle—this renders sketching the still invisible parts of EU law and predicting the future stance taken by the CJEU difficult.[22]

The Directive does not present complete EU rules on causal links and their evaluation.[23] The parts of the Directive which relate to matters bordering on the evaluation of causation are relevant EU law, and the related national rules are based on applicable EU law, but areas which are only partially or not at all dealt with by the Directive are still governed by a combination of EU rules and principles, and national law.

The provisions of the Directive which are or may be of relevance in the process of evaluating causation include at least Article 3 on the right to full compensation; Article 2 on the definitions of the terms used in the Directive, including, for instance, an attempt to define 'injured party'; Article 11 on joint and several liability as well as 'harm caused by the infringement of competition law'; Articles 12–16 on passing-on, indirect purchasers and the treatment of claims presented by actors of different market levels in the context of the same infringement, and noting that guidelines for estimating overcharges that were passed on shall be issued by the Commission; and Article 17 on the quantification of harm.

Furthermore, the Recitals of the Directive include some noteworthy passages, such as Recital 11 in which it is noted that where Member State systems provide other conditions for compensation, 'such as imputability, adequacy or culpability, they should be able to maintain such conditions in so far as they comply with the case-law of the Court of Justice, the principles of effectiveness and equivalence, and this Directive'. Also, for instance, Recitals 12–13 on, among other things, compensable losses and interest, and on avoiding overcompensation, are of relevance. As are Recitals 39–41 and 43–46 which discuss, among other issues, proving the amount of damages and the role of national law in that context.

The exact effects that the statements of the Directive (and the national laws implementing them) are supposed to have when a national court is resolving causation-related matters in a concrete case are neither obvious

[21] See, for instance, *Courage* (n 2) paras 28–31; *Manfredi* (n 2) paras 90–100; *Kone* (n 2) paras 21–24 and 32–37. The two last mentioned cases and the role of EU requirements are discussed further in the section on the principle of effectiveness and EU law requirements below.

[22] These issues are discussed more closely below, in s 3.

[23] See also the Communication from the Commission on quantifying harm in actions for damages based on breaches of Article 101 or 102 of the Treaty on the Functioning of the European Union [2013] C167/7 (13 June 2013), paras 5–9, and rec 46 of the Directive. These passages highlight the role of national law, but also the principles of effectiveness and equivalence in causation-related matters, in the context of quantifying damages.

nor clarified in any detail by the Directive. The national court still has a bulk of rules, principles and presumptions, of both EU and national background, to organise and 'crystallise' to form applicable law with some kind of hierarchy.

Relatively open central questions as regards causation and the acceptability of decisions by national courts include matters like when the test for existence of a causal relationship is too strict so that applying it, for instance, signifies infringing the principle of effectiveness. You might say that a law or interpretation which would always result in a causal link not being established would be incompatible with EU law. Defining which other solutions are unacceptable is an intricate issue.

In the case law of the CJEU, numerous references have been made regarding the possibility of *claiming compensation*[24] but there is much less available on the likelihood of succeeding with your claim and *receiving compensation,* and on the evaluation of the national law in this respect.[25] The requirement regarding the possibility of *claiming* compensation is of course closely tied to the idea of the potential results of a claim. In addition to recent cases, the Directive appears to underline the practical possibility of receiving compensation.[26] Nevertheless, it is difficult to evaluate whether—from the point of view of the requirements of EU law—the chances of some actors obtaining compensation are too insignificant, even though the law would not preclude those actors' claims.[27]

In the same vein, it may be remarked that the Directive introduces presumptions which deal with causal link related matters, but also recognises that rebuttal is possible.[28] At what point is rebutting too easy?

Parts of the Directive, as well as certain passages of some earlier preparatory documents, and for instance the *Otis* judgment, seem to suggest that approaches where a causal link forms a high threshold for obtaining damages are also compatible with EU law.[29] On the other hand, judgments like the one made in *Kone* call for a cautious analysis. Moreover, it should be borne in mind that before we enter into a discussion on, for instance,

[24] See, for example, *Courage* (n 2) para 26; *Manfredi* (n 2) paras 60–61; *Otis* (n 2) paras 41–44; *Kone* (n 2) paras 21–24.

[25] See, for instance, *Donau Chemie* (n 2) paras 32–33; *Kone* (n 2) paras 31, 34 and 37.

[26] See the Directive Arts 2 and 3 and, for example, recs 4–6, 12–13. See also similarly the speech by Commissioner J Almunia, 'Looking Back at Five Years of Competition Enforcement in the EU', Global Antitrust Enforcement Symposium, Washington, 10 September 2014).

[27] Moreover, EU law does not seem to take a stand concerning the claimant's responsibility as regards to formulating the claims and asserting the most favourable legal basis. These matters relate to evaluating different domestic law options and their relationship to EU law.

[28] See, in particular, the Directive Art 17(2) on the presumption that cartels cause harm. Note also the rules on passing-on and indirect purchasers in Arts 12–16.

[29] See, for instance, Directive Arts 3(3) and 12(2) on overcompensation. As to earlier documents, see Commission Staff Working Paper (Annex to the Green Paper Damages actions for breach of the EC antitrust rules) SEC(2005) 1732, paras 274–76. As regards *Otis* (n 2), see para 65.

national causation tests and the principle of effectiveness, the national approach to causation may be rendered (partially) incompatible with EU law because of the contradictions it presents when compared to more exact EU rules, on, for instance, claim (or damages) entitled actors or compensable losses. For example, national traditions according to which, in the context of pure economic loss, legally significant causal relationships may not include too many steps with different actors, may conflict both with the existing EU case law and the provisions of the Directive.

2.3 Notes on (the Basis of) Finnish Cases

In the cases that have been dealt with by Finnish courts, several causation-related issues touching upon the relationship and interaction of EU and national law have been encountered, either explicitly or implicitly.

One of the dilemmas which is indirectly raised by the cases brought to Finnish courts, and which potentially has a broad significance across the Member States, is when does law provide an effective enough chance *to actually obtain compensation*? This theme could also be discussed in the following section on the principle of effectiveness and EU law requirements, but as it also touches upon the evaluation of causal connection, it can justifiably be brought up now in the context of tangential Finnish cases. Relevant EU law as regards causation, the practical possibility of *receiving* damages and national solutions have already been discussed above.

In the *Asphalt cartel damages claims* case[30] the Helsinki District Court had to evaluate whether a limitation to the applicability of a provision in the former Act on Competition Restrictions (480/1992)—the competition restriction damages provision 18a being applicable only to relationships between undertakings—resulted in a conflict with EU law as several of the claimants could have been regarded as something other than an undertaking (non-undertaking public authorities). The Court reasoned that restricted applicability of one provision is not problematic from the point of view of EU case law when other legal bases for awarding damages are available.[31] The Court did not proceed to evaluate in detail whether the other asserted legal bases were as *effective* as EU law required.

[30] A case entity where the Helsinki District Court heard 41 damages and comparable claims by the State of Finland, and Finnish cities and municipalities after a nationwide (and EU law-infringing) asphalt cartel had been found against in public enforcement. On 28 November 2013 the Court issued 41 judgments (collectively: *Asphalt cartel damages claims*). Amongst the judgments were L 09/10623 on the claim by the city of Helsinki, L 09/49467 on the claim by the city of Espoo, and L 11/2572 on the claim by the city of Kemi. All the judgments of the entity decided on 28 November 2013, except for the judgment on the claim by the city of Kemi, are under appeal and pending before the Helsinki Appellate Court.

[31] See the judgment on the claim by the city of Espoo, ibid, 254–57 (ss 4.5.4–4.5.5).

Anyhow, it should be noted that in the context of legal bases which are 'secondary' or general and maybe not optimal for competition restriction cases, it may be central to assess whether some of the conditions for awarding compensation actually, according to the usual interpretation tradition, result in too high a threshold for receiving damages when seen from the point of view of EU law. It may be wise to analyse whether the national tradition or established interpretation should be rethought in the competition restriction context. In the Finnish *Asphalt cartel damages claims* case, these issues could have been of particular importance if the damages claims had been assessed to a significant extent under general tort law, in the context of which pure economic loss is compensated only if special criteria are fulfilled and the approach to legally significant causal relationships is strict and pertains only to rather 'short' and obvious causal relationships to justify compensation.[32]

Generally in the *Asphalt cartel damages claims* judgments, the approach to causal relationships is, in any case, relatively claimant-friendly. On the basis of most of the economic evidence and a significant part of the other evidence provided, the Court's point of departure was that the cartel had raised prices by 15–20 per cent.[33]

The extent to which the effects of any (alleged) competition restriction should be distinguished from the effects of other phenomena is a subtheme of legally relevant causal links. Alternative and cumulative reasons for 'damages' form a typically challenging theme in the evaluation of causal relationships.[34] In the Finnish *Car spare parts damages claims* case,[35] the claimant argued that it had suffered considerable economic damage and losses due to attempts by the defendants to hamper the claimant's cooperation with a retail chain. It had been established in public enforcement proceedings that a cartel or concerted practice, which also infringed EU law, had indeed taken place. The Helsinki District Court concluded that the claimant had obviously encountered some loss of profit and difficulties in its business operations, but noted that it had failed to establish a legally significant connection between the competition restriction and any alleged illegally caused damage. Other reasons for the unwanted developments were not excluded to a sufficient extent.[36]

[32] Some authors also suggest that if compensation for pure economic loss is justified under the criterion 'especially weighty reasons for compensating the damage', which would be the applicable criterion in most competition cases if assessed under general tort law, the approach to legally significant causal relationships is even stricter. See, for instance, P Ståhlberg and J Karhu, *Suomen vahingonkorvausoikeus* (Helsinki, Talentum, 2013) 383–84.

[33] See, for instance, the judgment on the claim by the city of Espoo (n 30) 309–12 (s 9.2); the judgment on the claim by the city of Helsinki (n 30) 241–46 (ss 7.2–7.3).

[34] See also, for example, Van Dam, *European Tort* (Oxford, Oxford University Press, 2013) 329–37 and 323–24.

[35] Helsinki District Court, L 07/33936 on 31 March 2014. The judgment has been appealed and the case is pending before the Helsinki Appellate Court.

[36] See ibid, 171–80.

A decision like this could obviously constitute a problem when evaluated in the light of EU law if the facts clearly pointed towards a competition restriction like the cause of loss of profit. But in situations where competition restriction evidently plays a marginal role, a solution like this one may be perceived as the normal application of a causal relationship. Analysing the middle ground between these extremes is, with the current state of EU law, rather a challenge.

Of course, 'easy' causal link evaluations are also possible regardless of the complex combination of applicable EU and national law. For example, in the *Asphalt cartel damages claims* case, the Helsinki District Court found that the city of Kemi was not entitled to compensation as the contract prices it had paid were based on contract terms that were drafted before the competition restriction affected the price level.[37]

3. THE PRINCIPLE OF EFFECTIVENESS AND OUTER LIMITS OF EU LAW REQUIREMENTS

3.1 Preliminary Remarks

The principle of effectiveness (national rules must not render relying on EU law practically impossible or excessively difficult) has developed into its current wording from a prohibition against 'practical[38] impossibility'.[39] The current long wording of the core contents of the principle of effectiveness clearly refers to the *impossibility* or *considerable difficulty* of effectively relying on EU law. The reason why the principle of effectiveness is or should be of particular interest in the competition restriction damages context is the obscurity of the outer limits of the requirements the principle (or EU law otherwise) sets for national systems. Matters touching upon this issue have already been mentioned in the section on causal links above.

Some of the conclusions drawn on the basis of the principle of effectiveness raise, at least to a certain extent, the question whether also requirements which are not actually explained by the wording of the core contents of the principle[40] are prospective conclusions from the principle in the future. Furthermore, it may be justified to understand some of the apparent applications of the principle of effectiveness as actually including requirements which are additional to the principle, even though the requirements

[37] This is the only asphalt cartel damages claims judgment of 28 November 2013 which was not appealed.

[38] Or 'virtual', see, for example, Case 199/82 *San Giorgio* [1983] ECR 3595.

[39] See, for instance, Case 68/79 *Just* [1980] ECR 501, para 18, which still mentions mere practical impossibility. Compare to *San Giorgio*, paras 12–14. Para 12 also includes references to earlier case law that only mentions practical impossibility.

[40] Examples from competition damages cases are discussed in the next subsection.

are presented by the CJEU in an unstructured way.[41] This, and the related lack of clarity, makes evaluating the EU law compatibility of a national solution highly challenging. Requirements which may be regarded as new or additional are possible, among other things, in the light of the classic formulation '*in the absence of Community rules* governing the matter; it is for the domestic legal system of each Member State' to lay down the necessary rules.[42]

3.2 Intriguing Appearances in the Competition Restrictions Damages Context

It is central to note, for example, that in *Manfredi* the discussion on compensable types of losses has been constructed as the application of the principle of effectiveness.[43] Furthermore, in *Kone*, it seems that the principle of effectiveness plays a part in concluding that 'the victim of umbrella pricing may obtain compensation for the loss caused by the members of a cartel'.[44] If the principle of effectiveness, or all EU law requirements applied together with the principle, may lead to these results, what kind of conclusions made on the basis of national law are not captured by the EU requirements? It is evident that an analysis against the background of the mere 'may not render relying on EU law practically impossible or excessively difficult' will not yield a trustworthy answer.

For instance, in *Kone*, one could have reasoned that, in general, relying on EU law is possible and not even excessively difficult, even though national rules on compensation would not result in awarding damages to so-called *umbrella customers*, which are connected to the competition-infringing behaviour only by a 'long' and complex causal link—and applying a causal

[41] On potential additional or particularly stringent requirements, see S Prechal and R Widdershoven, 'Redefining the Relationship between "Rewe-effectiveness" and Effective judicial Protection' (2011) 4 *Review of European Administrative Law* 31; P Van Cleynenbreugel, 'Transforming Shields into Swords: The VEBIC Judgment, Adequate Judicial Protection Standards and the Emergence of Procedural Heteronomy in EU Law' (2011) 18 *Maastricht Journal of European and Comparative Law* 511; K Havu, 'Private Enforcement of EU (Competition) Law—Remarks and Outlooks Regarding the Intertwinement of EU and National Law' (2014) 150 *Tidskrift utgiven av Juridiska Föreningen i Finland* 55, 59–64.

[42] *Courage* (n 2) para 29 (emphasis added).

[43] See *Manfredi* (n 2) paras 95–100. See also, in the context of vertical liability, Joined Cases C-46/93 and C-48/93 *Brasserie du Pêcheur* [1996] ECR I-1029, paras 83, 87–90.

[44] *Kone* (n 2) para 34, determining whether liability was left up to the national system. See also para 37 on liability towards umbrella customers, including the remark 'the answer to the question referred to is that Article 101 TFEU must be interpreted as meaning that it precludes the interpretation and application of domestic legislation enacted by a Member State which categorically excludes, for legal reasons, any civil liability of undertakings belonging to a cartel'. In *Kone*, 'full effect and practical effect of competition law' reasoning merges with procedural autonomy principles focused reasoning: see paras 24–26 and 32–37. See similarly *Donau Chemie* (n 2) in particular, paras 27 and 47–49.

link as a condition for liability is, as a starting point, acceptable. Nevertheless, it should be noted that in *Kone*, part of the problem, according to the CJEU, appears to be the impossibility of even *claiming* compensation.[45] This justifies the use of the principle of effectiveness or similar principles at least to the extent that prevents a situation where access to justice is denied. As to observations on *Manfredi*, requirements such as those presented on compensable losses in the case are not necessarily the logical result of the (core contents) of the principle of effectiveness. Foreseeing the statements on the basis of the wording of the principle was probably not common, at least not before the principle was used in this way in vertical liability case law.

Again, the area of potential claimants and recipients of compensation is a matter which contains possibly interesting relevant elements, like the situation of potential buyers who were priced out of the market or otherwise did not buy the product affected by competition restriction for reasons which derive from the competition infringement.[46] If EU law requires that umbrella customers may receive compensation, is the correct interpretation of the requirements that claimants like the ones mentioned above should also be afforded this possibility? How about potential umbrella customers who did not purchase the relevant product? Further questions relate to the issue of how easy it should be to obtain compensation.

Article 4 of the Directive discusses the principles of effectiveness and equivalence explicitly, stating their relevance and core contents. Nevertheless, the interface of the conditions for liability and EU law requirements continue to be puzzling. As can be noted above in the context of causal links, the exact interrelationships of the principles and the provisions of the Directive and the national laws implementing them, as well as the significance of the principles in the context of the national rules 'surrounding' and complementing the Directive-based rules, remain vague and do not directly translate into solutions which national courts may safely adopt.[47]

3.3 Notes on (the Basis of) Finnish Cases

Taking EU law highlights presented above into account, there are evidently numerous difficulties in evaluating whether a national solution infringes the principle of effectiveness or other strong requirements which appear in the

[45] See *Kone* (n 2) para 37 and paras 3–15, 21–24 (compare, however, paras 31 and 34). Of course, the question that arises here is what not being able to claim even is. As regards the CJEU's perceptions of the domestic state of law, it must be borne in mind that the CJEU answers the preliminary ruling questions within the framework set by the referring national court—this emphasises the relevance of the CJEU's understanding or description of the (main case) legal context.

[46] See on these 'victims', in particular, WPJ Wils, 'Should Private Antitrust Enforcement be Encouraged in Europe?' (2003) 26 *World Competition* 473, 487–88.

[47] See also, for instance, the Directive recs 11 and 46.

same contexts. For example, as regards applications for other, in principle acceptable, conditions for liability: is *requiring that the claimant shows fault* (intention or negligence) on the part of the defendant contrary to the EU requirements, even, for instance, in an abuse of dominance case with a 'surprisingly' narrow market definition?[48] And, again regarding the condition of a causal link: is *denying compensation because the claimant failed to completely exclude other possible reasons* for a loss of profit unacceptable? Is it unacceptable only in some particular situations and if so, which situations?[49]

In the Finnish court cases, one of the most obvious difficulties relating to the requirements of EU law and acceptable national solutions was related to a matter which is in addition to the potential challenges of applying conditions for liability: damages liability succession in a situation where a company has acquired business activities in the context of which competition law has been infringed. The issue was brought to the fore with the *Asphalt cartel damages claims* case. Relevant EU law did not include clearly applicable concrete rules on the possibility of transferring the liability from the infringing company to the acquirer. Nor was it possible to base the transferral of liability on national provisions: national law would have led to the result that private damages liability was not transferred.[50]

The question regarding whether EU law nevertheless required the possibility of the acquirer's damages liability may be seen as a question on the full effectiveness of EU law and on the implications of the principle of effectiveness as well as, even though it is not recommended as a question on EU

[48] As to the post-Directive state of law, note the vagueness of rec 11 of the Directive. After highlighting that the national solutions should comply with the principles of effectiveness and equivalence, it is noted that: 'Where Member States provide other conditions for compensation under national law, such as imputability, adequacy or culpability, they should be able to maintain such conditions in so far as they comply with the case-law of the Court of Justice, the principles of effectiveness and equivalence, and this Directive'. There is also potential for a conflict between remarks like the ones in the rec and the stringent applications of the principle of effectiveness, or of other EU law requirements, already made by the CJEU. In the Finnish *Asphalt cartel damages claims* case, the relevant infringement was a hard-core arrangement which rendered evaluating fault rules in the light of EU (case) law practically irrelevant as fault was in any case found to be present so that requiring (showing) fault would not constitute any real threshold for obtaining damages. It is interesting to note, however, that in Finnish law, several applicable legal bases require fault (intention or negligence) on the part of the actor who allegedly caused the damage. In the context of competition restrictions which are not as blameworthy as cartels, compatibility with EU law, or how to interpret the national law uniformly with EU law, may be an issue.

[49] See also the discussion on the Finnish judgment in the *Car spare parts damages claims* case in the section on causal links above. Against the background of the facts of the case, finding that other reasons for the loss of profit were not excluded by the claimant and, thus, no relevant causal connection established appears to be a reasonable conclusion. The Directive and the presumption that cartel infringements cause harm (Art 17(2)) form a step towards an answer to the issue of alternative causes. Nevertheless, the detailed evaluation in cartel cases and all evaluation in non-cartel situations remain open.

[50] See the judgment in the claim by the city of Espoo (n 30) 277–86 (ss 5.4.2.2–5.4.4).

requirements on sanctions. All of the above are based on the principle of sincere cooperation (now Article 4(3) of the Treaty on European Union) and on case law interpreting the principle.[51] Also, for instance, Article 47 of the Charter of Fundamental Rights of the EU and the general principle of effective judicial protection could be relevant from the claimants' point of view.[52]

In the *Asphalt cartel damages claims* case, the Helsinki District Court focused on 'the system of legal consequences of EU competition law infringements' and concluded that it was now necessary to find that liability had been transferred to the companies that had acquired the business activities. The explicit discussion on the relevant EU law requirements is brief and the reliance on analogy as regards the *transferability of liability for fines* in the context of public enforcement is strong.[53] You may wonder whether the result was something EU law required even though neither explicit stand nor evident interpretation on the meaning of the relevant EU law in this type of situation was available.[54] If EU law did not require a conclusion like the one now made, the judgment was, for this part, not based on any law.

4. CONCLUDING REMARKS

This contribution briefly discusses issues of the interface of EU and national law in damages cases that are based on EU competition law. The focus is on the lack of clarity surrounding the evaluation of causal links and the outer limits of requirements set for national remedial and procedural solutions, especially by the principle of effectiveness. These matters are discussed as problems caused by unclear EU law and its interplay and intertwinement with national law. Moreover, the practical implications of the ambiguity of the relevant EU law are studied and also discussed together with problems encountered in the Finnish damages cases.

As the reasons for challenges in correctly recognising the whole of applicable law amongst EU principles and rules and national law lie in EU law itself, practical difficulties such as the ones highlighted here might possibly be relevant in any Member State. While the Directive on competition damages actions provides some additions to the state of EU law, it does not exhaustively resolve the problem of attuning EU and national law.

[51] See, for instance, Case 33/76 *Rewe-Zentralfinanz eG et Rewe-Zentral AG* [1976] ECR 1989, para 5; Case 14/83 *Von Colson* [1984] ECR 1891, paras 21–28. See also *Donau Chemie* (n 2), paras 22, 27 and 42.

[52] The internal structure and hierarchy of the EU requirements are not discussed here at any length, but it can be stressed that one of the difficulties underpinning the theme of requirements for national remedial solutions is the difficulty of discerning the relevant parts of EU law and their significance.

[53] See the judgment on the claim by the city of Espoo (n 30) in particular, 286–92 (ss 5.4.5.1–5.4.5.3).

[54] See also Havu, 'Private Enforcement' (n 41) 67–68 and 71–72.

13

Practical Private Enforcement: Perspectives from Greece and the Netherlands

AGISILAOS KARPETAS*

1. INTRODUCTION

HABEMUS DIRECTIVE. THE long-awaited Directive on competition damages actions,[1] which is the by-product of intense and constructive debate, public consultations and guidance papers,[2] was officially signed into law on 26 November 2014 and published in the Official Journal of the European Union on 5 December 2014. The Directive is the focal point of the broader package[3] of proposals aimed at facilitating private actions for damages (particularly those stemming from competition law infringements) in the EU. The aim of the Directive is twofold: firstly, to ensure full compensation for harm caused by competition law infringements

* Agisilaos Karpetas, LLM Europa Institute, Leiden University. The authorship of this chapter was supported by the Hellenic Scholarships Foundation scholarship programme 'Education and lifelong learning' in association with the European Social Fund and NSRF 2007–13. All views expressed are personal. The author would like to express his gratitude to Ms Elsbeth Beumer, doctoral candidate at the Europa Institute of Leiden University, who co-authored the parts on the Dutch provisions. Without her expertise on Dutch competition rules and enforcement framework, this publication would have not been possible. The law is as it stands on January 2015.

[1] Directive 2014/104/EU of the European Parliament and of the Council of 26 November 2014 on certain rules governing actions for damages under national law for infringements of the competition law provisions of the Member States and of the European Union [2014] OJ L349/1.

[2] Full list of relevant documents available at ec.europa.eu/competition/antitrust/actions damages/documents.html.

[3] The full initiative includes a Communication on quantifying harm in actions for damages based on breaches of Arts 101 or 102; a Practical Guide on Quantifying Harm in Actions for damages based on breaches of Arts 101 or 102; an Impact Assessment Report and a Recommendation urging Member States to put collective redress mechanisms in place to ensure effective access to justice. All documents are available at ec.europa.eu/competition/antitrust/actionsdamages/documents.html.

through rules fostering undistorted competition and removing obstacles to the proper functioning of the internal market while avoiding overcompensation. Secondly, to coordinate the enforcement of competition rules by competition authorities and national courts.[4] The Directive provides, in essence, a general common framework that will govern actions for damages stemming from competition law infringements following its implementation into national legal orders. At the same time, it addresses and provides (at least a certain level of) clarity with regard to several contentious issues that have arisen during the decade-long debate, which mostly relates to the balancing of and smooth interaction between public and private enforcement of EU competition law.

This chapter will focus on a selection of such issues that have been central during the trilogue negotiations. The provisions of the Directive will be examined in light of the existing competition law and competition enforcement rules of Greece and the Netherlands. The two selected jurisdictions stand on different sides of the competition enforcement spectrum among EU Member States. On the one hand, the Netherlands has an advanced and highly praised competition enforcement framework in place, a successful leniency programme and a considerable number of private actions for damages brought before national courts. Greece, on the other hand, has a significantly less tested and experienced enforcement framework that, to a large extent, is still being refined. The first successful leniency application was only made as late as 2007,[5] whereas relevant cases have been extremely rare.[6]

The possible conflicts that the new rules create with the existing national frameworks and the identification of any common or diverging features or trends will be used as a platform for a preliminary constructive assessment of the Directive.

The following (selected) issues will be examined: (1) the disclosure of evidence; (2) limitation periods; (3) the effect of national decisions; (4) joint and several liability; (5) passing-on defence; and (6) consensual dispute resolution.

[4] Art 1 of the Directive.

[5] See Hellenic Competition Commission's (HCC) Decision 369/V/2007 (in Greek) on the milk cartel. Note that the application by MEVGAL was made under the previous leniency programme and, notably, in a non-confidential manner and only after dawn raids by the HCC to the premises of participating undertakings.

[6] Private enforcement has been extremely rare and mostly in the form of shield litigation (ie the competition law claim has been raised in defence to an action in contract or tort). See more in BJ Rodger and MA Fernández (eds), *Article 234 and Competition Law: An Analysis* (Alphen aan de Rijn, Kluwer, 2008) 574 ff.

2. A PRELIMINARY POINT: THE LEGAL BASIS OF THE RIGHT TO DAMAGES

Law 3959/2011 on the Protection of Free Competition[7] offers no explicit statutory basis for actions for damages originating from EU or national competition law infringements. Article 914 of the Greek Civil Code ('CC') establishing tort liability remains the basis for such actions.[8] There are no limitations on the standing of natural or legal persons, associations of persons or entities that do not have legal personality (also from other jurisdictions) for bringing an action for damages under Article 914 CC before Greek Civil Courts (whether a Single or a Multi-Member Civil Court will be competent is determined based on the value of the claim). Three cumulative substantive requirements must be met: the existence of (a) an unlawful act; (b) damage; and (c) a causal link between the unlawful act and the damage. Two forms of compensation are available: pecuniary damages and reasonable pecuniary satisfaction.[9] Both stand-alone and follow-on actions for damages are, in principle, possible.

In a similar fashion, since both jurisdictions follow the Germanic system, Article 6:162 of the Dutch Civil Code (*Burgerlijk Wetboek*, 'DCC') establishing tort liability provides the legal basis for damages actions (stand-alone or follow-on) stemming from competition law infringements under Dutch law. Breach of the European or national competition rules is an unlawful act that can create a right to compensation. According to Article 3:303 DCC, standing is limited to damage claimants that can show 'sufficient interest'.[10] Dutch courts have jurisdiction if the defendant is domiciled in the Netherlands or if the competition law infringement that caused the damage took place in the Netherlands.

[7] Which replaced Law 703/1977.

[8] See an interesting comment on the rationale of this choice by the legislator in Apostolopoulos, 'Towards a New Unfair Competition Law in Greece' (2007) 8–9 *Dikaio Epicheiriseon and Etaireion* 900–11 (in Greek). It is questionable, but exceeds the scope of the present contribution, whether a different choice of a statutory basis by the Greek legislator would be more suitable in light of the goals of modern competition law. See more on the goals of competition law in G Triantafyllakis, 'Economic Freedom or Effectiveness as the Protected Legal Interest in Competition Law' (2012) 7 *Dikaio Epicheiriseon and Etaireion* 628–38 (in Greek).

[9] Pecuniary damages relate to injury to goods having an economic value and can be paid either in kind (*in natura* restitution) or, most commonly, through monetary compensation. Reasonable pecuniary satisfaction is awarded in case of moral damage, ie damage to non-pecuniary goods.

[10] Existence of 'sufficient interest' is generally presumed.

3. DISCLOSURE OF EVIDENCE

3.1 The Relevant Provisions in the Directive

According to Article 5 of the Directive on competition damages actions, disclosure of evidence should, in principle, be subject to strict and active judicial control as regards its necessity, scope and proportionality. The evidence, access to which is sought, must be relevant in terms of substantiating a plausible claim[11] and a request for disclosure should be limited to specific evidence or relevant categories of evidence that are as precise and narrow as possible.[12] The legitimate interests of all parties concerned (including third parties) must be taken into account.[13] When performing the strict necessity and proportionality test, national courts should, in particular, consider the extent to which the claim or defence is supported by available facts and evidence justifying the disclosure request, the scope and cost of disclosure and protection of confidential information.[14] Evidence containing business secrets or otherwise confidential information should in principle be available for disclosure but must receive an appropriate (higher) level of protection.[15] National courts shall ensure that full effect is given to applicable legal professional privilege in disclosure orders[16] and guarantee the right to be heard of the addressee(s) of a disclosure request.[17]

Article 6 deals specifically with evidence included in the file of a competition authority and provides additional guidance to national courts as regards the performance of the proportionality test as well as the widely disputed 'grey' and 'black list' derogations. In addition to the requirements set out in Article 5(3), national courts must consider whether the request has been clearly formulated with regard to the nature, subject matter or contents of evidence, whether the party is requesting disclosure in relation to an action for damages before a national court and to take into account the need to safeguard the effectiveness of the public enforcement of competition law when access to evidence contained in the file of a competition authority is sought.[18] Article 6(6) provides that (a) leniency corporate statements; and (b) settlement submissions are 'black-listed', ie they can never

[11] Art 5(1) of the Directive.
[12] Art 5(2) ibid.
[13] Art 5(3) ibid.
[14] The provision is clearer when read in conjunction with rec 18 of the Preamble. Proportionality should also be carefully assessed when disclosure may unravel a competition authority's investigation strategy. The generic disclosure of documents contained in the file of a competition authority should thus be deemed disproportionate.
[15] Art 5(4) of the Directive. Interestingly, the term 'business secrets' is only mentioned in rec 18 of the Preamble.
[16] Art 5(6) ibid.
[17] Art 5(7) ibid.
[18] Art 6(4) ibid.

be disclosed.[19] Article 6(5) introduces a 'grey list' of evidence, disclosure of which may only be ordered after the competition authority has closed its proceedings.[20]

3.2 The Relevant Provisions Under Greek Law

There is no single clear provision in Greek law on third party access to evidence in competition law infringement cases. Claimants may seek access through provisions related to the disclosure of evidence in general that can be found in different legislative acts.

Article 15(9) of the Regulation of the Functioning and Management of the Competition Commission ('RFMCC')[21] prohibits third party access to the Hellenic Competition Commission's ('HCC') files for pending cases. Limited access may be given to complainants. The HCC has stated that access to documents is in principle denied to complainants or third parties even when they are part of the HCC procedure.[22] The HCC cites the protection of business secrets and the general public interest to protect competition law as overriding requirements to limit the rights of complainants (as PepsiCo in that particular case) or third parties to access its file. Just recently, there has been a request for access to the complete administrative record with the aim of initiating a follow-on action for damages by a complainant who already enjoyed limited access as a party of the proceedings before the HCC.

Law 3959/2011 and the Greek Leniency Programme[23] are silent on the issue of third party access to documents contained in the leniency application file.[24] Third parties can request to be part of the procedure before the HCC, according to Article 23(4) RFMCC, if they can prove legitimate interest in the outcome of the case. The HCC can accept or reject the request on the basis of the ability of the requesting party to contribute to the discovery of the truth on the given case. Third parties admitted to the procedure may

[19] Substance should prevail over form as the national court may itself, upon a reasoned request, access 'black-listed' evidence in order to assess that their contents corresponds to the definitions set out in Art 2 of the Directive.

[20] The 'grey list' refers to information that was prepared specifically for the proceedings of a competition authority (eg, replies to requests for information by the competition authority) and information that was drawn up by a competition authority in the course of its proceedings (eg, a Statement of Objections).

[21] *Κανονισμός Λειτουργίας και Διαχείρισης της Επιτροπής Ανταγωνισμού* (Regulation of the Functioning and Management of the Competition Commission), published in the Official Gazette of the Government on 16 January 2013 (FEK B' 2507/16.1.2013).

[22] Decision 309/V/2006, where PepsiCo requested access to the HCC file in a case against CocaCola-3E (in Greek).

[23] As established by the HCC in Decision 526/VI/2011(in Greek).

[24] Point 45 of the Leniency Programme only provides access to copies of the oral statements of the applicant after the HCC has communicated its Initial Statement on the case to the parties. Access is then only permitted at the HCC premises.

be allowed access to the non-confidential versions of the submissions of the other parties by the HCC. This seems to be a rather rocky path for damage claimants in light of the reluctance of the HCC to allow access to its files,[25] particularly considering, in most cases, the limited (if any at all) contribution to the discovery of the truth. Access to the HCC files of non-pending cases can be sought through Article 5 of the Code of Administrative Proceedings ('CAP'),[26] which provides a general right of access for citizens to documents of the Administration and to private documents that are kept by the Administration.[27] Paragraph 3, however, introduces an absolute exception in cases where access would breach confidentiality guaranteed by specific legal provisions (as for example those set by the RFMCC). This provision is in line with the black and grey lists introduced in the Directive and in fact goes even beyond them as it precludes access to any document the HCC has decided to identify as confidential.[28] It is hard to reconcile this provision with *Pfleiderer*[29] and *Donau Chemie*[30] or Article 5(1) as it allows no room for the administrative judge to perform the weighing of interests exercise put forward by the Court of Justice of the European Union ('CJEU').[31] No relevant case has arisen thus far, which could perhaps lead to a reference for a preliminary ruling.

Damage claimants may also seek access to documents through civil courts as a side step to a pending action for damages.[32] Article 107 CCP provides that the Civil Court can, on its own motion, order discovery by one or more of the means of evidence recognised by the CCP. According to Articles 450–52 CCP, a litigant may bring a separate action before the

[25] See in that regard Decision 369/V/2007 of the HCC, para 68 where the HCC stated that access to documents is not an absolute right whereas applications for leniency and elements of the leniency programme must remain confidential (in Greek). Confidentiality cannot be breached and access cannot be granted to the other parties, as this would be contrary to the very purpose of confidentiality, which is to help the HCC perform its tasks and protect undertakings/witnesses that have collaborated with the authorities.

[26] Law 2690/99, FEK 45 A' 1999.

[27] This right stems from Arts 5A and 10 of the Greek Constitution. The CAP must be distinguished from the Code of Administrative Procedure, which governs the adjudication of substantive administrative disputes from the ordinary administrative courts only. The Council of State has recently clarified that the HCC is not an administrative court but an administrative authority and thus the provisions of the Code of Administrative Procedure are not applicable. The Council of State, Case 1324/2013, NOMOS database (in Greek).

[28] In accordance with the provisions of Art 16 RFMCC.

[29] Case C-360/09 *Pfleiderer* EU:C:2011:389.

[30] Case C-536/11 *Donau Chemie* EU:C:2013:366.

[31] In fact, the Greek provision presents some similarities with the Austrian provision in *Donau Chemie* in the sense that in both cases the legislator has made a conscious choice prohibiting disclosure without allowing room for the national judge to perform the *Pfleiderer* weighing exercise.

[32] See also Areios Pagos, Case 204/2010, NOMOS database (in Greek). Access through Arts 901–02 CC (if no damage action is pending) does not seem possible in light of Case 673/2009 where the Athens Court of Appeal rejected the legitimate interest of the applicant, when his request to present documents was in order to establish the facts for the first time.

competent court requesting an order against another litigant or a third party to present documents in the possession of the latter, which may provide evidence regarding the litigant's allegations. Such documents need to be identified in accordance with the general rule of Article 216 CCP, which provides that pleadings must clearly identify the subject matter of the dispute, the facts on which a claim is based and the legal grounds justifying the claim.[33] There seems to be some uncertainty regarding the threshold set by the Courts concerning the details demanded when seeking the production of documents.[34] The HCC could be considered a third party towards which such an action could be addressed. Article 452(3) CCP only excludes access to confidential documents that are in the possession of the administrative authorities if they are related to national security and external relations. No relevant cases have arisen so far. It seems that the civil judge would, in principle, enjoy discretion to decide on disclosure in line with Article 5 of the Directive and the CJEU jurisprudence. It is interesting and highly debatable, however, whether judges would be willing to rule contrary to the public interest argument (which looms behind the HCC's decision to declare documents confidential), particularly taking into account that civil judges are not specialised in competition law cases.

3.3 The Relevant Provisions Under Dutch Law

The right to ask the judge to order disclosure of information is not revolutionary under Dutch law. Dutch procedural law does not provide for an absolute right to information, but requires instead the balancing of different interests (disclosure versus confidentiality). The provision that reflects the disclosure regime most clearly is Article 843a of the Dutch Civil Procedure Act, 'CPA' (*Wetboek Burgerlijke Rechtsvordering*).[35] This Article provides that a party with a legitimate interest may, on its own account, claim access to a copy or an extract of specific documents concerning a legal relationship between the requesting party or its predecessors, and the person in whose control or custody the evidence lies. This basic rule is supplemented with provisions regulating the discretionary power of the court to determine the way in which access is put forward (paragraph 2), the privilege

[33] Accordingly, a request for the production of documents requires a precise description of the contents of the document(s) and the relevance to the case (See Areios Pagos 681/2007, Areios Pagos 953/2002, NOMOS database (in Greek)). Access can also be sought through the injunctive relief procedure of Art 731 CCP, see in that regard Case 9/2014 First Instance Court of Veria, NOMOS database (in Greek).

[34] See more in I Symplis, 'Damages Actions in Private Antitrust Enforcement: Greek Report' in B Cortese (ed), *EU Competition Law—Between Public and Private Enforcement* (Alphen aan den Rijn, Kluwer, 2014) 283.

[35] Other relevant provisions are Arts 21, 22, 85 and 126 CPA.

of non-disclosure (paragraph 3) and the reasons to refuse disclosure of the documents (paragraph 4). Non-compliance with an order of the court to disclose certain documents can result in a sanction being imposed by the court (see for example Articles 21 and 22 CPA).

However, the disclosure of documents on the basis of Article 843a CPA is limited. A claimant seeking access to particular documents should fulfil certain conditions. Firstly, the claimant should have a legitimate interest in obtaining access to the requested documents, for example, by identifying that the documents are essential for establishing the damage. Secondly, the claimant should specify, as precisely as possible, which documents should be disclosed ('fishing expeditions' are prohibited). Thirdly, the documents must concern a legal relationship to which the claimant is a party. A legal relationship on the basis of a wrongful act satisfies this criterion. The Court will assess whether these conditions are met and if there are overriding reasons (such as the need to protect confidential information)[36] to refuse access to the requested documents.[37] For example, documents that fall under the 'legal professional privilege'[38] will not be disclosed. It is interesting to note that in the Netherlands (in contrast to European practice) the legal professional privilege also covers documents from in-house lawyers.[39]

In two recent damage action cases, Dutch district courts discussed the scope of Article 843a CPA. In *TenneT v Alstom*, the District Court of Arnhem refused to grant Alstom (defendant in the case) access to documents related to the investigation of the European Commission and documents on the damage that TenneT had suffered. According to the District Court, Alstom failed to specify the requested documents.[40] In *CDC v Shell*, the District Court of The Hague affirmed that there is no general right to access to documents and that disclosure only relates to specific documents that can actually contribute to the damages action, provided that (i) there are no overriding interests in the non-disclosure of documents or (ii) the fair administration of justice cannot be served without granting access.[41]

More recently, in *Pilkington and Scheuten Glass v ACM*, the District Court of Rotterdam found the leniency statements to be unreliable for two

[36] Provided that partial access to the confidential documents is not possible. See eg, *Compagnie de Manutentation Ro-Ro (CdMR) BV v Scheldepoort BV and others*, judgment of the District Court of Middelburg of 6 July 2006 NL:RBMID:2006:AZ0501.

[37] Overriding reasons to refuse the requested documents will not be easily accepted.

[38] See for the application of the 'legal professional privilege' in EU competition law procedures the judgment of the CJEU in Case C-550/07 *Akzo Nobel Chemicals Ltd and Akcros Chemicals Ltd v Commission* EU:C:2010:512.

[39] *Vaal en Van 't Hoft v Stichting H9 Invest e.a*, judgment of the Dutch Supreme Court of 15 March 2013 NL:HR:2013:BY6101.

[40] *TenneT v Alstom*, judgment of the District Court of Arnhem of 16 May 2012 NL:RBARN:2012:BW7445.

[41] *CDC v Shell and others*, judgment of the District Court of The Hague of 1 May 2013 NL:RBDHA:2013:CA1870.

reasons: (i) the ACM had asked leading questions and provided considerable information to the leniency applicants before asking questions; and (ii) there were inconsistencies between the statements of the leniency applicants.[42] Other evidence contained in the file could not confirm the allegations to a sufficient degree. More interestingly, the District Court also found that Pilkington should not have been refused access to the full leniency statements contained in the case file. The District Court sided with Pilkington in their argument that leniency statements regarding other glass markets and other periods were relevant for the assessment of the reliability of the statements which resulted in a violation of their rights of defence. It seems that, in practice, it is rather difficult to obtain access to documents under Article 843a CPA. A balance of interests has to be struck between the interests of the applicant and the defendant, whereby the applicant must specify to which documents the request relates (which basically implies that the applicant should have knowledge of the existence and the context of the requested documents).[43]

Although the CPA does leave room for weighing the different arguments for and against disclosure, it does not preclude corporate statements and settlement submissions from entering into the public domain. Also, the Government Information (Public Access) Act of the Netherlands (*Wet Openbaarheid Bestuur*, 'Wob'),[44] which can be the legal basis for claiming access to documents that are in the possession of the Dutch Competition Authority (Authority for Consumers & Markets 'ACM'), does not guarantee such absolute protection. One of the relative exceptions[45] to the general rule of public access to government information, Article 10(2)d Wob, protects the interests of inspection, control and supervision. According to settled case law, this exception only applies to cases where the disclosure of documents interferes with the enforcement tasks of the public authority. The ACM can only rely on this exception where it can prove that its enforcement tasks will be effectively undermined when a third party receives access to

[42] *Pilkington and Scheuten Glass v ACM*, judgment of the District Court of Rotterdam of 3 March 2014 NL:RBROT:2014:2273.

[43] This approach seems to be in line with the *Pfleiderer* and *Donau Chemie* judgments (nn 29 and 30) where the Court of Justice held that a national law must not preclude any possibility for the national court to perform such a balancing exercise of the interests involved when determining whether to provide (leniency) documents to third-party claimants.

[44] The Wob is the equivalent of Regulation 1049/2001 of the European Parliament and of the Council of 30 May 2001 regarding public access to European Parliament, Council and Commission documents [2001] OJ L145/43.

[45] The grounds for denying access to documents are listed in Arts 10 and 11 Wob. The grounds for refusal contained in Art 10(1) Wob are absolute grounds for refusal, ie access to the file will always be denied in relation to documents falling within one of the categories mentioned in that provision. The grounds for refusal of Art 10(2) Wob are relative grounds for refusal. The disclosure of information shall not take place when its importance does not outweigh the interests enumerated in Art 10(2) Wob.

the corporate statements and settlement submissions. It is, however, still questionable whether the disclosure of corporate statements will actually deter undertakings from applying for leniency (acknowledging the huge fines that will otherwise be imposed upon them). The exception regarding inspection, control and supervision can, however, be used as grounds for refusal during ongoing administrative proceedings.[46] The grey-listed exception of Article 6(5) of the Directive, ensuring that national courts will not order the disclosure of documents in pending competition law proceedings, is part of standard practice under the Wob.[47]

The final version of the relevant provisions regarding the disclosure of documents in the Directive as (re)formulated following the intensive trilogue meetings between the three institutions involved in the legislative process, and particularly the provisions added during the last round of negotiations on the explicit prohibition of fishing expeditions in Article 5(3)(b), protection of confidential information in Article 5(3)(c), and protection of the legal privilege in Article 5(6), do not seem to conflict with the provisions already in place.[48]

4. THE BINDING EFFECT OF NATIONAL DECISIONS

4.1 The Relevant Provisions in the Directive

Article 9(1) of the Directive on competition damages actions awards binding conclusive force to final decisions of the national competition authorities finding an infringement for the purposes of an action for damages brought before their national courts. The binding effect of a decision of a competition authority does not extend to other Member State jurisdictions; rather it can be used as at least prima facie evidence. This change to the original proposal addresses questions of principle (ie whether it is right that a national court is bound by a decision of a competition authority of another Member State) that have been voiced.[49]

[46] In combination with Art 10(2)(c) and (g).

[47] See eg, the following decisions of the ACM: Decision of 20 December 2007, Case 6259 (*Wob-verzoek rapport* 5697_1/102); and Decision of 9 July 2008, Case 6407 (*Wob-verzoek inzake Heijmans & IBC*).

[48] A comparative read of the original draft of the Commission proposal, the later versions during the trilogue negotiations and the final text of the Directive illustrates the steps made towards more elaborate safeguarding tools, which have been drafted in detail (at times surprisingly so for a Directive).

[49] See AP Komninos, *EC Private Antitrust Enforcement. Decentralised Application of EC Competition Law by National Courts* (Oxford, Hart Publishing, 2008) 16; and E-J Zippro, *Privaatrechtelijke handhaving van mededingingsrecht* (Deventer, Kluwer, 2009) 632.

4.2 The Relevant Provisions Under Greek Law

According to Article 30 of Law 3959/2011, decisions of the HCC can be appealed before the Athens Administrative Court of Appeal. The parties can seek annulment of the judgment of the Court of Appeal before the Council of State in accordance with Article 32 Law 3959/2011. Judgments of the Athens Administrative Court of Appeal and the Council of State have the force of '*res judicata*', ie they are binding for civil courts.[50] If no appeal against the decision of the HCC has been lodged, civil courts can only incidentally decide on the validity of the HCC decision but are bound by the HCC's decision on all substantive issues.[51]

The final version of Article 9(2) of the Directive, according to which the final decisions of the competition authorities of other Member States must be regarded as prima facie evidence (in contrast to the initial proposal that would have extended the binding effect to such decisions as well), seems to be in line with Articles 338–440 CCP under which public documents issued by the Greek or foreign state authorities are regarded as rebuttable conclusive evidence on all statements of fact that their author had a duty to ascertain. However, courts enjoy the right to freely evaluate statements of opinion, expert testimonies and personal testimonies contained in public documents.[52]

4.3 The Relevant Provisions Under Dutch Law

There is no existing provision on binding effect of the ACM decisions under Dutch law. In practice, the courts would hardly ever deviate from the findings of an ACM decision. It is interesting to note that the '*Masterfoods* defence'[53] has not been successful in the Netherlands. The Appeal Court of Amsterdam concluded in *Equilib v KLM* that the Dutch Civil Court is only prescribed to suspend the proceedings when the outcome of the damage action (ie the relevant factual and legal issues of the case) depends on the validity of a decision of the European Commission. The fact that the suspension of the proceedings is not always required complies (following the Dutch Appeal Court) with the legislation in force[54] and the *Masterfoods*

[50] Art 35 Law 3959/201.

[51] See in that regard, Case 18/2002 Court of Appeal of Patras, NOMOS database (in Greek).

[52] As noted by Symplis (n 34) 279, 'the criterion of the distinction seems to be empiricist and pragmatic rather than conceptual […] this approach seems both unsatisfactory and unlikely to be adopted'.

[53] Referring to the judgment in Case C-344/98 *Masterfoods Ltd v HB Ice Cream Ltd* EU:C:2000:689 where the Court held that national courts cannot make a decision that is contrary to a decision of the Commission.

[54] Art 16 (1) of Regulation 1/2003 on the implementation of the rules on competition laid down in Arts 101 and 102 TFEU [2003] OJ L1/1.

judgment,[55] as they both leave a certain discretion to the national court to assess whether there is reasonable doubt that the decision of the Commission is not valid (which could trigger the suspension of the national procedure).[56]

5. LIMITATION PERIODS

5.1 The Relevant Provisions in the Directive

Article 10 of the Directive on competition damages actions sets out the limitation periods applicable for bringing actions for damages. Member States must ensure that there is a minimum limitation period of five years for damages claims.[57] The limitation period cannot begin to run before the infringement has ceased and the claimant knows or can reasonably be expected to know of the existence of the infringement, the fact that the infringement caused harm to him/her and the identity of the infringer.[58] Article 10 further stipulates the suspensory effect on the limitation period of an investigation of a competition authority with regard to the infringement to which the action for damages relates. In addition, according to Article 18(1) of the Directive, the limitation period for bringing an action for damages is suspended for the duration of any consensual dispute resolution process. This specific type of suspension is only applicable to parties that 'are or were involved or represented in the consensual dispute resolution'.[59]

5.2 The Relevant Provisions Under Greek Law

Greek law seems to be in line with this requirement. Article 937 CC sets the limitation period for Article 914 CC claims at five years. The limitation period commences on the date when the injured party became aware of the damage and of the identity of the party liable to compensation.[60]

[55] Referring to para 57 of *Masterfoods* (n 53).

[56] See *Equilib v KLM and others*, judgment of the Dutch Court of Appeal of Amsterdam of 24 September 2013 NL:GHAMS:2013:3013. For a similar judgment see *CDC v Shell and others* (n 41). In the second judgment, the Court held that suspension was not necessary, because there were other legal issues at stake that bore no relation to the Decision of the Commission, such as the forum choice, the claimed several liability and the validity of the cession. In addition, the Court referred to the Union's obligation of loyal cooperation and the principles of good administration, which require the prevention of an undue delay of proceedings.

[57] Art 10(3) of the Directive.

[58] Art 10(2) ibid.

[59] This may in practice lead to different limitation periods being applicable for different claimants with regard to undertakings that participate in the consensual dispute resolution proceedings.

[60] The five-year limitation period is also applicable to future damage, which could, under the normal course of events, be anticipated as a result of the unlawful act, apart from that which could not be reasonably foreseen. Decisions 53/2002 and 949/2002 of the Supreme Court, NOMOS database (in Greek).

Such claims are further subject to a general limitation period of 20 years commencing on the date that the unlawful act was committed.

Article 937 CC provides for an extended limitation period in case the tort is also a criminal offence under Greek Criminal law. In such a case, the limitation period for raising an action for damages is extended accordingly.[61] The criminal offence in Article 44 Law 3959/2011 is a misdemeanour, which according to Article 111 of the Greek Criminal Code is also subject to a limitation period of five years. Claimants will, however, need to be careful since the starting points of the criminal and civil limitation periods may not always coincide. Suspension of the limitation period is also possible in accordance with the general rules of Article 255 et seq. Article 260 et seq provide for the interruption of the limitation period (ie the limitation period is reset and recommences in accordance with the specific provisions on interruption).[62]

A suspension period as described in Article 10(4) of the Directive is not available in the CC or in Law 3959/2011. Article 42 of Law 3959/2011 sets a limitation period of five years from the date the infringement ceased for the HCC to impose sanctions on the perpetrators. Article 42(3) extensively lists actions from the HCC or another competition authority that trigger a suspension. Perhaps the scope of this provision will have to be extended in order to cover follow-on actions for damages and ensure compatibility with Article 10(4).

5.3 The Relevant Provisions Under Dutch Law

The limitation period of Article 10(3) of at least five years is *grosso modo* in line with Dutch law, particularly Article 3:310 of the Dutch Civil Code (*Burgerlijk Wetboek* 'DCC'). Similarly to the Greek CC, there is also a limitation period of 20 years that commences on the date the unlawful act causing the damage took place. The limitation period would be interrupted by raising a legal action (section 3:316 DCC) through a written warning (section 3:317 DCC) or because of a collective action (section 3:305 DCC but only applicable to the claimants represented under Dutch law in the collective action). An open legal question under Dutch law is, however, how to determine when the limitation period begins to run. In this context, in a

[61] Nevertheless, suspension of the criminal limitation period does not automatically suspend the civil limitation period; see Case 21/2003 Supreme Court (Grand Chamber), available at NOMOS database (in Greek).

[62] For example, according to Art 261 CC, the limitation period for a damage claim will be interrupted once the claim is properly raised in accordance with the procedural requirements. The limitation period will be reset and recommence after the last procedural act by the parties or the court.

few recent cases, the Dutch courts have arrived at different conclusions. In *CEF v FEG*, the District Court of Rotterdam ruled that the claimants should have started the damage action as soon as possible and should not have waited for the European Commission to reach a final decision. The District Court concluded that the damage claim was barred, as the claimants were fully aware of the proceedings of the European Commission.[63]

In *TenneT v ABB* the District Court rejected the claim of ABB that the limitation period started to run when the European Commission announced (in a press release) the start of an investigation into the gas insulated switchgear projects market. According to the District Court, TenneT could not have been expected, on the basis of that press release, to realise that the successor company was a victim of that cartel. Relevant to the outcome of this case was the finding of the European Commission that the cartel participants had taken effective measures to hide their cartel activities.[64] In another case, where the parties claimed the annulment of contracts[65] with undertakings that were part of the 'elevators cartel', the District Court concluded that the limitation period began to run the moment the European Commission published its final infringement decision.[66] It remains to be seen to what extent Dutch courts will take the conditions for qualifying the starting point of the limitation period set out in the Directive into consideration. Meanwhile, in *ASR v Achmea*, the Supreme Court ruled that the limitation period for a contribution claim (ie a claim which arises when a jointly and severally liable defendant contributes to the compensation of damages in excess of its actual share in those damages) is also five years starting from the moment of the excessive contribution.[67] This judgment may also impact damage claims.

6. JOINT AND SEVERAL LIABILITY

6.1 The Relevant Provisions in the Directive

Article 11 of the Directive on competition damages actions regulates joint and several liability. The principle provision in the first paragraph provides for joint and several liability of undertakings that have infringed

[63] *CEF v FEG*, judgment of the District Court of Rotterdam of 7 March 2007 NL:RBROT:2007:BA0926.

[64] *TenneT v ABB*, judgment of the District Court East-Netherlands of 16 January 2013 NL:RBONE:2013:BZ0403.

[65] Arguing the absence of consensus, Art 6:229 DCC.

[66] *VVE 'Het Schip' and others v Otis*, judgments of the District Court Centre-Netherlands of 13 March 2013 NL:RBMNE:2013:CA1922.

[67] See *ASR v Achmea*, judgment of the Supreme Court of 6 April 2012 NL:HR:2012:BU3784.

competition law through joint behaviour (ie full compensation by any of the co-infringers until the injured party has been fully compensated). Two types of derogations are introduced in paragraphs 2 and 4. Firstly, where the infringer is a small or medium-sized enterprise ('SME'),[68] its liability is limited only to its direct and indirect purchasers when the following two cumulative requirements are met: (a) its market share in the relevant market is below five per cent at any time during the infringement; and (b) the application of the principal provision on joint and several liability would irretrievably jeopardise its economic viability unless the SME was the leader of the competition law infringement or has coerced other undertakings to participate therein or in case the SME is a repeated offender.[69]

Secondly, the liability of an immunity recipient through a successful leniency application shall be extended to injured parties other than its own direct or indirect purchasers or providers (in case of a buyer's cartel) only where these other parties are unable to obtain full compensation from the other cartel participants.[70] The Directive also imposes an obligation on the Member States to make contributions for an infringer, recoverable on the basis of their relative responsibility for the harm caused. Immunity recipients' contributions cannot exceed the harm to its direct and indirect customers or providers. Meanwhile, Article 19(2) on consensual settlements protects co-infringers from further liability and recovery as regards the remaining claims of the settling party. This derogation is revoked by way of the exception provided in Article 19(3) where non-settling co-infringers cannot pay the damages that correspond to the remaining claim unless this is expressly excluded under the terms of the consensual settlement. Lastly, in accordance with Article 19(4), national courts shall take into account damages paid pursuant to a consensual settlement when determining the amount of the contribution of the settling co-infringer that is recoverable by other co-infringers.

6.2 The Relevant Provisions Under Greek Law

The CC provides for joint and several liability where: (a) the damage has been the result of a joint act; or (b) more than one party is at the same time liable for the same damage; or (c) more than one party has acted simultaneously or consecutively and it cannot be determined whose act has caused the damage.[71] Each party is liable for the entire amount of damages, but the

[68] As defined in Commission Recommendation 2006/361/EC of May 6, 2003 concerning the definition of micro, small and medium-sized enterprises [2003] OJ L124, 36.
[69] Art 11(3) of the Directive.
[70] Art 11(4) ibid.
[71] Art 480 et seq CC.

claimant is entitled to claim such an amount only once.[72] Where one of the liable parties compensates the entire amount of damages, this party has a right of restitution against the other joint defendants either on the basis of the degree of fault of each one as determined by the national court or, if the degree of fault cannot be determined, in equal parts.[73]

Article 71 CC provides that a legal entity is liable for compensation under Article 914 CC for acts or omissions of its representatives when they perform their duties. Such representatives remain jointly and severally liable alongside the legal entity. In addition to liability under Article 71 CC, the lawful representatives of a legal entity which breaches Article 1 of Law 3959/2011 are subject to criminal liability in the form of a pecuniary penalty.[74] These individuals could be further sued for damages on the basis of Article 914 CC.

There is intense criticism with regard to the concept of criminal liability in cartel cases as set out in Article 44(1), read in conjunction with Article 1 Law 3959/2011. It is argued that the terminology used to describe the competition law infringements is intrinsically vague and thus not in conformity with Article 7 of the Greek Constitution which encompasses the '*nullum crimen nulla poena sine lege*' doctrine.[75] There is further criticism that the incarceration time (of at least two years) and criminal fines ranging from a hundred thousand to one million euros are disproportionate. It needs to be noted that not one case has been reported so far where such criminal penalties have been imposed. It remains to be seen whether such cases will arise in the future and the impact criminal convictions may have on follow-up actions for damages. Despite the fact that the civil judge can freely assess a criminal conviction when examining a damage claim, the chances of a successful follow-on damage claim increase significantly in practice.

At the moment, there is no provision awarding special protection as regards the limitation of liability for successful leniency applicants as prescribed in Article 11(4) of the Directive.

6.3 The Relevant Provisions Under Dutch Law

In the Netherlands, joint and several liability follows from Article 6:6 DCC and Article 6:102, paragraph 1, DCC.[76] Dutch law does not specifically provide for a rule securing successful leniency applicants limited liability

[72] Art 481 ibid.
[73] Arts 926 and 927 ibid.
[74] Art 44(1) Law 3959/2011.
[75] And particularly the *sine lega certa* qualification of the doctrine.
[76] The latter reads as follows: 'When two or more persons are individually liable for the same damage, then they are joint and severally liable for it.'

as prescribed by the derogation of Article 11(4) of the Directive. In fact, Article 6:13 DCC stipulates that when recovery from one of the debtors proves to be impossible, the irrecoverable part will be imputed to the other debtors in proportion with the part of the joint obligation. Recovery of excessive contributions by co-infringers is possible, in line with the provision of Article 11(5) of the Directive.

An issue that the Directive does not touch upon, but is currently a 'hot potato' under Dutch law, relates to the civil liability of entities that belong to the same undertaking. Under EU and Dutch competition law, parent companies are presumed to be liable for cartel violations committed by their wholly owned subsidiaries (based on the 'single economic entity' doctrine).[77] *A contrario*, Dutch corporate law prescribes that an entity is only liable to injured parties if that entity can be blamed, independently, for the damage. In *TenneT v ABB*, the Dutch District Court emphasised that ABB could only be liable to the injured parties if it was actually aware of the cartel. Thus, being part of a particular parent company was not sufficient for holding the company responsible for the damage.[78]

7. PASSING-ON DEFENCE

7.1 The Relevant Provisions in the Directive

Articles 12 to 16 of the Directive on competition damages actions clarify the passing-on defence in light of the twofold goal of ensuring full compensation for injured parties while at the same time avoiding overcompensation. Article 13 recognises, in principle, the passing-on defence with regard to the whole or part of the overcharge. The burden of proof concerning whether the overcharge was passed on rests with the defendant. In the case of claims brought up by indirect purchasers, the burden of proof concerning the existence and the scope of passing-on shifts to the claimant.[79] The claimant will need to prove that the defendant committed an infringement of competition law, that this infringement resulted in an overcharge for the direct purchaser(s) and that the claimant has purchased the goods or services that were the object of the infringement or goods or services derived from or containing them. Article 15 further calls for coordination between

[77] See eg, Joined Cases C-628/10 and C-14/11 *Alliance One International Inc and Standard Commercial Tobacco Co Inc v Commission and Commission v Alliance One International Inc and Others* EU:C:2012:479 and Case C-97/08 *Akzo Nobel NV and Others v Commission* EU:C:2009:539.

[78] *TenneT v ABB*, judgment of the District Court East-Netherlands of 16 January 2013 NL:GHAMS:2013:BZ0403. See for a discussion of this case B Braat, 'Kartelschade in Nederland, een eerste aanzet' (2013) 9 *Nederlands Tijdschrift voor Europees Recht* 318–25 (in Dutch).

[79] Art 14(1) of the Directive.

and control by national courts when faced with multiple damage claims from different levels of the supply chain. In accordance with Article 16, the Commission shall issue further guidelines on the estimation of the passed-on overcharge.

7.2 The Relevant Provisions Under Greek Law

The passing-on defence is examined by a Greek civil court in the context of proof of damage.[80] No presumption exists that the overcharge has been passed on and that, therefore, the claimant has not incurred any or has incurred limited (partial) damage. The concept of 'indirect purchasers' may prove to be more challenging. Damage claimants, according to Article 914 CC, must prove a causal link between the unlawful act and the damage suffered. A party that suffered injury, not because of the unlawful act but as a consequence of the damage that the unlawful act caused to the directly injured party, is not entitled to damages.[81] Indeed, there is a risk that indirect purchasers may not be able to claim damages through Article 914 CC.[82] There may be little room in such cases for a damages action to be based on Article 919 CC, according to which compensation can be sought for damages caused intentionally and in breach of '*bonos mores*'[83] and where there is a causal link between the act or omission by the defendant and the damage suffered.[84] Of crucial importance is whether the passing-on of the overcharge breaks the causal link between the infringement and the damage of the indirect purchaser. There has been no clear-cut answer in the jurisprudence thus far.[85]

7.3 The Relevant Provisions Under Dutch Law

The provisions on the passing-on of overcharge (as well as on the quantification of harm) relate, to a large extent, to the question of who has the burden

[80] To the author's knowledge, the argument has not yet been invoked before Greek civil courts in relation to a damage claim for a competition law infringement.

[81] A Georgiadis and M Stathopoulos, *Interpretation of the Civil Code* (Athens, Sakkoulas, 1982) 710.

[82] The indirect purchaser may have recourse to Art 904 CC on unjust enrichment against the direct purchaser in cases where the direct purchaser was (over)compensated for damages that were actually passed-on to the indirect purchaser.

[83] ie the moral and social principles prevailing at a certain time in the society as understood by the average citizen.

[84] See in that regard, Case 2265/2011 First Instance Court of Athens, NOMOS database (in Greek).

[85] See, nevertheless, Areios Pagos 439/2012, NOMOS database (in Greek), where the indirect damage of the manufacturer was not recognised in a tortious claim against the defendant who had provided misleading information regarding the chemical composition of a pesticide, gives an indication that the answer may be in the affirmative.

to prove that the overcharge (resulting from the infringement) was passed on. In the Netherlands, a provision that is similar to the passing-on defence can be found in Article 6:100 of the DCC, according to which '[w]hen the injured person has not only suffered damage from an event, but also a benefit, then this benefit has to be subtracted, as far as this is reasonable, from the damage that has to be compensated to him.'

This provision illustrates that the compensation of damages actually incurred is the guiding principle in the Netherlands and that possible benefits (ie the passing-on of overcharges) should be subtracted from the damage. The burden of proof concerning whether the overcharge was passed-on lies with the defendant (in line with Article 13 of the Directive). The difficulty with this provision, as suggested by the District Court in the *TenneT v ABB* case, is to prove that the benefit is the direct consequence of the anticompetitive conduct that caused the damage. In *TenneT v ABB* the benefit that TenneT (the claimant) received came at the expense of the indirect purchasers (and not of ABB, ie the defendant). It is, however (according to the District Court), fair that ABB has to pay the full damages (including the damages that the indirect purchasers suffered), provided that such compensation will, eventually, benefit the indirect purchasers by having to pay lower prices to TenneT.[86] On appeal, however, the second-instance Court stated that not allowing the passing-on defence was premature since the defendant had not been given the chance to counter-argue the economic report on which the District Court's reasoning was based.[87] The approach of the District Court seems to be more in line with the early version of Article 12(2) of the Commission's Proposal,[88] which stipulated that the passing-on defence could not be invoked in cases where the indirect purchaser is legally unable to seek compensation (because of national rules on causality) in an attempt to protect indirect purchasers that are at a level of the supply chain that is remote from the infringement. This provision has been deleted from the final text of the Directive. The ruling of the Court of Appeal seems to be in line with the final version of Article 13 of the Directive on the passing-on defence, which contains no such exception to the applicability of the passing-on defence as the one prescribed in Article 12(2) of the Commission's Proposal.

[86] Whether the claimant (TenneT) will indeed lower the prices is, however, uncertain.

[87] *TenneT v ABB*, judgment of the Court of Appeal of Arnhem-Leeuwarden of 2 September 2014 NL:GHARL:2014:6766.

[88] Available at eur-lex.europa.eu/LexUriServ/LexUriServ.do?uri=OJ:C:2013:167:0019:0021:EN:PDF.

8. CONSENSUAL DISPUTE RESOLUTION

8.1 The Relevant Provisions in the Directive

Articles 18 and 19 of the Directive on competition damages actions provide a framework for facilitating consensual dispute resolution in damage claims cases. In brief, since elements of both provisions have already been mentioned in earlier parts, Article 18 provides for two different types of suspensory effect: on the one hand, the limitation period for bringing actions is suspended for the duration of any consensual dispute resolution process while on the other, national courts may suspend proceedings pending before them for up to two years where the parties are involved in a consensual dispute resolution process with regard to the claim covered by the pending action for damages. Article 18(3) further provides the competition authorities discretion to consider consensual settlements prior to their decision being issued as a mitigating factor when imposing fines.[89]

8.2 The Relevant Provisions Under Greek Law

Article 871 CC is the basis of consensual settlements. Law 3994/2011[90] amended Article 214A CCP, which in its previous form imposed a procedural obligation on the parties to attempt a consensual settlement before commencing court proceedings;[91] the amended version allows the parties at any point prior or even after court proceedings have commenced to settle the dispute.

Settlements are rather underdeveloped in Greek legal practice. The most recent amendment to the Code of Lawyers[92] introduces in Article 35 an obligation for lawyers to inform their clients on alternative dispute resolution mechanisms and mediation in particular. Arbitration (which, of course, requires an agreement on an arbitration clause by the parties) is another option. There are no records of the numbers of out of court settlements or of their success rate.

Settlements could be a success in the Greek legal order, particularly considering the often excessive length of court proceedings (which affects both the claimants who may only receive compensation long after the infringement and the defendants who are burdened with excessive interest). The provision of Article 19(1), however, that the defendant can still be sued

[89] With regard to Art 19 see s 6.

[90] Law 3994/2011 on the Modernisation of the Code of Civil Procedure, FEK A 165/25.7.2011.

[91] Despite the unquestionable good intentions of the legislator, the provision was, in fact, 'dead wood' that merely added to the administrative burden.

[92] Law 4194/2013 as amended by Art 7 Law 4205/2013.

by the claimant when the non-settling co-infringers are not able to pay the damages that correspond to the remaining claim, seems to create some uncertainty. It partly takes away one of the greatest benefits of settlements, namely certainty about the amount of damages to be paid and may thus deter undertakings from settling. The final clause of Article 19(3) that the derogation of Article 19(1) 'may be expressly excluded under the terms of the consensual settlement' that was introduced after the latest trilogue discussions addresses these concerns to a large extent; it is hard to consider that any consensual dispute resolution process will not include such an explicit statement.

8.3 The Relevant Provisions Under Dutch Law

Alternative dispute resolution is a well-developed concept under Dutch law. In principle, arbitration can be agreed for all types of dispute. The arbitration procedure is codified in section 1020 et seq CPA. Settlement agreements are governed by Articles 7:900 et seq CC. Furthermore, there is a special 'mass damage' settlement procedure available in accordance with the provisions of section 7:907 et seq CC.[93] There is no obligation to engage in alternative dispute resolution prior to the start of court proceedings. However, section 3:305a CC provides that a collective action is not admissible if the representative entity has not made a sufficient attempt to achieve the objective of the action through consultations with the defendant. A similar provision to that of Article 19(1) where the claim of the settling injured party shall be reduced by the settling co-infringer's share of the harm can be found in Article 6:14 DCC. This Article holds that

> the creditor may release a solidary debtor towards another solidary debtor from this internal obligation by committing himself towards this other solidary debtor to reduce his debt-claim against him with the amount that this other solidary debtor could have demanded as an internal contribution from the debtor on whose behalf the creditor has waived his rights.

Kortmann and Wesseling raised similar concerns as regards the earlier version of the provisions on consensual dispute resolution. The main concern was that parties that follow the Dutch proportionate share reduction methodology (Article 6:14 DCC) in their individual settlement agreement might

[93] The Amsterdam Court of Appeal is the competent court for such a procedure. If it declares such a 'mass damage' settlement binding, all parties affected by the agreement will be bound by it unless they choose to opt out within the time limit set by the court. See also *Converium and others*, judgment of Amsterdam Court of Appeal of 12 November 2010 NL:GHAMS:2010:BO3908 and of 17 January 2012 NL:GHAMS:2012:BV1026 where the Court found it had jurisdiction even though the majority of the injured parties to the relevant 'mass damage' settlement were not domiciled in the Netherlands.

have been deterred from reaching a settlement agreement due to reasonable fear that they may be forced to pay further damage claims.[94]

9. CONCLUSIONS

In conformity with its twofold goal, the Directive on competition damages actions seems, at first glance, to contribute to a more harmonised system of private enforcement of competition law.[95] As a first concluding remark, it has been illustrated that Greek as well as Dutch law are to a large extent already in line with the majority of the provisions of the Directive. It is to be expected that certain tweaks will be necessary. However, neither jurisdiction seems to require a major overhaul of its enforcement system.

As regards Greece, the multitude of relevant (and in some cases unclear) applicable provisions in different sections of the Greek legislative framework remain a primary concern. In this regard, the example of rules on access to evidence is quite illustrative. In 2010, there were public announcements by high-ranking Greek officials on a legislative initiative concerning a regulatory framework for damage claims due to competition law infringements. The initiative never materialised and even the recent amendment to Greek Competition law through Law 3959/2011 provides little to no clarity on the matter. The implementation of the Directive may be an opportunity for the legislator to simplify a seemingly overcomplicated (despite being underdeveloped in terms of volume of cases) enforcement system and make the adjustments necessary.[96] The development of an effective settlement system should be a priority, particularly in light of the average length of court proceedings in Greece. As regards the Netherlands, certain amendments in Dutch law will also be necessary as indicated in the substantive analysis above, for example, on the disclosure of evidence (excluding corporate statements from possible disclosure), the effect of national decisions, and the joint and several liability.

In light of these observations, it is interesting to note some similarities on issues that remain controversial for both an advanced and a rather underdeveloped jurisdiction. Causality (ie the proof of the causal link between the competition infringement and the damages), particularly in the case of

[94] J Kortmann and R Wesseling, 'Two Concerns Regarding the European Draft Directive on Antitrust Damage Actions' (2013) 1 *CPI Antitrust Chronicle* 1,1–9.

[95] It is, of course, early days for a concrete assessment, and it remains to be seen what problems may be encountered by Member States during the implementation period, as well as the first references for preliminary rulings based on the new rules in the future in order to be able to evaluate the Directive more positively.

[96] The HCC and the Greek Government were strong advocates of the adoption of the Directive and gave it top priority during the Greek Presidency of the Council of the EU in the first semester of 2014.

indirect purchasers, seems to be at the top of the list. A second common issue relates to the 'short' limitation period of five years available to both jurisdictions. Depending on the circumstances of the case, it may be possible that the limitation period, which starts when the claimant becomes aware of the damages and the liable person, may run out before the competent competition authority has reached a final decision establishing whether there has been a breach of the competition rules or not. Furthermore, the increased volatility of the limitation period applicable to different applicants and defendants, due to all the possible suspensions based on the pending investigation(s), litigation and/or consensual dispute resolution proceedings, gives rise to concern among practitioners.[97] Thirdly, there seems to be a need to crystallise the rules on the passing-on defence for which no jurisdiction has clear provisions but where all accept it in principle.[98] A fourth common denominator, despite the glaring differences in terms of the relevant existing jurisprudence, relates to the rules on access to evidence where (particularly in light of the black and grey list exemptions) clarity and precision in the implementation of the new rules will be of paramount importance in order to provide national judges with a working framework to perform the balancing exercise and the proportionality test(s) prescribed.

On this note, the (in)experience of civil judges to deal with antitrust damage claims may prove pivotal alongside clear and careful transposition of the new rules in national legal orders. Antitrust damage claims are extremely fact-intensive and fact-specific by nature. They further require an understanding of the functioning of the market where the infringement occurred and, more often than not, advanced techniques on quantification of the harm and the damages are necessary. The familiarisation of civil judges with such concepts or even specialised courts dealing with such cases may bridge the gap between different jurisdictions. Forum shopping, however, will hardly be avoided in the author's view. The Netherlands is, and is expected to remain, one of the most attractive jurisdictions regarding cartel damage claims,[99] largely thanks to the fast and efficient court

[97] There have been suggestions of a fixed instead of an open-ended limitation period, see for example Kortmann and Wesseling (n 94).

[98] There has been considerable academic debate in the legal literature on whether the passing-on defence should be available in light of the general principle of compensation being made available 'for actual loss suffered'.

[99] Despite the recent trend of the ACM towards 'alternative enforcement', ie means of administrative (public) enforcement with a more horizontal approach where undertakings agree to cooperate with the competition authority and adjust their behaviour without a public decision (eg, a decision with regard to a fine) being made available. See more on 'alternative enforcement' in E Lachnit, 'Alternative Enforcement of Competition Law—Balancing Legal Requirements in Practice', RENFORCE Working Paper, available at renforce.rebo.uu.nl/wp-content/uploads/2013/11/RENFORCE-Working-Paper-Settlements.pdf.

proceedings,[100] the already existing framework for collective redress (which in the case of Greece is not at all available) and settlements and the clarity of rules applicable.[101] The new rules on consensual dispute resolution are expected to further enhance the importance and role of settlements as the most time (and, quite possibly, cost) efficient means of resolving such damages disputes.

As a final remark, it may be worth considering the introduction of a specific statutory provision on antitrust damages (at least at the academic level) in light of the substantive reshaping of competition law enforcement at the EU level through the Commission's initiative and the on-going discussion on the goals of competition law and competition law enforcement. It could be argued that a separate statutory provision accompanied by procedural provisions more tailored towards the specificities of antitrust damage claims could circumvent some of the issues arising in general tort litigation and, potentially, take some burden off non-expert national civil judges. This option may be more intriguing particularly in jurisdictions where private enforcement of competition law remains rather underdeveloped (such as Greece) as it can create a less complex, time and cost efficient framework for all parties involved that would guarantee the effective exercise of the right to full compensation for harm caused by an infringement of EU competition law as set forth in Article 1 of the Directive.

[100] See more on the average duration of court proceedings (which decreased steadily between 2005 and 2010) in the Netherlands in the report prepared by the Council for the Judiciary, available at www.rechtspraak.nl/Actualiteiten/Persinformatie/Documents/Rechtspraak-%20doorlooptijden%202005-2010.pdf.

[101] There are currently collective follow-on actions pending before Dutch courts (most notably related to the cartels in the elevators and the air-cargo markets). Professional antitrust litigation vehicles that collect claims from alleged injured parties have initiated the damages proceedings in some of the pending cases.

Part V

Harm, Indirect Purchasers, and Alternative Redress

14

Indirect Purchasers—Is there Anything New in the Directive? An Introductory Overview of the Current and Future Status of Indirect Purchasers in the EU

ELISABETH EKLUND*

1. INTRODUCTION

WITH THE INTRODUCTION of the EU Directive on competition damages actions and its common framework for anti-trust damages claims in all the Member States, what will be the standing of indirect purchasers and will it result in something new? Already in 2001, the Court of Justice of the European Union in its landmark ruling, *Courage v Crehan*, determined that 'anyone' had the right to obtain competition law damages, including a broad category of various indirect purchasers. As will be further developed in this chapter, this view fundamentally deviates from the rights of indirect purchasers in the US, where these rights have been blocked by the Supreme Court since the 1970s. However, the rights of indirect purchasers must be seen in conjunction with the possibility of invoking or claiming a passing-on defence. This option has now been introduced with the new Directive, while it is barred in the US. This chapter aims to outline the developments so far in the EU and the US. Moreover, practical experience is also drawn from Sweden, one Member State where the right to seek competition damages was already introduced in 1993, albeit with a rather minor impact on indirect purchasers. This leads to the question: why is this the case? The future possibilities of indirect purchasers to obtain

* Elisabeth Eklund, partner at the law firm Advokatfirman Delphi, Stockholm, Sweden (elisabeth.eklund@delphi.se). The author wishes to thank senior associate Oscar Jansson for comments on a draft of this chapter. The usual disclaimer applies.

damages and the problems they may face will also be analysed, together with an assessment of the risks competition law infringers face from indirect purchasers.

Firstly, this chapter provides a short background and overview of the Directive on competition damages actions ('the Directive').[1] There follows a summary of the Court of Justice of the European Union's ('the ECJ') case law on competition damages. We subsequently look across the Atlantic for a brief overview of US case law. The next section deals with the future treatment of indirect purchasers in the EU—a summary of the relevant provisions in the Directive which is followed by a description of various categories of indirect purchasers. Thereafter, relevant experiences from Sweden are dealt with, and lastly, I will give my concluding remarks.

2. THE DIRECTIVE—A SHORT BACKGROUND AND OVERVIEW

The EU has a long-standing history of public enforcement. However, private enforcement has been less widespread in this regard despite the case law of the ECJ, further developed below. In 2005, the Commission, in its Green Paper on Damages actions for breach of the antitrust rules, stated that 'While Community law demands an effective system for damages claims for infringements of antitrust rules, this area of the law in the 25 Member States presents a picture of total underdevelopment'.[2] After many years of analysis and internal drafts, the Directive was presented by the European Commission in June 2013 and an amended version was adopted by the Parliament in April 2014. The Member States have two years from its entry into force to transpose the Directive into national law. As will be discussed below, the question is how this will affect the possibilities for indirect purchasers to obtain damages. And going further, if this can be characterised as something new?

The compensation model outlined in the Directive is based on compensation through single damages for the harm suffered, with interest. Thus, the model used in the US with treble damages as an incentive for private enforcement has not been adopted. It is explicitly stated in Article 3(3) of the Directive that:

> Full compensation under this Directive shall not lead to overcompensation, whether by means of punitive, multiple or other types of damages.

[1] Directive 2014/104/EU of the European Parliament and of the Council of 26 November 2014 on certain rules governing actions for damages under national law for infringements of the competition law provisions of the Member States and of the European Union [2014] OJ L349/1.

[2] Commission, 'Green Paper on Damages actions for breach of the EC antitrust rules' COM(2005) 672 final.

The Directive's other key features cover the need for, inter alia, efficient processes for the disclosure of evidence and the binding effect of final decisions of competition authorities and courts in subsequent damages actions in the Member State in question. The provisions are said to balance rights and obligations of both the claimant and the defendant and to include safeguards against abuses of litigation.

The Directive aims at removing practical obstacles to full compensation for all victims of infringements of EU competition law. The provisions of the Directive will apply to all damages actions, be it individual or collective, which are available in the Member States. The proposal also seeks to optimise the relationship between the private enforcement of the EU competition rules through damages actions and the public enforcement of those rules by the Commission and national competition authorities. In that context the protection of leniency applicants has been an important element, following the ECJ's ruling in the *Pfleiderer* case.[3]

The Commission has a dual goal of enforcement, which has now been further implemented through the Directive. Firstly, deterrence through high fines for breaches of the competition rules.[4] The Directive on competition damages actions enforces the additional kind of deterrence originally introduced by the ECJ where the infringer pays for the damage caused by the infringement. This will give full effect to the EU competition rules and also ensure the proper functioning of the internal market (see Recital 49 of the Directive). This is further mirrored in Article 1 of the Directive which stipulates that the Directive, alongside full compensation,

> sets out rules fostering undistorted competition in the internal market and removing obstacles to its proper functioning, by ensuring equivalent protection throughout the Union for anyone who has suffered such harm.

The fines for competition law infringements in the EU have increased substantially for a number of years, thus increasing the stakes for companies contemplating anti-competitive conduct.[5] In addition to these existing remedies, the infringer must now to a greater extent than before take into account the risk of having to pay damages. Large damages have already been awarded in several Member States, in particular the UK, Germany and the Netherlands, but mainly to direct purchasers so far. Depending on the circumstances, the indirect purchasers may be the actual victims of the anti-competitive behaviour, and very large sums are sometimes at stake in damages. A number of circumstances determine, however, whether it is

[3] Case C-360/09 *Pfleiderer AG v Bundeskartellamt* [2011] ECR I-5161.

[4] See Commission, 'Guidelines on the method of setting fines imposed pursuant to Article 23(2)(a) of Regulation No 1/2003' [2006] OJ C210/02.

[5] The maximum fines amount so far to EUR 1.47 billion for a cartel, Case T-91/13 LG Electronics v Commission (not yet reported) and EUR 1.06 billion for abuse of a dominant position, see Case T-286/09 *Intel* EU:T:2014:547.

worthwhile for an indirect purchaser to take action or not. This will be developed further below.

The notion of private enforcement is, however, broader than damages proceedings. Recital 5 of the Directive on competition damages actions underlines that

> Actions for damages are only one element of an effective system of private enforcement of infringements of competition law and are complemented by alternative avenues of redress, such as consensual dispute resolution and public enforcement decisions that give parties an incentive to provide compensation.

The question is, however, when an indirect purchaser is considered to be too far from the infringement to be entitled to damages. Questions regarding causality are not regulated by the Directive but left open for national procedural rules. However, the rules regarding efficiency and equal treatment as developed further below in Section five must always be taken into account in such assessments.

3. ECJ CASE LAW ON ANTITRUST DAMAGES

As an introductory remark it can be noted that a large number of products pass through several stages in the distribution chain before they reach the final consumer, be it an undertaking or an individual. If a cartel or an abuse of a dominant position leads to an increase in price, this will probably trickle down through the distribution chain, albeit to a varying extent depending on the kind of product or service concerned. Thus, not only the direct purchaser, but several levels of indirect purchasers, may suffer damage from the same competition law infringement. This principle has been recognised by the ECJ in its case law.

In September 2001, the ECJ delivered its ruling in the *Courage v Crehan* case.[6] In this landmark ruling, the ECJ declared that:

> The full effectiveness of Article 85 of the Treaty [now Article 101 TFEU] ... would be put at risk if it were not open to any individual to claim damages for loss caused to him by a contract or by conduct liable to restrict or distort competition.[7]

This wording was reiterated by the ECJ in the *Manfredi* case in 2006 (para 60):

> [A]s regards the possibility of seeking compensation for loss caused by a contract or by conduct liable to restrict or distort competition, it should be recalled that the full effectiveness of Article 81 EC and, in particular, the practical effect of the prohibition laid down in Article 81(1) EC would be put at risk if it were not

[6] Case C-453/99 *Courage v Crehan* [2001] ECR I-6297.

[7] ibid para 26.

> open to any individual to claim damages for loss caused to him by a contract or by conduct liable to restrict or distort competition (*Courage and Crehan*, cited above, paragraph 26).[8]

Thus, the ECJ already made it clear in 2001 that the right to claim damages belongs to 'any individual' who has suffered damage and has since then upheld that principle. The Court's ruling may be seen as the starting point in the process of turning private enforcement into a realistic complement to the public enforcement of the EU competition rules. It may, however, be noted that the possibility of indirect purchasers bringing damages actions was only recently opened up in several of the larger Member States. For example, it was in June 2011 that the German Supreme Court explicitly recognised that indirect purchasers have standing and that defendants can invoke passing on.[9]

In this regard it is interesting to note that indirect purchasers making purchases of the same kind of product from several sources may also be entitled to compensation in relation to purchases from purchasers not part of the cartel in question due to the ECJ's recent judgment opening up for so-called umbrella pricing.[10]

How indirect purchasers are treated in the Directive will be developed further below, but let us first travel across the Atlantic where indirect purchasers have been barred from bringing antitrust damages claims for a long time.

4. THE US EXPERIENCE

Article 4 of the Clayton Act states that

> any person who shall be injured in his business or property by reason of anything forbidden in the antitrust laws may sue.

Consequently, the Clayton Act does not limit standing to certain groups of plaintiffs.

It is often believed that the EU antitrust rules have been inspired by the US rules. It is true that the US has a long-standing tradition of private enforcement. However, as regards the rights of indirect purchasers, the EU has taken a different route than the US courts. This is based on long-standing two-tier case law from the US Supreme Court, which substantially limits the broad wording of the Clayton Act.

[8] Joined Cases C-295/04 to C-298/04 *Vincenzo Manfredi et al* [2006] ECR I-6619.

[9] See S Wisking, K Dietzel and M Herron, 'European Commission Finally Publishes Measures to Facilitate Competition Law Private Actions in the European Union' (2014) 35 *European Competition Law Review* 185, referring to case no KZR 75/10.

[10] Case C-557/12 *Kone AG and Others v ÖBB-Infrastruktur AG* EU:C:2014:1317.

The first stage in this case law was the barring of a passing-on defence for defendants in *Hanover Shoe* (1968).[11] Passing-on means the practice of an injured party reducing its actual losses by passing them on, entirely or partially, to its own purchasers. In such situations the losses, which have been passed on, no longer constitute harm for which the party that passed them on has to be compensated. As will be developed further below, it follows from the Directive that it is therefore appropriate to allow an infringer to invoke the passing-on of actual loss as a defence against a claim for damages, and at the same time allow indirect purchasers to claim that they have suffered harm due to the fact of passing-on, on behalf of the supplier.[12] Thereafter, the US Supreme Court banned indirect purchasers' actions in federal courts in *Illinois Brick* (1977).[13]

In the *Hanover Shoe* case, action had been brought under § 4 of the Clayton Act against a manufacturer of shoe machinery by one of its customers, a manufacturer of shoes. In his defence, the shoe machinery manufacturer sought to show that the plaintiff had not been injured in its business as required by § 4 because it had passed on the claimed illegal overcharge to those who bought shoes from it. According to the defendant's theory, the illegal overcharge was absorbed by the plaintiff's customers—the indirect purchasers of the defendant's shoe machinery—who were the persons actually injured by the antitrust violation. In *Hanover Shoe*, the Supreme Court rejected the argument that the indirect, rather than the direct, purchasers were the parties injured by the antitrust violation. The Court held that, except in certain limited circumstances, a direct purchaser suing for treble damages under § 4 of the Clayton Act is injured within the meaning of § 4 by the full amount of the overcharge paid by it, and that the antitrust defendant is not permitted to introduce evidence that indirect purchasers were in fact injured by the illegal overcharge.[14]

In the subsequent ruling in *Illinois Brick* the background was the following; the petitioners manufactured and distributed concrete blocks in the Greater Chicago area. They sold the concrete primarily to masonry contractors, who submitted bids to general contractors for the masonry parts of construction projects. The general contractors, in turn, submitted bids for these projects to customers such as the respondents, the State of Illinois and 700 local governmental entities in the Greater Chicago area, including counties, municipalities, housing authorities, and school districts. The respondents were thus indirect purchasers of concrete blocks, which passed through two separate levels in the chain of distribution before reaching them. The concrete was purchased directly from the petitioners by

[11] *Hanover Shoe* 392 US 481 (1968).
[12] The role of passing-on is described in recs 34 and 35 of the Directive.
[13] *Illinois Brick Co v Illinois* 431 US 720 (1977).
[14] *Hanover Shoe* (n 11) 494.

masonry contractors and used by them to build masonry structures; those structures were incorporated in entire buildings by general contractors and sold to the respondents. The respondent State of Illinois, on behalf of itself and local government entities, brought an antitrust treble damages action under § 4 of the Clayton Act, alleging that the petitioners had engaged in a combination and conspiracy to fix the prices of concrete blocks in violation of § 1 of the Sherman Act. The complaint alleged that the amounts paid by the respondents for concrete blocks were more than $3 million higher by reason of this price-fixing conspiracy.

The Supreme Court held that

> The first reason for the Court's rejection of this offer of proof [on passing on] was an unwillingness to complicate treble damages actions with attempts to trace the effects of the overcharge on the purchaser's prices, sales, costs, and profits, and of showing that these variables would have behaved differently without the overcharge. A second reason for barring the pass-on defense was the Court's concern that unless direct purchasers were allowed to sue for the portion of the overcharge arguably passed on to indirect purchasers, antitrust violators 'would retain the fruits of their illegality' because indirect purchasers 'would have only a tiny stake in the lawsuit,' and hence little incentive to sue.[15]

Since the defendants were unable to use the passing-on defence, the Court arrived at the conclusion that the same principles bar indirect purchasers' actions, except in three narrow circumstances.[16]

While this elimination of recovery under federal law enabled the Supreme Court to both simplify Sherman Act cases, by limiting recovery to direct purchasers only, and maintain consistency between the *Hanover Shoe* and *Illinois Brick* judgments, it simultaneously created what some call an unfair system of recovery.[17] However, more than half of the states have passed state legislation which allows indirect purchasers to seek damages under state law.[18]

Professor Hovenkamp notes the downside of not permitting indirect purchasers' actions by stating:

> Permitting indirect purchasers actions would increase the costs of litigation and may result in overdeterrence. However, the Illinois Brick rule clearly deprives injured parties of their claim to damages. (...) In the great majority of situations

[15] *Illinois Brick* (n 13) 725.

[16] See A Hamilton and D Henry, 'Bricks, Beer and Shoes: Indirect Purchaser Standing in the European Union and the United States' (2012) 5 *Global Competition Litigation Review* 111, 115.

[17] See L Finn, 'The Developing Role of State Indirect Purchaser Statutes: The Current and Future Status of Indirect Purchaser Remedies using *Mylan Laboratories* as a Benchmark' available at web.law.columbia.edu/sites/default/files/microsites/career-services/The%20Developing%20Role%20of%20State%20Indirect%20Purchaser%20Statutes.pdf 1.

[18] Hamilton and Henry (n 16).

> the indirect purchaser rule gives the entire damage action to the person who suffered the smaller injury—or, in some cases, no injury at all.[19]

It is, however, held by some scholars that the problem of overcompensation is not a problem in practice due to the low levels of damages.[20]

The Antirust Modernization Committee recommended in 2007 that the *Hanover Shoe* and the *Illinois Brick* doctrines should be overruled through legislative amendments, but this has so far not led to any legislation.[21]

Thus, indirect claims are still barred in federal damages suits but exist in more than half of the states due to state legislation. As a last remark on the US, it may be added that the situation is not the same across the US border. The Canadian Supreme Court recently allowed antitrust damages claims by indirect purchasers.[22]

5. THE FUTURE TREATMENT OF INDIRECT PURCHASERS IN THE EU—RELEVANT PROVISIONS IN THE DIRECTIVE

After having outlined the US perspective, I will now describe how the situation of indirect purchasers is dealt with in the Directive. As in the ECJ's case law, the Directive clearly states in Article 1(1) that:

> This Directive sets out certain rules necessary to ensure that anyone who has suffered harm … ensuring equivalent protection throughout the Union for anyone who has suffered such harm (emphasis added).

The right to full compensation for anyone that has suffered harm due to a competition law infringement is further developed in Article 3:

> Member States shall ensure that any natural or legal person who has suffered harm caused by an infringement of competition law is able to claim and to obtain full compensation for that harm.
>
> Full compensation shall place a person who has suffered harm in the position in which that person would have been had the infringement of competition law not been committed. It shall therefore cover the right to compensation for actual loss and for loss of profit, plus the payment of interest (emphasis added).

The question regarding causality is not regulated by the Directive. However, Article 4 in the Directive requires that the principles of effectiveness and the principle of equivalence shall be applied, which means that Member States

[19] See H Hovenkamp, *Federal Antitrust Policy: The Law of Competition and its Practice*, 4th edn (St Paul, MN, West Acamedic Publishing, 2011) 681.

[20] RH Lande, 'The Proposed Damages Directive: The Real Lessons from the United States' (2014) 2 *CPI Antitrust Chronicle* 2, has remarked that 'if the U.S. experience is a guide, the relatively modest payments that will be made to indirect victims won't cause the sum of payments to direct and indirect purchasers to exceed 100 percent of the overcharges'.

[21] Antitrust Modernization Commission, 'Report and Recommendations', available at govinfo.library.unt.edu/amc/report_recommendation/introduction.pdf, 18.

[22] *Option Consommateurs v Infineon Technologies AG*, 2013 SCC 59.

shall not treat claims under EU law in a less favourable way than national claims.

> In accordance with the principle of effectiveness, Member States shall ensure that all national rules and procedures relating to the exercise of claims for damages are designed and applied in such a way that they do not render practically impossible or excessively difficult the exercise of the Union right to full compensation for harm caused by an infringement of competition law. In accordance with the principle of equivalence, national rules and procedures relating to actions for damages resulting from infringements of Article 101 or 102 TFEU shall not be less favourable to the alleged injured parties than those governing similar actions for damages resulting from infringements of national law.

The definition of indirect purchasers is found in Article 2 (24):

> 'indirect purchaser' means a natural or legal person who acquired, not directly from an infringer, but from a direct purchaser or a subsequent purchaser, products or services that were the object of an infringement of competition law, or products or services containing them or derived therefrom.

Indirect purchasers are further included in the definition of 'injured parties' in Article 2(6), where it is stated that

> 'injured party' means a person that has suffered harm caused by an infringement of competition law.

Another definition of interest in this context is the definition of 'overcharge' in Article 2(20):

> 'overcharge' means the difference between the price actually paid and the price that would otherwise have prevailed in the absence of an infringement of competition law.

Article 16 provides that:

> The Commission shall issue guidelines for national courts on how to estimate the share of the overcharge which was passed on to the indirect purchaser.

No such guidelines have been issued so far.

The possibility to use the passing-on defence against direct purchasers, as well as indirect purchasers is developed in the next section.

Article 15 regulates how actions for damages for claimants from different levels in the supply chain shall be handled in order to avoid multiple liability or to absence of liability. This is important as indirect purchasers and direct purchasers may bring action in different proceedings, and also in different Member States. It is thereby stated in Article 15 that

> Member States shall ensure that … national courts seized of an action for damages are able, by means available under Union and national law, to take due account of any of the following:
>
> (a) actions for damages that are related to the same infringement of competition law, but are brought by claimants from other levels in the supply chain;

(b) judgments resulting from actions for damages as referred to in point (a);
(c) relevant information in the public domain resulting from the public enforcement of competition law.

2. This Article shall be without prejudice to the rights and obligations of national courts under Article 30 of Regulation (EU) No 1215/2012.

The impact of Regulation (EU) No 1215/2012, on jurisdiction and the recognition and enforcement of judgments in civil and commercial matters,[23] is specified in Recital 44:

> It is possible for actions pending before the courts of different Member States to be considered as related within the meaning of Article 30 of Regulation (EU) No 1215/2012 of the European Parliament and of the Council. Under that Article, national courts other than that first seized may stay proceedings or, under certain circumstances, may decline jurisdiction. This Directive is without prejudice to the rights and obligations of national courts under that Regulation.

Thus, national courts may stay proceedings or decline jurisdictions due to the fact that action has been brought in another Member State. This means that close monitoring of actions in other Member States will be important in the future.

The Directive further provides for rules in Article 12 in order to ensure that overcompensation does not take place.

2. In order to avoid overcompensation, Member States shall lay down procedural rules appropriate to ensure that compensation for actual loss at any level of the supply chain does not exceed the overcharge harm suffered at that level.
3. This Chapter shall be without prejudice to the right of an injured party to claim and obtain compensation for loss of profits due to a full or partial passing-on of the overcharge.
4. Member States shall ensure that the rules laid down in this Chapter apply accordingly where the infringement of competition law relates to a supply to the infringer.
5. Member States shall ensure that the national courts have the power to estimate, in accordance with national procedures, the share of any overcharge that was passed on.

Article 13 regulates the possibility for defendants to invoke the passing-on defence, at the same time placing the burden of proof on the defendant for the passing-on of the overcharge by the claimant:

> Member States shall ensure that the defendant in an action for damages can invoke as a defence against a claim for damages the fact that the claimant passed on the whole or part of the overcharge resulting from the infringement of competition

[23] Regulation (EU) No 1215/2012, on jurisdiction and the recognition and enforcement of judgments in civil and commercial matters, OJ L 351, 20.12.2012, 1–32.

> law. The burden of proving that the overcharge was passed on shall be on the defendant, who may reasonably require disclosure from the claimant or from third parties.

Article 14 specifically states that when a claimant claims that an overcharge was passed on by the defendant, the burden of proof shall rest with the claimant. When the claimant is an indirect purchaser it shall be deemed to have proven that a passing-on to it occurred where it has shown that (paragraph 2):

> (a) the defendant has committed an infringement of competition law;
> (b) the infringement of competition law has resulted in an overcharge for the direct purchaser of the defendant; and
> (c) the indirect purchaser has purchased the goods or services that were the object of the infringement of competition law, or has purchased goods or services derived from or containing them.

However, this presumption may be rebutted by the defendant according to the following paragraph, at the end of Article 14:

> This paragraph shall not apply where the defendant can demonstrate credibly to the satisfaction of the court that the overcharge was not, or not entirely, passed on to the indirect purchaser.

6. VARIOUS CATEGORIES OF INDIRECT PURCHASERS

Even if indirect purchasers are defined in the Directive, it is safe to say that this is no homogeneous group. Indirect purchasers may be close to the infringement, eg, because they purchase the final goods directly from a retailer of a cartel member. They may alternatively purchase the product further down the distribution chain and incorporate it in another product without even really paying attention to its existence, or buying the cartel goods much further down the supply chain. Indirect purchasers may further range from multinational corporations to SMEs and lastly to consumers.

When discussing indirect purchasers it is important to remember that it is not always a question of private undertakings. Another category of indirect purchasers is public authorities that often make substantial procurements of various products and services. These are actually listed in Recital 3 of the Directive as examples of indirect purchasers alongside consumers and undertakings. It is worth remembering that the ECJ held that the Commission was entitled to sue for damages in relation to the elevator cartel, which it had fined, but where it was a purchaser of the elevators in question.[24] In that situation it was, however, a direct purchaser.

[24] Case C-199/11 *Europese Gemeenschap v Otis NV and Others* EU:C:2012:684.

Below, the impact of a competition law infringement on various categories of indirect purchasers is illustrated, as well as the difficulties they may face; however, the examples are much more numerous.

6.1 Example 1

The first example relates to purchasers of the cartel goods; say, eg, a car manufacturer cartel, which buys the products from a retailer of a cartel member. The indirect purchasers in this situation are the car purchasers which may involve both B2B, ie business-to-business (such as eg taxi companies) and B2C, ie business-to-consumers. In this situation there is likely to be media attention if there is a public enforcement case and in such a case even individual customers in the form of consumers may become aware of the infringement. Unless there is public enforcement it is less likely that the indirect purchasers will become aware of the cartel infringement. It is also a lot less likely that an indirect purchaser, rather than a direct purchaser, will try to use a competition law defence in a contractual dispute, and thereby link that claim to damages.

Thus, it is unlikely that there will be numerous stand-alone cases brought by indirect purchasers. However, in this situation follow-on cases may be initiated, in particular by B2B customers.

Even if a car is one of the more expensive products an individual consumer ever purchases, besides a home, it is unlikely that a consumer will take action for damages, unless it is through collective redress through opt-out proceedings (which are rare in the EU and not promoted by the Commission, which proposes an opt-in system in its Collective Redress Recommendation).[25] Let us assume that the price of a new car is in the range of EUR 20–25,000 and that a plausible cartel overcharge is 10 per cent. That would lead to a claim per purchaser of about EUR 2–2,500, a sum for which it is not worth bringing damages proceedings in order to try to recoup the amount lost. However, a class action may be worth their while. The indirect purchasers are less likely to be involved in an opt-in system than in an opt-out system.

6.2 Example 2

It typically becomes more difficult for the indirect purchaser, in particular when it is a matter of a consumer, to identify the infringement and the extent

[25] Commission Recommendation 2013/396/EU of 11 June 2013 on common principles for injunctive and compensatory collective redress mechanisms in the Member States concerning violations of rights granted under Union Law [2013] OJ L201/60; see also Commission, 'Communication from the Commission to the European Parliament, the Council, The European Economic and Social Committee and the Committee of the Regions: Towards a European Horizontal Framework for Collective Redress' COM(2013) 401 final.

of the damage when products which are incorporated in other products are involved and the former are subject to the competition law infringement. Examples of such goods are, eg, various spare parts in relation to car purchasers. If we compare with the first example, the cartel is one step up in the retail chain, and thus does not exist between the car manufacturers but between the manufacturers of parts delivered to the car manufacturers. The direct and indirect purchasers would, however, be the same but the infringer in the previous example would have been turned into a direct purchaser and the then direct purchaser would have been turned into an indirect purchaser. It would therefore be much more difficult for the indirect purchasers to both identify the infringement and estimate the damage. Even in the case of public enforcement most consumers would probably not make a connection between the cartel they read about in the newspaper and the car parts in their car. Moreover, they are unlikely to understand that they are entitled to compensation, which is why it is essential that Member States provide information to the public if the Directive is to become an effective means of public enforcement.

6.3 Example 3

This third example illustrates a situation where the direct purchaser is not the actual victim due to the fact that there is full passing-on to the indirect purchaser. This example derives from a private enforcement case, via an injunction,[26] in which I represented the applicant, a local taxi company in Uppsala. The case concerned the abuse of a dominant position.

The background to the case was that the defendants, Swedavia AB (publ), owner of Stockholm Arlanda Airport, together with a contractor, the parking company Europark AB, had introduced fees for taxi companies operating the parking at Arlanda Airport, picking up pre-booked customers in the entrance hall of the airport. These companies were charged a fee of approximately EUR 5.

Since the taxi companies had previously accepted pre-orders free of charge, the additional fee was not included in the price of the taxi ride; instead the customers were charged this fee in full on top of the price of the ride.

In this situation, the taxi passengers could thus in theory have initiated proceedings for damages since there was a judgment laying down the infringement. The damage was, however, too small for the consumers and so far no major corporate taxi customers have taken action, almost four years after the proceedings, which is why this is unlikely to happen. Nor have any of the taxi companies brought an action for damages. Regardless of the fact that they passed on the full overcharge they suffered; the damage due to the

[26] MD 2011:28, *Uppsala Taxi 100 000 AB v EuroPark Svenska Aktiebolag and Swedavia AB*.

loss of passengers, as well as the increase in administrative costs due to the new registration system for pre-booked customers.

6.4 Challenges for Indirect Purchasers

In conclusion, as regards the various categories of indirect purchasers, it is interesting to note that there are several common challenges, some of which are also of relevance to direct purchasers. Firstly, the infringement must be identified, which is generally more difficult for indirect than direct purchasers. In addition, the amount of the damage and possible passing-on must be assessed. If direct purchasers have already taken action, the indirect purchasers should coordinate their actions in relation to the direct purchasers. An assessment must also be made to see whether there are national rules on causality that render a claim by the indirect purchaser difficult or even bar such a claim depending on the circumstances.

Both direct and indirect purchasers will have to assess their situation when it comes to establishing evidence for both the infringement as such, and the size of the damages claimed.

One of the major issues which needs to be addressed, provided that there is evidence, is to prove the infringement, but it is almost equally important to establish whether it is worth litigating the claim with regard to the damages at stake, the expected litigation costs and the chances of success.

7. THE SWEDISH EXPERIENCE

The Swedish legislation regarding the private enforcement of the competition rules is unique in that the first legislative measures which were taken to encourage private actions were adopted more than 20 years ago. Since then a number of legislative measures have been adopted to encourage those who have suffered damage to take action.

The Swedish competition rules mirror Articles 101 and 102 TFEU and were implemented in Sweden through the old Competition Act which entered into force on 1 July 1993.[27] The current Competition Act[28] entered into force on 1 November 2008.

Unlike the EU competition rules, the Swedish competition rules include an explicit damage provision, and have done so since the former Competition Act entered into force in 1993. Just like the Directive, the Swedish model is based on compensation through single damages. Victims of competition

[27] Swedish Competition Act (*Konkurrenslag* 1993:20).
[28] ibid 2008: 579.

law infringements are entitled to full compensation, including the right to interest in accordance with the Interest Act.[29]

Even though the legislative possibility regarding initiating action for competition damages had already been introduced when the Swedish Competition Act was first enacted in 1993, it took more than 10 years before the possibility for indirect purchasers to take action was introduced through a legislative amendment in 2005.[30] The notion regarding who is entitled to sue for damages was thereby widened. Previously, only contracting parties and companies were entitled to damages for competition law infringements, but the provision was amended to include everyone who has suffered loss, ie encompassing consumers and indirect purchasers as well.[31] In my view, the amendments made sense in order to cover for a number of inconsistencies in the damages provisions. The original proposal also contained a method to ensure access to evidence, but this proposal was not part of the final legislative package.[32]

The current damages provisions are found in Chapter 3, sections 25 and 26 of the Competition Act, which mirror the wording in the previous Act.[33] Despite the amendments described above, the number of damages actions is not increasing in Swedish courts. Since August 2005, when the amendments entered into force, fewer than 25 cases have been brought before the Stockholm City Court, which is the main legal forum even if standing is also provided in the District Court where the defendant has its location. Only four of these cases have led to a judgment, but damages were only awarded in two joined cases.[34] The limited number of claims for damages can be explained by a number of factors. The most important ones are described below.

Despite the fact that the damage provisions in the Competition Act have been in place for 20 years, and have also been amended over the years to

[29] Swedish Act on Interest (*räntelagen* 1975:635).

[30] Prop 2004/05:117 *Skadestånd enligt konkurrenslagen* (Swedish Government Bill on Damages in accordance with the Competition Act).

[31] In addition, the period of limitation was extended from five to 10 years. It also became possible to sue for damages due to an infringement of the EU competition rules and not only in relation to breaches of the Swedish competition rules.

[32] See the proposal in the SOU 2004:10 (Swedish Government Inquiry) 104 125; cf prop. 2004/05:117 (n 30) 45 where the Government states that the reasons for implementing the proposal were not strong enough.

[33] Inauthentic translation of Arts 25 and 26 by the Swedish Competition Authority: 'If an undertaking intentionally or negligently infringes any of the prohibitions contained in Chapter 2, Article 1 or 7, or in Article 101 or 102 in the Treaty, the undertaking shall compensate the damage that is caused thereby. The right to such damages shall lapse if no action is brought within ten years from the date when the damage was caused.

The Stockholm City Court shall always be competent to examine cases relating to damages pursuant to Article 25.'

[34] See the joined cases *Euroclear Sweden AB v Europe Investor Direct AB and others*, Case no T 10012-08 of 19 January 2011. The case was appealed to the Supreme Court, Case no T 792-11, but leave for appeal was not granted.

create further incentives for victims to seek redress, there is hardly any case law at all. Some cases have been initiated and subsequently settled, but even these are very limited in number. So far no case has been granted leave for appeal to the Supreme Court. The Svea Court of Appeal has only issued one joint judgment where damages were awarded. This was a stand-alone case where Euroclear (previously VPC Aktiebolag) was found to have abused its dominant position in the market for information concerning the addresses of shareholders in Swedish joint-stock companies by refusing to supply the information. The three applicants that used the information requested in their business activities were awarded damages of SEK 1.9 million (approximately EUR 200 000), plus interest which was approximately 25 per cent of the amount claimed. The Court stated that, as a general rule, the damage should be equal to the profit lost. Since the applicants had failed to show the actual profit, the Court applied the rule in the Swedish Code of Judicial Procedure, providing that if it is difficult to fully prove a loss, the Court shall estimate the damage to a reasonable amount. The Court of Appeal considered the extent of the effects of the abuse and that it took some time for the businesses to recover after the abuse had ended.

A damages action is handled by general courts under the provisions of the Code of Judicial Procedure regarding actions which are not amenable to out-of-court settlements. These conditions include provisions on the duty of disclosure, ie an opportunity for a party to request the other party to submit certain documents or evidence in a procedure. The Swedish rules also include the principles of the free production of evidence and free evaluation of evidence. Sweden has for many years applied rules about class actions which makes it possible for a number of businesses or consumers to seek damages jointly. So far, this possibility has not been used in any competition case.[35] The Group Proceedings Act is based on the opt-in principle, meaning that only those that actively express their intention to be included in the action have the right to damages.

Despite these favourable conditions to pursue damage claims, there has so far been only one case where damages have been awarded by a court in Sweden, the so-called *VPC* or *Euroclear* case mentioned above. A number

[35] Rules on collective redress were introduced in January 2003 through the Swedish Group Proceedings Act (*lag* (2002:599) *om grupprättegång*). The Group Proceedings Act, which is not specifically aimed at competition cases, has a long history. Government-run activities supporting consumers are well established in Sweden, and an important aspect when maintaining a high level of consumer protection is to ensure easy access to redress. The first proposals concerning collective redress, which resembled the American concept, were made nearly 25 years ago. Not too surprisingly, the idea of collective redress in a form similar to the American 'class action' concept was met with considerable resistance from both the Swedish Business Society and the legal profession. As a consequence, it took more than a decade of deliberations and redrafting before the proposals materialised into a final legislative product. In many aspects the original proposal was significantly amended, the legislator finally opting for a far more cautious compromise version.

of other damages claims have been settled, including claims for damages from municipalities affected by the so-called asphalt cartel (a bid-rigging cartel affecting a large part of the market for asphalt in Sweden). In several judgments, the plaintiffs have failed to demonstrate that there has been a competition law infringement which is why the claims for damages have been rejected.

Despite the long-standing damage provisions in Swedish competition law, the damage cases are very rare. Despite the fact that indirect purchasers have been able to bring action for almost 10 years now, no damage cases have been brought by consumers as far as I am aware, nor have any cases been brought by undertakings as indirect purchasers. Why is this the case? The main reason for the lack of indirect purchaser actions seems to be the small number of actions brought by the Swedish Competition Authority. Since 2005, only three cartel actions brought by the Swedish Competition Authority have been decided by the Swedish Courts and only two cases regarding abuse of dominant position. Thus, there is very little substance for follow-on damages. In addition, in some cases it may be difficult to obtain evidence. There are limited disclosure rules and these do not allow fishing. Another hurdle, in particular for consumers to bring action, is the often small amount of total damages for each customer. Sweden has collective redress legislation but it has so far not been applied in a competition law context and also on very few other damages actions in other areas. It should also be noted that contingency fees are not allowed and the loser-pays principle applies in Swedish courts. Thus, even with the Directive, it is likely that there will continue to be few damage cases in Swedish courts in the future, unless the Competition Authority brings successful cases to court more often.

Since the EU has opted against the imposition of compulsory rules on class actions and in favour of a recommendation to the Member States, it seems unlikely that collective redress actions will be widely used by consumers or SMEs in the next few years.

8. CONCLUDING REMARKS

As has been outlined above, the right of indirect purchasers to bring damage claims is not a new phenomenon and it is an avenue that will probably be promoted more and thus also used more with the explicit provisions in the Directive addressing these issues, which will subsequently be implemented in the national legislation of the Member States. There may, however, be no effective private enforcement in the EU unless there is effective public enforcement, as the two routes run in parallel. The room for indirect purchasers to bring action will continue to be fairly limited, in particular when these indirect purchasers are consumers, due to both difficulties in identifying and proving the infringement and in calculating the damages.

The main possibility for indirect purchasers to bring actions for damages becomes possible when it is question of follow-on damages when the claimants do not need to prove the infringement. On the other hand, such actions may include complicated assessments regarding causality. In other cases there may, however, be a very obvious causality between the infringement and the damage caused and even full disclosure of the passing on.

Nevertheless, as is the case for direct purchasers as well, the damage in question must entail such a substantial amount that it is worth initiating litigation, which may take years to resolve. In many situations, that is simply not the case, due to the fact that competition litigations are costly in many different contexts, in particular if the competition law infringement as such needs to be established and in addition to that the damages too.

However, the rules on binding decisions in follow-on actions as well as the disclosure rules will hopefully help to enable damaged parties to bring action. It will be very interesting to see the upcoming developments due to the implementation of the Directive. Even if it remains difficult for indirect purchasers to bring damages claims, competition law infringers must definitively take such possible claims seriously in their risk assessments.

15

Beyond the Competition Damages Directive: What Room for Competition Law Restitution?

MAGNUS STRAND*

1. INTRODUCTION

AT THE SWEDISH Network for European Legal Studies (SNELS) conference held in Uppsala on 15 and 16 May 2014, it was discussed whether or not the new EU Competition Damages Directive[1] would encompass actions for restitution for a breach of competition law. Views differed: Some argued that, in order to achieve effective harmonisation of private enforcement of competition law in the EU, the Directive should be interpreted as encompassing any claim for damages or restitution alike. Others, including this author, argued that damages actions should be distinguished from restitutionary actions, and that the wording and purpose of the Directive should not be interpreted as encompassing the latter. This contribution picks up on that discussion.

Restitution could function as an alternative to damages where the anti-competitiveness of a contract renders such a contract null and void pursuant to Article 101(2) TFEU, and plausibly also in the event of a breach of Article 102 TFEU. Needless to say, damages and restitution are distinct legal actions and different criteria apply to them under the legal traditions of the EU Member States. While an award of damages traditionally seeks to repair harm caused, restitution traditionally seeks to reverse a transaction for which there was no legal basis. In other words, the payment of an overcharge constitutes harm for which damages are payable, but the payment of an overcharge may also lack legal basis (being contrary to competition law)

* Magnus Strand is Doctor of Laws and Junior Lecturer at Uppsala University.

[1] Directive 2014/104/EU of the European Parliament and of the Council of 26 November 2014 on certain rules governing actions for damages under national law for infringements of the competition law provisions of the Member States and of the European Union [2014] OJ L349/1.

and under such circumstances that payment should be reversed. In certain instances, both could plausibly apply in parallel to the reclaim of an overcharge exacted in breach of competition law.

The case law of the European Court of Justice on restitution for a breach of EU competition law is almost non-existent. There are thus far only three cases, all with particular limitations. The first two, *Société de Vente*[2] and *VAG France*,[3] are both somewhat dated and the relevant holdings of the Court have not been confirmed in more recent case law. In the third, *GT-Link*,[4] the defendant was not a private individual, but a state-owned company. Therefore, the action in *GT-Link* was for the repayment of illegal charges levied by (an emanation of) a Member State contrary to EU law, which is a distinct action under EU law,[5] making it difficult to draw conclusions for the purposes of actions for restitution from private parties for a breach of competition law.

In this contribution, the stakes involved will be examined and the elements of restitution will be outlined. Then, it will be discussed whether restitutionary redress falls within the scope of the Competition Damages Directive. Assuming that restitutionary redress is an alternative which does not fall within the scope of the Directive, particular possibilities and problems will be discussed. It will also be discussed whether existing restitutionary remedies in national law should, or indeed must, be available for a breach of EU competition law. Finally, some summarising conclusions will be drawn.

2. WHY AND WHEN IS RESTITUTION AN OPTION?

The Competition Damages Directive introduces a strong preference for compensatory damages, which has not been present in preceding EU case law. By contrast, in *Manfredi*, the Court of Justice explicitly held that if exemplary or punitive damages were available to actions under national law, which were sufficiently similar to actions for damages for an infringement of EU competition law, an award of such damages also had to be available

[2] Case 319/82 *Société de Vente de Ciments et Bétons de l'Est SA v Kerpen & Kerpen GmbH und Co KG* [1983] ECR 4173.

[3] Case 10/86 *VAG France SA v Établissements Magne SA* [1986] ECR 4071.

[4] Case C-242/95 *GT-Link A/S v De Danske Statsbaner (DSB)* [1997] ECR I-4449.

[5] On this action, see A Jones, *Restitution and European Community Law* (London, Mansfield Press, 2000), or M Strand, *The Passing-On Problem in EU Law Damages and Restitution* (Uppsala University (diss), 2015) Ch 6. I wish to thank Professor Jones for her comments on restitutionary aspects at the public defence of my book, which have also inspired this contribution.

in the latter actions.[6] This holding, however, is overruled by the new Directive, as its Article 3(3) introduces a ban on heads of damages designed to serve deterrence rather than compensation. Furthermore, the provisions on passing-on in Articles 12 and 13 have the effect of precluding any possibility to award restitutionary damages. Combined with the ban in Article 3(3), that leaves compensatory heads of damages as the only heads of damages available under the Directive. Furthermore, the soft-law instruments accompanying the Competition Damages Directive (the Communication on quantifying harm in actions for damages for a breach of EU competition law[7] and the more detailed Practical Guide on the same subject)[8] also stay within the paradigm of compensatory heads of damages.[9]

However, the Directive does not explicitly exclude the possibility of bringing other actions for payment, instead of—or combined with, as the case may be—an action for damages. For example, a direct purchaser (of goods or services that have been the object of an infringement of competition law resulting in an overcharge for those goods or services) may wish instead to bring an action for restitution of the overcharge. Indeed, where the claimant is a direct purchaser who has paid an overcharge, the circumstances may be such that an action for restitution or unjust enrichment is preferable to an action for damages. However, it should be borne in mind that restitution cannot remedy a loss of sales caused by the infringement. For such losses, damages are the only viable option.

As noted by Howard and Blackwood, an action to recover illegal gains from an infringer may be more advantageous for certain claimants than an action for compensation for harm, or easier to prove.[10] Komninos has clarified that claimants for restitution do not need to prove harm and causation,

[6] Joined Cases C-295/04 to 298/04 *Vincenzo Manfredi v Lloyd Adriatico Assicurazioni SpA* (C-295/04), *Antonio Cannito v Fondiaria Sai SpA* (C-296/04) and *Nicolò Tricarico* (C-297/04) and *Pasqualina Murgolo* (C-298/04) *v Assitalia SpA* [2006] ECR I-6619, Operative part para 5. The 2004 Ashurst Study (D Waelbroeck, D Slater and G Even-Shoshan, 'Ashurst Study on the Conditions of Claims for Damages in Case of Infringement of EC Competition Rules: Comparative Report' (Brussels, 2004) 84, available at ec.europa.eu/competition/antitrust/actionsdamages/comparative_report_clean_en.pdf (last accessed 1 March 2015) reported exemplary damages to be available in Cyprus, the United Kingdom, and in Ireland, but also that they were rarely awarded. Punitive damages were available in Cyprus and seemed to be awarded more often than exemplary damages.

[7] Commission, 'Communication from the Commission on quantifying harm in actions for damages based on breaches of Art 101 or 102 of the Treaty on the Functioning of the European Union' [2013] OJ C167/19.

[8] Commission, 'Staff Working Document—Practical Guide on quantifying harm in actions for damages based on breaches of Art 101 or 102 of the Treaty on the Functioning of the European Union' SWD(2013) 205.

[9] See eg OJ C167/19 (n 7) para 6.

[10] A Howard and A Blackwood, 'Litigating Infringements in the National Courts' in V Rose and D Bailey (eds), *Bellamy & Child: European Union Law of Competition*, 7th edn (Oxford, Oxford University Press, 2013) 1254.

but only enrichment of the defendant to the disadvantage of the claimant.[11] If nothing else, an action for restitution may be preferable in order to escape the rules on passing-on in the Directive. In particular, such a possibility would be of great interest to direct purchasers as the defence of passing-on is alien to, or at least controversial in, the law of restitution and unjust enrichment.[12] Therefore, if such alternative means of redress were sought by direct purchasers, the rules in the Directive on passing-on could plausibly be circumvented, and the direct purchaser claimants might thus acquire a much larger award than would be available under the damages regime of the Directive.

To indirect purchasers, the availability of restitution is less crucial, as the Competition Damages Directive serves to make it easier for indirect purchasers to bring an action for damages.[13] Moreover, a direct restitutionary action by an indirect purchaser against the infringer of competition law, leapfrogging the direct purchaser, would be an oddity in European private law.[14] In an attempt to bridge the gap, the Berlin Kammergericht has reportedly held that if a restitutionary action were successfully brought by a direct purchaser against an infringer of competition law, subsequent restitution actions against the direct purchaser should be available to indirect purchasers.[15]

The preliminary issue, however, is the scope of the Competition Damages Directive. If the Directive encompasses restitutionary actions, there will be no need to proceed to discussing the elements of restitution for a breach of competition law. Therefore, it is now time to examine the scope of the Directive.

[11] AP Komninos, *EC Private Antitrust Enforcement* (Oxford, Hart Publishing, 2008) 219.

[12] The issue has been debated to some extent among common law scholars, see eg, P Birks, *Unjust Enrichment*, 2nd edn (Oxford, Oxford University Press, 2005) 219–21; and M Rush, *The Defence of Passing-on* (Oxford, Hart Publishing, 2006).

[13] See Directive 2014/104/EU (n 1) Arts 12(1), 14 and 15.

[14] The concept of restitution commonly presupposes a direct transaction from the claimant to the defendant, see Draft Common Frame of Reference (C von Bar and E Clive (eds), *Principles, Definitions and Model Rules of European Private Law: Draft Common Frame of Reference (DCFR) Full Edition* (6 vols, Munich, Sellier European Law Publishers, 2009)) 4036 and 4039–42; G Dannemann, *The German Law of Unjustified Enrichment and Restitution* (Oxford, Oxford University Press, 2009) 34; and Rush (n 12) 210–11. However, in EU case law on the repayment of illegal charges, indirect taxpayers may be able to bring an action for repayment of charges levied in breach of EU law against the Member State itself; Case C-94/10 *Danfoss A/S and Sauer-Danfoss ApS v Skatteministeriet* [2011] ECR I-9963 Operative part para 1.

[15] Howard & Blackwood (n 10) 1257. See also AP Komninos, 'Private Enforcement in the EU with Emphasis on Damages Actions' in I Lianos and D Geradin (eds), *Handbook on European Competition Law: Enforcement and Procedure* (Cheltenham, Edward Elgar Publishing, 2013) 249.

3. EXPLORING THE SCOPE OF THE COMPETITION DAMAGES DIRECTIVE

The scope and purpose of the Directive is explained in Article 1, which states that it provides 'certain rules necessary to ensure that anyone who has suffered harm caused by an infringement of competition law (...) can effectively exercise the right to claim full compensation for that harm', and that it therefore sets out rules coordinating public enforcement of competition law with private 'enforcement of those rules in damages actions'. Further, Article 3(2) explains that '[f]ull compensation shall place a person who has suffered harm in the position in which that person would have been had the infringement not been committed'. This is easily recognised as the standard phrase for compensation through damages. Article 12 on the passing-on of overcharges and the right to full compensation also consistently speaks of 'harm' and 'compensation'. Moreover, Article 13 on the passing-on defence explicitly applies in 'an action for damages'. The same term is used in the following Articles, 14 and 15, on indirect purchasers and parallel actions. For the purposes of the new Directive, an 'action for damages' is defined in Article 2(4) as meaning 'an action under national law by which a claim for damages is brought', and a 'claim for damages' is defined in Article 2(5) as meaning 'a claim for compensation for harm caused by an infringement of competition law'.

If it is accepted that a claim for restitution concerns the return of something (money, commodity or its value), and that a claim for unjust enrichment concerns the reversal of such an enrichment, a literal interpretation of the relevant Articles suggests that such restitutionary actions should fall outside the scope of the Competition Damages Directive.[16] If, as was suggested at the Uppsala conference, the Commission wished for such actions to fall within the scope of the Directive, it has nevertheless failed to include any legal provisions in the text that would be able to secure such an interpretation.

Of course, it is ultimately for the European Court of Justice to decide on the scope of the Directive. In that regard, a relevant comparison can be made with actions against a Member State. There, the Court of Justice has consistently held that it is for the claimants to bring an action to specify the nature and basis of their actions, under the supervision of the national court.[17] There is no case law on this issue in the context of competition law. Until such case law emerges, it can neither be assumed that the case law on

[16] Definitions will of course vary between jurisdictions. These two definitions or descriptions are roughly based on P Birks, *An Introduction to the Law of Restitution* (Oxford, Oxford University Press, 1985) 11, and DCFR (n 14) Art VII.-1:101(1), respectively.

[17] See Joined Cases C-397/98 and C-410/98 *Metallgesellschaft Ltd and Others* (C-397/98), *Hoechst AG and Hoechst (UK) Ltd* (C-410/98) *v Commissioners of Inland Revenue and HM Attorney General* [2001] ECR I-1727, para 81; and Case C-446/04 *Test Claimants in the*

actions against Member States will be adopted for the purposes of competition law claims nor that that case law will be ignored by the Court of Justice in the interest of the effective harmonisation of private enforcement of competition law.

In the personal opinion of this author, restitutionary awards should be distinguished from awards of damages, not only for their differences in purpose, but also for their corresponding differences with regard to the applicable criteria for the establishment of a right to an award, as well as for the estimation of the award. While it is true that the same set of circumstances may sometimes allow claimants a choice between the two remedies, this will not always be the case. The choice—when available—will not be without consequence regarding the claimant's prospects of successful litigation. Therefore, I would conclude that the action must be distinguished. By reason of the wording of the Directive, I would further conclude that restitutionary actions fall outside its scope of application. Accordingly, restitution should remain an alternative to competition law damages.

Still, the particular possibilities and problems in respect of restitution in the context of competition law must be examined further. An outline of those possibilities and problems follows in the next section.

4. POSSIBILITIES AND PROBLEMS

4.1 Introducing Restitution in the Competition Law Context

Assuming that my conclusions in the previous section are correct, and (accordingly) in the absence of EU law rules governing restitutionary remedies for a breach of competition law, such remedies will remain governed by national law—albeit subject to the requirements of Article 47 of the EU Charter and the EU law principles of equivalence and effectiveness.[18] In that regard, it must be kept in mind that, pursuant to Article 101(2) TFEU, agreements or decisions prohibited pursuant to Article 101 TFEU are automatically void. In principle, where parties to a contract which is declared void have conferred benefits to each other in accordance with the contract, such benefits should be restored.[19]

The laws of the Member States offer a number of possibilities in restitution that would be suitable for private enforcement of competition law.[20]

FII Group Litigation v Commissioners of Inland Revenue [2006] ECR I-11753, para 201. Cf R Williams, *Unjust Enrichment and Public Law: A Comparative Study of England, France and the UK* (Oxford, Hart Publishing, 2011) 113–18; and Strand (n 5) 87–92.

[18] Of course, national law implementing provisions of Directive 2014/104/EU (n 1) may be applied *mutatis mutandis* to restitutionary actions by the national courts, eg Art 9 on the effect of decisions of a national competition authority.

[19] It seems safe to assume that this applies generally in European private law; cf DCFR (n 14) Art II.-7:303, VII.-1:101 and, in particular, VII.-2:101(2).

[20] Jones (n 5) 152–54 lists English case law and summarises the findings on restitutionary actions in a private enforcement survey published by the European Commission (AJ Braakman

The crucial issue for claimants, however, is to establish how the infringement of competition law is connected to the price of a product or service bought. The situation will seem fairly straightforward where prices have been inflated: The restitutionary claim would be for the return of the aggregate amount of the overcharge paid. In more complicated cases, the contract may be void in its entirety, and all benefits conferred under the contract may accordingly have to be reversed. Moreover, goods purchased might be consumed, resold to the next level of the supply chain, incorporated in the production line of the buyer so as to make it unreasonably difficult and/or expensive to return them, or otherwise unavailable.[21] Under such circumstances, the detailed national rules on the unwinding of performances will apply.[22]

Furthermore, although claimants for restitution may be better off than damages claimants insofar as they do not need to prove harm and causation, they will still need to establish that the prices were inflated and the precise or at least approximate amount of such inflation, in order for the national court to award restitution of the overcharge. Unless the overcharge can be identified in the form of price discrimination, as a specific item on invoices, or somehow with similar certainty, the identification of an overcharge on a complex market may prove quite difficult. Of course, this is a difficulty which is not particular to restitution, but which is shared with damages claimants.[23]

However, there are further complicating factors. First, the sanction in Article 101(2) TFEU targets the contract (or decision or practice) which is contrary to Article 101 TFEU. Accordingly, a classic price-fixing cartel agreement may be void by virtue of Article 101(2) TFEU, but that does not mean that sales contracts entered into by the members of the cartel (so-called linked contracts) are void even though the prices in those contracts may be inflated by the cartel. Indeed, the European Court of Justice has held that the automatic nullity now provided for by Article 101(2) TFEU applies only to those contractual provisions which are incompatible with Article 101 TFEU.[24] Accordingly, under EU law, linked contracts are not automatically

and N Dutilh (eds), *The Application of Articles 85 and 86 of the EC Treaty by National Courts in the Member States* (Brussels, European Commission, 1997)). A few German cases are listed in L Ritter and WD Braun, *European Competition Law: A Practitioner's Guide* (3rd edn, The Hague, Kluwer Law International, 2004) 1174, fn 1151. See also Komninos (n 11) 219.

[21] Arguably, the most common situation where the enrichment can be returned as such is where it consists of real estate. Intellectual property can also be returned as such, but will trigger the model rule of the DCFR (n 14) Art VII.-5:104 in particular.

[22] In the DCFR (n 14) the return of benefits transferred under a void contract is governed by model rules on unjustified enrichment in its Book VII; see Art II.-7:303(1). In Book VII, see Ch 5 in particular.

[23] See SWD(2013) 205 (n 8), part 3 s II on how to quantify overcharges.

[24] Case 56/65 *Société Technique Minière (LTM) v Maschinenbau Ulm GmbH (MBU)* [1966] ECR 235, 250. The Court further held that the issue of severability is governed by national law. See also *Société de Vente* (n 2) Operative part para 2.

void by virtue of their connection with a cartel.[25] Nevertheless, they may be void or avoidable under national law. Second, with regard to vertical agreements that include an infringement of competition law, the illegality of the contract might render restitution unavailable in some Member States. The purpose of such national rules is to avoid offering legal redress to the parties of illegal or immoral contracts.[26] Such a national rule was at issue in *Courage*, where it was reported that English law would not allow a party to an illegal agreement to claim damages from the other party.[27]And third, it has never been confirmed by the Court of Justice that contracts that are contrary to Article 102 TFEU are void in the same manner as under Article 101(2) TFEU. It is often assumed that in principle, they should be, although it is uncertain whether a contract contrary to Article 102 TFEU is automatically void or whether it is avoidable.[28]

It follows that it is necessary to proceed to examine under what circumstances restitution may be a legally and practically viable alternative remedy. Beginning with claims under Article 101 TFEU, it will first be discussed when restitutionary redress can be used to reverse the payment of overcharges pursuant to an anti-competitive vertical agreement, and then if restitutionary redress can be available where an overcharge is the result of an anti-competitive horizontal agreement (a cartel). Thereafter, it will be examined whether restitution can be available where an overcharge is the result of abuse of a dominant position contrary to Article 102 TFEU. The discussion will be inspired by relevant materials from the national jurisdictions of the Member States, even though these are not EU law materials *sensu stricto*.

4.2 Restitution Pursuant to Nullity of a Vertical Agreement

In a vertical agreement, contractual clauses which are contrary to Article 101 TFEU, and which are not exempted by virtue of the block exemption for

[25] Where there is a particularly close connection between a horizontal agreement and vertical agreements, however, both may be void pursuant to Art 101(2) TFEU; cf Case C-32/11 *Allianz Hungária Biztosító Zrt and Others v Gazdasági Versenyhivatal* EU:C:2013:160, para 45, where the Court held that vertical agreements 'implementing' a horizontal agreement partitioning the market would be unlawful (and thus void under Art 101(2) TFEU).

[26] DCFR (n 14) Art VII.-6:103; see also 547–50 and 4167–74.

[27] Case C-453/99 *Courage Ltd v Bernard Crehan and Bernard Crehan v Courage Ltd and Others* [2001] ECR I-6297, para 11. See further D Beard and A Jones, 'Co-Contractors, Damages and Article 81: The ECJ Finally Speaks' (2002) 23 *European Competition Law Review* 246, 247–48.

[28] On Art 102 TFEU in this context, see U Bernitz, 'The Sanction of Voidness under Article 102 TFEU and its Relation to Damages' in U Bernitz, *Europarättens genomslag* (Stockholm, Norstedts Juridik, 2012) 276–77 (also available in A Ezrachi (ed), *Article 82 EC: Reflections on its Recent Evolution* (Oxford, Hart Publishing 2009)); and Jones (n 5) 169.

vertical agreements in Regulation 330/2010[29] or any other exemption of general application, are automatically void in accordance with Article 101(2) TFEU. If the illegal clause cannot be severed from the other clauses of the contract, the contract in its entirety will be null and void. In circumstances where severance is possible under national law, and the illegal aspects of the vertical agreement include the payment of an overcharge (eg the infamous beer tie in *Courage* and other English pub tenancy cases, or unlawful upfront access payments),[30] it would follow that the payment of such an overcharge must be reversed. Under such circumstances, an action for restitution may be a plausible option for claimants.

However, as mentioned above, the illegality of the contract might render restitution unavailable in some Member States. For example, common law distinguishes several such defences of illegality to an action for restitution including the strong *ex turpi causa non oritur actio* (from a disgraceful cause arises no action), as well as the weaker *in pari delicto* rule.[31] The compatibility of such rules with EU law was discussed by the European Court of Justice in *Courage*.[32] The Court stressed the horizontal direct effect of Articles (now) 101 and 102 TFEU, and that it was settled case law that the nullity of a contract which is prohibited under Article 101 TFEU could be relied on by anyone. It followed, the Court held, that 'any individual can rely on a breach of Article [101 TFEU] before a national court even where he is a party' to the contract at issue.[33] Therefore, the Court would not accept any absolute bar against actions for damages brought by a party to the anti-competitive contract, but would nevertheless allow national courts to deny claimants to obtain damages from co-contractors in circumstances where it was established that the claimant bore 'significant responsibility for the distortion of competition'.[34] With regard to the details of the assessment, the Court of Justice instructed national courts to

> ... ascertain whether the party who claims to have suffered loss through concluding a contract that is liable to restrict or distort competition found himself in a markedly weaker position than the other party, such as seriously to compromise or even eliminate his freedom to negotiate the terms of the contract and his

[29] Commission Regulation (EU) No 330/2010 of 20 April 2010 on the application of Article 101(3) of the Treaty on the Functioning of the European Union to categories of vertical agreements and concerted practices [2010] OJ L102/1.

[30] See Commission, 'Guidelines on Vertical Restraints' [2010] OJ C130/1, paras 203–08.

[31] See eg A Burrows, *The Law of Restitution*, 3rd edn (Oxford, Oxford University Press, 2011) 488–89; and Birks (n 12) 247–53.

[32] In *Courage* (n 27), the original action in the main proceedings was for restitution or damages, but the restitution claims had been dropped before the reference to the Court of Justice was made. The ruling of the Court thus concerned the *in pari delicto* rule in damages. However, there seems to be no reason why the ruling of the Court of Justice in *Courage* would not apply *mutatis mutandis* to an action for restitution.

[33] ibid paras 22–24.

[34] ibid paras 28 and 31.

capacity to avoid the loss or reduce its extent, in particular by availing himself in good time of all the legal remedies available to him.

Such a rule seems to be quite suitable for the purposes of competition law restitution, and furthermore seems compatible with the approaches of the national laws of most Member States as reported in the DCFR.[35]

4.3 Restitution and Linked Contracts Pursuant to Nullity of a Horizontal Agreement

It was demonstrated above that price inflations caused by cartels are not easily remedied by way of restitution. However, for the purposes of such circumstances, it has been discussed to what extent national law may allow private enforcement in the form of restitution.

An ambitious survey of some Member State jurisdictions carried out by Caroline Cauffman indicates considerable variance on the issue of linked contracts.[36] Although the details of the survey cannot be reported here, a few summarising comments should suffice to illustrate the problems involved: In German law, linked contracts that serve to implement a prohibited agreement (*Ausführungsverträge*) are distinguished from linked contracts that contain consequences of the prohibited agreement (*Folgeverträge*). In principle, *Ausführungsverträge* are equally void as the prohibited agreement, while *Folgeverträge* are valid, although this state of affairs is the subject of some discussion.[37] The nullity of a cartel agreement does not seem to render linked contracts void neither in English nor Dutch law, while the matter is unclear in French and Belgian law.[38] Cauffman has similarly found that the rules of national contract law will rarely cause linked contracts to be void or avoidable, although damages for the breach of competition law might be available in some instances. However, under German law, bid-rigging amounts to fraud. It would therefore be possible to nullify the contract at issue.[39]

The Swedish Supreme Court has ruled that the issue of whether nullity pursuant to competition law extends to follow-on contracts[40] cannot be

[35] DCFR (n 14) 548–50.

[36] C Cauffman, 'The Impact of Voidness for Infringement of Article 101 TFEU on Linked Contracts' (2013) *Maastricht European Private Law Institute Working Paper* No 2013/3, available at ssrn.com/abstract=2204954 (last accessed 25 May 2015).

[37] ibid 5–6.

[38] ibid 3–7 and 22–23.

[39] ibid 23.

[40] By 'follow-on contracts' (perhaps 'follow-on clauses' would have been a better option), the Supreme Court referred to contracts that included standard clauses negotiated within a trade association, where the horizontal agreement on the standard clause at issue is subsequently held incompatible with Art 101 TFEU (or the national equivalent) and therefore void. Under the circumstances, however, the Supreme Court held that there was no binding horizontal agreement on the standard clause at issue, and hence that it could not be nullified as such.

answered generally, but that it must be determined in the individual case. According to the Supreme Court, the factors to be considered were the connection between the prohibited agreement and the follow-on contract, and the weight to be assigned to the public interest of fair competition.[41] It has been commented that these *dicta* give some directions but not much detailed guidance for the assessment.[42]

In sum, linked contracts are rarely void or avoidable by virtue of the nullity of a horizontal agreement up (or down) stream. Consequentially, restitution will equally rarely be an available option for claimants who have contracted with cartelists.

4.4 Restitution and Article 102 TFEU

The direct or indirect imposition of unfair purchase or selling prices is one of the examples of an abuse of a dominant position, explicitly provided in Article 102 TFEU. For instance, a dominant seller might have discriminated between customers, imposing higher prices on those customers who were also competitors of the dominant seller on other relevant markets. The practical circumstances under which restitution for a breach of Article 102 is a plausible option to damages thus seem to be quite similar to those discussed in Section 4.2. And yet, as mentioned above, it has never been confirmed by the European Court of Justice that contractual clauses that are contrary to Article 102 TFEU are void in the same manner as under Article 101(2) TFEU.

It has been argued by Bernitz that contractual clauses in breach of Article 102 TFEU should be void and/or unenforceable, by virtue of the direct effect of Article 102 and by analogy with Article 101(2).[43] Komninos has similarly argued that the reason why there is no provision on nullity in Article 102 TFEU is because 'the behaviour prohibited therein does not usually take the form of an agreement', but that nullity of contractual clauses in breach of Article 102 is necessary in order to safeguard 'the "system" of the two basic competition rules of the Treaty and (…) the effectiveness and efficiency' of Article 102.[44] Commentators often mention that agreements contrary to Article (now) 102 TFEU have been declared null and void in Sweden[45] and the United Kingdom.[46]

[41] NJA 2004 s 804, 825.

[42] J Andersson, 'HD, konkurrensbegränsande avtal och följdavtals ogiltighet' (2005) 8 *Europarättslig tidskrift* 364, 369.

[43] Bernitz (n 28) 276. This view is shared by A Jones and B Sufrin, *EU Competition Law*, 7th edn (Oxford, Oxford University Press, 2014) 1100; and by Howard and Blackwood (n 10) 1232 fn 187.

[44] Komninos (n 11) 159–60.

[45] Case T 33-00 *SAS v Luftfartsverket* (Göta Hovrätt Swedish Court of Appeal judgment delivered 27 April 2001).

[46] *English Welsh & Scottish Railway v E ON UK* [2007] EWHC 599.

Under Article 102 TFEU, the contractual relationship between the dominant and the other contractor is direct. Thus, the problems arising in the context of cartels are avoided. This seems to open the door to restitution of performances rendered in accordance with a contractual clause which includes abuse of a dominant position. By analogy with case law under Article 101 TFEU,[47] it would be for national law to govern the unwinding of performances, subject to the principles of effectiveness and equivalence.

As with restitution pursuant to the nullity of a vertical agreement in breach of Article 101 TFEU, the illegality of the contract might render restitution unavailable in some Member States.[48] In the context of Article 102, however, the *Courage* rule—under which claims brought by co-contractors cannot be barred unless they bear significant responsibility for the breach of competition law—should ensure that restitution is kept available to deserving victims of an abuse of a dominant position on the relevant market.

5. MUST NATIONAL RESTITUTIONARY REMEDIES BE MADE AVAILABLE?

From the perspective of EU law, it is a crucial question whether national courts can somehow be required to extend the scope of application of national restitutionary remedies to circumstances where the contract or contract clause is void because it is contrary to EU competition law.[49] The proper strategy through which to pursue an answer to that question—and indeed the answer itself—differs, depending on whether or not restitutionary remedies are available under national law in similar circumstances.

Where rights conferred on individuals by EU competition law have been infringed, it is well known that EU law requires that an effective remedy is made available to the individual. However, as explained in the '*Butter Buying Cruises*' case and more recently in *Unibet* and *Inuit*, the right to an effective remedy is not a right to any remedy.[50] With regard to infringements of EU competition law, the point of departure should be that the rights of individuals are safeguarded by the combined forces of public enforcement and the harmonised damages regime for private enforcement

[47] *Société de Vente* (n 2).

[48] See further s 4.2.

[49] In this chapter, the concept of a remedy signifies a legal action brought before a court or administrative body with a view to enforcing a right. One way of doing so is to bring an action, the purpose of which is to secure a certain form of redress; eg, an injunction or the award of damages or restitution.

[50] Case 158/80 *Rewe-Handelsgesellschaft Nord mbH and Rewe-Markt Steffen v Hauptzollamt Kiel (Butter Buying Cruises)* [1981] ECR 1805, para 44 and Operative part para 7; Case C-432/05 *Unibet (London) Ltd and Unibet (International) Ltd v Justitiekanslern* [2007] ECR I-2271, paras 40–41; Case C-583/11 P *Inuit Tapiriit Kanatami and Others v European Parliament and Council of the European Union* EU:C:2013:625, paras 103–04.

created by the Competition Damages Directive and the accompanying soft-law instruments. Before the adoption of the Competition Damages Directive and the accompanying soft-law instruments, it was sometimes debated whether the need for effective judicial protection of EU law rights did not require restitution to be available.[51] Under the present circumstances, if by chance the new competition law damages regime cannot adequately ensure the effective judicial protection of the claimant and there is no effective restitutionary action in the jurisdiction at issue, the Court might plausibly require national courts to make available an action of restitution in the circumstances. However, this author fails to envisage such a scenario, not only because the new harmonised damages regime offers judicial protection, but also because it should be safe to assume that relevant restitutionary remedies are available in all Member States.

In that regard, it should be recalled that existing alternative redress mechanisms that are already available in national law are also addressed by EU law requirements. In the *Butter Buying Cruises* case, a right to equivalent remedies for the infringement of rights guaranteed by (now) EU law provisions with direct effect was proclaimed by the Court of Justice.[52] This right to equal access to remedies was settled in the operative part of the judgment in *Butter Buying Cruises* and is still generally acknowledged.[53] However, the *Butter Buying Cruises* case did not touch upon whether the duty of national courts was to extend all remedies known to the national jurisdiction to claims based on EU law. The limitations settled with regard to the principle of equivalence might plausibly apply *mutatis mutandis* in this context, so that it would not be required of the national courts to extend any remedies known to their jurisdiction to all claims based on EU law,[54] but only those applying in relevantly similar circumstances. If so, it might also be presumed, for instance, that the pertinent national remedy to extend to an action for restitution brought against a private undertaking pursuant to an infringement of EU competition law would not be a national restitutionary

[51] See eg Komninos (n 11) 219–20; Jones (n 5) 149–53 and 187–92, Bernitz (n 28) 282, and V Milutinovic, *The 'Right to Damages' under EU Competition Law: From* Courage v Crehan *to the White Paper and Beyond* (Alphen aan den Rijn, Wolters Kluwer, 2010) 170.

[52] *Butter Buying Cruises* (n 50) para 44, and Operative part para 7.

[53] See eg, K Lenaerts, I Maselis and K Gutman (JT Nowak (ed)), *EU Procedural Law* (Oxford, Oxford University Press, 2014) 118; S Prechal, *Directives in EC Law*, 2nd edn (Oxford, Oxford University Press, 2006) 146; and T Andersson, *Rättsskyddsprincipen: EG-rätt och nationell sanktions- och processrätt ur ett svenskt civilprocessuellt perspektiv* (Uppsala, Iustus förlag, 1997) 79.

[54] cf Case C-231/96 *Edilizia Industriale Siderurgica Srl (Edis) v Ministero delle Finanze* [1998] ECR I-4951, para 36; and Joined Cases C-279/96, C-280/96 and C-281/96 *Ansaldo Energia SpA v Amministrazione delle Finanze dello Stato, Amministrazione delle Finanze dello Stato v Marine Insurance Consultants Srl* and *GMB Srl and Others v Amministrazione delle Finanze dello Stato* [1998] ECR I-5025, para 29.

action available against the state, but a general restitutionary action available against private individuals.[55]

As Articles 101 and 102 TFEU have horizontal direct effect,[56] the *Butter Buying Cruises* logic leads to the conclusion that restitutionary actions available under national law will also need to be made available for the purposes of claims based on a breach of Article 101 and/or 102 TFEU. As Arnull notes, in *Butter Buying Cruises*, the Court of Justice seemed to assume 'that all developed legal systems would have a sophisticated array of remedies which could if necessary be adapted to the requirements of [EU] law'.[57]

Accordingly, where restitutionary actions are available under national law, it is concluded that the rights conferred on individuals by EU competition law should be enforceable through the use of such restitutionary actions. In the absence of EU law harmonisation, the rules and conditions of national law governing such actions will apply, albeit subject to the requirements of Article 47 of the EU Charter and the EU law principles of equivalence and effectiveness.

In cases where the breach of competition law is by a vertical agreement in breach of Article 101 TFEU or a contractual clause which includes abuse of a dominant position, the discussion above has revealed that restitution may be a viable option to damages. Still, as is evident from the many question marks in this discussion, matters are not quite clear. Where appropriate, therefore, reference should be made to the Court of Justice for a preliminary ruling on the extension of national restitutionary actions to claims based on an infringement of EU competition law.

6. CONCLUSIONS

As noted above, the Competition Damages Directive does not explicitly exclude the possibility of bringing other actions for payment instead of or combined with an action for damages. For example, a direct purchaser might instead wish to bring an action for the restitution of an overcharge, where such an action is available under national law, while indirect purchasers might instead wish to rely on the Directive.[58] Accordingly, it is expected that direct purchasers will attempt to bring restitutionary actions rather than damages actions where preferable.

However, with the development of the action for damages, from *Courage* and now through the Competition Damages Directive and the accompanying

[55] cf *Edis* (n 54) para 37; *Ansaldo Energia* (n 54) para 29.

[56] Case 127/73 *Belgische Radio en Televisie and société belge des auteurs, compositeurs et éditeurs v SV SABAM and NV Fonior* [1974] ECR 51, para 16.

[57] A Arnull, *The European Union and its Court of Justice*, 2nd edn (Oxford, Oxford University Press, 2006) 273.

[58] cf Williams (n 17) 179–81.

soft-law instruments, the Court of Justice should not be expected to require that a certain remedy be available before national courts if another one, which is capable of safeguarding the protection of rights conferred on the claimant by EU law, is already available. Therefore, future case law of the Court of Justice is expected to determine first of all whether national actions for restitution fall within or outside the scope of application of the new Competition Damages Directive. If it is decided by the Court that they fall outside the scope of the Directive, the next problem will be to decide on the impact of Article 47 of the EU Charter and the EU law principles of equivalence and effectiveness on the details of such national actions.

In view of the differences in both the purposes and the conditions governing damages and restitution, this author has taken the view that restitutionary actions should not fall within the scope of application of the new Competition Damages Directive. It is submitted that restitutionary actions might be capable to contribute to the private enforcement of competition law in Europe, although within the limits set by the scope of nullity and by its capacity of meeting the interests of individual claimants. It will be very interesting to follow future restitutionary developments beyond the Competition Damages Directive.

16

The Presumption and Quantification of Harm in the Directive and the Practical Guide

MARIOS C IACOVIDES*

1. INTRODUCTION

ONE OF THE beneficial innovations for claimants introduced by the Directive on competition damages actions (or the Directive),[1] is the rebuttable presumption of harm in cartel cases enshrined in Article 17(2). Especially for follow-on claimants, that is to say claimants who base their case on a cartel case that has already been brought successfully by the European Commission (the Commission) or by a national competition authority, the presumption of harm will be of the greatest utility. Not having to prove the infringement,[2] nor that the cartel has resulted in some harm, will leave them with the need to only show loss, causation and quantum.[3] Stand-alone claimants will need to prove the infringement of EU (or national) competition law in addition to that.

The estimation of the quantum of damages in competition law cases can be costly in terms of time, effort and resources, due to the complexity of the economic data and the methods of transforming it into legally meaningful

* Marios C Iacovides (marios.iacovides@jur.uu.se) LLB (King's College London) LLM (Stockholm University) is a doctoral candidate in European Law at Uppsala University, Sweden, and Marie Curie Early Stage Research fellow at Università Bocconi, Milan, Italy. This chapter was partly authored with support from the project 'Dispute Settlement in Trade: Training in Law and Economics' (www.dissettle.org), a Marie Curie Initial Training Network funded under the EU Seventh Framework Programme (Grant Agreement No FP7-PEOPLE-2010-ITN_264633).

[1] Directive 2014/104/EU of the European Parliament and of the Council of 26 November 2014 on certain rules governing actions for damages under national law for infringements of the competition law provisions of the Member States and of the European Union [2014] OJ L349/1.

[2] Art 9 of the Directive on competition damages actions, ibid.

[3] A Howard, 'Too Little, too Late? The European Commission's Legislative Proposals on Anti-Trust Damages Actions' (2013) 4 (6) *Journal of European Competition Law & Practice* 455, 458. See Case C-199/11 *Europese Gemeenschap v Otis NV* EU:C:2012:684, para 65.

indicators of damage. The estimation is also inherently speculative, since it involves a counterfactual—what would have been the competitive situation in the market but for the infringement? Thus, the general improvement of claimants' position under EU competition law brought about by the Directive would be chimeric if claimants were not somehow facilitated in the quantification of the harm they suffered as a result of the infringement of competition rules.

As a result, although the existence of harm and its quantification are two distinct elements of a successful claim for damages, the benefits from the former depend to a great extent on the latter. This was realised by the drafters of the Directive, who included in Article 17 an obligation on national courts to estimate the harm and an option for national competition authorities to assist in its calculation.[4] These guarantee renewed interest in the Practical Guide on quantifying harm in actions for damages based on breaches of Article 101 or 102 of the TFEU (the Practical Guide),[5] which has hitherto been largely overlooked by the academic community of competition law scholars.

Against this backdrop, this chapter discusses the relationship between the presumption of harm and its quantification, and by extension also the relationship between the Directive on competition damages actions and the Practical Guide. It is organised as follows: Section two gives some background from the preparatory work leading up to the proposal for the Directive and presents the provisions of the Directive that are relevant to the topic; Section three gives an overview of the Practical Guide and explains the Directive's relation to it; Section four identifies the major issues that are likely to be litigated by national courts and the Court of Justice of the European Union (CJEU) in the years following the coming into force of the Directive and discusses the compatibility of the Practical Guide with the Directive; and Section five provides a summary and short conclusions.

2. THE QUANTIFICATION OF HARM AND THE DIRECTIVE

2.1 The Green and White Papers

The Commission already identified the quantification of harm, along with the scope of damages, as a key issue for private enforcement in 2005 when it issued the Green Paper on damages actions for breach of the EC

[4] Respectively Arts 17(1) and 17(3) of the Directive on competition damages actions (n 1).

[5] European Commission, 'Commission Staff Working Document—Practical Guide: Quantifying Harm in Actions for Damages Based on Breaches of Article 101 or 102 of the Treaty on the Functioning of the European Union' SWD(2013) 205 (Strasbourg, 11 June 2013).

antitrust rules (the Green Paper on damages actions).[6] The Staff Working Paper accompanying the Green Paper as an Annex (the Green Paper Staff Working Paper) portrayed the quantification of harm as one of the major obstacles that the Commission wished to tackle with its legislative initiatives in private enforcement.[7] Through these two documents, the Commission sought the reactions of stakeholders on a number of issues relating to the quantification of harm, such as whether it should publish guidelines on the matter, whether split proceedings on the liability of the infringer and on the quantum of damages should be introduced, and whether courts should have the power to assess quantum on the basis of an equitable approach.[8] The majority of the responses to the Green Paper on damages actions were positively disposed to the issuing of guidelines for the quantification of harm.[9]

The Green Paper on damages actions was followed by a White Paper on damages actions for breach of the EC antitrust rules (the White Paper on damages actions)[10] in 2008. Section 2.5 thereof dealt with the issue of the quantification of harm. Meanwhile, between the Green and the White Papers on damages actions, the Court of Justice (ECJ, or the Court) had ruled in *Manfredi* that compensation from infringements of EU competition law should be available not only for actual losses as a result of the price increase attributable to the infringement (*damnum emergens*), but also for the loss of profit as a result of any reduction of sales (*lucrum sessans*), plus interest.[11] Since the scope of damages was settled by the Court, in the White Paper on damages actions the Commission simply expressed its wish to codify the case law and to instead put more emphasis on the calculation of the quantum of damages. In that regard, it identified three issues: first, that the calculation of damages is often very cumbersome; second, that the calculation can become excessively difficult or even practically impossible if national law requires that the exact amount of the harm suffered must always be precisely calculated; and third, that far-reaching calculation

[6] European Commission, 'Green Paper on Damages Actions for Breach of the EC Antitrust Rules', COM(2005) 672 final (Brussels, 19 December 2005).

[7] European Commission, 'Commission Staff Working Paper—Annex to the Green Paper Damages Actions for Breach of the EC Antitrust Rules' SEC(2005) 1732 (Brussels, 19 December 2005) para 37.

[8] Green Paper on damages actions (n 6) s 2.3, Questions 18–20.

[9] European Commission, 'Commission Staff Working Paper Accompanying the White Paper on Damages Actions for Breach of the EC Antitrust Rules' SEC(2008) 404 (Brussels, 2 April 2008) (White Paper Staff Working Paper), para 184. There were 149 responses to the Green Paper. For the full list see ec.europa.eu/competition/antitrust/actionsdamages/green_paper_comments.html (last accessed 1 January 2015).

[10] European Commission, 'White Paper on Damages Actions for Breach of the EC Antitrust Rules', COM(2008) 165 final (Brussels, 2 April 2008). There were 172 responses to the White Paper. For the full list see ec.europa.eu/competition/antitrust/actionsdamages/white_paper_comments.html (last accessed 1 January 2015).

[11] Joined Cases C-295/04 to C-298/04 *Manfredi v Lloyd Adriatico Assicurazioni SpA and Others* [2006] ECR I-6619, paras 95–97.

requirements can be disproportionate to the amount of damage suffered.[12] Hence, the Commission expressed its determination to issue non-binding guidance on the quantification of damages in antitrust cases[13] and even suggested that simplified methods of damages calculation could be utilised, including average cartel overcharges as guidance to national courts for the quantum of damages.[14]

2.2 The Directive—Article 17

The consultation resulted in a proposal for a Draft Directive in 2013.[15] The Directive on competition damages actions, after amendments by the European Parliament and the Council, was adopted in 2014. Given how intertwined all the aspects of a competition law case are, there are several provisions in the Directive that are relevant for the quantification of antitrust harm. Most important of these is Article 17.

2.2.1 The Presumption of Harm

Article 17(2) of the Directive introduces a rebuttable presumption of harm in 'cartel'[16] cases. The presumption of harm resulting from cartels did not appear in the Green Paper on damages actions, which only discussed in general terms whether the claimant's burden of proof could be somehow alleviated for all damages claims based on infringement decisions by competition authorities in the Member States, or where information asymmetries between the claimant and the defendant exist.[17] It did not appear in the White Paper on damages actions either, which only noted that in cases of cartels and other restrictions of competition by object, negative effects

[12] White Paper on damages actions (n 10) 5.

[13] ibid. See also White Paper Staff Working Paper (n 9) paras 199–200.

[14] White Paper Staff Working Paper (n 9) para 200.

[15] Proposal for a Directive of the European Parliament and of the Council on certain rules governing actions for damages under national law for infringements of the competition law provisions of the Member States and of the European Union, COM(2013) 404 final (Strasbourg, 11 June 2013) (Draft Directive on competition damages actions), Explanatory Memorandum, s 4.5. The choice of legislating through a Directive was not met with universal approval: A-M Van Den Bossche, 'Private Enforcement, Procedural Autonomy and Article 19(1) TEU: Two's Company, Three's a Crowd' (2014) 33(1) *Yearbook of European Law* 41, 74–78.

[16] A cartel is defined in Art 2(14) of the Directive as 'an agreement or concerted practice between two or more competitors aimed at coordinating their competitive behaviour on the market or influencing the relevant parameters of competition through practices such as, but not limited to, the fixing or coordination of purchase or selling prices or other trading conditions, including in relation to intellectual property rights, the allocation of production or sales quotas, the sharing of markets and customers, including bid-rigging, restrictions of imports or exports or anti-competitive actions against other competitors'.

[17] Green Paper on damages actions (n 6) Questions 8 and 9.

can be presumed.[18] Thus, it seems that the presumption of harm and the difficulties faced by claimants in the quantification of harm were not seen as interlinked at that stage.

They appear to have been linked sometime between the White Paper consultation and the formulation of the Draft Directive.[19] At the outset, the linking of the presumption of harm and its quantification may appear somewhat puzzling. After all, the two issues are clearly distinct, and creating the presumption that harm results from cartels does not in any way assist the claimant in its quantification. The Preamble of the Directive on competition damages actions suggests that the inclusion of a presumption of harm as a result of cartel infringements of competition law is intended to remedy the information asymmetry between claimants and defendants which results from the secret nature of cartels. According to the Preamble, the exclusion of such a presumption for other infringements of competition law is also explained by the secret nature of cartels.[20] The presumption relates in particular to an increase in prices for the cartelised goods or services, or alternatively the prevention of a lowering of prices that would have occurred but for the cartel.[21] Yet, given that—as the Preamble also acknowledges—the presumption does not cover the concrete amount of the harm, it is unclear how the information asymmetry 'and some of the difficulties associated with quantifying harm'[22] are ameliorated by a presumption as to the existence of harm, or how the presumption makes it easier for claimants to obtain evidence necessary to prove the quantum of harm.

The inclusion of a presumption of harm for cartel cases was heavily influenced by the findings of a study commissioned by the Commission[23] that showed that approximately nine out of 10 cartels led to overcharges.[24] Although some authors have criticised the study, its findings, and the Commission's reliance on it,[25] in our opinion there is nothing new here, as the practice since the first years of EU competition law enforcement has been to view cartels as inherently harmful for competition. In particular, there is a long history of cartels being treated as 'by object' restrictions of competition,

[18] White Paper Staff Working Paper (n 9) para 88.

[19] Draft Directive on competition damages actions (n 15) Explanatory Memorandum, s 4.5.

[20] Rec 47 of the Directive on competition damages actions (n 1).

[21] ibid.

[22] ibid.

[23] Draft Directive on competition damages actions (n 15) Explanatory Memorandum, s 2.2.

[24] Oxera and a multi-jurisdictional team of lawyers led by A Komninos, 'Quantifying Antitrust Damages—Towards Non-Binding Guidance for Courts, available at ec.europa.eu.ezproxy.its.uu.se/competition/antitrust/actionsdamages/quantification_study.pdf (last accessed 1 January 2015) 91.

[25] CF Weidt, 'The Directive on Actions for Antitrust Damages after Passing the European Parliament' (2014) 35(9) *European Competition Law Review* 438, 442, arguing that the Oxera study results are questionable due to the study's heavy reliance on JM Connor, 'Price-Fixing Overcharges: Revised 3rd Edition' (24 February 2014), available at ssrn.com/abstract=2400780 (last accessed 31 December 2014).

meaning that no effects have to be shown to prove an infringement of Article 101(1) TFEU. Today, this is generally accepted across the board and also finds textual support in EU primary law,[26] secondary law such as Block Exemption Regulations, and several other documents such as Notices and Guidelines.[27] This is not an arbitrary choice on the part of the competition law enforcers as economic theory and prior experience have demonstrated that most cartels do indeed cause harm by increasing prices and limiting output.[28] The upshot is that the presumption of harm is not really controversial and should be welcomed for the enhancement it brings about to the position of claimants.

The downside is that being uncontentious also means that the presumption of harm does not really add much in practice for damages claimants.[29] Its value lies in that it places on the defendant the burden of showing that the cartel did *not* cause harm. But supposing that the cartel member does not manage to rebut the presumption (as will most probably be the case in the majority of cases), or even that the defendant concedes that there was harm, the benefit for the claimant will simply be that the harm is not equal to zero. This does not strike us as particularly helpful, especially since the

[26] Art 101(1) TFEU applies to restrictions by 'object', of which cartels are a clear example.

[27] There is significant overlap of 'object restrictions' under Art 101(1) TFEU and 'cartels' according to the definition in Art 2(14) of the Directive (see n 16). Horizontal agreements whereby prices are fixed, output is limited, and markets and customers are shared, are included in the object box: Commission Notice on agreements of minor importance which do not appreciably restrict competition under Article 101(1) of the Treaty on the Functioning of the European Union (De Minimis Notice) [2014] OJ C291/01, para 13; Commission Guidelines on the applicability of Article 101 of the Treaty on the Functioning of the European Union to horizontal co-operation agreements [2011] OJ C11/1 (2011 Horizontal Co-Operation Guidelines), paras 128, 160, 205, 234, and 274. Other conduct that results in price-fixing, output limitation, or market or customer sharing is also to be classified as restriction by 'object'. Such conduct includes the exchange of information that reduces uncertainty about future behaviour (2011 Horizontal Co-Operation Guidelines, paras 73–74; Case C-8/08 *T-Mobile Netherlands BV, KPN Mobile NV, Orange Nederland NV and Vodafone Libertel NV v Raad van bestuur van de Nederlandse Mededingingsautoriteit* [2009] ECR I-4529, para 43; Case T-588/08 *Dole Food Company, Inc. and Dole Germany OHG v European Commission* EU:T:2013:130, paras 51–82); research and development agreements and joint purchasing agreements that serve merely as disguised cartels (2011 Horizontal Co-Operation Guidelines, paras 128 and 205); and the use of standardisation agreements and the offering of standard terms with the aim of excluding competitors (2011 Horizontal Co-Operation Guidelines, paras 173–75).

[28] P Van Cleynenbreugel, 'Article 101 TFEU and the EU Courts: Adapting Legal Form to the Realities of Modernization?' (2014) 51 (5) *Common Market Law Review* 1381, 1417; Case C-67/13 P *Groupement des cartes bancaires (CB) v European Commission* EU:C:2014:2204, paras 49–51; Case C-8/08 *T-Mobile*, ibid, para 29; Case C-209/07 *The Competition Authority v Beef Industry Development Society Ltd and Barry Brothers (Carrigmore) Meats Ltd* [2008] ECR I-8637, para 17; and Case C-226/11 *Expedia Inc v Autorité de la concurrence and Others* EU:C:2012:795, para 36. See also Commission Guidelines on the application of Article 81(3) of the Treaty [2004] OJ C101/97, para 20.

[29] E Clark and R Sander, 'Navigating the Quantum Minefield in Cartel Damages Cases' (advance access article published 23 December 2014) (2014) *Journal of European Competition Law & Practice* 1, 3 are of the same opinion.

Commission dropped its initial suggestion of allowing quantification based on average presumptive cartel overcharges.[30] At the end of the day, the claimant will still need to show the magnitude of the harm she has suffered.

This is when the connection between the presumption of harm and its quantification becomes apparent, revealing the logic that inspired its lumping together with the other two paragraphs of Article 17 of the Directive, dealing with the empowerment of national courts to estimate the harm when it is not possible for the claimant to do so (Article 17(1)), and with the possibility for national competition authorities to assist in the quantification (Article 17(3)). We turn our attention to these two below.

2.2.2 *The Empowerment of National Courts to Estimate Harm*

Article 17(1) of the Directive obliges Member States to ensure that neither the burden nor the standard of proof required for the quantification of harm renders the exercise of the right to damages 'practically impossible or excessively difficult'. Moreover, for cases where it is established that a claimant has suffered harm as a result of an infringement of competition law but it is 'practically impossible or excessively difficult' to quantify that harm with precision on the basis of the evidence available, Member States are obliged by Article 17(1) to ensure that their courts have the power to estimate the amount of competitive harm caused by the infringement.

In this author's opinion, the principle of effectiveness, which follows from the case law of the CJEU[31] and is now also enshrined in Article 4 of the Directive, would already necessitate the estimation of an approximate harm when its exact quantification is impossible. The added value of Article 17(1) of the Directive is that it clarifies the point that no action for damages is unsuccessful simply because the claimant cannot estimate the harm caused to her with precision, and elaborates on the meaning of the principle of effectiveness.

Of course, the important legal question arising out of Article 17(1) of the Directive is when a national court can be satisfied that it is 'practically impossible or excessively difficult' for the claimant to calculate the precise harm. A liberal reading of this requirement would suggest that it is always satisfied since the counterfactual calculation of damages is—by its nature—an unverifiable approximation of what would have happened but for the infringement.

[30] This practice is followed in Hungary. Section 8/8 of the Hungarian Competition Act adopts a presumptive overcharge for infringements of competition law, set at 10%. For a discussion of the appropriateness of the overcharge presumption, see R Noble and S Pilsbury, 'Is 10 Per Cent the Answer? The Role of Legal Presumptions in Private Competition Litigation' (2008) 1(3) *Global Competition Litigation Review* 124.

[31] Case C-453/99 *Courage Ltd v Crehan* [2001] ECR I-6297, para 29; *Manfredi* (n 11) para 62.

Furthermore, questions arise as to what the empowerment of national courts to estimate the harm entails and what requirements it places on Member States and their competent courts in practice. Is it enough for Member States to empower their courts legally where this is not already the case under national law? How about the actual capacity to make the estimates? Does Article 17(1) of the Directive require courts to have sitting judges that are trained economists? Does it suffice if the Member State ensures that its judges dealing with competition law cases receive some training in economics? Take one of the Member States as an illustrative example. In Sweden, *Konkurrenslagen* (the Swedish Competition Act), requires that *Stockholms tingsrätt*, which is the competent court in competition law matters, be comprised of two judges with legal expertise and two judges who are economic experts in cases in which one of the parties is *Konkurrensverket* (the Swedish Competition Authority). In cases between private parties, the court is instead comprised of either one or three judges, all of whom are lawyers.[32] Could the empowerment of national courts pursuant to Article 17(1) of the Directive now be interpreted as meaning that an economist ought to serve in *all* competition law cases?

2.2.3 *Assistance by National Competition Authorities in the Quantification of Damages*

Arguably, the Directive itself, in Article 17(3), sanctions one manifestation of the national courts' empowerment to estimate the damages. The Article calls upon Member States to ensure that, in proceedings relating to an action for damages, a national competition authority may—if this is requested by the national court seized on the matter—assist that court with respect to the determination of the quantum of damages. The assistance only has to be provided by the national competition authority in those cases where it considers it to be 'appropriate'.

The assistance of national competition authorities in the quantification of harm will certainly enhance the interplay between public and private enforcement; that is a positive development. However, it may also increase the complexity of cases already at the public enforcement stage, since a competition authority that is anticipating the possibility of being called upon by the national courts to provide assistance with the quantification of harm may find it convenient to quantify the effects of the anti-competitive behaviour already while striving to prove the infringement, although it may not strictly need to do so either because the conduct it is investigating is an agreement, concerted practice, or decision of an association of undertakings

[32] See c 8 s 8 in conjunction with c 7 s 2 of *Konkurrenslagen* (2008: 579).

that by object restricts Article 101(1) TFEU,[33] or unilateral conduct that per se breaches Article 102 TFEU in the absence of objective justifications.[34] As the controversy surrounding the Commission Decision[35] and the judgment of the General Court[36] in *Intel* shows,[37] increasing the complexity of a case by engaging in econometric analysis (*in casu* an as-efficient-competitor-test spanning 151 pages of the Decision)[38] when this is not necessarily required, puts an unnecessary strain on the competition authority, and needlessly increases litigation and litigation costs.[39] This increases legal uncertainty, hardly a desirable side effect of the Directive.

Additionally, it is far from clear in what circumstances a national competition authority may deem it to be 'appropriate' to assist the national court in the quantification of damages. Most probably, national competition authorities will have to flesh out the details and predetermine the conditions, always in line with the requirements of effectiveness and equivalence.[40] One can envisage litigation being spurred by disgruntled claimants who were denied assistance in the quantification of harm by their national competition authorities, and vice versa by defendants when the national competition authority does decide to lend a hand. Again, legal certainty may be reduced as a result.

[33] Case 246/86 *SC Belasco and others v Commission of the European Communities* [1989] ECR 2117, paras 15–16, holding that economic effects, such as actual raising of the prices are irrelevant in object cases. For an overview of some of the cases that confirm this, see D Bailey, 'Restrictions of Competition by Object under Article 101 TFEU' (2012) 49(2) *Common Market Law Review* 559, 587.

[34] It is beyond the scope of this chapter to discuss whether per se abuses exist, a matter of great debate and controversy among competition law scholars. For unilateral conduct whose anti-competitive effects are inferred, see Communication from the Commission Guidance on the Commission's enforcement priorities in applying Article 82 of the EC Treaty to abusive exclusionary conduct by dominant undertakings [2009] OJ C45/7, para 22. The CJEU has never stated that there are per se abuses; instead the courts stress that objective justifications are always available: Case T-286/09 *Intel Corp v European Commission* EU:T:2014:547, para 94.

[35] Commission Decision D(2009) 3726final (13 May 2009), Intel [2009] COMP/C-3/37.990.

[36] *Intel* (n 34). As expected, the case has been appealed to the Court of Justice as Case C-413/14 P *Intel Corporation v Commission* (appeal pending).

[37] See R Whish, 'Intel v Commission: Keep Calm and Carry on!' (2014) 6 (1) *Journal of European Competition Law & Practice* 1; WPJ Wils, 'The Judgment of the EU General Court in Intel and the So-Called "More Economic Approach" to Abuse of Dominance' (2014) 37 (4) *World Competition* 405; and JS Venit, 'Case T-286/09 Intel v Commission—The Judgment of the General Court: All Steps Backward and No Steps Forward' (2014) 10(2) *European Competition Journal* 203.

[38] Commission Decision, Intel (n 35) 302–453.

[39] *cf* B Veronese, 'European Public and Private Antitrust Enforcement: It Takes Two to Tango' (2014) 5(8) *Journal of European Competition Law & Practice* 563, 565–66.

[40] These are now also found in Art 4 of the Directive. See also the case law cited above in n 31.

2.3 Other Relevant Provisions in the Directive

Beyond Article 17, a few other provisions in the Directive also indirectly regulate the quantification of harm, especially the apportionment thereof to claimants at different levels of the supply chain.

Article 3(3) of the Directive stipulates that 'full compensation' under the Directive should not lead to overcompensation, for example through punitive, or multiple damages. A specific application of this general principle for the passing-on of overcharges is Article 12 of the Directive. Article 12(1) requires, inter alia, that compensation of harm exceeding that caused by the infringement of competition law to the claimant be avoided. Moreover, in order to avoid overcompensation, Article 12(2) places a duty upon Member States to lay down appropriate procedural rules to ensure that compensation for actual loss at any level of the supply chain does not exceed the overcharge harm suffered at that level. Accordingly, Member States are instructed by Article 12(5) to ensure that their national courts have the power to estimate the share of the overcharge that was passed on down the supply chain. Additionally, passing-on is presumed.[41]

Obviously, quantification under Article 17 of the Directive has to be seen in this light. Although Article 3(3) seems to allow for national law that imposes punitive or multiple damages, Article 12(1) is stricter since it stipulates that compensation over and above the harm caused by the infringement should be avoided. Accordingly, the national court(s) imposing damages on defendants for a multiplicity of claims at different levels of the supply chain will need to ensure that the damages do not collectively exceed the actual harm caused by the infringement. A task that is by no means an easy one, especially considering that this will require national courts to be aware of passing-on rates, and cases pending or having been decided in their legal system as well as in other Member States.

Finally, another relevant provision of the Directive is Article 16, which calls upon the Commission to issue guidelines for national courts on the estimation of the share of the overcharge that was passed on to indirect purchasers. This Article is slightly puzzling given that the Practical Guide on quantifying harm already contains guidance on this exact point.[42] Most probably, by reason of this provision, the Commission will issue more

[41] Art 14(2) of the Directive (n 1). The claimant only needs to show that: (a) the defendant has committed an infringement of competition law; (b) the infringement of competition law has resulted in an overcharge for the direct purchaser of the defendant; and (c) the indirect purchaser has purchased the goods or services that were the object of the infringement of competition law, or has purchased goods or services derived from or containing them. The presumption can be rebutted.

[42] Practical Guide on quantifying harm (n 5) paras 161–71. This Art did not appear in the Commission's Draft Directive. It was inserted by the European Parliament.

comprehensive and specific guidance on the passing-on rate than what is already contained in the Practical Guide.

In any case, the Practical Guide can be expected to receive more attention in the aftermath of the adoption of the Directive. For this reason, in the section that follows, we look more closely at the Practical Guide, the methods it suggests for quantifying harm, their application, benefits and shortcomings.

3. THE PRACTICAL GUIDE ON QUANTIFYING HARM

The Practical Guide on quantifying harm and the related Communication from the Commission on quantifying harm in actions for damages based on breaches of Article 101 or 102 of the TFEU (the Communication on quantifying harm in antitrust damages actions),[43] were issued by the Commission simultaneously with the Draft Directive on competition damages actions. Surprisingly, given the strong association of the Practical Guide and the Directive, the former is not mentioned in the latter, not even in its Preamble.

The aim of the Practical Guide is to offer assistance to national courts and parties, to provide insights, to set out information on the methods and techniques available to quantify harm typically caused by anti-competitive practices, and to facilitate the consensual resolution of disputes.[44]

To achieve its aim, the Practical Guide explains the features, strengths and weaknesses of various methods and techniques available to quantify harm and gives practical examples on how to quantify the overcharge and the harm caused by the volume effect of cartels and exclusionary practices, while recognising that methods and techniques may evolve over time and economic insights on harm can change.[45] Thus, the Practical Guide does not purport to be comprehensive or definite.[46] On the contrary, the Commission stresses that the Practical Guide is purely informative, does not bind national courts or parties, does not alter the legal rules of the Member States, does not affect rights and obligations, and does not raise or lower the standard or burden of proof or the level of detail of the factual submissions required from parties.[47]

The Practical Guide gives an overview of three types of methods for quantifying competitive harm: (i) comparator-based methods; (ii) simulation

[43] Communication from the Commission on quantifying harm in actions for damages based on breaches of Article 101 or 102 of the Treaty on the Functioning of the European Union [2013] C167/19.

[44] Practical Guide on quantifying harm (n 5) para 6.

[45] ibid, para 10.

[46] ibid; Communication on quantifying harm in antitrust damages actions (n 43) para 16.

[47] Communication on quantifying harm in antitrust damages actions (n 43) para 12; Practical Guide on quantifying harm (n 5) paras 7 and 9.

methods; and (iii) cost-based and finance-based methods. In what follows we present these different methods, with most emphasis on the comparator-based method, which is the most common.

3.1 Comparator-Based Methods

A comparator-based method of quantifying competitive harm may be based on a comparison across time, across geographical markets, or across different products. The comparison may also be of a difference in the different time periods, geographical markets, or product markets.

3.1.1 The Various Comparator-Based Methods

In a time-based comparison, data from different points of reference are taken and subsequently compared with the same data from the cartel period. The points of reference may be the unaffected pre-infringement period, the unaffected post-infringement period, or both unaffected periods.[48] As the Practical Guide acknowledges, 'it is only possible to identify a *sufficiently similar time period* that allows a likely non-infringement scenario to be reasonably approximated';[49] no period of reference will be exactly the same as the ideal counterfactual. Moreover, there may be uncertainty as to when an infringement begins and ends, since the infringement may be phased in gradually and the non-infringement equilibrium may take some time to be reached post-infringement.[50] This will be especially problematic where other structural problems exist in the market: in oligopolies, knowledge gained during the infringement period may lead to tacit coordination post-infringement.[51] It may also be the case because of the existence of long-term contracts.[52] Despite these concerns, a comparison across different time periods is in any case good for obtaining a safe estimate of the minimum harm suffered.[53]

In a geographical market-based comparison, data from different geographical markets are retrieved and subsequently compared with the same data from the geographical market where the infringement took place. The more a geographical market is similar to the infringement geographical market, the more suitable it will be for comparison. Thus, for the comparison

[48] Practical Guide on quantifying harm (n 5) para 39.
[49] ibid, para 43 (emphasis added).
[50] ibid, paras 43–44.
[51] ibid, para 45.
[52] Organisation for Economic Co-Operation and Development, Directorate for Financial and Enterprise Affairs, Competition Committee, 'Quantification of Harm to Competition by National Courts and Competition Agencies', DAF/COMP(2011)25 (27 November 2012) 35–36.
[53] Practical Guide on quantifying harm (n 5) para 46.

to be useful, the products traded in the two geographical markets should be the same, or sufficiently similar, and competitive characteristics should generally be similar, except for the infringement.[54] As the Practical Guide points out, the comparison is most suitable for markets that are national or smaller (local or regional).[55] The likelihood of similarity increases in neighbouring local or regional markets in the same Member State, but at the same time there may be uncertainties about the geographical scope of the infringement since neighbouring markets may be affected by an infringement in one of them. For instance, due to less competitive pressure from the affected market, prices may rise in the neighbouring market, rendering it unsuitable for comparison. Despite these concerns, a comparison across different geographical markets is good for obtaining lower-bound estimates of the competitive harm.[56]

In a product market-based comparison, data for different products are retrieved and subsequently compared with the same data for the product that was subject to the infringement. What makes the comparison meaningful is the identification of products that share similar market characteristics. Mutatis mutandis, the comparison based on data from another product market is vulnerable to the same problems as a geographical market comparison. In addition, the nature of the products, the way they are traded, and characteristics of the market such as concentration levels, buying power, and cost structures must be kept in mind.[57]

Finally, the 'difference in differences' method combines comparisons over time and across markets. For instance, it may trace the difference of price over time in the infringement market compared with difference of price over time in another geographical market. The benefit of utilising this method is that it excludes all the factors that are the same in both markets and thus isolates the influence of the antitrust breach. However, its negative feature is that it rests on the assumption that changes in the market affect both markets in the same way.[58]

3.1.2 The Application of the Comparator-Based Methods

The Practical Guide divides the methods of conducting the comparison into simple methods and sophisticated methods involving regression.

The simpler methods consist predominately of individual data observations: the comparison with this method is direct, and can be executed even without adjustments to the data. Naturally, the amount of data will

[54] ibid, para 50.
[55] ibid, para 51.
[56] ibid, para 53.
[57] ibid, para 55.
[58] ibid, para 58. Eg, an assumption might be that a drop in the price of an input will have had the same impact on both markets.

vary depending on availability. The more data observations the better but, according to the Practical Guide, even single data observations may suffice if they can be accepted as representative of the period.[59] The data can be used as is or as averages. The Practical Guide states that efforts should be made to compare like with like. Hence, data from the same months, or from the same type of customer will yield more reliable results.[60]

Linear interpolation and extrapolation are appropriate where comparison over time has produced a series of data (eg, prices over time). Comparator values for the infringement period are used. The difference between the interpolated/extrapolated (estimated) price and the actual price is the overcharge. The estimated price may be adjusted for known differentiating factors other than the infringement, such as cyclical patterns, and seasonal variations. It can also be adjusted in a more sophisticated way through regression analysis.[61]

Regression analysis is a statistical technique that helps investigate patterns in the relationship between economic variables and to measure to what extent a certain variable of interest is influenced by the infringement or other variables that are not affected by the infringement. Hence, it is a way of accounting for alternative causes for the differences observed through a comparison of data.[62] There are two approaches to regression: the forecasting approach and the dummy-variable approach. The forecasting approach involves regression pre and post-infringement to establish the statistical relationship between variables in the form of an equation. This is subsequently used to forecast the values during the infringement period and find the difference. In the dummy-variable approach, data from the infringement period is used too, the three steps of the forecasting approach are combined, and the regression equation indicates how much the variable of interest changed during the infringement period after accounting for the effect of other variables.[63]

According to the Practical Guide, in order to properly carry out regression analysis a few requirements have to be met. First, sound knowledge of various statistical techniques is necessary. Second, regression analysis requires a good understanding of the industry concerned. Third, it relies on a sufficient number of data observations, with disaggregated data being preferable.[64] The Commission also mentions some best practices to be followed where possible, such as explicitly acknowledging imperfections, giving intervals instead of point estimates, giving confidence intervals (95 per cent likelihood that a specific interval contains the true value regarded as a high

[59] ibid, para 64.
[60] ibid, para 66.
[61] ibid, para 67.
[62] ibid, para 69.
[63] ibid, para 71.
[64] ibid, paras 81–82.

degree of certainty), and calculating 'statistical significance' by using a null hypothesis.[65]

3.2 Simulation Models

Simulation draws on economic models of market behaviour; that is to say how markets function and how firms compete with each other. The models range from perfect competition models to monopoly models with intermediate models such as the Bertrand model (oligopoly model with few firms, high barriers to entry and competition on price), the Cournot model (oligopoly model with few firms, high barriers to entry and competition on output), and the dynamic oligopoly model (takes into account game theory and repeated interaction).[66]

Such models can be built to estimate the prices or other variables that are likely to have prevailed in the counterfactual market. In order to succeed, they must replicate the most significant factors influencing supply and the cost structure of firms and demand conditions.[67] Accordingly, simulations based on these models can be demanding in terms of data and rely heavily on assumptions.[68] That said, these shortcomings are not *ipso facto* a reason to dismiss the estimates arrived at from simulation models since they can still provide useful insights.[69]

3.3 Cost-Based and Finance-Based Methods

These methods consist of determining the production cost per unit of product and estimating a reasonable profit margin to be added to the per unit production costs. Thus, an expected competitive price for the product is arrived at, allowing an analysis of the financial situation (in particular the profitability) of the claimant undertaking before and after the infringement. This will enable an estimation of the harm suffered because of the antitrust infringement.

4. SOME INTERESTING QUESTIONS LYING AHEAD

This section offers some thoughts on the Practical Guide on quantification of harm's complex relationship and compatibility with the Directive on

[65] ibid, paras 84–88.
[66] ibid, paras 97–98.
[67] ibid, para 100. See also OECD, 'Quantification of Harm' (n 52) 37–39.
[68] As recognised by the Practical Guide on quantifying harm (n 5) para 102.
[69] ibid, para 105.

competition damages actions. It highlights the issues that will need to be clarified in the future, and the questions that are likely to give rise to litigation in national courts and that might eventually reach the ECJ through Article 267 TFEU.

4.1 Inherent Limitations of Counterfactuals versus No Overcompensation

It is important to appreciate that it is impossible to know how a market would have evolved but for the infringement of Articles 101 or 102 TFEU and that 'prices, sales volumes, and profit margins depend on a range of factors and complex, often strategic interactions between market participants that are not easily estimated'.[70] This is also recognised by the Court (albeit in a different context), which has held that in the calculation and the evaluation of damages, given the hypothetical nature of counterfactuals, courts have 'a broad discretion as to both the figures and the statistical data to be chosen and also, above all, as to the way in which they are to be used'.[71]

The inherent limitations of counterfactuals raise some interesting questions. The first one, as touched upon above,[72] has to do with the requirement in Article 17(1) of the Directive placed on Member States to empower their national courts to estimate the harm '*if it is established* that a claimant suffered harm but it is practically impossible or excessively difficult precisely to quantify the harm suffered' based on the available evidence.[73] If, as the Practical Guide on quantification of harm recognises, the quantification of harm is subject to considerable limits as to the degree of certainty and precision that can be expected and no single 'true' value of the harm suffered can be obtained, and if the best that even a court could arrive at are estimates relying on assumptions and approximations,[74] does that not mean that—in the large majority of cases and bar the odd situation where evidence on the record identifies unequivocally the overcharge that the cartel members decided to impose—the requirement ought to be automatically satisfied? Put simply, it is unclear what there is to establish when the claimant can simply point to the nature of counterfactuals, with support lent from the Practical Guide.

The second interesting question that arises from the inherent uncertainty of counterfactuals is how that might shape the requirements for avoiding

[70] ibid, para 16.
[71] Joined Cases C-104/89 and C-37/90 *JM Mulder and others and Otto Heinemann v Council of the European Communities and Commission of the European Communities* [2000] ECR I-203, para 79.
[72] See s 2.2.2 above.
[73] Emphasis added.
[74] Practical Guide on quantifying harm (n 5) paras 17 and 123.

overcompensation enshrined in Articles 3(3) and 12 of the Directive. In particular, what procedural rules could a Member State lay down in order to satisfy the requirement found in Article 12(2) that 'compensation for actual loss at any level of the supply chain does not exceed the overcharge harm suffered at that level' when it is practically impossible to estimate a 'true' value of the overcharge? Given the broad discretion courts will enjoy in the calculation of harm, this requirement may too be rendered empty of substance.

4.2 Different Approaches to Passing-On

A second issue that will require clarification in the future is that despite the close connection between the Practical Guide and the Directive, there appear to be inconsistencies in their respective approach to passing-on.[75]

On the one hand, the Directive seems to treat price increases being passed on down the supply chain as normal commercial practice.[76] On the other hand, the Practical Guide adopts a much more nuanced and careful approach to passing-on, focusing on the various criteria and factors that determine not only the degree of passing-on but also its existence.[77] It also points to at least one scenario under which it is likely that the direct customer will normally not be able to pass on the increase in cost due to the cartel.[78] Of course, the Directive's approach may be justified simply as a choice to side with the indirect purchaser and facilitate her claim against the competition law infringer. That said, it is unclear why the law should show preference for the indirect purchaser whose level of compensation might limit the availability of redress for direct purchasers, who may also be victims of the infringement.

4.3 The Mutual Recognition of Different Methods of Quantification

A third issue that may arise has to do with the choice of different methods for the quantification of harm. It is easy to appreciate that given the different assumptions and models used in each of the methods, the choice of

[75] M Strand, 'Indirect Purchasers, Passing-On and the New Directive on Competition Law Damages' (2014) 10 (2) *European Competition Journal* 361, 384 also suggests that Art 14(2) of the Directive shows a preference for the econometric approach to quantification of harm rather than the comparator-based methods. This would run counter to the Directive's wish to respect national procedural autonomy in the matter of choice of quantification method.

[76] Art 14(1) of the Directive on competition damages actions (n 1).

[77] Practical Guide on quantifying harm (n 5) paras 168 and 171.

[78] ibid, para 169.

method for the calculation of antitrust damages will in all certainty have an impact on the quantum of damages.[79]

The issue with the variety of methods and quanta may also be exacerbated by the requirement placed on national courts by Article 15 of the Directive to take due account of other actions for damages related to the same infringement brought by claimants from other levels in the supply chain, related judgments, and information in the public domain from the enforcement of competition rules by national competition authorities. This will mean that national courts will be called upon to mutually recognise the methods and estimates of damages of other courts within the EU, as well as the calculations of effects and harm by competition authorities. Where these methods and estimates differ a great deal, it will be hard for the national court to make necessary comparisons,[80] putting in question the wisdom of preserving national procedural autonomy in these matters.[81]

5. CONCLUSIONS

In this chapter we have discussed the presumption of harm in Article 17 of the Directive on competition damages actions and its relevance (along with other provisions) for the quantification of harm. We have briefly presented the Practical Guide on quantifying harm and its relationship and consistency with the Directive. The chapter poses a large number of questions, and offers few answers. Readers are asked to show understanding; a dearth of answers is to be expected given the scarcity of private enforcement in EU competition law and the infancy of the measures discussed here. In typical EU law fashion, questions will eventually reach the ECJ through Article 267 TFEU, and in time many of the issues identified in this chapter will be resolved.

By way of conclusion we offer a few prognoses.[82] First, we think it doubtful that the presumption of harm in cartels will make much practical difference in the case law. The positive impact will instead come from the national courts' power to estimate the harm, and the national competition

[79] G Notaro, 'Methods for Quantifying Antitrust Damages: the Pasta Cartel in Italy' (2013) 10(1) *Journal of Competition law & Economics* 87 demonstrates how different methods of quantifying damages stemming from the Italian pasta cartel case would affect the quantum of damages.

[80] Howard, 'Too Little, Too Late?' (n 3) 459.

[81] While recognising at the same time that preserving diversity in the application of EU competition law may be a value worth preserving: See in general C Townley, 'Coordinated Diversity: Revolutionary Suggestions for EU Competition Law (and for EU Law too)' (2014) 33(1) *Yearbook of European Law* 194.

[82] The Greek word 'prognosis' for these predictions best reveals their character: they come before knowledge (pro- 'before' + gignōskein 'know'). Readers, you have been warned!

authorities' possibility to assist therewith. It is expected that defendants with the right incentives and resources will try to test the limits of both these developments. Second, a further integration of public and private enforcement, and a drive towards more effects—even in cases that do not strictly require it—can be expected. After all, a competition authority that has not identified any effects because the conduct restricts competition by object (Article 101(1) TFEU) or is per se abusive (Article 102 TFEU) will have little to offer in terms of assistance to affected claimants. Third, issues that will need clarification include the avoidance of overcompensation and how that relates to inherent difficulties in calculating harm, and the preferred approach to passing-on. Finally, it will be interesting to see which quantification methods catch on and how competent courts will deal with a multiplicity of decisions made by national competition authorities and judgments by other national courts.

Appendix

I

(Legislative acts)

DIRECTIVES

DIRECTIVE 2014/104/EU OF THE EUROPEAN PARLIAMENT AND OF THE COUNCIL

of 26 November 2014

on certain rules governing actions for damages under national law for infringements of the competition law provisions of the Member States and of the European Union

(Text with EEA relevance)

THE EUROPEAN PARLIAMENT AND THE COUNCIL OF THE EUROPEAN UNION,

Having regard to the Treaty on the Functioning of the European Union, and in particular Articles 103 and 114 thereof,

Having regard to the proposal from the European Commission,

After transmission of the draft legislative act to the national parliaments,

Having regard to the opinion of the European Economic and Social Committee [1],

Acting in accordance with the ordinary legislative procedure [2],

Whereas:

(1) Articles 101 and 102 of the Treaty on the Functioning of the European Union (TFEU) are a matter of public policy and should be applied effectively throughout the Union in order to ensure that competition in the internal market is not distorted.

(2) The public enforcement of Articles 101 and 102 TFEU is carried out by the Commission using the powers provided by Council Regulation (EC) No 1/2003 [3]. Upon the entry into force of the Treaty of Lisbon on 1 December 2009, Articles 81 and 82 of the Treaty establishing the European Community became Articles 101 and 102 TFEU, and they remain identical in substance. Public enforcement is also carried out by national competition authorities, which may take the decisions listed in Article 5 of Regulation (EC) No 1/2003. In accordance with that Regulation, Member States should be able to designate administrative as well as judicial authorities to apply Articles 101 and 102 TFEU as public enforcers and to carry out the various functions conferred upon competition authorities by that Regulation.

(3) Articles 101 and 102 TFEU produce direct effects in relations between individuals and create, for the individuals concerned, rights and obligations which national courts must enforce. National courts thus have an equally essential part to play in applying the competition rules (private enforcement). When ruling on disputes between private individuals, they protect subjective rights under Union law, for example by awarding damages to the victims of infringements. The full effectiveness of Articles 101 and 102 TFEU, and in particular the practical effect of the prohibitions laid down therein, requires that anyone — be they an individual, including consumers

---

[1] OJ C 67, 6.3.2014, p. 83.

[2] Position of the European Parliament of 17 April 2014 (not yet published in the Official Journal) and decision of the Council of 10 November 2014.

[3] Council Regulation (EC) No 1/2003 of 16 December 2002 on the implementation of the rules of competition laid down in Articles 81 and 82 of the Treaty (OJ L 1, 4.1.2003, p. 1).

and undertakings, or a public authority — can claim compensation before national courts for the harm caused to them by an infringement of those provisions. The right to compensation in Union law applies equally to infringements of Articles 101 and 102 TFEU by public undertakings and by undertakings entrusted with special or exclusive rights by Member States within the meaning of Article 106 TFEU.

(4) The right in Union law to compensation for harm resulting from infringements of Union and national competition law requires each Member State to have procedural rules ensuring the effective exercise of that right. The need for effective procedural remedies also follows from the right to effective judicial protection as laid down in the second subparagraph of Article 19(1) of the Treaty on European Union (TEU) and in the first paragraph of Article 47 of the Charter of Fundamental Rights of the European Union. Member States should ensure effective legal protection in the fields covered by Union law.

(5) Actions for damages are only one element of an effective system of private enforcement of infringements of competition law and are complemented by alternative avenues of redress, such as consensual dispute resolution and public enforcement decisions that give parties an incentive to provide compensation.

(6) To ensure effective private enforcement actions under civil law and effective public enforcement by competition authorities, both tools are required to interact to ensure maximum effectiveness of the competition rules. It is necessary to regulate the coordination of those two forms of enforcement in a coherent manner, for instance in relation to the arrangements for access to documents held by competition authorities. Such coordination at Union level will also avoid the divergence of applicable rules, which could jeopardise the proper functioning of the internal market.

(7) In accordance with Article 26(2) TFEU, the internal market comprises an area without internal frontiers in which the free movement of goods, persons, services and capital is ensured. There are marked differences between the rules in the Member States governing actions for damages for infringements of Union or national competition law. Those differences lead to uncertainty concerning the conditions under which injured parties can exercise the right to compensation they derive from the TFEU and affect the substantive effectiveness of such right. As injured parties often choose their Member State of establishment as the forum in which to claim damages, the discrepancies between the national rules lead to an uneven playing field as regards actions for damages and may thus affect competition on the markets on which those injured parties, as well as the infringing undertakings, operate.

(8) Undertakings established and operating in various Member States are subject to differing procedural rules that significantly affect the extent to which they can be held liable for infringements of competition law. This uneven enforcement of the right to compensation in Union law may result not only in a competitive advantage for some undertakings which have infringed Article 101 or 102 TFEU but also in a disincentive to the exercise of the rights of establishment and provision of goods or services in those Member States where the right to compensation is enforced more effectively. As the differences in the liability regimes applicable in the Member States may negatively affect both competition and the proper functioning of the internal market, it is appropriate to base this Directive on the dual legal bases of Articles 103 and 114 TFEU.

(9) It is necessary, bearing in mind that large-scale infringements of competition law often have a cross-border element, to ensure a more level playing field for undertakings operating in the internal market and to improve the conditions for consumers to exercise the rights that they derive from the internal market. It is appropriate to increase legal certainty and to reduce the differences between the Member States as to the national rules governing actions for damages for infringements of both Union competition law and national competition law where that is applied in parallel with Union competition law. An approximation of those rules will help to prevent the increase of differences between the Member States' rules governing actions for damages in competition cases.

(10) Article 3(1) of Regulation (EC) No 1/2003 provides that '[w]here the competition authorities of the Member States or national courts apply national competition law to agreements, decisions by associations of undertakings or concerted practices within the meaning of Article [101(1) TFEU] which may affect trade between Member States within the meaning of that provision, they shall also apply Article [101 TFEU] to such agreements, decisions or concerted practices. Where the competition authorities of the Member States or national courts apply national competition law to any abuse prohibited by Article [102 TFEU], they shall also apply Article [102 TFEU].' In the interests of the proper functioning of the internal market and with a view to greater legal certainty and a more level playing field for undertakings and consumers, it is appropriate that the scope of this Directive extend to actions for damages based on the infringement of national competition law where it is applied pursuant to Article 3(1) of Regulation (EC) No 1/2003. Applying differing rules on civil liability in respect of infringements of Article 101 or 102 TFEU and in respect of infringements of rules of national competition law which must be applied in the same cases in parallel to Union competition law would otherwise adversely affect the position of

claimants in the same case and the scope of their claims, and would constitute an obstacle to the proper functioning of the internal market. This Directive should not affect actions for damages in respect of infringements of national competition law which do not affect trade between Member States within the meaning of Article 101 or 102 TFEU.

(11) In the absence of Union law, actions for damages are governed by the national rules and procedures of the Member States. According to the case-law of the Court of Justice of the European Union (Court of Justice), any person can claim compensation for harm suffered where there is a causal relationship between that harm and an infringement of competition law. All national rules governing the exercise of the right to compensation for harm resulting from an infringement of Article 101 or 102 TFEU, including those concerning aspects not dealt with in this Directive such as the notion of causal relationship between the infringement and the harm, must observe the principles of effectiveness and equivalence. This means that they should not be formulated or applied in a way that makes it excessively difficult or practically impossible to exercise the right to compensation guaranteed by the TFEU or less favourably than those applicable to similar domestic actions. Where Member States provide other conditions for compensation under national law, such as imputability, adequacy or culpability, they should be able to maintain such conditions in so far as they comply with the case-law of the Court of Justice, the principles of effectiveness and equivalence, and this Directive.

(12) This Directive reaffirms the *acquis communautaire* on the right to compensation for harm caused by infringements of Union competition law, particularly regarding standing and the definition of damage, as stated in the case-law of the Court of Justice, and does not pre-empt any further development thereof. Anyone who has suffered harm caused by such an infringement can claim compensation for actual loss (*damnum emergens*), for gain of which that person has been deprived (loss of profit or *lucrum cessans*), plus interest, irrespective of whether those categories are established separately or in combination in national law. The payment of interest is an essential component of compensation to make good the damage sustained by taking into account the effluxion of time and should be due from the time when the harm occurred until the time when compensation is paid, without prejudice to the qualification of such interest as compensatory or default interest under national law and to whether effluxion of time is taken into account as a separate category (interest) or as a constituent part of actual loss or loss of profit. It is incumbent on the Member States to lay down the rules to be applied for that purpose.

(13) The right to compensation is recognised for any natural or legal person — consumers, undertakings and public authorities alike — irrespective of the existence of a direct contractual relationship with the infringing undertaking, and regardless of whether or not there has been a prior finding of an infringement by a competition authority. This Directive should not require Member States to introduce collective redress mechanisms for the enforcement of Articles 101 and 102 TFEU. Without prejudice to compensation for loss of opportunity, full compensation under this Directive should not lead to overcompensation, whether by means of punitive, multiple or other damages.

(14) Actions for damages for infringements of Union or national competition law typically require a complex factual and economic analysis. The evidence necessary to prove a claim for damages is often held exclusively by the opposing party or by third parties, and is not sufficiently known by, or accessible to, the claimant. In such circumstances, strict legal requirements for claimants to assert in detail all the facts of their case at the beginning of an action and to proffer precisely specified items of supporting evidence can unduly impede the effective exercise of the right to compensation guaranteed by the TFEU.

(15) Evidence is an important element for bringing actions for damages for infringement of Union or national competition law. However, as competition law litigation is characterised by an information asymmetry, it is appropriate to ensure that claimants are afforded the right to obtain the disclosure of evidence relevant to their claim, without it being necessary for them to specify individual items of evidence. In order to ensure equality of arms, those means should also be available to defendants in actions for damages, so that they can request the disclosure of evidence by those claimants. National courts should also be able to order that evidence be disclosed by third parties, including public authorities. Where a national court wishes to order disclosure of evidence by the Commission, the principle in Article 4(3) TEU of sincere cooperation between the Union and the Member States and Article 15(1) of Regulation (EC) No 1/2003 as regards requests for information apply. Where national courts order public authorities to disclose evidence, the principles of legal and administrative cooperation under Union or national law apply.

(16) National courts should be able, under their strict control, especially as regards the necessity and proportionality of disclosure measures, to order the disclosure of specified items of evidence or categories of evidence upon request of a party. It follows from the requirement of proportionality that disclosure can be ordered only where a claimant has made a plausible assertion, on the basis of facts which are reasonably available to that claimant, that the claimant has suffered harm that was caused by the defendant. Where a request for disclosure aims to obtain a category of evidence, that category should be identified by reference to common features of its constitutive elements such as the nature, object or content of the documents the disclosure of which is requested, the time during which they were drawn up, or other criteria, provided that the evidence falling within the category is relevant within the meaning of this Directive. Such categories should be defined as precisely and narrowly as possible on the basis of reasonably available facts.

(17) Where a court in one Member State requests a competent court in another Member State to take evidence or requests that evidence be taken directly in another Member State, the provisions of Council Regulation (EC) No 1206/2001 (1) apply.

(18) While relevant evidence containing business secrets or otherwise confidential information should, in principle, be available in actions for damages, such confidential information needs to be protected appropriately. National courts should therefore have at their disposal a range of measures to protect such confidential information from being disclosed during the proceedings. Those measures could include the possibility of redacting sensitive passages in documents, conducting hearings in camera, restricting the persons allowed to see the evidence, and instructing experts to produce summaries of the information in an aggregated or otherwise non-confidential form. Measures protecting business secrets and other confidential information should, nevertheless, not impede the exercise of the right to compensation.

(19) This Directive affects neither the possibility under the laws of the Member States to appeal disclosure orders, nor the conditions for bringing such appeals.

(20) Regulation (EC) No 1049/2001 of the European Parliament and of the Council (2) governs public access to European Parliament, Council and Commission documents, and is designed to confer on the public as wide a right of access as possible to documents of those institutions. That right is nonetheless subject to certain limits based on reasons of public or private interest. It follows that the system of exceptions laid down in Article 4 of that Regulation is based on a balancing of the opposing interests in a given situation, namely, the interests which would be favoured by the disclosure of the documents in question and those which would be jeopardised by such disclosure. This Directive should be without prejudice to such rules and practices under Regulation (EC) No 1049/2001.

(21) The effectiveness and consistency of the application of Articles 101 and 102 TFEU by the Commission and the national competition authorities require a common approach across the Union on the disclosure of evidence that is included in the file of a competition authority. Disclosure of evidence should not unduly detract from the effectiveness of the enforcement of competition law by a competition authority. This Directive does not cover the disclosure of internal documents of, or correspondence between, competition authorities.

(22) In order to ensure the effective protection of the right to compensation, it is not necessary that every document relating to proceedings under Article 101 or 102 TFEU be disclosed to a claimant merely on the grounds of the claimant's intended action for damages since it is highly unlikely that the action for damages will need to be based on all the evidence in the file relating to those proceedings.

(23) The requirement of proportionality should be carefully assessed when disclosure risks unravelling the investigation strategy of a competition authority by revealing which documents are part of the file or risks having a negative effect on the way in which undertakings cooperate with the competition authorities. Particular attention should be paid to preventing 'fishing expeditions', i.e. non-specific or overly broad searches for information that is unlikely to be of relevance for the parties to the proceedings. Disclosure requests should therefore not be deemed to be proportionate where they refer to the generic disclosure of documents in the file of a competition authority relating to a certain case, or the generic disclosure of documents submitted by a party in the context of a particular case. Such wide disclosure requests would not be compatible with the requesting party's duty to specify the items of evidence or the categories of evidence as precisely and narrowly as possible.

---

(1) Council Regulation (EC) No 1206/2001 of 28 May 2001 on cooperation between the courts of the Member States in the taking of evidence in civil or commercial matters (OJ L 174, 27.6.2001, p. 1).

(2) Regulation (EC) No 1049/2001 of the European Parliament and of the Council of 30 May 2001 regarding public access to European Parliament, Council and Commission documents (OJ L 145, 31.5.2001, p. 43).

(24) This Directive does not affect the right of courts to consider, under Union or national law, the interests of the effective public enforcement of competition law when ordering the disclosure of any type of evidence with the exception of leniency statements and settlement submissions.

(25) An exemption should apply in respect of any disclosure that, if granted, would unduly interfere with an ongoing investigation by a competition authority concerning an infringement of Union or national competition law. Information that was prepared by a competition authority in the course of its proceedings for the enforcement of Union or national competition law and sent to the parties to those proceedings (such as a 'Statement of Objections') or prepared by a party thereto (such as replies to requests for information of the competition authority or witness statements) should therefore be disclosable in actions for damages only after the competition authority has closed its proceedings, for instance by adopting a decision under Article 5 or under Chapter III of Regulation (EC) No 1/2003, with the exception of decisions on interim measures.

(26) Leniency programmes and settlement procedures are important tools for the public enforcement of Union competition law as they contribute to the detection and efficient prosecution of, and the imposition of penalties for, the most serious infringements of competition law. Furthermore, as many decisions of competition authorities in cartel cases are based on a leniency application, and damages actions in cartel cases generally follow on from those decisions, leniency programmes are also important for the effectiveness of actions for damages in cartel cases. Undertakings might be deterred from cooperating with competition authorities under leniency programmes and settlement procedures if self-incriminating statements such as leniency statements and settlement submissions, which are produced for the sole purpose of cooperating with the competition authorities, were to be disclosed. Such disclosure would pose a risk of exposing cooperating undertakings or their managing staff to civil or criminal liability under conditions worse than those of co-infringers not cooperating with the competition authorities. To ensure undertakings' continued willingness to approach competition authorities voluntarily with leniency statements or settlement submissions, such documents should be exempted from the disclosure of evidence. That exemption should also apply to verbatim quotations from leniency statements or settlement submissions included in other documents. Those limitations on the disclosure of evidence should not prevent competition authorities from publishing their decisions in accordance with the applicable Union or national law. In order to ensure that that exemption does not unduly interfere with injured parties' rights to compensation, it should be limited to those voluntary and self-incriminating leniency statements and settlement submissions.

(27) The rules in this Directive on the disclosure of documents other than leniency statements and settlement submissions ensure that injured parties retain sufficient alternative means by which to obtain access to the relevant evidence that they need in order to prepare their actions for damages. National courts should themselves be able, upon request by a claimant, to access documents in respect of which the exemption is invoked in order to verify whether the contents thereof fall outside the definitions of leniency statements and settlement submissions laid down in this Directive. Any content falling outside those definitions should be disclosable under the relevant conditions.

(28) National courts should be able, at any time, to order, in the context of an action for damages, the disclosure of evidence that exists independently of the proceedings of a competition authority ('pre-existing information').

(29) The disclosure of evidence should be ordered from a competition authority only when that evidence cannot reasonably be obtained from another party or from a third party.

(30) Pursuant to Article 15(3) of Regulation (EC) No 1/2003, competition authorities, acting upon their own initiative, can submit written observations to national courts on issues relating to the application of Article 101 or 102 TFEU. In order to preserve the contribution made by public enforcement to the application of those Articles, competition authorities should likewise be able, acting upon their own initiative, to submit their observations to a national court for the purpose of assessing the proportionality of a disclosure of evidence included in the authorities' files, in light of the impact that such disclosure would have on the effectiveness of the public enforcement of competition law. Member States should be able to set up a system whereby a competition authority is informed of requests for disclosure of information when the person requesting disclosure or the person from whom disclosure is sought is involved in that competition authority's investigation into the alleged infringement, without prejudice to national law providing for *ex parte* proceedings.

(31) Any natural or legal person that obtains evidence through access to the file of a competition authority should be able to use that evidence for the purposes of an action for damages to which it is a party. Such use should also be allowed on the part of any natural or legal person that succeeded in its rights and obligations, including through the acquisition of its claim. Where the evidence was obtained by a legal person forming part of a corporate group constituting one undertaking for the application of Articles 101 and 102 TFEU, other legal persons belonging to the same undertaking should also be able to use that evidence.

(32) However, the use of evidence obtained through access to the file of a competition authority should not unduly detract from the effective enforcement of competition law by a competition authority. In order to ensure that the limitations on disclosure laid down in this Directive are not undermined, the use of evidence of the types referred to in recitals 24 and 25 which is obtained solely through access to the file of a competition authority should be limited under the same circumstances. The limitation should take the form of inadmissibility in actions for damages or the form of any other protection under applicable national rules capable of ensuring the full effect of the limits on the disclosure of those types of evidence. Moreover, evidence obtained from a competition authority should not become an object of trade. The possibility of using evidence that was obtained solely through access to the file of a competition authority should therefore be limited to the natural or legal person that was originally granted access and to its legal successors. That limitation to avoid trading of evidence does not, however, prevent a national court from ordering the disclosure of that evidence under the conditions provided for in this Directive.

(33) The fact that a claim for damages is initiated, or that an investigation by a competition authority is started, entails a risk that persons concerned may destroy or hide evidence that would be useful in substantiating an injured party's claim for damages. To prevent the destruction of relevant evidence and to ensure that court orders as to disclosure are complied with, national courts should be able to impose sufficiently deterrent penalties. In so far as parties to the proceedings are concerned, the risk of adverse inferences being drawn in the proceedings for damages can be a particularly effective penalty, and can help avoid delays. Penalties should also be available for non-compliance with obligations to protect confidential information and for the abusive use of information obtained through disclosure. Similarly, penalties should be available if information obtained through access to the file of a competition authority is used abusively in actions for damages.

(34) Ensuring the effective and consistent application of Articles 101 and 102 TFEU by the Commission and the national competition authorities necessitates a common approach across the Union on the effect of national competition authorities' final infringement decisions on subsequent actions for damages. Such decisions are adopted only after the Commission has been informed of the decision envisaged or, in the absence thereof, of any other document indicating the proposed course of action pursuant to Article 11(4) of Regulation (EC) No 1/2003, and if the Commission has not relieved the national competition authority of its competence by initiating proceedings pursuant to Article 11(6) of that Regulation. The Commission should ensure the consistent application of Union competition law by providing, bilaterally and within the framework of the European Competition Network, guidance to the national competition authorities. To enhance legal certainty, to avoid inconsistency in the application of Articles 101 and 102 TFEU, to increase the effectiveness and procedural efficiency of actions for damages and to foster the functioning of the internal market for undertakings and consumers, the finding of an infringement of Article 101 or 102 TFEU in a final decision by a national competition authority or a review court should not be relitigated in subsequent actions for damages. Therefore, such a finding should be deemed to be irrefutably established in actions for damages brought in the Member State of the national competition authority or review court relating to that infringement. The effect of the finding should, however, cover only the nature of the infringement and its material, personal, temporal and territorial scope as determined by the competition authority or review court in the exercise of its jurisdiction. Where a decision has found that provisions of national competition law are infringed in cases where Union and national competition law are applied in the same case and in parallel, that infringement should also be deemed to be irrefutably established.

(35) Where an action for damages is brought in a Member State other than the Member State of a national competition authority or a review court that found the infringement of Article 101 or 102 TFEU to which the action relates, it should be possible to present that finding in a final decision by the national competition authority or the review court to a national court as at least prima facie evidence of the fact that an infringement of competition law has occurred. The finding can be assessed as appropriate, along with any other evidence adduced by the parties. The effects of decisions by national competition authorities and review courts finding an infringement of the competition rules are without prejudice to the rights and obligations of national courts under Article 267 TFEU.

(36) National rules on the beginning, duration, suspension or interruption of limitation periods should not unduly hamper the bringing of actions for damages. This is particularly important in respect of actions that build upon a finding by a competition authority or a review court of an infringement. To that end, it should be possible to bring an action for damages after proceedings by a competition authority, with a view to enforcing national and Union competition law. The limitation period should not begin to run before the infringement ceases and before a claimant knows, or can reasonably be expected to know, the behaviour constituting the infringement, the fact that the infringement caused the claimant harm and the identity of the infringer. Member States should be able to maintain or introduce absolute limitation periods that are of general application, provided that the duration of such absolute limitation periods does not render practically impossible or excessively difficult the exercise of the right to full compensation.

(37) Where several undertakings infringe the competition rules jointly, as in the case of a cartel, it is appropriate to make provision for those co-infringers to be held jointly and severally liable for the entire harm caused by the infringement. A co-infringer should have the right to obtain a contribution from other co-infringers if it has paid more compensation than its share. The determination of that share as the relative responsibility of a given infringer, and the relevant criteria such as turnover, market share, or role in the cartel, is a matter for the applicable national law, while respecting the principles of effectiveness and equivalence.

(38) Undertakings which cooperate with competition authorities under a leniency programme play a key role in exposing secret cartel infringements and in bringing them to an end, thereby often mitigating the harm which could have been caused had the infringement continued. It is therefore appropriate to make provision for undertakings which have received immunity from fines from a competition authority under a leniency programme to be protected from undue exposure to damages claims, bearing in mind that the decision of the competition authority finding the infringement may become final for the immunity recipient before it becomes final for other undertakings which have not received immunity, thus potentially making the immunity recipient the preferential target of litigation. It is therefore appropriate that the immunity recipient be relieved in principle from joint and several liability for the entire harm and that any contribution it must make vis-à-vis co-infringers not exceed the amount of harm caused to its own direct or indirect purchasers or, in the case of a buying cartel, its direct or indirect providers. To the extent that a cartel has caused harm to those other than the customers or providers of the infringers, the contribution of the immunity recipient should not exceed its relative responsibility for the harm caused by the cartel. That share should be determined in accordance with the same rules used to determine the contributions between infringers. The immunity recipient should remain fully liable to the injured parties other than its direct or indirect purchasers or providers only where they are unable to obtain full compensation from the other infringers.

(39) Harm in the form of actual loss can result from the price difference between what was actually paid and what would otherwise have been paid in the absence of the infringement. When an injured party has reduced its actual loss by passing it on, entirely or in part, to its own purchasers, the loss which has been passed on no longer constitutes harm for which the party that passed it on needs to be compensated. It is therefore in principle appropriate to allow an infringer to invoke the passing-on of actual loss as a defence against a claim for damages. It is appropriate to provide that the infringer, in so far as it invokes the passing-on defence, must prove the existence and extent of pass-on of the overcharge. This burden of proof should not affect the possibility for the infringer to use evidence other than that in its possession, such as evidence already acquired in the proceedings or evidence held by other parties or third parties.

(40) In situations where the passing-on resulted in reduced sales and thus harm in the form of a loss of profit, the right to claim compensation for such loss of profit should remain unaffected.

(41) Depending on the conditions under which undertakings are operating, it may be commercial practice to pass on price increases down the supply chain. Consumers or undertakings to whom actual loss has thus been passed on have suffered harm caused by an infringement of Union or national competition law. While such harm should be compensated for by the infringer, it may be particularly difficult for consumers or undertakings that did not themselves make any purchase from the infringer to prove the extent of that harm. It is therefore appropriate to provide that, where the existence of a claim for damages or the amount of damages to be awarded depends on whether or to what degree an overcharge paid by a direct purchaser from the infringer has been passed on to an indirect purchaser, the latter is regarded as having proven that an overcharge paid by that direct purchaser has

been passed on to its level where it is able to show prima facie that such passing-on has occurred. This rebuttable presumption applies unless the infringer can credibly demonstrate to the satisfaction of the court that the actual loss has not or not entirely been passed on to the indirect purchaser. It is furthermore appropriate to define under what conditions the indirect purchaser is to be regarded as having established such prima facie proof. As regards the quantification of passing-on, national courts should have the power to estimate which share of the overcharge has been passed on to the level of indirect purchasers in disputes pending before them.

(42) The Commission should issue clear, simple and comprehensive guidelines for national courts on how to estimate the share of the overcharge passed on to indirect purchasers.

(43) Infringements of competition law often concern the conditions and the price under which goods or services are sold, and lead to an overcharge and other harm for the customers of the infringers. The infringement may also concern supplies to the infringer (for example in the case of a buyers' cartel). In such cases, the actual loss could result from a lower price paid by infringers to their suppliers. This Directive and in particular the rules on passing-on should apply accordingly to those cases.

(44) Actions for damages can be brought both by those who purchased goods or services from the infringer and by purchasers further down the supply chain. In the interest of consistency between judgments resulting from related proceedings and hence to avoid the harm caused by the infringement of Union or national competition law not being fully compensated or the infringer being required to pay damages to compensate for harm that has not been suffered, national courts should have the power to estimate the proportion of any overcharge which was suffered by the direct or indirect purchasers in disputes pending before them. In this context, national courts should be able to take due account, by procedural or substantive means available under Union and national law, of any related action and of the resulting judgment, particularly where it finds that passing-on has been proven. National courts should have at their disposal appropriate procedural means, such as joinder of claims, to ensure that compensation for actual loss paid at any level of the supply chain does not exceed the overcharge harm caused at that level. Such means should also be available in cross-border cases. This possibility to take due account of judgments should be without prejudice to the fundamental rights of the defence and the rights to an effective remedy and a fair trial of those who were not parties to the judicial proceedings, and without prejudice to the rules on the evidenciary value of judgments rendered in that context. It is possible for actions pending before the courts of different Member States to be considered as related within the meaning of Article 30 of Regulation (EU) No 1215/2012 of the European Parliament and of the Council ([1]). Under that Article, national courts other than that first seized may stay proceedings or, under certain circumstances, may decline jurisdiction. This Directive is without prejudice to the rights and obligations of national courts under that Regulation.

(45) An injured party who has proven having suffered harm as a result of a competition law infringement still needs to prove the extent of the harm in order to obtain damages. Quantifying harm in competition law cases is a very fact-intensive process and may require the application of complex economic models. This is often very costly, and claimants have difficulties in obtaining the data necessary to substantiate their claims. The quantification of harm in competition law cases can thus constitute a substantial barrier preventing effective claims for compensation.

(46) In the absence of Union rules on the quantification of harm caused by a competition law infringement, it is for the domestic legal system of each Member State to determine its own rules on quantifying harm, and for the Member States and for the national courts to determine what requirements the claimant has to meet when proving the amount of the harm suffered, the methods that can be used in quantifying the amount, and the consequences of not being able to fully meet those requirements. However, the requirements of national law regarding the quantification of harm in competition law cases should not be less favourable than those governing similar domestic actions (principle of equivalence), nor should they render the exercise of the Union right to damages practically impossible or excessively difficult (principle of effectiveness). Regard should be had to any information asymmetries between the parties and to the fact that quantifying the harm means assessing how the market in question would have evolved had there been no infringement. This assessment implies a comparison with a situation which is by definition hypothetical and can thus never be made with complete accuracy. It is therefore appropriate to ensure that national courts have the power to estimate the amount of the harm caused

([1]) Regulation (EU) No 1215/2012 of the European Parliament and of the Council of 12 December 2012 on jurisdiction and the recognition and enforcement of judgments in civil and commercial matters (OJ L 351, 20.12.2012, p. 1).

by the competition law infringement. Member States should ensure that, where requested, national competition authorities may provide guidance on quantum. In order to ensure coherence and predictability, the Commission should provide general guidance at Union level.

(47) To remedy the information asymmetry and some of the difficulties associated with quantifying harm in competition law cases, and to ensure the effectiveness of claims for damages, it is appropriate to presume that cartel infringements result in harm, in particular via an effect on prices. Depending on the facts of the case, cartels result in a rise in prices, or prevent a lowering of prices which would otherwise have occurred but for the cartel. This presumption should not cover the concrete amount of harm. Infringers should be allowed to rebut the presumption. It is appropriate to limit this rebuttable presumption to cartels, given their secret nature, which increases the information asymmetry and makes it more difficult for claimants to obtain the evidence necessary to prove the harm.

(48) Achieving a 'once-and-for-all' settlement for defendants is desirable in order to reduce uncertainty for infringers and injured parties. Therefore, infringers and injured parties should be encouraged to agree on compensating for the harm caused by a competition law infringement through consensual dispute resolution mechanisms, such as out-of-court settlements (including those where a judge can declare a settlement binding), arbitration, mediation or conciliation. Such consensual dispute resolution should cover as many injured parties and infringers as legally possible. The provisions in this Directive on consensual dispute resolution are therefore meant to facilitate the use of such mechanisms and increase their effectiveness.

(49) Limitation periods for bringing an action for damages could be such that they prevent injured parties and infringers from having sufficient time to come to an agreement on the compensation to be paid. In order to provide both sides with a genuine opportunity to engage in consensual dispute resolution before bringing proceedings before national courts, limitation periods need to be suspended for the duration of the consensual dispute resolution process.

(50) Furthermore, when parties decide to engage in consensual dispute resolution after an action for damages for the same claim has been brought before a national court, that court should be able to suspend the proceedings before it for the duration of the consensual dispute resolution process. When considering whether to suspend the proceedings, the national court should take into account the advantages of an expeditious procedure.

(51) To encourage consensual settlements, an infringer that pays damages through consensual dispute resolution should not be placed in a worse position vis-à-vis its co-infringers than it would otherwise be without the consensual settlement. That might happen if a settling infringer, even after a consensual settlement, continued to be fully jointly and severally liable for the harm caused by the infringement. A settling infringer should in principle therefore not contribute to its non-settling co-infringers when the latter have paid damages to an injured party with whom the first infringer had previously settled. The corollary to this non-contribution rule is that the claim of the injured party should be reduced by the settling infringer's share of the harm caused to it, regardless of whether the amount of the settlement equals or is different from the relative share of the harm that the settling co-infringer inflicted upon the settling injured party. That relative share should be determined in accordance with the rules otherwise used to determine the contributions among infringers. Without such a reduction, non-settling infringers would be unduly affected by settlements to which they were not a party. However, in order to ensure the right to full compensation, settling co-infringers should still have to pay damages where that is the only possibility for the settling injured party to obtain compensation for the remaining claim. The remaining claim refers to the claim of the settling injured party reduced by the settling co-infringer's share of the harm that the infringement inflicted upon the settling injured party. The latter possibility to claim damages from the settling co-infringer exists unless it is expressly excluded under the terms of the consensual settlement.

(52) Situations should be avoided in which settling co-infringers, by paying contribution to non-settling co-infringers for damages they paid to non-settling injured parties, pay a total amount of compensation exceeding their relative responsibility for the harm caused by the infringement. Therefore, when settling co-infringers are asked to contribute to damages subsequently paid by non-settling co-infringers to non-settling injured parties, national courts should take account of the damages already paid under the consensual settlement, bearing in mind that not all co-infringers are necessarily equally involved in the full substantive, temporal and geographical scope of the infringement.

(53) This Directive respects the fundamental rights and observes the principles recognised in the Charter of Fundamental Rights of the European Union.

(54) Since the objectives of this Directive, namely to establish rules concerning actions for damages for infringements of Union competition law in order to ensure the full effect of Articles 101 and 102 TFEU, and the proper functioning of the internal market for undertakings and consumers, cannot be sufficiently achieved by the Member States, but can rather, by reason of the requisite effectiveness and consistency in the application of Articles 101 and 102 TFEU, be better achieved at Union level, the Union may adopt measures, in accordance with the principle of subsidiarity as set out in Article 5 TEU. In accordance with the principle of proportionality, as set out in that Article, this Directive does not go beyond what is necessary in order to achieve those objectives.

(55) In accordance with the Joint Political Declaration of 28 September 2011 of Member States and the Commission on explanatory documents ([1]), Member States have undertaken to accompany, in justified cases, the notification of their transposition measures with one or more documents explaining the relationship between the components of a directive and the corresponding parts of national transposition instruments. With regard to this Directive, the legislator considers the transmission of such documents to be justified.

(56) It is appropriate to provide rules for the temporal application of this Directive,

HAVE ADOPTED THIS DIRECTIVE:

CHAPTER I

SUBJECT MATTER, SCOPE AND DEFINITIONS

Article 1

Subject matter and scope

1. This Directive sets out certain rules necessary to ensure that anyone who has suffered harm caused by an infringement of competition law by an undertaking or by an association of undertakings can effectively exercise the right to claim full compensation for that harm from that undertaking or association. It sets out rules fostering undistorted competition in the internal market and removing obstacles to its proper functioning, by ensuring equivalent protection throughout the Union for anyone who has suffered such harm.

2. This Directive sets out rules coordinating the enforcement of the competition rules by competition authorities and the enforcement of those rules in damages actions before national courts.

Article 2

Definitions

For the purposes of this Directive, the following definitions apply:

(1) 'infringement of competition law' means an infringement of Article 101 or 102 TFEU, or of national competition law;

(2) 'infringer' means an undertaking or association of undertakings which has committed an infringement of competition law;

(3) 'national competition law' means provisions of national law that predominantly pursue the same objective as Articles 101 and 102 TFEU and that are applied to the same case and in parallel to Union competition law pursuant to Article 3(1) of Regulation (EC) No 1/2003, excluding provisions of national law which impose criminal penalties on natural persons, except to the extent that such criminal penalties are the means whereby competition rules applying to undertakings are enforced;

(4) 'action for damages' means an action under national law by which a claim for damages is brought before a national court by an alleged injured party, or by someone acting on behalf of one or more alleged injured parties where Union or national law provides for that possibility, or by a natural or legal person that succeeded in the right of the alleged injured party, including the person that acquired the claim;

(5) 'claim for damages' means a claim for compensation for harm caused by an infringement of competition law;

(6) 'injured party' means a person that has suffered harm caused by an infringement of competition law;

([1]) OJ C 369, 17.12.2011, p. 14.

(7) 'national competition authority' means an authority designated by a Member State pursuant to Article 35 of Regulation (EC) No 1/2003, as being responsible for the application of Articles 101 and 102 TFEU;

(8) 'competition authority' means the Commission or a national competition authority or both, as the context may require;

(9) 'national court' means a court or tribunal of a Member State within the meaning of Article 267 TFEU;

(10) 'review court' means a national court that is empowered by ordinary means of appeal to review decisions of a national competition authority or to review judgments pronouncing on those decisions, irrespective of whether that court itself has the power to find an infringement of competition law;

(11) 'infringement decision' means a decision of a competition authority or review court that finds an infringement of competition law;

(12) 'final infringement decision' means an infringement decision that cannot be, or that can no longer be, appealed by ordinary means;

(13) 'evidence' means all types of means of proof admissible before the national court seized, in particular documents and all other objects containing information, irrespective of the medium on which the information is stored;

(14) 'cartel' means an agreement or concerted practice between two or more competitors aimed at coordinating their competitive behaviour on the market or influencing the relevant parameters of competition through practices such as, but not limited to, the fixing or coordination of purchase or selling prices or other trading conditions, including in relation to intellectual property rights, the allocation of production or sales quotas, the sharing of markets and customers, including bid-rigging, restrictions of imports or exports or anti-competitive actions against other competitors;

(15) 'leniency programme' means a programme concerning the application of Article 101 TFEU or a corresponding provision under national law on the basis of which a participant in a secret cartel, independently of the other undertakings involved in the cartel, cooperates with an investigation of the competition authority, by voluntarily providing presentations regarding that participant's knowledge of, and role in, the cartel in return for which that participant receives, by decision or by a discontinuation of proceedings, immunity from, or a reduction in, fines for its involvement in the cartel;

(16) 'leniency statement' means an oral or written presentation voluntarily provided by, or on behalf of, an undertaking or a natural person to a competition authority or a record thereof, describing the knowledge of that undertaking or natural person of a cartel and describing its role therein, which presentation was drawn up specifically for submission to the competition authority with a view to obtaining immunity or a reduction of fines under a leniency programme, not including pre-existing information;

(17) 'pre-existing information' means evidence that exists irrespective of the proceedings of a competition authority, whether or not such information is in the file of a competition authority;

(18) 'settlement submission' means a voluntary presentation by, or on behalf of, an undertaking to a competition authority describing the undertaking's acknowledgement of, or its renunciation to dispute, its participation in an infringement of competition law and its responsibility for that infringement of competition law, which was drawn up specifically to enable the competition authority to apply a simplified or expedited procedure;

(19) 'immunity recipient' means an undertaking which, or a natural person who, has been granted immunity from fines by a competition authority under a leniency programme;

(20) 'overcharge' means the difference between the price actually paid and the price that would otherwise have prevailed in the absence of an infringement of competition law;

(21) 'consensual dispute resolution' means any mechanism enabling parties to reach the out-of-court resolution of a dispute concerning a claim for damages;

(22) 'consensual settlement' means an agreement reached through consensual dispute resolution.

(23) 'direct purchaser' means a natural or legal person who acquired, directly from an infringer, products or services that were the object of an infringement of competition law;

(24) 'indirect purchaser' means a natural or legal person who acquired, not directly from an infringer, but from a direct purchaser or a subsequent purchaser, products or services that were the object of an infringement of competition law, or products or services containing them or derived therefrom.

Article 3

Right to full compensation

1. Member States shall ensure that any natural or legal person who has suffered harm caused by an infringement of competition law is able to claim and to obtain full compensation for that harm.

2. Full compensation shall place a person who has suffered harm in the position in which that person would have been had the infringement of competition law not been committed. It shall therefore cover the right to compensation for actual loss and for loss of profit, plus the payment of interest.

3. Full compensation under this Directive shall not lead to overcompensation, whether by means of punitive, multiple or other types of damages.

Article 4

Principles of effectiveness and equivalence

In accordance with the principle of effectiveness, Member States shall ensure that all national rules and procedures relating to the exercise of claims for damages are designed and applied in such a way that they do not render practically impossible or excessively difficult the exercise of the Union right to full compensation for harm caused by an infringement of competition law. In accordance with the principle of equivalence, national rules and procedures relating to actions for damages resulting from infringements of Article 101 or 102 TFEU shall not be less favourable to the alleged injured parties than those governing similar actions for damages resulting from infringements of national law.

CHAPTER II

DISCLOSURE OF EVIDENCE

Article 5

Disclosure of evidence

1. Member States shall ensure that in proceedings relating to an action for damages in the Union, upon request of a claimant who has presented a reasoned justification containing reasonably available facts and evidence sufficient to support the plausibility of its claim for damages, national courts are able to order the defendant or a third party to disclose relevant evidence which lies in their control, subject to the conditions set out in this Chapter. Member States shall ensure that national courts are able, upon request of the defendant, to order the claimant or a third party to disclose relevant evidence.

This paragraph is without prejudice to the rights and obligations of national courts under Regulation (EC) No 1206/2001.

2. Member States shall ensure that national courts are able to order the disclosure of specified items of evidence or relevant categories of evidence circumscribed as precisely and as narrowly as possible on the basis of reasonably available facts in the reasoned justification.

3. Member States shall ensure that national courts limit the disclosure of evidence to that which is proportionate. In determining whether any disclosure requested by a party is proportionate, national courts shall consider the legitimate interests of all parties and third parties concerned. They shall, in particular, consider:

(a) the extent to which the claim or defence is supported by available facts and evidence justifying the request to disclose evidence;

(b) the scope and cost of disclosure, especially for any third parties concerned, including preventing non-specific searches for information which is unlikely to be of relevance for the parties in the procedure;

(c) whether the evidence the disclosure of which is sought contains confidential information, especially concerning any third parties, and what arrangements are in place for protecting such confidential information.

4. Member States shall ensure that national courts have the power to order the disclosure of evidence containing confidential information where they consider it relevant to the action for damages. Member States shall ensure that, when ordering the disclosure of such information, national courts have at their disposal effective measures to protect such information.

5. The interest of undertakings to avoid actions for damages following an infringement of competition law shall not constitute an interest that warrants protection.

6. Member States shall ensure that national courts give full effect to applicable legal professional privilege under Union or national law when ordering the disclosure of evidence.

7. Member States shall ensure that those from whom disclosure is sought are provided with an opportunity to be heard before a national court orders disclosure under this Article.

8. Without prejudice to paragraphs 4 and 7 and to Article 6, this Article shall not prevent Member States from maintaining or introducing rules which would lead to wider disclosure of evidence.

Article 6

Disclosure of evidence included in the file of a competition authority

1. Member States shall ensure that, for the purpose of actions for damages, where national courts order the disclosure of evidence included in the file of a competition authority, this Article applies in addition to Article 5.

2. This Article is without prejudice to the rules and practices on public access to documents under Regulation (EC) No 1049/2001.

3. This Article is without prejudice to the rules and practices under Union or national law on the protection of internal documents of competition authorities and of correspondence between competition authorities.

4. When assessing, in accordance with Article 5(3), the proportionality of an order to disclose information, national courts shall, in addition, consider the following:

(a) whether the request has been formulated specifically with regard to the nature, subject matter or contents of documents submitted to a competition authority or held in the file thereof, rather than by a non-specific application concerning documents submitted to a competition authority;

(b) whether the party requesting disclosure is doing so in relation to an action for damages before a national court; and

(c) in relation to paragraphs 5 and 10, or upon request of a competition authority pursuant to paragraph 11, the need to safeguard the effectiveness of the public enforcement of competition law.

5. National courts may order the disclosure of the following categories of evidence only after a competition authority, by adopting a decision or otherwise, has closed its proceedings:

(a) information that was prepared by a natural or legal person specifically for the proceedings of a competition authority;

(b) information that the competition authority has drawn up and sent to the parties in the course of its proceedings; and

(c) settlement submissions that have been withdrawn.

6. Member States shall ensure that, for the purpose of actions for damages, national courts cannot at any time order a party or a third party to disclose any of the following categories of evidence:

(a) leniency statements; and

(b) settlement submissions.

7. A claimant may present a reasoned request that a national court access the evidence referred to in point (a) or (b) of paragraph 6 for the sole purpose of ensuring that their contents correspond to the definitions in points (16) and (18) of Article 2. In that assessment, national courts may request assistance only from the competent competition authority. The authors of the evidence in question may also have the possibility to be heard. In no case shall the national court permit other parties or third parties access to that evidence.

8. If only parts of the evidence requested are covered by paragraph 6, the remaining parts thereof shall, depending on the category under which they fall, be released in accordance with the relevant paragraphs of this Article.

9. The disclosure of evidence in the file of a competition authority that does not fall into any of the categories listed in this Article may be ordered in actions for damages at any time, without prejudice to this Article.

10. Member States shall ensure that national courts request the disclosure from a competition authority of evidence included in its file only where no party or third party is reasonably able to provide that evidence.

11. To the extent that a competition authority is willing to state its views on the proportionality of disclosure requests, it may, acting on its own initiative, submit observations to the national court before which a disclosure order is sought.

Article 7

Limits on the use of evidence obtained solely through access to the file of a competition authority

1. Member States shall ensure that evidence in the categories listed in Article 6(6) which is obtained by a natural or legal person solely through access to the file of a competition authority is either deemed to be inadmissible in actions for damages or is otherwise protected under the applicable national rules to ensure the full effect of the limits on the disclosure of evidence set out in Article 6.

2. Member States shall ensure that, until a competition authority has closed its proceedings by adopting a decision or otherwise, evidence in the categories listed in Article 6(5) which is obtained by a natural or legal person solely through access to the file of that competition authority is either deemed to be inadmissible in actions for damages or is otherwise protected under the applicable national rules to ensure the full effect of the limits on the disclosure of evidence set out in Article 6.

3. Member States shall ensure that evidence which is obtained by a natural or legal person solely through access to the file of a competition authority and which does not fall under paragraph 1 or 2, can be used in an action for damages only by that person or by a natural or legal person that succeeded to that person's rights, including a person that acquired that person's claim.

Article 8

Penalties

1. Member States shall ensure that national courts are able effectively to impose penalties on parties, third parties and their legal representatives in the event of any of the following:

(a) their failure or refusal to comply with the disclosure order of any national court;

(b) their destruction of relevant evidence;

(c) their failure or refusal to comply with the obligations imposed by a national court order protecting confidential information;

(d) their breach of the limits on the use of evidence provided for in this Chapter.

2. Member States shall ensure that the penalties that can be imposed by national courts are effective, proportionate and dissuasive. The penalties available to national courts shall include, with regard to the behaviour of a party to proceedings for an action for damages, the possibility to draw adverse inferences, such as presuming the relevant issue to be proven or dismissing claims and defences in whole or in part, and the possibility to order the payment of costs.

CHAPTER III

EFFECT OF NATIONAL DECISIONS, LIMITATION PERIODS, JOINT AND SEVERAL LIABILITY

Article 9

Effect of national decisions

1. Member States shall ensure that an infringement of competition law found by a final decision of a national competition authority or by a review court is deemed to be irrefutably established for the purposes of an action for damages brought before their national courts under Article 101 or 102 TFEU or under national competition law.

2. Member States shall ensure that where a final decision referred to in paragraph 1 is taken in another Member State, that final decision may, in accordance with national law, be presented before their national courts as at least prima facie evidence that an infringement of competition law has occurred and, as appropriate, may be assessed along with any other evidence adduced by the parties.

3. This Article is without prejudice to the rights and obligations of national courts under Article 267 TFEU.

Article 10

Limitation periods

1. Member States shall, in accordance with this Article, lay down rules applicable to limitation periods for bringing actions for damages. Those rules shall determine when the limitation period begins to run, the duration thereof and the circumstances under which it is interrupted or suspended.

2. Limitation periods shall not begin to run before the infringement of competition law has ceased and the claimant knows, or can reasonably be expected to know:

(a) of the behaviour and the fact that it constitutes an infringement of competition law;

(b) of the fact that the infringement of competition law caused harm to it; and

(c) the identity of the infringer.

3. Member States shall ensure that the limitation periods for bringing actions for damages are at least five years.

4. Member States shall ensure that a limitation period is suspended or, depending on national law, interrupted, if a competition authority takes action for the purpose of the investigation or its proceedings in respect of an infringement of competition law to which the action for damages relates. The suspension shall end at the earliest one year after the infringement decision has become final or after the proceedings are otherwise terminated.

Article 11

Joint and several liability

1. Member States shall ensure that undertakings which have infringed competition law through joint behaviour are jointly and severally liable for the harm caused by the infringement of competition law; with the effect that each of those undertakings is bound to compensate for the harm in full, and the injured party has the right to require full compensation from any of them until he has been fully compensated.

2. By way of derogation from paragraph 1, Member States shall ensure that, without prejudice to the right of full compensation as laid down in Article 3, where the infringer is a small or medium-sized enterprise (SME) as defined in Commission Recommendation 2003/361/EC [1], the infringer is liable only to its own direct and indirect purchasers where:

(a) its market share in the relevant market was below 5 % at any time during the infringement of competition law; and

(b) the application of the normal rules of joint and several liability would irretrievably jeopardise its economic viability and cause its assets to lose all their value.

3. The derogation laid down in paragraph 2 shall not apply where:

(a) the SME has led the infringement of competition law or has coerced other undertakings to participate therein; or

(b) the SME has previously been found to have infringed competition law.

4. By way of derogation from paragraph 1, Member States shall ensure that an immunity recipient is jointly and severally liable as follows:

(a) to its direct or indirect purchasers or providers; and

(b) to other injured parties only where full compensation cannot be obtained from the other undertakings that were involved in the same infringement of competition law.

Member States shall ensure that any limitation period applicable to cases under this paragraph is reasonable and sufficient to allow injured parties to bring such actions.

---

[1] Commission Recommendation 2003/361/EC of 6 May 2003 concerning the definition of micro, small and medium-sized enterprises (OJ L 124, 20.5.2003, p. 36).

5. Member States shall ensure that an infringer may recover a contribution from any other infringer, the amount of which shall be determined in the light of their relative responsibility for the harm caused by the infringement of competition law. The amount of contribution of an infringer which has been granted immunity from fines under a leniency programme shall not exceed the amount of the harm it caused to its own direct or indirect purchasers or providers.

6. Member States shall ensure that, to the extent the infringement of competition law caused harm to injured parties other than the direct or indirect purchasers or providers of the infringers, the amount of any contribution from an immunity recipient to other infringers shall be determined in the light of its relative responsibility for that harm.

CHAPTER IV

THE PASSING-ON OF OVERCHARGES

Article 12

Passing-on of overcharges and the right to full compensation

1. To ensure the full effectiveness of the right to full compensation as laid down in Article 3, Member States shall ensure that, in accordance with the rules laid down in this Chapter, compensation of harm can be claimed by anyone who suffered it, irrespective of whether they are direct or indirect purchasers from an infringer, and that compensation of harm exceeding that caused by the infringement of competition law to the claimant, as well as the absence of liability of the infringer, are avoided.

2. In order to avoid overcompensation, Member States shall lay down procedural rules appropriate to ensure that compensation for actual loss at any level of the supply chain does not exceed the overcharge harm suffered at that level.

3. This Chapter shall be without prejudice to the right of an injured party to claim and obtain compensation for loss of profits due to a full or partial passing-on of the overcharge.

4. Member States shall ensure that the rules laid down in this Chapter apply accordingly where the infringement of competition law relates to a supply to the infringer.

5. Member States shall ensure that the national courts have the power to estimate, in accordance with national procedures, the share of any overcharge that was passed on.

Article 13

Passing-on defence

Member States shall ensure that the defendant in an action for damages can invoke as a defence against a claim for damages the fact that the claimant passed on the whole or part of the overcharge resulting from the infringement of competition law. The burden of proving that the overcharge was passed on shall be on the defendant, who may reasonably require disclosure from the claimant or from third parties.

Article 14

Indirect purchasers

1. Member States shall ensure that, where in an action for damages the existence of a claim for damages or the amount of compensation to be awarded depends on whether, or to what degree, an overcharge was passed on to the claimant, taking into account the commercial practice that price increases are passed on down the supply chain, the burden of proving the existence and scope of such a passing-on shall rest with the claimant, who may reasonably require disclosure from the defendant or from third parties.

2. In the situation referred to in paragraph 1, the indirect purchaser shall be deemed to have proven that a passing-on to that indirect purchaser occurred where that indirect purchaser has shown that:

(a) the defendant has committed an infringement of competition law;

(b) the infringement of competition law has resulted in an overcharge for the direct purchaser of the defendant; and

(c) the indirect purchaser has purchased the goods or services that were the object of the infringement of competition law, or has purchased goods or services derived from or containing them.

This paragraph shall not apply where the defendant can demonstrate credibly to the satisfaction of the court that the overcharge was not, or was not entirely, passed on to the indirect purchaser.

Article 15

Actions for damages by claimants from different levels in the supply chain

1. To avoid that actions for damages by claimants from different levels in the supply chain lead to a multiple liability or to an absence of liability of the infringer, Member States shall ensure that in assessing whether the burden of proof resulting from the application of Articles 13 and 14 is satisfied, national courts seized of an action for damages are able, by means available under Union or national law, to take due account of any of the following:

(a) actions for damages that are related to the same infringement of competition law, but that are brought by claimants from other levels in the supply chain;

(b) judgments resulting from actions for damages as referred to in point (a);

(c) relevant information in the public domain resulting from the public enforcement of competition law.

2. This Article shall be without prejudice to the rights and obligations of national courts under Article 30 of Regulation (EU) No 1215/2012.

Article 16

Guidelines for national courts

The Commission shall issue guidelines for national courts on how to estimate the share of the overcharge which was passed on to the indirect purchaser.

CHAPTER V

QUANTIFICATION OF HARM

Article 17

Quantification of harm

1. Member States shall ensure that neither the burden nor the standard of proof required for the quantification of harm renders the exercise of the right to damages practically impossible or excessively difficult. Member States shall ensure that the national courts are empowered, in accordance with national procedures, to estimate the amount of harm if it is established that a claimant suffered harm but it is practically impossible or excessively difficult precisely to quantify the harm suffered on the basis of the evidence available.

2. It shall be presumed that cartel infringements cause harm. The infringer shall have the right to rebut that presumption.

3. Member States shall ensure that, in proceedings relating to an action for damages, a national competition authority may, upon request of a national court, assist that national court with respect to the determination of the quantum of damages where that national competition authority considers such assistance to be appropriate.

CHAPTER VI

CONSENSUAL DISPUTE RESOLUTION

Article 18

Suspensive and other effects of consensual dispute resolution

1. Member States shall ensure that the limitation period for bringing an action for damages is suspended for the duration of any consensual dispute resolution process. The suspension of the limitation period shall apply only with regard to those parties that are or that were involved or represented in the consensual dispute resolution.

2. Without prejudice to provisions of national law in matters of arbitration, Member States shall ensure that national courts seized of an action for damages may suspend their proceedings for up to two years where the parties thereto are involved in consensual dispute resolution concerning the claim covered by that action for damages.

3. A competition authority may consider compensation paid as a result of a consensual settlement and prior to its decision imposing a fine to be a mitigating factor.

Article 19

Effect of consensual settlements on subsequent actions for damages

1. Member States shall ensure that, following a consensual settlement, the claim of the settling injured party is reduced by the settling co-infringer's share of the harm that the infringement of competition law inflicted upon the injured party.

2. Any remaining claim of the settling injured party shall be exercised only against non-settling co-infringers. Non-settling co-infringers shall not be permitted to recover contribution for the remaining claim from the settling co-infringer.

3. By way of derogation from paragraph 2, Member States shall ensure that where the non-settling co-infringers cannot pay the damages that correspond to the remaining claim of the settling injured party, the settling injured party may exercise the remaining claim against the settling co-infringer.

The derogation referred to in the first subparagraph may be expressly excluded under the terms of the consensual settlement.

4. When determining the amount of contribution that a co-infringer may recover from any other co-infringer in accordance with their relative responsibility for the harm caused by the infringement of competition law, national courts shall take due account of any damages paid pursuant to a prior consensual settlement involving the relevant co-infringer.

CHAPTER VII

FINAL PROVISIONS

Article 20

Review

1. The Commission shall review this Directive and shall submit a report thereon to the European Parliament and the Council by 27 December 2020.

2. The report referred to in paragraph 1 shall, inter alia, include information on all of the following:

(a) the possible impact of financial constraints flowing from the payment of fines imposed by a competition authority for an infringement of competition law on the possibility for injured parties to obtain full compensation for the harm caused by that infringement of competition law;

(b) the extent to which claimants for damages caused by an infringement of competition law established in an infringement decision adopted by a competition authority of a Member State are able to prove before the national court of another Member State that such an infringement of competition law has occurred;

(c) the extent to which compensation for actual loss exceeds the overcharge harm caused by the infringement of competition law or suffered at any level of the supply chain.

3. If appropriate, the report referred to in paragraph 1 shall be accompanied by a legislative proposal.

Article 21

Transposition

1. Member States shall bring into force the laws, regulations and administrative provisions necessary to comply with this Directive by 27 December 2016. They shall forthwith communicate to the Commission the text thereof.

When Member States adopt those measures, they shall contain a reference to this Directive or be accompanied by such a reference on the occasion of their official publication. Member States shall determine how such reference is to be made.

2. Member States shall communicate to the Commission the text of the main provisions of national law which they adopt in the field covered by this Directive.

Article 22

Temporal application

1. Member States shall ensure that the national measures adopted pursuant to Article 21 in order to comply with substantive provisions of this Directive do not apply retroactively.

2. Member States shall ensure that any national measures adopted pursuant to Article 21, other than those referred to in paragraph 1, do not apply to actions for damages of which a national court was seized prior to 26 December 2014.

Article 23

Entry into force

This Directive shall enter into force on the twentieth day following that of its publication in the *Official Journal of the European Union.*

Article 24

Addressees

This Directive is addressed to the Member States.

Done at Strasbourg, 26 November 2014.

For the European Parliament	For the Council
The President	*The President*
M. SCHULZ	S. GOZI

Index

NB—figures in **bold** make reference to information in tables

abuse of dominant position, 8, **68–69**
  Finland, 233
  IMS Health case, 126–27, 130–33
  intellectual property rights, 126–27
  Magill case, 126–27
  Poland, 204
  SEPs and, 135–36
  Sweden, 277
access to leniency documents, 32, 92–93
  see also leniency programmes
  absolute bar, 36, **41**
  balancing private and public enforcement, 95–96
  barrier to private enforcement, as a, 32–33
  cartel members, 165–67
  cartel victims, 10–11, 165–67
  coherence of the system, 180
  Damages Directive, 96, 119, 176, 180
    evidence held by individuals, 176–77
    evidence held by National Competition Authorities, 176–77
    protecting leniency programmes, 93, 177–80
  ECJ case law, 167–68
    Commission files:
      court access to, 172–76
      individual access, 168–69
    ECJ judgments, 171–72
    General Court judgments, 170–71
    individual access, 168–69
      Commission files, 169–172
      court files, 168–69
      National Competition Authority files, 168–69
  effectiveness principle, 92, 96
  equivalence principle, 92
  friction between public and private enforcement, 91–93
  limits, 9
  national courts and, 107–08
  Poland, 211–13
  private enforcement, 32–33
  rights of cartel victims and members, 165–66
    background, 166–67
  Statements of Objection, 174, 180
    access to evidence post-SO, 182–84
  weighing of interests, 148–55, 92
Ashurst Study, 5–6

balancing private and public enforcement, 95–97
  access to leniency statements and settlement submissions, 95–96
  effectiveness principle, 96
  friction between public and private enforcement, 90–93
binding effect of national decisions, 6, 116, 217, 244
  cartel decisions, 195
  follow-on actions and, 278
  Greece, 245
  Netherlands, 245–46
  Sweden:
    Directive's impact on national law, 71–72
  Poland, 207–08
  public enforcement cases, 71–72, 73, 80
black list, 257
  disclosure of evidence, 161, 238–39
  leniency statements, 161

cartel members:
  see also access to leniency documents
  access to documents:
    Damages Directive and, 176–80
    ECJ and, 167–76
  rights of access to documents, 165–67
cartel victims:
  see also access to leniency documents
  access to documents:
    Damages Directive and, 176–80
    ECJ and, 167–76
  indirect purchasers, 272
  Kone case, 160
  rights of access to documents, 165–67
cartels:
  leniency programmes, 144–45
    US programmes, 145
  overcharges, 74–77

fines, 76
quantification of harm, 75
rights of cartel victims and members, 165–66
background, 166–67
causation, **40**, 222–24, 256–57
competition restriction cases, 224
ECJ case law, 225–28
national courts, 225–26
evaluation of, 29, 226
follow-on actions, 35–36
class actions, *see* collective redress
Clayton Act, 19, **39–40**, 265–67
collective redress, **40**, 88
Commissions proposals, 37–38
non-binding principles, 18
differences of opinion, 6–7, 201
Netherlands, 257–58
Poland (opt-in model), 213
advantages, 213–14
disadvantages, 214–15
reform, 215–16
Portugal, 197–98
opt-out model, 198–200
private enforcement, 88
SMEs, 37
Sweden, 62–63, 79–80, 277
Communication and Practical Guide 2013:
quantification of harm, 305–06
comparator-based methods, 306–09
cost-based methods, 309
finance-based methods, 309
simulation models, 309
competition law, 3–4
enforcement legal framework, 83–97
objectives, 48–51
private enforcement, 15–41
intellectual property cases, 121–39
restitution, 279–93
compensation for damage, *see* right to full compensation
complex markets:
welfare effects of damages, 52–54
consensual dispute resolution, 4, 36, 254, 257–58
Greece, 254–55
Netherlands, 255–56
Poland, 219
suspension of limitation periods, 111, 246
costs to private litigants, 30–31, **40**
Clayton Act, 19
recovery of costs for successful claimants, 19–20
cost v benefit, 88–90
effect of Damages Directive, 94–95
Portugal, 194
Courage case, 5, 87, 264–65
Art 101 TFEU, 48
Art 102 TFEU, 290
causal damage due to excessive prices, 160
English law and, 286–87
indirect purchasers, 261
national procedural autonomy, 100–02, 104–05
right to full compensation, 28, 166, 188
Sweden and, 60

damages:
see also restitution; right to full compensation
exemplary damages, 280–81
multiple damages, **39**
punitive damages, **39**, 280–81
prohibition of, 36
restitution compared, 279–80, 285
welfare effects of the right to damages:
antitrust liability, 60
collective redress, 62–63
competition law, 48–51
complex market settings, 52–54
concept, 44–47
damages for antitrust injury, 54–56
disclosure of evidence, 60–62
forum rules, 56
impact of Damages Directive, 47–48
indirect customers, 59
limitation periods, 59–60
passing-on of overcharges, 59
persons entitled to damages, 57–58
private litigation and claims, 63–64
quantification of harm, 57
simplified market setting, 51–52
Damages Directive, 3–4, 11–13
see also individual countries
adoption, 3
delays, 6–7
background, 5–6
concerns, 34–38
direct purchasers, 35
effect on interplay between private and public enforcement, 93–97
features, 4, 7–9, 66
follow-on litigation, 9
indirect purchasers, 35, 268–71
joint and several liability, 4, 8–9, 217–18, 249–51
national procedural autonomy, 112
limitation periods, 4, **40**, 72–73, 246–48
national procedural autonomy, 111–12
national courts:
competition restriction cases, 225–26
duties, 34–36
overcompensation, 35, 270
passing-on of overcharges, 9–10, **39**, 59, 78, 251–53, 257
national procedural autonomy, 112
procedural provisions:
impact on Swedish law, 71–73

quantification of harm, 4, **40**, 57, 67–71, **68–70**, 74–77, 295–97
Art 17, 302–03
empowerment of national courts to estimate harm, 301–02
presumption of harm, 298–301
other provisions, 304–05
Communication and Practical Guide 2013, 305–09
inherent limitations of counterfactuals, 310–11
mutual recognition of different methods of quantification, 311–12
national procedural autonomy, 113
passing-on of overcharges, 311
presumption of harm, 302–03, 312
right to compensation for harm, 3–4, 8, 34
right to full compensation, 4, 7–8, 34, 35
scope, 283–84
US Antitrust law compared, 4–5, 16–17
welfare effects of damages, 47–48
de minimis, 217–18
deadweight loss, 45–46, 89
Sweden, 78
direct purchasers, 35
passing-on of overcharges, 112
restitution, 292
enrichment of defendant and, 281–82
loss of sales and, 281
overcharge for goods, 281
Directive on Competition Damages Actions, *see* Damages Directive
disclosure of evidence, **40**, 113–14, 238
access to leniency documents, 10–11
black list, 161, 238–39
common and civil law compared, 10
Greece, 239–41
civil courts, 240–41
grey list, 161–62, 238–39
intellectual property rights, 123–24
leniency programmes, 10–11
national procedural autonomy:
proportionality, 114–16
proportionality test, 10, 114–16
Sweden, 60–62
Directive's impact on national law, 71
white list, 162
Donau Chemie case, 11, 32, 169
access of third parties to competition authority files, 212
access to leniency documents, 92, 96–97, 153
national procedural autonomy, 107–08

economic incentives, 66, 79
deadweight loss, 78
overcharge approximations, 73–77
passing-on of overcharges, 78
payment of interest, 77–78
procedural provisions and, 71–73
role of Damages Directive, 94
effectiveness and equivalence principles, 29–30, 32, **39–41**, 89, 96, 230–31, 301–03
access to leniency documents, 92–93, 96
causation and, 225–28
clarification of antitrust liability, 60
competition restriction cases, 231–32
Finland, 221–22, 228, 232–34
indirect purchasers, 268–69
mutatis mutandis, 291
national procedural autonomy, 100, 101–06
positive obligations, 110, 117–18
restitution, 291–92
scope of the right to damages, 94
umbrella pricing, 231–32
enforcement:
see also private enforcement; public enforcement
decentralisation of enforcement systems, 17, 236
fines, 85–86, 263
cartels, 76
sanctions, 52, 85–86, 247
equivalence principle, *see* effectiveness and equivalence principles
essential facilities doctrine, 127–30, 132–33
estimation of harm, *see* quantification of harm
European Court of Justice:
access to leniency documents:
case law, 152, 154–55, 167–68, 170–72, 182–83
court access:
Commission files, 172–76
individual access, 168–69
Commission files, 169–172
court files, 168–69
National Competition Authority files, 168–69
barriers to private litigation, 27–32
causation:
competition restriction cases, 225–28
competition damages, 264–65
essential facilities doctrine, 129–30
General Court judgments, 150–51, 170–71
ex turpi causa non oritur actio, 287
exemplary damages, 106, 280–81
see also punitive damages
expert evidence, **41**
assessment of quantitative damages, 193

fair, reasonable and non-discriminatory terms, *see* FRAND terms
Finland, 221–22

causation, 228–30
effectiveness principle, 232–34
follow-on litigation, 9, **40**, 60, **69**, 277–78
access to leniency documents:
cartel members, 180–84
cartel victims, 165–80
cartel activity and, 63–64, 67
friction between public and private enforcement, 90–91
Greece, 239
Poland, 206, 210
Portugal, 192–93
public enforcement, 95
rebuttal presumption of harm, 295
Sweden, 288–89
forum shopping, 56, 116–18, 196, 200, 257–58
FRAND terms:
injunctive relief, 138–39
Commission's approach, 135–36
existence of a dominant position, 134–35
German approach, 135
Huawei case, 136–38
standard setting, 133–34
SEPs and, 133–135
Commission's approach, 135–36
dominant position, 138–39
German approach, 135
full compensation:
Courage case, 28, 166, 188
interest payments, 77–78
Manfredi case, 166
Pfleiderer case, 167
right to, 4, 7–8, 34, 35

Greece, 237, 256–58
binding effect of national decisions, 245
consensual dispute resolution, 254–55
disclosure of evidence, 239–41
civil courts, 240–41
joint and several liability, 249–50
leniency programme, 239–40
limitation periods, 246–47
passing-on defence, 252
Green Paper on Damages Actions for Breach of the EC Antitrust Rules (Green Paper), 6, 166, 296–97
grey list, 257
disclosure of evidence, 161–62, 238–39
leniency statements, 161–62

IMS Health case:
abuse of dominant position, 126–27
ECJ ruling, 130–33
ECJ ruling:
abuse of dominant position, 130–33
essential facilities doctrine, 129–30
essential facilities doctrine, 127–28, 129
ECJ ruling, 129–30
indirect purchasers, 35, **39**, 261–64, 277–78
see also passing-on of overcharges
cartel victims, 272
case law, 264–65
categories, 271–72
consumers, 272–73
full passing-on to indirect purchasers, 273–74
purchasers of cartel goods, 272
challenges, 274
definition, 269
effect of Damages Directive, 268–71
injured parties, 269
passing-on defence, 269, 270–71
Sweden, 59
recognition and enforcement of judgments, 270
restitution, 282
Sweden, 59, 274–77
US law, 265–68
barring the passing-on defence, 266
Clayton Act, 265
welfare effects of the right to damages, 59
infringements of competition law:
right to compensation for harm, 3–4
Sweden, 60–62
Directive's impact on national law, 71–73
injunctive relief:
FRAND terms, 138–39
Commission's approach, 135–36
existence of a dominant position, 134–35
German approach, 135
Huawei case, 136–38
standard setting, 133–34
intellectual property rights:
abuse of dominant position:
IMS Health case, 126–27
Magill case, 126–27
competition law:
defence, as a, 121–22, 123, 124–25
IMS Health case, 126–27
Magill case, 126–27
private competition law claims, 123
disclosure, 123–24
exclusion of direct competition, 121
FRAND terms, 138–39
Commission's approach, 135–36
existence of a dominant position, 134–35
German approach, 135
Huawei case, 136–38
standard setting, 133–34
injunctive relief, 122–23, 133–39
remedies, 122–23

standard setting, 133–34
Intellectual Property Rights Directive (IPRED), 166
interest payments, 35, 77–78, 79, 94, 268

joint and several liability, 4, 37, **41**, 248–49
  Greece, 249–50
  national procedural autonomy:
    positive obligations, 112
  Netherlands, 250–51
  special derogations, 8
  small and medium-sized businesses, 8, 55, 112, 181, 190, 217
    leniency programmes, 8–9
  Poland, 209–10, 217–18
  procedural obligations:
    positive obligations, 112

Kone case, 12
  follow-on actions, 190
  effectiveness principle, 231–32
  national procedural autonomy, 108
  private applicants as victims of cartels, 160

legal costs, 30–31, **40**
  Clayton Act, 19
    recovery of costs for successful claimants, 19–20
  cost v benefit, 88–90
  effect of Damages Directive, 94–95
  Portugal, 194
Leniency Notice 2006, 148, 150–51
leniency programmes, **41**, 143–44, 162–63
  access to leniency documents, 10–11, 115–16
    barrier to private enforcement, as a, 32–33
    categories of information, 149
    exceptions, 150
    necessity of access, 152
    refusal to grant access, 151
    transparency, 149–50
    weighing of interests and, 148–55
  black list, 161
  cartels, 144–45
  CDC Hydrogene Peroxide case, 151–52
  Commission's discretion, 146–47
  disclosure of evidence, 10–11
  effect of Damages Directive, 155–56, 166–67
    scope and condition of access to files, 156
    weighing of interests, 157–58
    transparency, 158–59
  EnBW Energie case, 150–51
    General Court, 150–51
    ECJ appeal, 152
  grey list, 161–62
  modernisation, 147–148
  perceived lack of transparency and certainty, 145–46
  Pfleiderer case, 154
  protection of leniency programmes, 177–80
  small and medium-sized businesses, 8–9
  US programmes and cartel activity, 145
  whistleblowing, 145
  white list, 162
limitation periods, 4, **40**, 246
  Greece, 246–47
  national procedural autonomy:
    positive obligations, 111–12
  Netherlands, 247–48
  Poland, 210
  Portugal, 196–97
  Sweden, 59–60
    Directive's impact on national law, 72–73
  US antitrust laws, 19

Manfredi case:
  causal damage due to excessive prices, 160
  national procedural autonomy, 105–06
  right to full compensation, 166
multiple damages, 7, 35, **39**, 48, 94, 251–52, 262, 304

national competition authorities:
  access to NCA documents, 168–69, 176–77
  binding force of decisions, 6
  effects of decisions, 195–96
  follow-on actions, 95
  imposition of fines, 85
  quantification of harm, 302–03
  regulation of public enforcement, 84
national courts:
  access to leniency documents and, 107–08, 175, 179
    National Courts Notice, 175, 179
  competition restriction cases, 225–26
  duties, 34–36
  quantification of harm, 301–02
National Courts Notice:
  access to leniency documents, 175–79
national procedural autonomy:
  barrier to private enforcement, as a, 28–30
  case law, 104–09
  effectiveness principle, 101–06, 110, 117–18
  equivalence principle, 103
  impact of Damages Directive, 117–19
  positive obligations, 110–11, 117–18
    joint and several liability, 112
    limitation periods, 111–12

passing-on of overcharges, 112
quantification of harm, 113
requirement for procedural rules, 111
settling claims, 112–13
private enforcement:
key features, 100–01
procedural obligations:
case law, 104–09
positive obligations, 110–13
scope, 109
proportionality:
duty of disclosure, 114–16
right of an individual to claim damages:
negative and positive procedural obligations, 103–04
scope, 101–03
shortcomings, 109
Netherlands, 237, 256–58
binding effect of national decisions, 245–46
consensual dispute resolution, 255–56
disclosure of evidence, 241–42
case law, 242–43
limitations, 242
weighing-up, 243–44
joint and several liability, 250–51
limitation periods, 247–48
passing-on defence, 252–53

Otis case:
binding effect of finding an infringement, 72
causation, 225–27
directness requirement, 225
overcharges:
see also passing-on of overcharges
cartels, 74–77
fines, 76
quantification of harm, 75
direct purchasers:
restitution, 281
passing-on of overcharges, 9–10, **39**, 251–52, 257
follow-on claimants, 9
Greece, 252
national procedural autonomy, 112
Netherlands, 252–53
provisions, 78
Sweden, 59
overcompensation, 7, 35, 48, 59, 66, 94, 226, 236, 251, 270, 304
inherent limitations of counterfactuals and, 310–11
Oxera Report, 76

pari delicto doctrine, **39**, 287
passing-on of overcharges, 9–10, **39**, 251–52, 257
follow-on claimants, 9
Greece, 252
indirect purchasers, 269, 270–71, 273–74
Sweden, 59
national procedural autonomy:
positive obligations, 112
Netherlands, 252–53
provisions, 78
Sweden, 59
US law, 265–68
barring the passing-on defence, 266
Pfleiderer case, 32, 91–93, 174–75
access to leniency documents, 154, 167–68
balancing test, 114, 160–62
national procedural autonomy, 106–07
right to full compensation, 167
Poland:
private enforcement, 219–20
access to documents, 211–13
approach of the courts, 205–09
background, 203–05
collective redress (opt-in model), 213
advantages, 213–14
disadvantages, 214–15
future developments, 215–17
joint or several liability, 217–18
leniency programmes, 218–19
joint or several liability, 209–10
lack of legal framework, 209–10
limitation periods, 210
Portugal:
collective redress, 197–98
opt-out model, 198–200
limitation period rules, 196–97
National Competition Decisions, effects of, 195–96
private enforcement, 187–88, 200–01
effect of Damages Directive, 188–91
follow-on actions, 192
legal costs, 194
mass damages claims, 192–93
procedure, 193–95
quantification of harm, 194
settlement, 194–95
presumption of harm, 298–301, 312
see also quantification of harm
right to rebut, 8, 36, 57, 74–75, 95, 112, 189–90, 227, 271, 295
private enforcement, 15–16, 86, 97
barriers in the EU, 17, 26–27, 33–34
access to leniency evidence, 32–33
Commission's right to grant exemptions, 28
cost and risk of litigation, 30–31
effectiveness principle, 30
equivalence principle, 30

lack of clarity, 28
national procedural autonomy, 28–30
relationship between public and private enforcement, 31–32
whether private rights of action for damages, 27
collective redress, 88
Commission proposals:
actions to resolve issues, 34–38
draft Directive, 18
non-binding principles for collective redress mechanisms, 18
practical guide on quantification of harm, 18
corrective justice and, 87–88
cost v benefit, 88–90
effectiveness principle, 30, 96
friction with public enforcement, 90–93
national procedural autonomy, 100–09
promotion of deterrence, 88
relationship between public and private enforcement, 31–32, 33
terminating ongoing infringements, 87
US antitrust laws, 19–26
Clayton Act, 19
compared, 16–17
injunctive relief, 19
judgments as *prima facia* evidence, 19
limitation periods, 19
recovery of costs for successful claimants, 19–20
treble damages, 19
procedural obligations, 116–17
national procedural autonomy:
scope, 109
positive obligations, 110–13
procedural provisions, 4, 73
see also consensual dispute resolution; disclosure of evidence
binding effect of finding an infringement, 71–72
disclosure of evidence, 71
limitation periods, 72
proportionality, 10, 189
disclosure of evidence, 159, 238
national procedural autonomy, 114–17
public enforcement, 83–84, 97, 262
deterrence:
fines, 85–86
friction with private enforcement, 90–93
prevention of future prohibited conduct, 84–85
stopping ongoing infringements, 84
punitive damages, 7, 29, 35, **39**, 48, 106, 116, 194, 262, 280–81, 304
see also exemplary damages
prohibition of, 36

quantification of harm, **40**, 295–96
approximations in national courts, 73–77
Damages Directive:
Art 17:
assistance by NCAs in quantification of damages, 302–03
empowerment of national courts to estimate harm, 301–02
presumption of harm, 298–301
other provisions, 304–05
assistance by National Competition Authorities, 302–03
cartel overcharges, 74–77
Communication and Practical Guide 2013, 305–06
comparator-based methods, 306–09
cost-based methods, 309
finance-based methods, 309
simulation models, 309
Green Paper, 296–97
inherent limitations of counterfactuals, 310–11
mutual recognition of different methods of quantification, 311–12
national procedural autonomy:
positive obligations, 113
passing-on of overcharges, 311
presumption of harm, 312
Art 17 Damages Directive, 302–03
reversed burden of proof, 8
Sweden, 57
case law, 67–71, **68–70**
White Paper, 297–98

recognition and enforcement of judgments:
indirect purchasers, 270
stays of proceedings, 270
Regulation 1/2003 (implementation of the rules on competition):
decentralisation of enforcement systems, 17
remoteness doctrine, **39**
US federal antitrust law, 22
restitution, 279, 284–85, 292–93
damages compared, 279–80, 285
Damages Directive:
scope, 283–84
direct purchasers, 292
enrichment of defendant and, 281–82
loss of sales and, 281
overcharge for goods, 281
horizontal agreements, 288–89
indirect purchasers, 282
national remedies, 290–91
right to equivalent remedies, 291–92
TFEU and, 285–86
Art 102, 289–90
vertical agreements, 286–88, 292

right to compensation for harm, 3–4, 8, 34, 235–36
  balancing, 155–61
  effect of Damages Directive, 94
  interest payments, 77–78
  Sweden:
    private litigation, 63–64
    welfare effects of the right to damages:
      damages for antitrust injury, 54–56
      forum rules, 56
      indirect customers, 59
      limitation periods, 59–60
      passing-on of overcharges, 59
      persons entitled to damages, 57–58
      quantification of harm, 57
  prioritisation, 155–61
  welfare effects, 43–44
    Sweden, 54–64
right to full compensation, 4, 7–8, 34, 35
  Courage case, 28, 166, 188
  interest payments, 77–78
  Manfredi case, 166
  Pfleiderer case, 167

settlement:
  cartel settlements, 84
  consensual settlement, 112–13, 189–90, 249
    Greece, 254–55
  national procedural autonomy:
    positive obligations, 112–13
  Portugal, 194–95
  procedures, 96–97, 193–94
settlement submissions:
  see also leniency statements
  disclosure of, 95–96, 114, 116, 156, 178–80, 238
  national courts:
    non-disclosure, 95–96
  Netherlands, 243–44, 255–56
  Poland, 212–13
  protection of, 161–62, 163
simplified market:
  welfare effects of damages, 51–52
small and medium-sized businesses, *see* joint and several liability
standard essential patents (SEPs):
  dominant position and, 138–39
  FRAND terms, 133–135
    Commission's approach, 135–36
    German approach, 135
standard setting, 133–34
Statements of Objection, 174, 180
  access to evidence post-SO, 182–84
Sweden:
  antitrust liability, 60
  challenges in courts related to the Damages Directive, 65–66
  collective redress schemes, 62–63, 79–80
  courts:
    challenges in courts related to the Damages Directive, 65–66
    litigation on damages, 66–67
    quantification of harm cases, 67–71, **68–70**
  damages for antitrust injury:
    background, 54–56
    limitation periods, 59–60
    private litigation, 63–64
  economic incentives, 79
    deadweight loss, 78
    overcharge approximations, 73–77
    passing-on of overcharges, 78
    payment of interest, 77–78
    procedural provisions and, 71–73
  duty of disclosure, 60–62
  private litigation, 63–64
  welfare effects of the right to damages:
    damages for antitrust injury, 54–56
    forum rules, 56
    indirect customers, 59
    limitation periods, 59–60
    passing-on of overcharges, 59
    persons entitled to damages, 57–58
    quantification of harm, 57

transparency, 143–44
  leniency programmes, 32, 158–59
    access to leniency documents, 149–50
    perceived lack of transparency and certainty, 145–46
  third party access to Commission documents, 169–72
  uncertainty of leniency and liability, 144–48
Transparency Regulation, 152, 169–72, 176
Treaty on the Functioning of the European Union (TFEU), 3–4, 27
  arbitration awards in causation procedures, 56
  background to Damages Directive, 5–7
  disclosure of evidence, 10–11
  protection of confidential information and business secrets, 172
  quantification of harm
    empowerment of national courts, 57
  restitution, 285–86
    Art 102, 289–90
  transparency principle, 169
treble damages, 4–5, 7, 19, 24, **39**, 61, 262, 266–67
  see also Clayton Act

umbrella pricing, 9, 108, 191, 225, 231–32, 265
US federal antitrust law:
  Clayton Act, 19
    injunctive relief, 19

judgments as *prima facia* evidence, 19
limitation periods, 19
recovery of costs for successful claimants, 19–20
treble damages, 4–5, 7, 19, 24, **39**, 61, 262, 266–67
cartels:
leniency programmes, 145
coercive nature, 22
Damages Directive compared, 4–5, 16–17
factors impacting on, **39–41**
leniency programmes, 145
private enforcement, 19–26
class actions, 22
Clayton Act, 19
concerns about the system, 22
injunctive relief, 19
judgments as *prima facia* evidence, 19
limitation periods, 19
recovery of costs for successful claimants, 19–20
remoteness doctrine, 22
Supreme Court case law, 21, 23
treble damages, 19
recalibrating measures, 22–24

welfare effects of right to damages:
competition law, 48–51
complex market settings, 52–54
concept, 44–47
'welfare' defined, 44
effect of government intervention, 45
impact of Damages Directive, 47–48
measuring welfare effects, 45
simplified market setting, 51–52
Sweden:
damages for antitrust injury, 54–56
forum rules, 56
indirect customers, 59
limitation periods, 59–60
passing-on of overcharges, 59
persons entitled to damages, 57–58
private litigation, 63–64
quantification of harm, 57
theoretical scenarios, 46–47
whistleblowing, 8–9, 10
Leniency Notices, 148
leniency programmes, 145
white list:
disclosure of evidence, 162
leniency statements, 162
White Paper on Damages Actions for Breach of the EC Antitrust Rules (White Paper), 6, 297–98
European Parliament resistance, 166

www.ingramcontent.com/pod-product-compliance
Ingram Content Group UK Ltd.
Pitfield, Milton Keynes, MK11 3LW, UK
UKHW020133290926
15471UKWH00003B/449

9 781509 921164